Organizing the 20th-Century World

Organizing the 20th-Century World

International Organization and the Emergence of International Public Administration, 1920–60s

Karen Gram-Skjoldager, Haakon A. Ikonomou and Torsten Kahlert (eds.)

BLOOMSBURY ACADEMIC
LONDON • NEW YORK • OXFORD • NEW DELHI • SYDNEY

BLOOMSBURY ACADEMIC
Bloomsbury Publishing Plc
50 Bedford Square, London, WC1B 3DP, UK
1385 Broadway, New York, NY 10018, USA
29 Earlsfort Terrace, Dublin 2, Ireland

BLOOMSBURY, BLOOMSBURY ACADEMIC and the Diana logo are trademarks of
Bloomsbury Publishing Plc

First published in Great Britain 2020
This paperback edition published in 2022

Copyright © Karen Gram-Skjoldager, Haakon A. Ikonomou and Torsten Kahlert, 2020

Karen Gram-Skjoldager, Haakon A. Ikonomou and Torsten Kahlert (eds.) have
asserted their right under the Copyright, Designs and Patents Act, 1988, to
be identified as Authors of this work.

Series design by Tjaša Krivec
Cover image: Preparations for the Second Part of the United Nations
General Assembly, 01 March 1949, United Nations (Lake Success), New York
(UN Photo/Albert Fox)

All rights reserved. No part of this publication may be reproduced or
transmitted in any form or by any means, electronic or mechanical, including
photocopying, recording, or any information storage or retrieval system,
without prior permission in writing from the publishers.

Bloomsbury Publishing Plc does not have any control over, or responsibility for,
any third-party websites referred to or in this book. All internet addresses given in
this book were correct at the time of going to press. The author and publisher
regret any inconvenience caused if addresses have changed or sites have
ceased to exist, but can accept no responsibility for any such changes.

Every effort has been made to trace copyright holders and to obtain their permissions for
the use of copyright material. The publisher apologizes for any errors or omissions
and would be grateful if notified of any corrections that should be incorporated
in future reprints or editions of this book.

A catalogue record for this book is available from the British Library.

Library of Congress Cataloging-in-Publication Data
Names: Gram-Skjoldager, Karen, editor. | Ikonomou, Haakon A.,
editor. | Kahlert, Torsten, 1977- editor.
Title: Organizing the 20th-century world : international organizations and the
emergence of international public administration, 1920-1960s / Karen Gram-Skjoldager,
Haakon A. Ikonomou and Torsten Kahlert (eds.).
Description: London ; New York : Bloomsbury Academic, 2020. |
Series: Histories of internationalism | Includes bibliographical references and index.
Identifiers: LCCN 2020027559 (print) | LCCN 2020027560 (ebook) |
ISBN 9781350134577 (hardback) | ISBN 9781350192461 (paperback) |
ISBN 9781350134584 (ebook) | ISBN 9781350134591 (epub)
Subjects: LCSH: International agencies–History–20th century. |
International agencies–Political aspects.
Classification: LCC JZ4850 .O745 2020 (print) | LCC JZ4850 (ebook) |
DDC 341.209/04–dc23
LC record available at https://lccn.loc.gov/2020027559
LC ebook record available at https://lccn.loc.gov/2020027560

ISBN:	HB:	978-1-3501-3457-7
	PB:	978-1-3501-9246-1
	ePDF:	978-1-3501-3458-4
	eBook:	978-1-3501-3459-1

Typeset by Integra Software Services Pvt. Ltd.

To find out more about our authors and books visit www.bloomsbury.com
and sign up for our newsletters.

Contents

List of Figures	vii
List of Contributors	viii

1 Introduction *Karen Gram-Skjoldager, Haakon A. Ikonomou and Torsten Kahlert* 1

Part I Populating Administrations 13

2 Biographical Analysis: Insights and Perspectives from the *IO BIO* Dictionary Project *Bob Reinalda* 15
3 The Biography as Institutional Can Opener: An Investigation of Core Bureaucratic Practices in the Early Years of the League of Nations Secretariat *Haakon A. Ikonomou* 33
4 Prosopography: Unlocking the Social World of International Organizations *Torsten Kahlert* 49

Part II Learning and Norms 71

5 The Influence of the United States on the Rise of Global Governance in Education: The OEEC and UNESCO in the post–Second World War Period *Maren Elfert and Christian Ydesen* 73
6 Learning across Institutions: The Officials of the ECSC High Authority and EEC Commission *Katja Seidel* 91
7 Food and Nutrition: Expertise across International Epistemic Communities and Organizations, 1919–63 *Amy L. Sayward* 109

Part III Legitimacy and Legitimization 127

8 Legitimizing International Bureaucracy: Press and Information Work from the League of Nations to the UN *Emil Eiby Seidenfaden* 129
9 Between Publicity and Discretion: The International Federation of League of Nations Societies *Anne-Isabelle Richard* 145
10 An Uneasy Relationship: German Diplomats and Bureaucrats in the League of Nations *Michael Jonas* 163

Part IV Leadership and Administration   181

11 Secretaries-General and Crisis Management: Trygve Lie and Dag
    Hammarskjöld at the United Nations *Ellen J. Ravndal*   183
12 Leadership Styles and Organizing Principles in NATO: Ismay, Spaak
    and Wörner *Linda Risso*   199
13 The Making of the International Civil Servant *c.* 1920–60:
    Establishing the Profession *Karen Gram-Skjoldager and
    Haakon A. Ikonomou*   215

Notes   231
References   290
Index   315

Figures

1	Development of the personnel of the whole secretariat of the League of Nations	52
2	Development of officials of the first division (excluding temporary collaborators)	52
3	Member states (black line) and nationalities (grey line) in the whole secretariat	54
4	Relative distribution of all nationalities of the first division for the whole period 1919–46	55
5	Relative representation of officials in the first division from different continents	56
6	Relative representation of West, Middle and Eastern Europe in the first division	56
7	British in the first division	58
8	French in the first division	58
9	Italians in the first division	59
10	Germans in the first division	59
11	Status distribution of men and women in the whole secretariat	62

Contributors

Amy Sayward is Professor of History at Middle Tennessee State University and Executive Director of the Society for Historians of American Foreign Relations (SHAFR). She is also the author of two books on international organizations: *The Birth of Development: How the World Bank, Food and Agriculture Organization, and World Health Organization Changed the World, 1945–1965* (Kent State University Press, 2006) and *The United Nations in International History* (Bloomsbury, 2017).

Anne-Isabelle Richard is University Lecturer in History at Leiden University, the Netherlands. Her interests are situated at the intersection of European, global and international history, using transnational approaches. Her work has examined anti-colonial, European and socialist civil society networks, Dutch interwar foreign policy, and the influence of colonialism on the interwar European movement, which is the topic of her first book project. She currently leads a four-year Dutch Research Foundation project on African Perspectives on Eurafrica. Her work has been published in (among others) the *Journal of Global History*, *European Review of History* and *Low Countries Historical Review*. An edited collection, *Global Perspectives on the Dutch Empire: Intellectual History in Imperial Practice*, was published in the Cambridge Imperial and Post-colonial Studies Series with Palgrave in 2020.

Bob Reinalda is Fellow at the Department of Political Science, Radboud University, Nijmegen, the Netherlands. He has published *Routledge History of International Organizations: From 1815 to the Present Day* (2009) and has edited *Ashgate Research Companion to Non-state Actors* (2011) as well as *Routledge Handbook of International Organization* (2013). Alongside Kent J. Kille and Jaci Eisenberg, he is an editor of *IO BIO, Biographical Dictionary of Secretaries-General of International Organizations* (www.ru.nl/fm/iobio).

Christian Ydesen is Professor (WSR) at Aalborg University, Denmark. He is the PI of the project 'The Global History of the OECD in Education' funded by the Aalborg University talent programme and the project 'Education Access under the Reign of Testing and Inclusion' funded by the Independent Research Fund, Denmark. He has been a visiting scholar at the University of Edinburgh (2008–9, 2016), the University of Birmingham (2013), the University of Oxford (2019) and the University of Wisconsin-Madison (2020) and has published several articles on topics such as educational testing, international organizations, accountability, educational psychology, and diversity in education from historical and international perspectives. He currently serves as an executive editor of the *European Educational Research Journal*.

Ellen J. Ravndal is Associate Professor in political science at the University of Stavanger, Norway. She holds a DPhil in International Relations from the University of Oxford and has previously taught at Lund University and the Australian National University. Her research broadly focuses on international organizations (IOs), including the UN secretary-general, IO autonomy and the history of IOs and has appeared in journals such as *Global Governance*, *International History Review*, and *Review of International Studies*.

Emil Eiby Seidenfaden holds a PhD from Aarhus University 2019 on the League of Nations and international public opinion. Seidenfaden's interests include history of international organizations, European political history and intellectual history. He is a prospective postdoctoral researcher at the Oxford Centre for European History through the Carlsberg Foundation's Visiting Fellowship at University of Oxford. Here, he will examine the work of Danish journalists involved in the Allied war effort 1940–5 including their relations to other Europeans and how they drew on these transnational encounters when shaping post-war sentiments about international politics, 1945–80. Seidenfaden's focus has thus revolved around themes in twentieth-century history of the press and propaganda in the context of early twentieth-century European transnational history.

Haakon A. Ikonomou is Associate Professor in History at the Saxo Institute, University of Copenhagen. He received his PhD from the European University Institute, Florence, in April 2016. Between 2016 and 2019 he was doing his post-doctorate on the collective project 'The Invention of International Bureaucracy' at Aarhus University. He is co-director of the Rethinking European Integration research group and centre coordinator at the Centre for Modern European Studies (CEMES) at the Saxo Institute. Currently he is heading the NOS-HS workshop series on 'Scandinavian Internationalist Diplomacy, 1920s–1970s' and preparing a manuscript for the monograph *The International Bureaucrat in the Twentieth Century – A Transnational Biography of Thanassis Aghnides*. He is also review editor of *Diplomatica: A Journal of Diplomacy and Society* (Brill).

Karen Gram-Skjoldager is Associate Professor of European International History at Aarhus University, Denmark. She received her PhD from Aarhus University in 2009 and has been Jean Monnet Fellow at the European University Institute in Florence and visiting fellow at the Nobel Institute in Oslo and Fudan University, Shanghai. Her research interests cover Scandinavian foreign policy, interwar international organizations, diplomacy and international law. She has published widely in leading international journals such as *Contemporary European History*, *Diplomacy and Statecraft* and *Journal of Global History*. She is a member of the editorial board of *Diplomatica: A Journal of Diplomacy and Society* (Brill) and program director of the MA programme in International and Global History at Aarhus University. She is currently director of the research project Inventing International Bureaucracy. The League of Nations and the Creation of International Public Administration, c. 1920–1960.

Katja Seidel is Senior Lecturer in History at the University of Westminster. She has published widely on the history of European integration, including studies on European elites and European policies. She is the author of *The Process of Politics in Europe: The Rise of European Elites and Supranational Institutions* (I.B. Tauris 2010). Recent publications include 'The Challenges of Enlargement and GATT Trade Negotiations: Explaining the Resilience of the European Community's Common Agricultural Policy in the 1970s' in *International History Review* (2019) and 'Britain, the Common Agricultural Policy and the Challenges of Membership in the European Community: A Political Balancing Act' in *Contemporary British History* (2019). Her current research is going to result in a biography of the American diplomat and economist Miriam Camps.

Linda Risso is Senior Research Fellow at the Institute of Historical Research in London. She is an expert on the history of European defence and security in the twentieth century. Her research focuses on the historical development of the European Union and NATO. In 2018–19, Dr Risso worked as historical consultant at the Supreme Headquarters Allied Powers Europe to produce 'An Enduring Alliance', a podcast on the history of NATO produced by the Alliance to celebrate its seventieth anniversary. She is the author of *Propaganda and Intelligence in the Cold War: The NATO Information Service* (Routledge, 2014).

Maren Elfert is Lecturer in Education and Society in the School of Education, Communication and Society at King's College London, and a 2018 National Academy of Education/Spencer Postdoctoral Fellow. Her research focuses on global governance of education and the influence of international organizations on educational ideas and policies. She is submissions editor of the *International Review of Education*.

Michael Jonas is Associate Professor in Modern History at Helmut Schmidt University, Hamburg, Germany, and Adjunct Professor at the University of Helsinki, Finland. He has published widely on the history of international relations in the nineteenth and, in particular, twentieth centuries, on the diplomatic, political and military history of both world wars, and on Northern Europe and small states in the international system. He is the author of *Scandinavia and the Great Powers in the First World War* (Bloomsbury, 2019) and the editor of *Stabilität durch Gleichgewicht? Balance of Power im internationalen System der Neuzeit* (Schöningh, 2015, with Ulrich Lappenküper and Bernd Wegner).

Torsten Kahlert holds a PhD in the history of science from Humboldt University Berlin (2015). From 2016 to 2018, he was a postdoctoral researcher in the research project The Invention of Bureaucracy. The League of Nations and the Creation of International Public Administration at Aarhus University. His publications include the monograph *Big Style Projects – Organisation, Objectivity and Historicism in the 19th Century* (2017) on large-scale humanities research projects and articles in leading international journals. Kahlert's research interests include history of international organizations, history of humanities and history of the East German Secret Police 1950–90. He is currently a review editor on history of science at H-Soz-Kult (http://www.hsozkult.de) and works as a researcher and public lecturer for museums and memorials especially on East German history.

1

Introduction

Karen Gram-Skjoldager, Haakon A. Ikonomou
and Torsten Kahlert

Since the beginning of the twentieth century, more than 5,000 international organizations (IOs) have been created to deal with an ever-expanding range of political, economic and technical issues.[1] All of these international organizations depend on permanent international administrations inhabited by civil servants, preparing and implementing policies and securing institutional continuity. As a consequence, the twentieth century has witnessed how international executive power in the form of international administrative bodies has come to constitute an increasingly important feature of world politics. While indispensable to international life, these international bureaucrats have also become the object of political criticism for their lack of efficiency and the opaque, undemocratic power they (allegedly) wield.[2]

This volume offers the first historical exploration of the genealogy and anatomy of international public administrations. Focusing on the foundational period of international organizations from the 1920s to the 1960s, it covers the birth of the League of Nations and the emergence of the second-generation international organizations that still shape international politics today (the UN, NATO, OEEC/OECD, the European Coal and Steel Community/EU). Geographically, the book centres on European and Atlantic international organizations, reflecting the fact that the multilateralization of international relations in the mid-twentieth century played out more intensely in Europe and the Western hemisphere than in other regions of the world.

Equally important, the volume demonstrates a broad range of historiographical traditions and methodological approaches to the study of institutions in international history. It is our assumption that after several 'turns' (cultural, linguistic, material, transnational), international history is now better equipped to restate its core questions of policy and power with a view to their institutional dimensions. Making use of the new approaches that have emerged in the field over the past several decades, we wish to develop a new understanding of the specific powers and roles of international organization administrations by delving into their institutional make-up, leadership, procedures and human composition. Such elements have been neglected, often with the implicit assumption that the same dynamics that exist in domestic politics or the old diplomacy of monarchs and emperors can be transplanted to the complex international environment emerging in the twentieth century. We contend that the anatomy of these institutions varied and changed over time and that policy-making processes and transnational exchanges of ideas cannot be treated analytically separate from their institutional contexts and the social worlds they represent.

Towards a Connected History of International Public Administrations

Since the 2000s, historians have abandoned the assumption that international organizations were mere arenas for interstate competition and bargaining and have become increasingly interested in the history, role and significance of these organizations in their own right.[3]

Over the last fifteen years, the 'transnational turn' brought the historical role of international organizations, transnational actors and expertise into focus.[4] Exploring networks of expertise, knowledge and power, historians have uncovered the influence of transnationally organized scientists, lawyers, colonial administrators, engineers, economists and other professional and political groups in shaping interwar and post-war politics.[5]

A strand of this literature has sought to connect the first 'experiment' of international organization in the League of Nations, with the many 'second generation' IOs created in the 1940s and 1950s. A key example of this approach is Patricia Clavin's groundbreaking work on the League's economic and financial cooperation.[6] A more recent example is Simon Jackson and Alanna O'Malley's multi-authored volume on *The Institution of International Order. From the League of Nations to the United Nations*. Likewise, European integration studies in recent years have increasingly focused on its deeper historical foundations and attempted to connect the advances in organizations from the late nineteenth century with inter- and post-war international institutional developments.[7] This volume draws inspiration from these studies and explores the development of international organization and administration as a gradual, continuous development that transcended the caesura of the Second World War.

The book also speaks to the trend, promoted by researchers like Akira Iriye and Mark Mazower, that places the League of Nations and post-war international organizations in the broader nineteenth- and twentieth-century genealogy of internationalism, i.e. the beliefs and practices that sought to promote a more peaceful, secure international order through the strengthening of international mechanisms and institutions, without questioning the notion of nation states and national sovereignty as building blocks of the international order.[8] Historical literature on internationalism has flourished in recent years, and scholars have explored internationalist actors and practices in almost any imaginable policy field,[9] emphasizing the interlinking webs of people and ideas and exploring the cultural and ideational significance of IOs as hubs of internationalist endeavours.[10] This has allowed historians to usefully break down the analytical barriers between imperial, international and national politics to study them as part of a complex twentieth-century development producing a multitude of different and entangled forms of internationalisms.[11] As Martin Geyer and Johannes Paulmann have distinguished so eminently in their exploration of the term,[12] historians explore internationalism as both ideology and process (often not distinguishing between the two). This conceptual width is tied to an analytical ambition to see nineteenth- and early twentieth-century internationalism as the beginning of globalization processes and an emerging international society that are still shaping the world today.[13]

While the transnational scholarship on internationalism and IOs has been particularly successful in uncovering and tracing nodes of power and knowledge in twentieth-century global governance,[14] it has rarely engaged with the international public administrations and their set-up and functioning per se. Rather, institutions are often left as not very well-defined hubs, nodal points or arenas, that tie together and distribute knowledge and ideas between different transnational networks. Thus, the literature rarely explains how international administrative frameworks facilitated, suppressed or sustained certain networks, behaviours or knowledge regimes over time.[15] Moreover, it does not explore the distinct practices, roles and powers that the international public administrations themselves developed across the twentieth century, making them into significant actors and distinct social entities with their own sets of professional norms and practices. This volume grounds both the 'process' and 'ideology' of internationalism and the 'power' and 'expertise' of transnational networks in a third, greatly underappreciated feature of the trajectory of global governance, namely bureaucratic organization and international administration and the role it has come to play in these processes.

A relatively recent historical scholarship, focusing explicitly on international public administrations, has begun to do just that, by tracing the roots and role of international administrations back to the late nineteenth century and into the post-war era.[16] This body of work has also developed and applied new analytical tools to analyse the illusive powers of international bureaucrats. Thus, Gram-Skjoldager and Ikonomou have used Pierre Bourdieu's concept of fields to understand how different professional capitals gained hold in different parts of the League of Nations Secretariat and how the secretariat developed a shared normative system that integrated and mediated between these. Scholars like Katja Seidel, Emmanuel Mourlon Druol, Elisabetta Tollardo, Vera Fritz, Benjamin Auberer and Torsten Kahlert have used prosopography and group biographies to pry open the black box of singular international administrations and institutions and analyse generational changes, gender composition, networks and epistemic communities, and professional and educational backgrounds of the multinational staff.[17] Linda Risso has recently operationalized the work of Quentin Skinner to study the first secretary-general of NATO, Lord Ismay, as an 'innovative ideologist'.[18] Still, as this scholarship is in its infancy, it often focuses on piecing together how single IO administrations came into being and functioned. Aiming to break down the barriers between single IO studies, the present volume explores administrative traits such as leadership, composition, networks, and governance styles across several IOs in the period from the 1920s to the 1960s, explicitly connecting interwar and post-war developments and downplaying 1945 as a caesura in the development of international public administration.

The *Sattelzeit* of International Public Administrations

The period between the early 1920s and the late 1960s can be understood both as a foundational period in the genealogy of international public administrations and in a longer perspective as a sort of *Sattelzeit* of far-reaching transformations in international relations, away from the Metternichian diplomacy and imperial scrambles of the nineteenth century and towards the infrastructure of global governance that we know today.[19] The first international intergovernmental organization to develop a large-scale bureaucracy was the League of Nations. Set up after the First World War to 'promote international co-operation and to achieve international peace and security',[20] it covered a wide range of policy areas – from collective security over national minority protection to the promotion of transnational governance in areas as diverse as infrastructure, health, economy and finance.[21] With no precedents to build on, the creation of an administration of more than 700 people from around forty different countries[22] to manage these diverse international activities was, as one former employee summarized it, 'a uniquely adventurous journey into unexplored territory [...] with no familiar landmarks, mapped charts or itineraries to direct the traveller'.[23] By setting out on this journey, the League Secretariat came to have a long-term impact on how international administration developed throughout the twentieth century as it became an important reference point in discussions about the new international institutions created after the Second World War.[24] Indeed, a large number of League staff went to work for these organizations: the majority of the League officials who continued their careers in the post-war multilateral landscape were transferred to the UN, and political economists like Jean Monnet and Per Jacobsson are prominent examples of League staff who went to work in sectoral economic and monetary institutions like the European Coal and Steel Community (ECSC) and the International Monetary Fund (IMF).[25]

These international organizations – that we label the 'second generation' – were all created in the post-war years as part of a US-led construction of a global order in the Western image. At the same time, they are radically different organizations with very different starting points: the UN – with its many special agencies – was the direct descendant of the League of Nations.[26] Yet it would take on a very different role due to two transformative processes: first, the presence of two superpowers and the divisions of the Cold War, which acted as a catalyst for fierce competition and stalemates, expert-driven policy-making and the reformation of the UN system – developments that affected all of the IOs under scrutiny in this volume.[27] Second, the process of decolonization and the emergence of new actors and forces in the Global South – a development that completely altered the state system and challenged both the American/Western dominance and the East-West dichotomy, particularly within the UN system.[28] The OEEC was a new, and at first regional, organization, set up to distribute Marshall Aid[29] and would later develop into the OECD, the custodian of Western capitalism and one of the most influential producers of global socio-economic knowledge paradigms.[30] NATO, meanwhile, was a new Atlantic security organization forced into existence by Cold War tensions. Not initially imagined with a large civilian administration, it developed a fully fledged and highly specialized secretariat from 1952 onwards.[31] Last, the ECSC, and later the EC, was imagined as a conscious break with conventional international administrations and would gain unique powers due to the ideological thrust of the project, the supranational elements of the institutions and the legal prerogatives they would get at their disposal.[32]

Nonetheless, as this volume shows, the administrations of these international organizations intertwine, overlap, compete and connect in various ways, making them highly suitable for a connected and comparative set of studies.[33] In focusing on these organizations, the volume highlights Europe and the Atlantic world as a hub for multilateralism and supranationalism in the mid-twentieth century and takes a particular interest in how international organization bureaucracies changed as Europe shifted from being a region defined by multinational and global empires to one structured around the nation state. Europe as a region played a decreasing role in global affairs as the twentieth century marched on. Yet, as the main battleground of two World Wars and the initial seat of the Cold War, it remained a focal point of innovative international governance and ultimately transformed large parts of its territory into what is arguably the most radical attempt at international organization to date: the EU. The issue of how European administrative models and practices travelled to other parts of the globe as decolonization spurred new regional forms of cooperation in Africa, Asia and South America is a topic that is highly deserving of academic investigation but lies beyond the scope of this volume (cf. also this introduction below).

By the end of the 1960s, the structural conditions as well as the core characteristics of these international public administrations changed. For once, they had all moved past their early formative years and reached a level of maturity, routinization and proficiency so far unseen in international politics. This can be witnessed, for instance, in the merger of the ECSC, EURATOM and EEC into the European Community, and the transition of the OEEC into the OECD – just as the post-war era, dominated by the Keynesian socio-economic paradigm and demand-side economics, marked by strong faith in (government) planning, rational scientific methods and technocratic solutions – was overtaken by the tumultuous and globalizing 1970s.[34] This is where our edited volume concludes, with the building blocks of the institutional order we know today established; as the first generations of post-war international civil servants were retiring; and with the economic, social and political paradigms they had helped to articulate and uphold coming under increasingly intense criticism and scrutiny. This volume, in other words, tells the story of the early formative phase of international public administration centred on Europe and the United States.

Dissecting International Public Administrations – Four Perspectives

Based on the historiographical outline above, we may formulate three aims for the current volume: first, to break down the barriers between research on various international public administrations, to explore administrative traits and practices within several IOs across the Second World War. Second, as mentioned above, we wish to explore the 1920s to the 1960s as a formative period in the genealogy and development of international public administrations and how this related to a broader, transformative *Sattelzeit* in twentieth-century international relations. Last, we aim to explore the distinct practices, roles, norms and powers that the international public administrations developed; the new opportunities they offered for experts, diplomats and activists; and how they emerged as clearly defined social and political entities that gave international civil services a distinct role in multilateral diplomacy. The volume is organized into four main parts.

Populating Administrations

While all chapters in the volume deal with people working inside and around international administrations, the contributions in this first part focus explicitly on the people who inhabited these executive bodies, their careers, roles and relations to and within the institutions. Moving past the formal regulations and principles of the international civil service, the three contributions in this part reflect on how biographical and prosopographical methods can help develop our understanding of international public administrations. In the opening chapter of this part (Chapter 2), Bob Reinalda introduces us to the IO BIO Dictionary Project, a unique digital collection of short, structured biographies of executive heads of IOs from the nineteenth to the twenty-first century. Based in a set of theoretical reflections that show us how and why international secretariats and their executive heads are important, Reinalda lays out the aim and principles of the IO BIO project. Going further back than the arc of the *Sattelzeit* under scrutiny in this volume, Reinalda begins with the international secretariats that managed the river conventions of the early nineteenth century and then goes on to show how the League and UN secretariats formed part of a long tradition of international executive heads fighting to create autonomy and room for manoeuvre for themselves and their secretariats.

In Chapter 3, Haakon Ikonomou explores how the biographical approach can be used as an analytical 'can opener' – holding personal, institutional and transnational analytical scales together – to explore traits of an international public administration that are difficult to grasp with a meso- or macro-analysis. Following the international civil servant and diplomat Thanassis Aghnides's road from the Ottoman countryside to the League Secretariat in 1919 and his work with the Greco-Turkish population exchange, the chapter challenges typical assumptions about the bureaucratic process of recruiting staff and explores the subtle complexities of an official's required international loyalty.

Chapter 4 demonstrates an alternative approach to exploring international administrations. Based on a combination of qualitative biographical research and quantitative analysis of the expansive LONSEA database, holding biographical data on all employees of the League of Nations, Torsten Kahlert delivers the first prosopographical study of the League sectretariat's higher staff, a group of around 700 international civil servants. Analysing the group along classical sociological lines, mapping their gender, age and nationality, Kahlert's chapter shows us the social characteristics of the League Secretariat top officials, how the group changed over time and how some of them were carried into the post-war order as former League officials made it into the new multilateral institutions.

Learning and Norms

International public administrations are in essence bureaucracies and are as such governed by rules, norms and procedures that shape the people, practice and purpose of the institution. Political scientists have long had an interest in the 'bureaucratic behavior' of IO administrations, trying to uncover pervasive logics or 'ways of doing things' within the institution. Trondal and colleagues (2010) argue, for instance, that international public administrations are characterized by inbuilt tensions between competing behavioural logics. An organization such as the OECD, for instance, may be pulled between a classic Weberian logic of impartiality and objectivity, on the one hand, and a much more policy-formulating and policy-enforcing logic determined by a transnational epistemic community of economists and educators, on the other. Fine-grained historical studies based on primary sources, on the other hand, are few and far between, and there is particularly a need for investigations of bureaucratic logics across IO administrations. Accordingly, in this part, Christian Ydesen and Maren Elfert (Chapter 5) explore the influence of the United States in shaping the bureaucratic focus and production of the competing and connected organizations of the OEEC and UNESCO in the realm of education. Katja Seidel (Chapter 6), meanwhile, goes back to the formative interwar period, the experiences of the

Second World War and early post-war technocratic cooperation to unpack the administrative culture of the first officials within the ECSC and the EC Commission. Seidel shows how different lessons learned from early international public administration would lead to competing visions of what a European bureaucracy could and should look like. In Chapter 7, Amy Sayward examines the issue of nutrition, health and agriculture as they were institutionalized in the new Food and Agriculture Organization of the United Nations (FAO). The chapter explores how the connected issues of food, nutrition and agriculture emerged as an international policy issue in the interwar years. It describes how it was pedalled by Anglo-American nutritional experts and how they used the infrastructure of the League of Nations to promote these issues. In particular it demonstrates how the new policy agenda was enthusiastically embraced by Secretary-General Joseph Avenol in the late 1930s, when the League was in severe political crisis. However, by then, expert activists were already pushing for the creation of a specialized organization for nutrition, health and agriculture – something that was achieved with the creation of FAO after the war. As Sayward demonstrates, having a separate bureaucratic body pushing this agenda was no guarantee for political leverage and impact.

Legitimacy and Legitimization

The legitimacy of international organizations and the way the wider public perceived them and engaged with them have been intimately connected phenomena from the inception of the League of Nations onwards. The Wilsonian ideal of open covenants and transparent diplomacy informed the function and rationale of the League Secretariat, which worked under the assumption that its legitimacy derived from an inherently liberal world public, that had to be mobilized to keep member states to the promises of the Covenant.[35] After the Second World War and the destructive mass mobilization of fascism and national socialism the aims and hopes of the IOs in terms of public relations were perhaps more restricted, but nonetheless highly sophisticated and a vital part of the administrative rationale. Lacking the more traditional 'hard' tools of power, IOs are remarkably conscious of how they are interpreted in their contemporary world, seeing good standing with the (global) public and with states as sources of power.[36]

The three chapters in this third part explore the nexus of legitimation and public relations from three angles: Emil Seidenfaden (Chapter 8) looks inside the engine room of the League of Nations Information Section and United

Nations Department of Public Information to see how they legitimized the administrations' own existence through press and information work. In Chapter 9, Anne Isabelle Richard explores the role of the International Federation of League of Nations Societies as a broker between the League of Nations, the member states and the global public, arguing that the IFLNS had both a public-educational side and pursued a discreet and informal policy-shaping strategy vis-à-vis the League Secretariat and member states and showing the reciprocity, synergies and overlap in personnel and agendas that developed between the two.

Michael Jonas's chapter (Chapter 10) investigates how the German foreign policy establishment as well as the wider German public opinion perceived the League and challenges the narrative that the German League officials were first and foremost 'traitors' within the organization, serving their national political interest and aiming at dismantling the machinery upholding the *Versailles Diktat* from the inside. The chapter highlights the many instances of institutional adaptation in Germany's relations with the League even before membership and the gatekeeping mechanisms in the Auswärtiges Amt that controlled who was allowed into the League Secretariat during Germany's seven-year membership (1926–33). Here he shows how, on the one hand, internationalist, leftist candidates with roots in German pacifist organizations were kept out of the secretariat. On the other hand, he demonstrates how the German officials that took a harsh and uncompromising nationalist stance in the secretariat were quickly marginalized not only in relation to the leadership of the secretariat but also vis-à-vis their hinterland in Berlin.

Leadership and Administration

The fourth perspective in this volume highlights the issues of leadership and administration and the relationship between the two. Each of the three chapters in this part approaches the issue from different angles. Ellen Ravndal (Chapter 11) explores UN Secretaries-General Trygve Lie and Dag Hammarskjöld's institutional capacity and personal ability to resolve and address crisis – both internally and externally – in the formative years of the United Nations. Moments of crisis, so Ravndal argues, are particularly well suited to explore the limitations and possibilities to exert influence and power for a head (secretary-general) of an IO.

In Chapter 12, Linda Risso explores the leadership style and management principles of NATO's first two secretaries-general, Lord Ismay and Paul-Henri Spaak, and compares and contrasts them to Manfred Wörner, who was secretary-general when the Cold War ended. Challenging the dominant crisis-led approach to NATO that has focused on how the organization and its leadership have responded to external chocks and ruptures, Risso instead explores the less visible, but just as important question of how the secretaries-general shaped the organization and its relationship with and leverage towards its member states through weekly meetings and a continuous process of negotiations and diplomatic exchange. Comparing the first two secretaries-general of the organization, Lord Ismay (1952–7) and Paul Henri Spaak (1957–61), with Manfred Wörner's tenure as secretary-general at the end of the Cold War (1988–94), Risso offers the reader a glimpse into how the role of secretary-general changed over the course of the Cold War but also shows us how the basis laid by the early secretaries-general kept hold for the following decades.

Last, Karen Gram-Skjoldager and Haakon A. Ikonomou (Chapter 13) trace the establishment and evolution of the international civil servant as a professional figure, from the end of the First World War, via the tumultuous 1930s to the apex of professionalization in the post-war years. Analysing the development of the profession as inextricably linked to the building of the secretariat as an institution, Gram-Skjoldager and Ikonomou explore two competing trends throughout the period: on the one hand, the early conception of a politically neutral and internationally recruited secretariat, loyal only to the organization, which would be the model for every major IO following the League. On the other hand, the secretariat of the League and later the UN were shaped by the political conditions of its environment, and particularly the matter of loyalty was challenged in several turns. Between these two poles, the international civil servant's rights, duties, rules and norms were formalized at a steady pace to gain the traits that we know and recognize today.

A First Step

Like the other chapters in the volume, the final chapter by Gram-Skjoldager and Ikonomou confirms the important, formative role played by the mid-twentieth-century international organizations in the shaping of modern international public administration. However, the studies presented in this volume only represent a first exploration into the field of international civil service; a wide range of important topics and themes still remain to be explored. Three issues in particular stand out as interesting avenues for further research. Firstly, this volume has focused mostly on the history of Western European and transatlantic organizations, often seen as the vanguard of the liberal international order. Expanding investigations into the administrative infrastructures of the competing communist project such as the Cominform, the Comecon and the Warsaw Pact would add important new dimensions to our understanding of international administrations and cast a new light on the international administrations under scrutiny in this volume.[37]

In the same vein, this collection of studies has focused on the administrations related to intergovernmental organizations. However, the twentieth century also saw the emergence of a vast field of transnational voluntary associations, lobby groups, business associations and so on, which also developed considerable international bureaucratic structures and capabilities of their own. Exploring the characteristics of, variations in and development of these NGO administrations and how they compared to, and not least interlinked with, IO bureaucracies stands out as another topic worthy of scholarly interest.[38]

Likewise, and perhaps most importantly, it seems pressing to explore how the administrative models and practices developed predominantly in Europe and the United States explored in this volume intertwined with and were translated into other regional contexts. Firstly, while this is not the focus of the current volume, these global aspects are crucial because European powers operated vast empires well into the second half of the twentieth century, and internationalized colonial administration was part of the "civilizing mission" of both the League and the UN.[39] Thus, secondly, while Europe was the hub of mid-twentieth-century multilateralism, the multilateralization of international politics was a global phenomenon, and exploring how regional cooperative structures such as the Organisation of African Unity/the African Union and the Association of Southeast Asia/ASEAN that grew out of decolonization developed their own distinct regional executive capacities should also figure centrally on the research agenda. Indeed, while we are offering a first attempt at a connected history of international administration, what remains is a truly *global* history of international administration, as one of the key features of twentieth- and twenty-first century international relations.

Part One

Populating Administrations

2

Biographical Analysis: Insights and Perspectives from the *IO BIO* Dictionary Project

Bob Reinalda

What do individual life and career descriptions add to our understanding of international organizations (IOs)? Generally speaking, many international relations scholars describe IOs in impersonal ways: the institutions are seen as actors, whereas individuals and their leadership receive little to no attention. However, how an organization acts may depend on the individual, or group of senior staff, in charge of it. Temporary institutions may become permanent organizations as a result of their leadership, and the growth, decline and survival of organizations also depend on their guidance. The first executive heads of IOs are significant because they set up the secretariats and thus play a key role in creating the institution of international public administration. Analysing a large number of individual careers and their relationship to political and organizational developments over time, therefore, helps understand the history of IOs and their administrative bodies.

The first section of this chapter discusses the *IO BIO* project and its effort to enhance the understanding of executive heads of IOs. *IO BIO*, the *Biographical Dictionary of Secretaries-General of International Organizations*, has published over eighty individual entries, covering more than forty IOs.[1] The second section discusses IO secretariats as the institutional context of these executive heads and the third section uses *IO BIO* entries and other sources to explore the emergence of international public administration in a long-term perspective from its earliest beginnings in 1815 until c.1960.

The Short Biography and the *IO BIO* Project

International relations theory is strongly inclined to minimize the role of individuals and leave personal factors out when analysing policy-making processes, because individuals are not viewed as explaining variation in international relations.[2] However, American scholar and Secretary of State Henry Kissinger, who as a professor shared this opinion, acknowledged that in practice personalities do make a difference.[3] (Neo)realism holds a negative opinion about both IOs (at best a platform for major powers) and their executive heads (only interested in egoistically securing the continuity and health of their organizations).[4] But, although restrained by major states, IOs can be seen as actors that matter in international relations, with executive heads (named secretary-general, director, administrator or similar titles) playing prominent roles, just like top politicians do in national political systems or CEOs in businesses. Several authors have applied organization theory to IOs to discuss leadership and the room of manoeuvre executive heads may create. Among them are Ernst Haas (1964), Robert Cox (1969), Michael Schechter (2012) and Nina Hall and Ngaire Woods (2017), who mention assets that executive heads may use, such as mobilizing the organization's expertise, researching alternative policy solutions and strategies, using the organization as medium to communicate views (the 'bully pulpit' function), and identifying external enemies and supporters.[5]

The biographical literature on executive heads of IOs is limited, leaving us with an incomplete understanding of the variety of people who have held these positions and also of the interactions between them as a group of actors. Biographies can be extensive (books and lengthy articles) and small (obituaries and entries in biographical dictionaries). The *IO BIO* project is currently exploring the potential of systematically mapping IO executive heads through small, highly structured biographies.

Accurate and Comparable Descriptions

The 'short biography' is a genre by itself. *IO BIO*, edited by the author together with Kent Kille and Jaci Eisenberg since 2012, is not set up as a 'Who is Who' that offers large enumerations of functions and responsibilities of living persons, but as an alphabetical dictionary with short biographies or mini-sized portraits (between 800 and 3,600 words) that aim to present an accurate and coherent description of the lives and careers of those included. Although older examples exist, the dictionary with short biographies of individuals whose professional work contributed to the public sphere dates back to the nineteenth century. The *IO BIO* project takes its cue from this genre in its modern form and focuses on the personality of leaders, their perceptions of what is going on, and their capacity to lead and act. Relevant factors to be discussed are self-image (personal values, social and political preferences), personal characteristics (e.g. charisma), available knowledge and expertise, experience, legitimacy and authority as well as performance, both successful and unproductive. Descriptions are based on a combination of primary and secondary sources, including private information and interviews.

In producing these life and career descriptions, *IO BIO* has a strict format, explained in author instructions, which provide detailed directions about the elements that should be included in the three sections of each entry.[6] The first section contains personal details, the second one consists of the account of life and work, and the third section has details about archives, publications by the person described and relevant literature about him or her. Every entry discusses the entire life and all careers and should discuss elements such as youth, family, education, first jobs, becoming engaged in international relations, international activities, being executive head and life after the international career, with the time in office as executive head as central to the entry.

The *IO BIO* set-up assumes that authors are experts with regard to the chosen organization and its head, have sufficient information available, and also have an open mind with regard to discovering the various components of the entire career and life they are profiling. Most information may be available through original documents, literature, archives, interviews and expert knowledge. Entries should provide more than superficial information, as it is important to understand what the people described in the entries have done: their attempts, their successes but also their failures. The instructions also contain warnings, such as avoiding copying myths or reproducing established narratives not based in solid research. Autobiographies and interviews may be inclined towards positive outcomes and disregard less favourable issues and results.

Information about executive heads made available by IOs frequently proves to be restricted. IOs are closed entities and often anxious of showing internal controversies. Even if transparency is an official policy, archives may remain closed or documents are not provided. Furthermore, IOs are inclined to define their own histories by writing 'official' histories themselves (in books, their own overviews and on websites). Such official histories may be written by insiders, who lack a scientific or critical regard. Conflicts are barely mentioned in official descriptions, although other sources may inform us about them. Information from internet sources often is incomplete and uncritically copied from, or by, other sources. In particular missing in several sources are the political dimensions of international relations and the policies of executive heads and their outcomes. In order to 'reconstruct' individual careers authors need combinations of sources and familiarity with what happens within organizations. *IO BIO* has found such authors but also acknowledges that it is easier to find authors in Europe and Northern America than elsewhere.

Prosopographical Studies

IO BIO entries inform about individual careers. However, the combination of entries also tells us about the group of executive heads and helps to answer questions such as the following: What are the backgrounds of executive heads? How well educated are they? What is the relevance of their political and professional expertise? Have they taken independent political initiatives? Within which policy areas and in what ways? Have their strategies to solve problems been successful? Have they failed in adapting their organization when being criticized by member states? Have they played a role in the organization's survival in case of external shocks or bureaucratic failure? What mutual relationships have existed between executive heads? All these issues touch upon one form of prosopography, focusing on the group of heads and the relations between them based on their position as IO leaders. Another form of prosopography focuses on the group that is made up of the executive head and his or her senior staff. Here *IO BIO* has restrictions, although many entries mention senior staff. Thomas Weiss et al. analysed information based on interviews with United Nations (UN) secretaries-general and other UN professionals who contributed to the promotion of ideas within the UN system and thus show us what can be achieved by venturing further in that direction.[7] In this volume, Torsten Kahlert also demonstrates what insights can be gained by drawing up a group portrait of the most senior staff in an IO, in this case in the League of Nations (see Chapter 4).

An extension of this prosopographical idea encompasses inter-organizational relations (IORs). The study of relations between IOs is a new field,[8] but not a new topic, as Kent Kille and I discovered using *IO BIO* entries to map IORs and the roles of executive heads. IORs are a long-standing phenomenon that resulted from the evolution of IOs, the increase in their numbers and the complementarity and/or overlap of activities and mandates. Our article in the 2017 volume edited by Biermann and Koops demonstrates this across various periods.⁹

International Secretariats and Their Executive Heads

During the formation of the modern state system several philosophers put forward 'peace plans', such as Abbé de Saint Pierre, Jean Jacques Rousseau, Jeremy Bentham and Immanuel Kant (*Perpetual Peace*, 1795). They raised fundamental questions with regard to war and peace among sovereign states and advanced proposals for the creation of what are now called IOs through the designing of structures (a general assembly, an international court) and the assignment of functions to these structures. In 1713 Saint Pierre already expected that 'international bureaus' as part of a peace plan would produce political, military and statistical information and promote international trade law. He mentioned the relevance of an independent civil service, for which he proposed to hire only Dutchmen.¹⁰

The peace plans influenced the statesmen who designed the Concert of Europe during the Congress of Vienna (1814–5). The Congress created the first IO in the form of an international river commission and a system of multilateral conferences and follow-up conferences (meant to monitor the implementation of decisions taken by the previous conference) which later institutionalized.¹¹ The international administrative bodies of the early IOs and multilateral conferences need more attention, as the IO secretariats did have an international character and the secretariats of multilateral conferences were given an increasingly multinational composition since the Berlin Congress of 1878, following the Russo-Turkish War.¹²

International Secretariats and Continuity

An IO secretariat is a hierarchically organized organ that takes care of the organization's continuity, seeks to devote itself to its objectives and purposes and, given the awareness of path dependence, functions as the institutional memory of the IO's undertakings. It runs the headquarters and represents the organization vis-à-vis states, other IOs and other actors. Continuity matters for reasoned organizational growth, adaptation to changing situations and situations of survival. International secretariats rest on both a Weberian understanding of modern bureaucracy (rational-legal authority, impersonal rules) and national bureaucratic traditions brought into the organization by the first executive head and senior staff, already in a compromise form, and then mixed with traditions brought in by later executive heads. The result is a mixture of administrative principles and processes borrowed from national administrations and adapted to the IO's own unique requirements.

The evolution of IOs shows experiments, copying of good practices and path dependence regarding chosen directions. Institutions evolve through institutional layering (or adaptation) and institutional conversion (or learning). Institutional layering refers to the process where new arrangements are layered on top of pre-existing structures (or new activities added), preserving much of the core of the original institution. Institutional conversion or learning happens if institutions designed with a set of goals in mind are redirected to other ends and means.[13]

Constitutions and Agency Slack

When states create IOs, they intend to remain in control of the new organization. Negotiation results between governments are carefully written down in the constitution, assuming that precise wordings, particularly the description of objectives, fields of activity and powers of organs, as well as certain organs themselves (especially the governing board), guarantee continued state control. However, this realist assumption contrasts with the fact that founding states have not been strongly inclined to give precise and detailed instructions for the secretariat and its staff in IO constitutions, in which sections and articles on secretariats, executive heads and staff have been relatively short and undetailed.

Principal Agent theory explains this contradiction by recognizing that the agent may develop some independent action. Agency slack in the form of 'slippage' refers to a situation where an agent (here an IO, particularly the secretariat) shifts policy away from the preferred outcome of the principal (the member states) towards its own preferences. Because constitutional instructions for secretariat and staff are not detailed, it may be expected that slippage emerges already in the early stage of creating the secretariat and setting into motion the required organizational processes. Legal theory also allows room of manoeuvre through its ideas of an organization's 'distinct will' (*volonté distincte*), with the secretariat not only executing the tasks set by its member states but also helping to shape those tasks and to select among them.[14] Legal theory also assumes that agreements may be incomplete, vague or contradictory, which implies that, if a secretariat meets with such elements in the constitution and other relevant documents, it will try to solve these either from the perspective of expertise in the field of their IO or from a managerial approach, or they address an international court to decide.

Frontierspersons and Leadership

The first executive heads of IOs are a special group. Similar to the idea of American settlers who had just come to live on the edge of what they regarded unclaimed territory, the individuals who start as the IO's first executive head may be viewed as 'frontierspersons'. They are mapping the unclaimed international issue area and are tasked with building up the organization's administrative machinery, based on a constitution drawn up by the founding states, followed by a phase in which the organization develops its first activities and policy-making. At this early moment there are still many things that have to be arranged and decided upon. Frontierspersons are particularly relevant for the emergence of international public administration through their ideas about institutions and internationalism.

Leadership of an IO requires the combination of two forms of leadership. 'Internal leadership' (directing the bureaucracy and managing staffing, finances and reform) refers to hierarchical relations and a range of layers of management responsibilities within the IO and its secretariat. 'External leadership' (representing the IO in international politics and finding support for its policies and actions) has a strong political character and emerges when executive heads use assets which help the organization to acquire more room of manoeuvre from its environment and play a role of its own. *IO BIO* has developed the assumption that in order to play significant roles in international politics, executive heads must combine strong internal and strong external leadership capacities. Those heads who show only internal, or only external, leadership will prove to be unproductive leaders. Those showing both forms of leadership are, in this analytical vocabulary, 'combiners'.

Executive Heads and the Emergence of International Public Administration

This section discusses the contribution of executive heads, particularly frontierspersons, to the emergence of international public administration, based on *IO BIO* entries and other sources. It reviews international river commissions, public international unions, the League of Nations, wartime IOs, the UN and UN specialized agencies in the period from 1815 to c.1960.

International River Commissions

The oldest IOs are international river commissions: the first one was created in 1815. The initial steps towards international public administration and the prototype of an international civil servant date even back to the Octroi Convention on the navigation of the Rhine between France and the German Empire, signed in August 1804 and ratified in February 1805. Although one state is missing to comply with the generally accepted IO criterium of three or more states, the convention created a small international bureaucracy to administer the river as a unitary whole. Both parties jointly appointed the director general, who supervised toll collection, inspected the towpaths and issued provisional new regulations.[15] The director general was not responsible to his government but to 'the governments as a collective organization signatory to the treaty'.[16] Each party appointed two of the four inspectors and one-half of the various toll agents in twelve bureaus along the river. This bureaucratic model, developed by Charles Coquebert de Montbret, was picked up by the Congress of Vienna which moved the core of the Octroi practices to the Central Commission for the Navigation of the Rhine. This IO was based on the principle of freedom of navigation on international rivers and should remove tolls and other obstacles.

The seven governmental representatives to the new Rhine Commission had to learn how to cooperate in a multilateral setting and needed seventeen years to issue the commission's first constitution, the 1831 Act of Mainz, which vested both legislative and judicial powers in an enlarged commission. The then created chief inspector was an international civil servant, since he was appointed by the commission through a system of weighted voting for the member states, paid from a common treasury and sworn to obey the commission's rules. Publications about the commission mention names of commissioners but not J. B. von Auer as chief inspector. The judges of the (national) Rhine courts that were created were appointed nationally but took an oath to apply the Rhine regulations unrestricted by local jurisprudence. The commissioners met once a year, elected a president each year and proposed provisions that required ratification by member states. They did so with a modest group of international staff but with much larger groups of local personnel working for the commission.[17] The new 1868 Act of Mannheim eliminated the position of chief inspector (as all tolls had been removed) but continued its combination of international staff hiring local personnel. Based on the new constitution, drafted by the 1919 Versailles Peace Conference, this early international public administration was replaced by a permanent secretariat with a secretary-general in 1920.

Similar administrations were set up for other rivers. The European Commission for the Danube, set up by the 1856 Paris Peace Treaty, had seven equivalent commissioners as its executive committee. Unlike the annual leadership changes in the Rhine Commission, British commissioner John Stokes developed into the Danube Commission's frontiersperson and long-lasting leader of this collegial institution, its bureaucracy and local personnel (1856–71).[18] The commission under his guidance drafted legislation in a manner which accommodated Ottoman law. The inspector-general of navigation and the captain of the port of Salina, although originally appointed and paid by the Sultan of the Ottoman Empire, were considered as acting under the direction of the commission and being invested with an international character, which was strengthened over time when the commission alone appointed and paid the inspector-general, the captain and other staff. Hence, this case shows a similar combination of a small international staff and large groups of local employees. For its buildings and ships the commission used its own flag. After the Versailles Peace Conference and a special conference in 1920 the commission was given a permanent secretariat in 1921.

The 'Danubian model' was also embodied in the General Act of the 1885 Berlin Conference regarding Africa, although the provided Congo Commission never came into being. The river commissions had in common the fact that in order to secure freedom of navigation and improve transportation they developed international public administrations, led by a small group of international civil servants and employing larger numbers of local staff. Individual commissioners however functioned as IO leaders, rather than executive heads, either on an annual basis or for a longer period.

Public International Unions

Most public international unions (PIUs), as IOs were called at the time, arose out of series of multilateral conferences. The conferences and PIUs proved helpful instruments in regulating common problems as a response to the expansion of modern capitalism and technology. They filled the needs for comparative knowledge and standardization with regard to issues such as measuring the earth; establishing a standard time; equal weights and measures; the protection of intellectual property rights; telegraph and postal services; and common regulations for international shipping, railways and roads. Since 1865 the series of conferences went through a process of institutionalization, in which permanent organizations with regular general assembly meetings replaced the former ad hoc combination of conferences and follow-up conferences, while permanent staff members became responsible for the day-to-day running of the organizations, thus taking care of continuity.[19] The PIUs established international mechanisms for doing 'a kind of job that had never been done before', with the Bureau of the International Telegraph Union (ITU) establishing 'the prototype of the secretariat, the vital core of any modern international organization'.[20]

Frontiersperson Louis Curchod played a role in establishing the ITU in 1865 and was a pivotal figure in creating its Bureau in 1868, which the constitution had not foreseen.[21] He succeeded in stabilizing the organization and, in spite of the Swiss government's strong oversight role, enhanced the Bureau's position by obtaining faster proceedings through the secretariat as well as improved voting procedures and ways for approval of conference texts. His combined internal and external leadership made the organization and its secretariat more self-directing than what the founders, particularly Switzerland, had had in mind. The Bureau had four permanent staff members, but depending on the work, such as for the telegraphic vocabulary it published, hired temporary staff, in 1899 for instance thirty-four persons (ten male, twenty-four female).[22]

Institutionalization of series of conferences implied a fixed location in one country and raised the issue of surveillance of the administrative work between general assemblies. The first PIUs left general supervision to the government of the country where they were located, preferably neutral countries such as Switzerland and Belgium. This, however, created organizational side effects, particularly the practice of confining appointments to positions to Swiss and Belgian subjects as well as restrictions in the communication between the secretariat and the member-state governments for all matters beyond routine correspondence. The alternative to this oversight model became the establishment of a 'governing board' or 'executive committee', in which a group of member states ensured supervision of the administrative work. PIUs established at later moments than the early ones preferred governing boards to governmental oversight as these boards functioned more efficiently. The International Bureau of Weights and Measures was placed under the supervision of an International Committee representing the member states in 1878. The first two directors, Gilbert Govi and Ole Broch, were also International Committee members, but this combination did not work well and later directors were not. Other PIUs with a governing board were the International Union of American Republics (1890), the International Sugar Union (1902) and the International Office of Public Hygiene (1907).

The PIUs thus contributed to the development of the three main IGO organs: general assembly, secretariat and governing board. Leadership was not with government representatives, as in the river commissions, but with the directors. The general understanding regarding PIU leadership was that the executive heads were men of 'high intellectual and moral standing'.[23] Step by step, states began to select qualified personnel. Mangone speaks about 'an early nucleus of international administration': 'a corps of administrators and technicians, staffed and paid by the pooled resources of the nation-states, owing first allegiance to an international organization'.[24] Having a multinational staff contributed to trust in the organization. The secretariat of the International Institute of Agriculture showed weakness in this respect, since its members remained too directly responsible to their governments and its staff was not multinational enough, with, for instance in 1910, forty-two Italians out of a total of fifty-three employees.[25]

PIU secretariats nurtured transnational professional networks, with their staff members designing many new international arrangements and agreements. By 1890 international civil servants provided as much of the intellectual leadership needed to establish new arrangements 'as did professionals within national governments', according to Murphy. Their presumed professional neutrality gave staff members the authority needed to design agreements and to promote them to member states by appealing not only to the members' self-interest but also to the global good and the end of 'international lawlessness'.[26]

The League of Nations

Given the practice of river commissions and PIUs, as described above, claims that international secretariats and international civil servants did not exist before 1919 do not stand.[27] The nineteenth-century practice furthermore was extensively discussed during the First World War by, among others, the Fabians. In his book *International Government* (1916) Leonard Woolf examined the internationalization of administration in several fields, arguing that as a result of agreements between states international administration had been set up in international secretariats and also through governmental introduction of uniformity into national administrations.[28] He analysed the secretariats extensively, observing both successes and weaknesses, and concluded that under modern conditions national administrations in many fields were inadequate and that international administration was necessary and feasible.[29]

Since 1915 plans for a 'League of Nations' were being discussed in the UK, the United States and elsewhere by citizens and in government circles. The Allied powers cooperated in inter-Allied war councils in order to coordinate purchases, such as wheat supplies, and to make the most efficient use of available means of transportation. These were not IOs based on delegated authority, but rather parts of national administrations linked together for international work.[30] The secretariat of the Allied Maritime Transport Council founded in 1918 worked with seconded personnel. In June 1919 the Peace Conference in Versailles agreed upon the Covenant of the League of Nations as the first part of Peace Treaty.

Frontiersperson in the League Secretariat became Eric Drummond.[31] Relevant here is his role in the design of the secretariat. If Maurice Hankey, the British secretary of the Peace Conference, had accepted the position of secretary-general offered to him, he would have used his experience, as British cabinet secretary, with the inter-Allied war councils and, according to a memorandum of March 1919, created a group of secretariat members, nominated by each state represented on the League's council, who as 'principal secretaries' would serve as liaison agents between their respective governments and the secretary-general. They therefore needed the confidence of both sides. James Salter, secretary of the Allied Maritime Transport Council in 1918 and seen by the Americans as a candidate secretary-general, disagreed on this double allegiance. He discussed his ideas with American, French and British officials at the Peace Conference. The Americans, Jean Monnet and Harold Butler, agreed with him that the secretariat should be an international body.[32] In his memorandum of 10 May 1919 Salter argued for an ambitious League structure that was 'effectively international' and aspired to 'the developed stage of international administration'.[33] Drummond, chosen as secretary-general after Hankey's refusal, used several ideas developed by Hankey, but in a news release on 29 May also followed Salter regarding 'a truly international secretariat, whose members ... must divest themselves of national preconceptions and devote themselves wholeheartedly to the service of the League'.[34] Drummond thus constructed a secretariat with an international staff and managed to ward off attempts from member states to influence recruitments and promotions in the League. In May 1920 the council adopted Arthur Balfour's report, which officially defined League officials as international civil servants.[35]

Albert Thomas, director of the International Labour Office, also established in Versailles, used his position as a base for initiative in international social policy. Drummond and Thomas expected that the League Secretariat and the office would share central services as a matter of economy and efficiency, but circumstances rendered this sharing impracticable, to their disappointment. The two secretariats would function as 'entirely separate, often cooperating but sometimes rival, agencies'. However, Drummond and his staff had conceived of 'several functional agencies to be created in addition to the International Labour Organization (ILO) as integrated into the League through the Secretariat'.[36] This dynamic and open attitude explains how, soon after the League had launched, its economic and social activities comprised various commissions, institutes and offices that developed into separate bodies with two remarkable developments: their growing autonomous position and their secretariats (as part of the League Secretariat) as locations of leadership and 'slippage'.

Among the frontierspersons of these bodies were Salter (Communications and Transit Organization 1921–30; Economic and Financial Organization 1922–30), Rachel Crowdy (Social Questions and Opium Traffic Section 1919–31),[37] Fridtjof Nansen (High Commissioner for Refugees 1921–30)[38] and Ludwik Rajchman (Health Organization 1921–39).[39] The *IO BIO* entries show that Crowdy, Nansen and Rajchman combined internal and external leadership when setting up the necessary organizational structures and elaborating the League's social, humanitarian and health work. Their bodies also produced inter-organizational relations, among themselves, between themselves and the League, and with IOs outside the League. Relations between these bodies and the League were not simply hierarchical ones (subordination to the council or assembly), but rather relations between specialized agencies and a mother organization, able to adopt and give birth to new institutions and to tie these to its authority and principles by offering an umbrella function. The League 'system' thus foreshadowed the UN system.[40]

The international character of secretariats was a matter of practice and not yet of constitutions. The League's Covenant Article 6 does not mention the secretariat's international character. The ILO's Article 395 mentions that for reasons of efficiency the director should select 'persons of different nationalities'. However, when the League created the International Institute of Intellectual Cooperation in 1925, the director was instructed to ensure its 'international character' and direct it with 'complete impartiality' and staff selected from 'different countries'.[41] When for political reasons an Italian and a German official began to consider themselves as national representatives in the League secretariat, the League in 1932 demanded new secretariat officials to sign a declaration of fidelity to regulate their conduct 'with the interests of the League alone in view and not to seek or receive instructions from any Government or other authority external to the Secretariat'.[42] With Germany and Japan leaving the League, this declaration had little practical effect.

Wartime Organizations

Several later UN specialized agencies were created during the time of the Allied United Nations (1942–5), hence before the establishment of the UN Organization. The Final Act of the Hot Springs conference on food and agriculture in May and June 1943 did not mention the Interim Commission's international character. The director general of the United Nations Relief and Rehabilitation Administration (UNRRA), set up in November 1943, could appoint staff as 'he shall find necessary' (Article IV.4), but when director general Herbert Lehman in practice noted numerous national preferences, he drew on the League experience and, successfully, made all UNRRA staff sign a loyalty statement attesting that their actions would reflect the organization's needs and not those of their states.[43]

Both the International Monetary Fund and the International Bank for Reconstruction and Development (IBRD), set up at Bretton Woods in July 1944, arranged that their executive head and staff 'shall owe their duty entirely' to the Fund, respectively, Bank and 'to no other authority, with each member state respecting 'the international character of this duty' and refraining 'from all attempts to influence any of the staff in the discharge of his functions'.[44] The Convention on International Civil Aviation, concluded in Chicago in December 1944, also dealt with the international character of personnel, who 'shall not seek or receive instructions in regard to the discharge of their responsibilities from any authority external to the Organization'.[45]

While the staff's international character thus mattered in most IOs set up during the war, the October 1944 Dumbarton Oaks proposals for the establishment of a general IO (the later UN) did not mention this in its draft Chapter X on the secretariat. The four major powers discussed dual leadership for the secretariat (a president with political responsibility and a secretary-general for administrative matters) but dropped it and decided that the secretary-general should combine political and administrative tasks.[46]

The United Nations

Details more fully explaining the responsibilities of the UN secretariat were brought in through debates and amendments at the San Francisco Conference (April–June 1945). The secretariat became one of the UN's 'principal organs' (Charter, Article 7), placing it on a par with the primary political bodies. Article 99 in Chapter XV on the secretariat about bringing matters to the attention of the Security Council explicitly recognized the secretary-general's political prerogatives and distinguished this UN position from that of the League. Article 100 became the 'clear constitutional formulation of Sir Eric Drummond's initial notion of an international secretariat',[47] making UN officials international staff instead of national representatives.[48]

Although executive secretary of the Preparatory Commission, Gladwyn Jebb, had been acting secretary-general (in January 1946), Trygve Lie, secretary-general since February, was the frontiersperson who elaborated the UN secretariat's political and administrative roles. This had to be done in a short time. Lie presided over important administrative developments, leaving recruitment and running the secretariat to his senior staff. He expanded the political powers of the office by delivering legal memorandums to argue why the secretary-general should be able to act in a certain manner. He took advantage of several crises to expand the powers of the office and gain recognition for the secretary-general's political role. During the McCarthy years, however, Lie betrayed the secretariat's international and independent character (Article 100) by allowing the US government to screen US UN staff, which resulted in tensions with his staff and his resignation. Yet, as chief administrative officer, Lie succeeded in carving out a secretariat space for an active and expansionist secretary-general, establishing a number of precedents for his successors to build on.[49]

The UN Specialized Agencies

International responsibilities in wordings more or less similar to Article 100 were brought into the constitutions of most UN specialized agencies, such as the Food and Agriculture Organization (1945, Article VIII.2), UNESCO (1945, Article VI.5), the International Refugee Organization (1946, Article 9.3), the ILO (1946, Articles 9.4 and 9.5) and the World Health Organization (WHO) (1946, Article 37). UNICEF did not include them but mentioned an 'equitable geographical rotation' (1946, Rule 11). The Havana Charter of the proposed International Trade Organization did not include them either but mentioned 'a wide geographical basis' and 'impartiality' as standards (1948, Article 85). The director of the UN Relief and Works Agency for Palestine Refugees in the Near East should select and appoint his staff in accordance with general arrangements made in agreement with the UN secretary-general (1949, Article 9.b).

The PIUs that joined the UN system showed a variety of adaptation. The ITU replaced its Bureau by creating a general secretariat, including international responsibilities (1947, Article 9.6). The Universal Postal Union (UPU), however, entered the UN system in 1948 but kept its International Bureau under Swiss government supervision (Switzerland not being a UN member) until 1972, when its Executive Council began to draw new staff and financial regulations. In 1979 it stopped using Swiss government services for maintaining its finances and opted for a self-financing system similar to that of other UN specialized agencies. In 1984 the UPU amended its constitution to replace Swiss supervision by Executive Council control,[50] but the Swiss government still 'supervises, without charge, the book-keeping and accounting of the International Bureau' by appointing an external auditor.[51] Until 1964 the Swiss government proposed the director general and all senior staff, with its first non-Swiss head (Egyptian Michel Rahi) elected in 1967. The UPU adaptation process thus was enduring and complicated, resulting in exceptionally detailed staff regulations, without international responsibilities, just mentioning the 'equitable geographical distribution'.[52] When the World Meteorological Organization, which in another form dates back to 1891, became a UN specialized agency, it created a permanent secretariat, including international responsibilities (1951, Article 22.b). The World Intellectual Property Organization as successor of the intellectual property conventions of the 1880s elected its first non-Swiss director (Dutchman George Bodenhausen) in 1963 and ended Swiss supervision of its Bureau in 1970, becoming a specialized agency in 1974, including international responsibilities (Article 9.8).

Frontierspersons of the UN specialized agencies and bodies showed mixed results in elaborating their secretariats. Eugene Meyer, who launched the IBRD in 1945, met with such sharp disagreements over procedures with the national executive directors that he resigned within a year.[53] As a visionary person, Julian Huxley developed original ideas and inspired UNESCO's staff, but, given the little room the United States allowed him and his poor administrative skills, his term ended after two years in 1948.[54] Although Brock Chisholm was a visionary leader with regard to establishing the WHO in 1948, he did not succeed in leading it as an independent organization, since he had to yield to member states which decided on significant orientations. His external leadership thus was weaker than his internal one, which undermined the secretariat's position.[55] These three executive heads did not therefore combine strong internal and external leadership.

More successful was UNICEF's first executive secretary Maurice Pate. He accepted the position in 1947 but demanded a clear line of authority from the UN secretary-general and a free hand in the choice of his staff and in directing activities. Four UN specialized agencies and the US opposed UNICEF's existence and extension, but Pate, a strong and creative 'combiner', made it a permanent and worldwide organization.[56] Gunnar Myrdal, appointed as executive secretary of the UN Economic Commission for Europe in 1947, made his secretariat an independent and scientifically based organ, functioning well during ten years despite the Cold War. Myrdal saw facts as the greatest persuaders, published the *Economic Survey of Europe* and denied governments the right to modify reports.[57] Hugh Keenleyside on his turn took a low profile, given US and Soviet suspicion, and successfully elaborated the Technical Assistance Administration within the UN secretariat in 1950. His managerial and operational leadership style allowed the UN to position itself as primary actor in global economics and enhance the aspirations of developing countries.[58]

When looking for someone who actually built an organization from scrap, it is Eric Wyndham White who combined internal and external leadership capacities to turn the 1948 General Agreement on Tariffs and Trade into an IO. He initiated and regularized meetings of contracting parties, widened the secretariat's mandate and prepared for new rounds of tariff negotiations. Being in charge of tariff negotiations was not a customary role for an executive secretary.[59] UN high commissioner for refugees Gerrit Jan van Heuven Goedhart in 1951 met with strong US opposition, a lack of resources and competition from other IOs, but as a smart 'combiner', who secured his own funds and expertise and used windows of opportunities, managed to strengthen the marginalized UNHCR and turn it into a relevant and even for the US acceptable actor.[60]

Less fortunate was Paul Hoffman, who successfully set up both the UN Special Fund (1958) and the UN Development Programme (1965), but his decentralized internal leadership and centralized external leadership resulted in a misdirected administration and eventually his dismission.[61] Sterling Cole's impatience with protocol, diplomatic conventions and political consensus building within the International Atomic Energy Agency (1957) resulted in strong opposition to a second term and credits for actual accomplishments to his senior staff.[62]

Available *IO BIO* entries of UN frontierspersons thus show both weaknesses regarding the elaboration and leadership of international public administrations (Cole, Huxley, Meyer) and achievements based on combined internal and external leadership (Keenleyside, Myrdal, Pate, Van Heuven Goedhart, Wyndham White) as well as mixed results, such as success in creation but not in governance (Chisholm, Hoffman) and offending Article 100 (Lie).

Conclusion

Individual career descriptions of the first executive heads of IOs, available through *IO BIO*, have added to better understand the emergence of international public administration. In the nineteenth century, international river commissions established international administrations led by commissioners, whereas PIUs established permanent secretariats led by qualified executive heads. These secretariats performed international functions with some independence vis-à-vis the member states and staff members used their professional neutrality to prepare arrangements and agreements. The feasibility of such international administrations, with civil servants with first allegiance to the IO, was one lesson, the creation of governing boards rather than governmental oversight by one country another. The debate between Hankey and Drummond, who had quite different ideas about the structure and functioning of the League of Nations Secretariat, shows that outcomes cannot be predicted when IO constitutions are still being negotiated. Drummond's international secretariat model that emerged spread to later IOs, including the UN, and made older IOs adapt.

While the League tended to centralize its specialized agencies, the UN tried to bestow upon them a 'marked degree of independence which would then encourage them to show initiative in their particular sectors', according to Williams.[63] He describes the UN executive heads as extremely independent ('their powers have often been compared with those of feudal barons'), highly political animals, to be mainly concerned with their majority support in votes (rather than in finance) and with a role in hiring and firing that was 'usually more important than the regulations'.[64] The frontierspersons discussed here laid the foundation for Williams's characteristics of independence, but it should also be remarked that not being able to combine internal and external leadership was a serious disadvantage.

3

The Biography as Institutional Can Opener: An Investigation of Core Bureaucratic Practices in the Early Years of the League of Nations Secretariat

Haakon A. Ikonomou

The principles of recruitment, the loyalties and requirements of international civil servants working for the League of Nations Secretariat (1919–46) were relatively well defined from an early stage. Already from its creation, the first Secretary-General Eric Drummond settled on a functional division of labour within the secretariat, with multinational sections dealing with everything from health to disarmament. He also decided that the staff were to be loyal to the international organization alone, rather than working on behalf of a member state. From 1922 onwards, moreover, the officials had the staff regulations to browse through, where detailed requirements in terms of staffing practices, moral obligations, rights and duties, rules of conduct and administrative hierarchies were established. Equally important, the staffing of the League – handled by the so-called Appointments Committee, composed of senior officials and headed by the secretary-general – was to balance international *representation* to build and uphold legitimacy with its member states, with strict *meritocracy*, as increasingly became the standard of most national administrations, to retain professional autonomy. Formally, the secretary-general had the sole authority to recruit new

---

I am most grateful to Markos A. Bouketsidis-Skourtelis for translations from Greek to English of correspondence from the Venizelos Archives. Many thanks also to Dimitri H. Gondicas, Director of the Seeger Centre at Princeton University, and Christos Tsakas, for the kind invitation to come and talk about my forthcoming biography on Thanassis Aghnides and international civil servants at Princeton University in February 2019. Thanks for the many rewarding discussions in the ongoing Global Biographies project. A particular thanks goes to Laura Almagor and Gunvor Simonsen for many stimulating debates on the uses of biography. Lastly, thanks to Karen Gram-Skjoldager, Torsten Kahlert and Emil Seidenfaden of the Invention of International Bureaucracy research project for valuable input to this chapter and various previous papers on Aghnides.

officials. With higher staff, the appointments had to be approved by the League Council.[1] The long-lasting repercussions of these choices on international public administration are explored in Karen Gram-Skjoldager and Haakon A. Ikonomou's chapter in this volume.[2]

This chapter presents a different approach and argument. The aim is to explore how biography can be used to unpack and question these core traits of early international public administration within the League Secretariat by following the Greek diplomat and international civil servant Thanassis Aghnides through two formative and connected bureaucratic practices: getting hired and working on an assigned task. In doing so, the chapter also offers a historical contextualization and inroad into the League of Nations that is not often seen: by exploring the early professional career of Aghnides, we also situate the early years of the League Secretariat against the collapse of the Ottoman Empire and show how a cultural and political broker such as Aghnides with networks and experiences in the Ottoman world was crucial to the League's engagement with the territorial and national problems that the dismantling of the Ottoman Empire entailed.

Born in the Cappadocia, in the Anatolian highlands of the Ottoman Empire, in 1889, Aghnides got a job at the League of Nations Secretariat in 1919. After several years in the Political Section – working particularly with politically sensitive nationality, border and minorities issues – he became director of the challenging Disarmament Section in 1930. Thanassis Aghnides thus became the secretary for the infamous World Disarmament Conference, which was the direct cause for Nazi Germany's withdrawal from the League in October 1933. In 1939, he became the under-secretary-general of the, by then, diminished world organization. After a stint as Greek Ambassador to London during the Second World War, he returned to international bureaucracy as chairman of the International Civil Service Advisory Board (ICSAB) and became one of the chief architects of the United Nations civil service, a model that informed several other IOs.[3]

This chapter will focus on the early parts of his career and quite specifically address two questions: Why and how did Aghnides get into the League Secretariat? And why and how did he work with the Lausanne conference and the Greco-Turkish population exchange, an issue that was deeply personal to him? By answering these two questions from a biographical perspective the chapter makes three broader claims: In the last decades, historians have explored the transnational biographies of nineteenth- and twentieth-century protagonists and recently turned specifically towards international organizations, and the League of Nations in particular, as a site to be explored through the biographical lens.⁴ The first claim – building on these recent publications – is simply that biography is more than a narrative choice. Rather, the biography can be used as an analytical tool with specific abilities to question, unpack and rethink interpretations arrived at through meso- or macro-analyses. With regard to administrative institutions, it allows us to move our analysis from formal rules of how things *should work* to the intricate practices of how things *did work*. Underneath, I will argue that the biography's ability to connect different analytical scales across time helps in this endeavour.

In line with this, the second claim is that Aghnides's hiring shows the importance of considering the structural forces that brought him to Paris in 1919 and the personal beliefs and actions that made him a suitable candidate as inextricably connected. Equally, we need to further explore the dynamics between the breakdown of the Ottoman Empire and the distinct institutional capacity building this required of the League Secretariat. Excellent work has been done on this in the context of the Mandate System of the League of Nations and in relation to the NGOs working in the region.⁵ Yet work that links the perspectives of Ottoman studies, Middle Eastern Studies and the historiography of the League is still relatively rare.⁶ This chapter makes a contribution in this respect that decentres the question of expertise and institutional capacity in Geneva.

The third claim ties Aghnides's road to Geneva together with the work he conducted in relation to the Lausanne Treaty and the Greco-Turkish population exchange. The chapter shows that Aghnides's conflation of his prior experiences, ideological inclinations, personal networks and the task at hand made him a deeply invested, broadly connected and unique asset for the League Secretariat. This could only be so, however, if his loyalties and actions aligned with those of the League. This they did, and the chapter reveals the significance for international civil servants in 'curbing' and 'matching' personal or other professional loyalties with the requirements of the League rather than abandoning them all together. On a more institutional level it shows the limited *localized* knowledge of the Ottoman world in a predominantly West-centric organization, leaving the secretariat highly dependent on the skills of a singular, relatively junior, official.⁷

The Biographical Approach – Scalarity as Institutional Can Opener⁸

'The proper subject of biography', Oscar Handlin writes, 'is not the complete person or the complete society, but the point at which the two interact. There the situation and the individual illuminate one another.'⁹ One of the strengths of the biography is its ability to link the individual to the structural and thereby provide 'valuable sensors for general trends and changes in society'.[10] Moreover, the biography may serve to examine the particular intensity and grip of such general developments, highlighting, at times testing, claims made about their importance and distribution among social groups and particular spatial units. Opposite, it also contextualizes and embeds the protagonist in the cultural webs, institutional structures and social mores of a specific time and place. In other words, the biographical approach can operate at several analytical scales at once.[11]

However, the protagonist should not only *exemplify* broader structural forces. (S)he is not a mere pedagogical tool – there to make it all more understandable or engaging. The movements, practices and articulations of the protagonist are interchangeably productive *in* and produced *by* structures.[12] Just as Anne Gerritsen holds that a locality can be 'produced' on several scales – ranging from the local to the global – so we may engage with the individual as someone produced and engaging with several scales at once. Thus, analytical scales – as we historians apply them – also need to resonate with and bring forth actual scales. Connected to this is the fact that the biographical approach allows us to unpack layers of time and question temporalities of events unfolding on larger scales.[13] One reason for this is that the historian can distinguish between and connect what we call *experienced time* and *historical time* and analyse the interplay between them.[14] If we accept this, then the agency and experiences of the person under the historian's lens can be used to analytically grasp traits about broader phenomena – because they are productive in them.

If we turn to the two formative practices under scrutiny in this chapter, it means that the hiring of Thanassis Aghnides in the early days of the League and the work of Thanassis Aghnides on the Greco-Turkish population exchange will be explored by connecting the *personal*, *institutional* and *transnational* processes that shaped and connected both. Following Aghnides's road to the League Secretariat in 1919 and his work with the Lausanne Treaty and the Greco-Turkish population exchange, the chapter challenges typical assumptions about the bureaucratic process of recruiting staff and explores the subtle complexities of an official's required international loyalty.

Getting In – A Special Kind of Mobility and Mindset

Thanassis Aghnides received his early education at three different Christian institutions in the Ottoman Empire: one Greek Orthodox, one French Catholic and one American Protestant in the 1890s and early 1900s. He learned French and English fluently, math, history, rhetoric and philosophy and – not least – musical instruments, such as the piano, a social key to the upper layers of society. The education he received from these three institutions amounted to a practical introduction to ecumenical thinking, and particularly at the American Anatolia College (in Merzifon by the Black Sea), the students were taught that they should unite the peoples of the world – across cultures and religions – and work as God's instruments for the good of mankind.[15] There was nothing preordained, of course, in his path, but his religious faith and his musical interest remained important elements of his internationalism until his death.

As the Ottoman Empire went through deep reforms (the so-called *Tanzimat*) giving more rights to religious groups and modernizing its state administration and educational system,[16] and as its coastal cities were increasingly connected to global markets, by both imperial design and economic globalization, the Christian populations of the Cappadocia region, in the heart of the Anatolian plains, were pushed towards the Mediterranean shores.[17] Thanassis ended up living with extended family in Constantinople and, with excellent grades from his early education, qualified to study law.[18] However, due to his particular language skills, and the close ties between the foreign Christian schools and the diplomatic corps in Constantinople, Thanassis was also drawn into the British and French ex-pat community and started tutoring newly arrived diplomats in written and spoken Turkish and Greek.[19] One of his 'students' was the young British diplomat Harold Nicolson.

Like so many Orthodox Greeks, however, Thanassis left the Ottoman Empire in the 1910s. Coming from a relatively well-off and large Cappadocian family, he had both the means and networks for a rather extraordinary mobility. Together with his two brothers Elie and Nicolas, Thanassis left for Belgium, where they lived with a distant family member for a while.[20] Elie and Nicolas left for the United States, though seemingly at different points in time, to strike up very successful careers: Elie as an inventor and Nicolas as a professor in Islamic Economy and Law at Columbia University.[21] Thanassis, meanwhile, settled down in Paris. He retook his legal degree at the University of Paris but was increasingly drawn to the political work of the Ottoman Greeks of Paris.[22]

During the latter half of the First World War, Thanassis Aghnides wrote several music reviews on performances of Greek music. He used his reviews to convey a subtle, yet unmistakable preference for a Greece reconnecting with its ancient 'national' roots, turned towards the West, and a new world order without (Ottoman) imperial tutelage, but instead of peaceful coexistence between a brotherhood of well-defined nation states.[23] His artistic musings soon caught the eye of the liberal Greek statesman Eleftherios Venizelos, in Paris at the time. Venizelos, Greek prime minister from 1910 to 1915, from 1917 to 1920 and several times later on, was the main architect of the Greek entrance in the First World War on the side of the Entente and the near realization of the 'Megali Idea' (the ambition of a Greater Greece, including large parts of Asia Minor) and became a trusted partner and useful instrument for British and French designs in the Middle East towards the end of the war and, particularly, in the violent settlement of the war after the Ottoman Empire collapsed.[24] Sometime in 1915/16, Venizelos called Aghnides in for a meeting, under the pretence that he wanted to discuss an article written by Aghnides entitled 'Greek art itself again'.[25] The content of the article itself must have convinced Venizelos that Aghnides was of the right ideological persuasion, and Venizelos – typically for him – recruited the young Cappadocian to his personal entourage of diplomatic envoys.[26] Aghnides obliged – a decisive step from being an Ottoman emigré in Paris to being a Greek national in service of his government, though he would not gain his new citizenship before 1924.[27]

Towards the end of the First World War many Ottoman Greeks came to see the Greek state as a possible guarantor of their rights and security and became ardent supporters of the Venizelist conception of the 'Megali Idea'. After his recruitment, Aghnides was stationed to London as director of Communications for the Greek Embassy during the last years of the First World War. In particular, he reported on British and American views on Greece's territorial claims after a (potential) allied victory. Aghnides, in other words, played a crucial part in Venizelos's plans to win allied support for a 'Greater Greece'. Among other things, Aghnides wrote regularly to the periodical *La Méditerranée Orientale*, published by a group of Ottoman-Greeks based in Paris and London. Here, Aghnides started to use terms such as 'national self-determination', 'civilizational right', and 'minority protection'; he drew on and reviewed new scientific works on ethnicity, geography and the nation state and started to dress up his arguments in an explicitly Wilsonian rhetoric of a new international order of peaceful, liberal nations.[28]

By the end of the First World War, Aghnides had left the Foreign Service and returned to Paris and was looking for new work. Here he met the now well-established diplomat – his old Turkish student – Harold Nicolson, who worked for the British delegation at the Paris Peace Conference and had recently been recruited to the secretariat of the League of Nations by Eric Drummond. Nicolson, therefore, wrote to the secretary-general:

I wish to recommend to you a young Greek who would, I think, be extremely valuable on the International Secretariat [...] I have known him for the last six years as he used to give me Turkish lessons in Constantinople. [...] I can guarantee that he is exactly the sort of person you would want, and I think it would be a great pity if we failed to secure his services.[29]

Drummond had to act swiftly and create a functional League Secretariat even before the full extent of its tasks and functions had been defined. Thus, the newly appointed secretary-general – after such men as Eleftherios Venizelos himself and Secretary to the British (War) Cabinet Maurice Hankey had passed down the post – seized upon the opportunity, when the Paris Peace Conference drew to a close, to recruit a small team of employees that would shape the institution profoundly. One of these early recruits – via an early recruit – was Thanassis Aghnides.

The structural traits of the early secretariat meant that Aghnides was always relatively likely to start out in the Minorities Section.[30] The Minorities Section was charged with the task of dealing with the politically charged and intricate legal regulation of national minorities regimes. Out of the twenty-three members of section and directors working for the Minorities Section (1919–46), twelve came from various national foreign services and nine were jurists or had legal training. Five officials were diplomats *with a* legal training, which means that fifteen out of twenty-three higher officials were either a diplomat, a jurist or both.[31] The concentration of jurists and diplomats is explained by the tasks of the section: overseeing the Minorities Treaties signed by the new or re-established Central, Eastern and South-Eastern European states, securing certain religious, educational and linguistic rights to national minorities. The section applied and monitored new, abstract legal principles and treaty obligations to a mélange of ethnic, religious and political groups across multiple newly formed states in which all major Western powers had strong interests.[32] As I have shown elsewhere, the nationality of who worked in Minorities Section mattered a great deal.[33] Due to the contested nature of the regime and the many vested interests, no French, German, Central or Eastern European officials worked their (and only one British official) throughout its existence. Officials from these countries could not work directly with minorities issues as it would delegitimize the section's position as a 'neutral' broker. This left the section to officials of other nationalities. Particularly, the Minorities Section was dominated by Scandinavian officials, as they were seen as distant enough to deal with the politics impartially, yet close enough to understand the peculiarities of the situation and whom they should align their views with.[34] Aghnides, therefore, was an almost perfect match for the section: a diplomat-jurist coming from a smaller European country outside of Eastern and Central Europe. However, being Greek was not exactly a token of disinterest in minorities questions. Here, we can only speculate that his unique language skills and knowledge of religious minorities might have played a role, together with indications of a specific request from Greek Foreign Minister Nikolaos Politis (a close collaborator of Venizelos and one of the leading international legal minds of the League's efforts at collective security, disarmament and arbitration) that Aghnides be stationed at the Minorities Section.[35]

Now, what does this tell us about the early hiring practices of the League Secretariat? First, we may note that Aghnides's recruitment to the League Secretariat was based on imperial and diplomatic networks, personal recommendations and relatively subjective assessments of his qualifications. This is significant, as the first generation of international civil servants was small in numbers, would stay on for a long time and had relatively wide powers to shape the new secretariat. Aghnides's way into the secretariat thus exposes the truly unbureaucratic nature in which the League Secretariat was created.[36]

Second, we may note the co-constitutive combination of major structural forces and Aghnides's mobility and mindset that brought him to Geneva. With his language skills, legal degree and his brief diplomatic career, it is easy to see how Thanassis Aghnides in many ways was a highly suitable candidate for a newly established League Secretariat. This was helped, in fact, by his 'peripheral' background, which meant that he possessed a unique knowledge in demand as the League sought to build institutional capacity and expertise on the question of 'sovereignty governance' in a post-Ottoman Middle East, Asia Minor and Balkans. However, what propelled him towards the League were very different things. In addition to the networks mentioned above, it was decisive that he believed in – or at least aligned himself with – the right *world view* and *ideological persuasion*. It was his 'internationalist nationalism' that brought him to Venizelos, and it was his Venizelist loyalties that marked him as a person that would be attuned to British political interests and sensitive towards the responsibilities of the new world organization.

Equally important, it was his religious-ecumenical and musical education and the social mobility of his family that formed the language through which he would articulate these views towards the end of the war. There was nothing inescapable or causal in his trajectory, but it allows us to access and explore some of the violent forces that shaped his outlook: the economic globalization of coastal Anatolia in the late 1800s, which drew those with skills and resources from inland Cappadocia to the large port cities; the increasing politicization of the religious minorities in the Ottoman Empire; the importance of Paris as global hub of anti-colonial and anti-imperial nationalist intellectual movements;[37] the need for the League to build institutional capacity to deal with a post-Ottoman world; and the Paris Peace Conference as densely populated hub of networked diplomatic actors that could pull the 'right' people with the 'right' background and nationality into the secretariat.

Getting to Work – Productive, Personal and Professional

By diving into the question of how Aghnides came to work with the Lausanne Conference and the population exchange between Turkey and Greece and the multiple roles he came to play, the chapter displays the almost complete conflation of his personal experiences, his ideological convictions, his networks and loyalties, and his professional mission. Indeed, I argue, it was precisely this conflation that made him such a valued asset of the League Secretariat, which makes us realize that the qualities in *actual* demand from an international civil servant were very different from the formal norms and rules that defined the 'ideal' role of the same, a notion Aghnides reflects upon himself when he describes the need for 'amphibious employees'.

After having pursued the realization of 'Greater Greece' through military means, with the blessing of particularly the British government, 1922–3 became a major turning point for Greek Venizelists and Royalists alike. First came the defeat of the Greek army in the Greco-Turkish War, the burning of Smyrna and the violent displacement of the non-Muslim populations of a Turkey in formation. This was followed by, and partly overlapped with, the Convention concerning the Greco-Turkish Population Exchange and the Treaty of Lausanne, signed on 30 January and 24 July 1923, respectively. The latter was the first major revision of the Paris Peace settlement, replacing the Treaty of Sèvres, which had carved up, internationalized or handed out large parts of the Ottoman Empire's Anatolian lands to the Great Powers and its allies.[38] As a consequence of the compulsory population exchange, approximately 1,300,000 Orthodox Greeks were uprooted from the Turkish coastline and inner Asia Minor and arrived in Greece, while 350,000 Muslims, mainly from Macedonia and Thrace, were forced to move in the opposite direction.[39]

The League of Nations Secretariat initially played a rather marginal role in the execution of the Greco-Turkish population exchange. However, the League would, in addition to appointing the neutral members of the Mixed Commission overseeing the exchange, be involved in a number of ways not anticipated. As Mads Drange has shown, the Minorities Section, for instance, was involved from the very beginning to monitor, negotiate, collect information and advice on the many instances of violence and pressures against minorities.[40] Moreover, in a more general way, the League Secretariat – and particularly the Political Section – acted as a nodal point for the governments, relief organizations, international commissions and bodies, and others that sought to influence the execution and outcome of the population exchange.

Having begun in the Minorities Section, Aghnides was first transferred to the Disarmament Section, before ending up in the Political Section in 1922.[41] Drawing on his language skills, his knowledge of religious minorities, and a professional blend of legal and diplomatic expertise enhanced by his stint with the Minorities Section, Aghnides was tasked with monitoring 'national' disputes in the Balkans and Asia Minor, starting with the Greco-Bulgarian population exchange.[42] As the secretariat gained its role as a brokering agent in the implementation of the Treaty of Lausanne and the monitoring of the population exchange, Aghnides became one of its intermediaries, shuttling between the Mixed Commission overseeing the exchange, various refugee and humanitarian organizations, the League Secretariat and council, and the Greek and Turkish governments. As the secretariat's informal envoy, Aghnides helped define the presence of the League in the population exchange policy. Moreover, as the *only* Greek national and 'local' expert of the secretariat, he became an important informant of the council.[43]

A particularly important role that Aghnides maintained during these years was that of personal contact point for Eleftherios Venizelos – who returned to Greek politics as chief negotiator at the Lausanne Conference – within the League Secretariat, keeping the dialogue going between the Greek statesman and Drummond and the director of the Political Section Paul Joseph Mantoux in particular.[44] This was part of a broader 'interpreting' of Greek demands, concerns and politics within the League context and vice versa. A good example of this is when he wrote to one of Venizelos's people to explain that the political deals of the council were 'determined not officially or publicly before the Council, but instead in advance and informally. In fact, the Council [simply] authorises the decisions that have been determined in private'. Aghnides therefore urged member of Venizelos's negotiation team at Lausanne, Mr. Michalakopoulos, to make a trip to Geneva to discuss the matter of securing a loan from the Great Powers for the settlement and feeding of refugees in Greece before 'we will again appear unprepared before the League of Nations Council'. It may be noted that Aghnides refers to a collective 'we' – *us Greeks* – and he applied an honest and direct kind of pressure which he would never do with his colleagues in the secretariat, finishing the letter with a sarcastic comment: 'I guess the Greek government does not wish this particular matter of the loan to be successful.'[45]

He was also instrumental in keeping an informal backchannel between Fridtjof Nansen – high commissioner of refugees in the League of Nations and the chief architect of the forced population exchange agreement – and Venizelos before and during the Lausanne negotiations. Aghnides had been prompted by the deputy high commissioner for refugees (and thus most likely indirectly by Nansen himself), and communicated to Venizelos, that he 'could achieve a lot through […] direct correspondence with Nansen, as long as this is kept secret, otherwise the prestige of Mr. Nansen would be undermined at our own loss'.[46] A few days before the opening of the conference, Aghnides could deliver the confidential message to Venizelos from Nansen:

> The Turks depend on my [Nansen's] proposals for the voluntary exchange of populations (from the previous evacuation of Constantinople from Greeks), upon all the Greeks. Naturally, I mean this exchange is mandatory. Of course the Turks kept insisting on their claims because they knew that I will not accept them and if so […] they believed that they could achieve more easily what they aim for, since in this way the negotiations would be interrupted and the Turks – after concluding peace – would turn to their usual methods, creating panic amongst Christians, who sadly abandon their property and assets [fleeing elsewhere]. In this way Turks seize all the property of the Christians. Possibly they may also resort to the arson of Pera [Constantiople], as was the case in Smyrna.

Aghnides then preceded to set up a meeting between the two at Lausanne, with the message that Nansen considered that the issue of population exchange needed to be settled at the conference.[47] These early coordinations were instrumental in Venizelos's conclusion that a *mandatory* population exchange – no matter the many regrettable consequences – was a necessary step to consolidate the Greek nation state and avoid further conflicts with, or a potential withdrawal from the negotiations of, the new Turkish state.[48]

Aghnides's work with the population exchange was thus permeated by the peculiar traits of his education and very clearly by his Venizelist internationalism. However, having emigrated from an increasingly hostile Ottoman Empire only a decade or so earlier, the population exchange was also a deeply personal matter. Two examples might suffice in this chapter.

First, while working for the Political Section of the League Secretariat, Aghnides assisted in drumming up Greek official support for the relocation of his old alma mater, Anatolia College, from Merzifon near the Black Sea in Turkey to Thessaloniki in Greece following the forced population exchange. The president of the Anatolia College, George E. White, came to Geneva to seek the help of the former student, and Aghnides considered it a 'labour of love' to help, first putting White in contact with Venizelos and then asking Venizelos to write a letter endorsing his plan of relocating the school. Venizelos obliged, stating that if Aghnides knew 'the persons that undertook this matter to be serious people, then I am prepared to grant the required recommendation'.[49]

Aghnides drafted the letter on behalf of Venizelos, stressing that an 'educational crisis' had arisen due to the 'recent devastating events that have taken place in the Near East and the consequent influx of refugees to Greece'. 'I feel certain', Aghnides had Venizelos say, 'that all my fellow countrymen will welcome any movement organized to render assistance to these poor human victims, in order to ensure them and their children some opportunity of obtaining an education and of becoming thereby useful citizens to their country.'[50] Though Venizelos was living in Paris at the time, he was still one of Greece's most influential politicians, and Aghnides knew the 'the matter could be settled with despatch *only* if I could enlist the Cretan stateman's support'.[51] 'There can be no doubt', concludes the political scientist John O. Iatrides, 'that Venizelos' support was to prove decisive for White and his associates, as well as for the authorities in Greece'.[52] Aghnides's long-standing personal ties and allegiance to Anatolia College thus produced a concrete and significant exchange.

A second example was when Secretary-General Drummond sent Aghnides to report on the social, economic and political implication of the population exchange for Greece. To gain first-hand knowledge about the situation, Aghnides visited the refugee camps in the outskirts of Athens. He was struck by those who had lived comfortable or even affluent lives in the Ottoman Empire and now had to 'resign themselves to live [...] four people in a room and work to earn their daily bread'. The Anatolian Greek Orthodox upper middle class, which he had belonged to, uprooted in brutal fashion, had lost their former purpose and dignity. 'The fate of these people, especially those who belong to liberal professions, is really sad,' Aghnides maintained, as 'their capacities remain unused and as most of these refugees left their fortune in Asia Minor'. In what was an unusually emotionally charged report, often breaking with the bureaucratic form, Aghnides observed that these refugees 'have a lot of strength to show so much courage'. This did not mean, however, that he opposed the population exchange. On the contrary, he believed that the exchange would in the long run strengthen Greco-Turkish relations and mark a new dawn for a Greece on its way to becoming a democratic state in a liberal world order based on Wilsonian principles. 'In this ferment of ideas', Aghnides wrote, 'refugees play a very important role'.[53]

His ties with Venizelos and the international humanitarian organizations, his knowledge of the Greek and Turkish political, cultural and economic situation, and the circumstances of the refugees, then, made him a very efficient information gatherer and middleman. This was a fact that both the director of the Political Section and the secretary-general took particular notice of.[54] In fact, the many roles Aghnides was allowed to play and the degree to which the League Secretariat depended upon his 'local' expertise say a great deal about the Western gravity of the institution and its relative lack of expertise on the post-Ottoman Middle East and Balkans.[55]

'Amphibious Employees'

The way Aghnides's personal, national and international loyalties aligned is striking. This was no coincidence, for when we study his hiring and work from a biographical perspective, we see that he worked hard to align his internationalism, patriotic loyalties and personal ambitions. Upon his hiring, Aghnides, who until then had been an Ottoman citizen, asked Greek Foreign Minister Politis to facilitate his naturalization, promising him to 'serve the interests of our country, which luckily now is in perfect harmony with the noble aims that the League of Nations strives for'.[56] Aghnides was seemingly equally eager to *become* Greek as he was to *become* an international civil servant and equally bent on representing their interests.

In fact, during his first four or five years with the League Secretariat, he worked tirelessly to be recognized as part of the Greek Foreign Service in order for him to have the prestige to work efficiently between the government and the League. In these early days, Aghnides saw the senior staff of the secretariat as divided into two parts: those who before being hired by the League of Nations, served in various departments of their respective Ministries of Foreign Affairs; and the rest, who were internationalist zealots or 'fanatic cranks', as he called them, often coming from various international non-governmental organizations or internationalist movements. 'It seems it is for them the best way to consume their fortune and time,' he remarked, '[t]heir role is not so important'.[57] But his eagerness to be recognized by the foreign service also had a more practical side:

> The political and social, not to say general uncertainty, which arose from the World War, is constantly growing. This is why I consider it not only my right, but my pressing duty to take my precautions for the future. Imagine that after some time, or after 3 or 5 years, the League of Nations dissolves; I will then be 40 years old. Having no bond with any national ministry *du jour au lendemain* I live my life jobless. At 40 I will have to choose a new profession. [...] What I really want is security.[58]

Aghnides, therefore, went on to draft a legal text that the parliament could adopt to ensure that the Greek Foreign Service could, as so many other foreign services of member states, absorb officials leaving the secretariat at a rank and pay-grade equivalent to what they had in the League. His reasoning as to why this was a good idea is revealing. 'The common advantages that these "*amphibious employees*" provide to their respective governments are many,' Aghnides wrote:

> (a) they represent more directly their national views; (b) they enjoy maximum independence and therefore; (c) they are in a position to place more effectively and defend their national views; (d) due to their prestige they can clearly influence international decisions in favor of their country; (e) although financially independent of their respective Foreign Ministries [...] this [arrangement] certainly promotes their sense of solidarity with the interests and traditions of their respective National Ministries.

As if to warn his own government of the consequences if officials were not assimilated by their respective foreign services, he maintained that

> a clerk who is not supported by his own government [...] would inevitably be urged to focus on his own individual future instead of totally devoting himself and employing any possible means to safeguard national interests. [...] Undoubtedly, the cornerstone of the modern civilisation is a healthy individualism. A person '*unable to save himself*' can never be a saviour of social groups.[59]

Little over a year later, he was appointed councillor of the Embassy in Bern with special thanks from the Greek government for his 'eagerness and patriotic interest in defending and promoting our national interests vis-à-vis the League of Nations'.[60]

This is exceedingly important, because nationality in the broadest sense, when correctly aligned with the rhetoric and practice of Genevan internationalism, was one of the most important capitals of the League Secretariat. What would, for example, Eric Drummond be, if not for his deep connections and continuous dialogue with British officialdom? Could Eric Colban have acted as a semi-official diplomatic envoy of the Minorities Section without the semi-detached and neutral connotations of his Norwegian nationality? It was not a matter of either or, nor a balancing act; it was the hybrid mix of the two that gave power and influence as an international civil servant. With no support from or connections to one's country of origin (or some other country), one's ability to act as a broker between multilateral agreements, norms and principles deriving from the League system and national political and economic interests would be severely limited.

Opposite, if clearly instructed by one's country of origin to act as an agent for its cause, no matter what, the official would be forced – at some point – to openly break with the codex and rituals of the international civil service. Once the mask fell off, and naked national interest was revealed, the official's actual ability to insert his countries interests into an international discourse disappeared.[61] As the Greek Foreign Minister Loukas Kanakaris-Roufos wrote to Aghnides in 1926, the government was exceedingly happy because it could count on him as a higher official who 'in addition/besides the honest dedication to the League of Nations also manages to serve his fatherland'.[62] Thus, we may understand the 'imperative' of neutrality and internationality in the staff regulations of the League of Nations, as serving the purpose of always forcing the official to align the national with the international.

Conclusion

This chapter has sought to use the biography of Thanassis Aghnides to rethink how we may understand two core practices of the early League Secretariat, that of hiring officials and working on/being assigned a specific task. Using analytical scales (both temporal and spatial) actively, the chapter explores *personal*, *institutional* and *transnational* dynamics as interconnected while tracing Aghnides's road to the League Secretariat in 1919 and his work with the Lausanne Treaty and the Greco-Turkish population exchange.

Aghnides's road to Geneva was moulded by the interactions of the major structural changes of the two first decades of the twentieth century, his extraordinary mobility facilitated by familial, diplomatic and imperial networks, and his political views and allegiances. These developments came together in Paris in 1919, just as Drummond was putting together the nucleus of the first generation of League officials. Exploring the question of staffing/hiring through several analytical scales reveals that a comprehensive history of the first generation of international civil servants will have to pay attention to the informal practices that tied place, people and persuasions together. While staffing practices became deeply bureaucratized with time, those who would create these formal rules – the first men and women – came through the door in a very different way.

Investigating his work with the population exchange, it is evident that his prior experiences, personal networks and political beliefs made him a very useful official for the League Secretariat. Contrary to the formal demand of complete devotion to the organization, the chapter has shown that it was the 'overlapping' of interests and loyalties, in this case, that made a forceful and influential official. We have also seen how Aghnides took on multiple roles in this work, which shows that even though the breakdown of the Ottoman Empire set him on a path that led him to Geneva, and Drummond and Nicolson appreciated his unique skillset and geographical background, the secretariat remained a deeply West-centric institution with little 'local' expertise to deal with the fallout of a post-Ottoman world of minority treaties, forced population exchanges and imperial mandates.

Last, the chapter looked at one aspect of Aghnides's personal experience of getting hired and working in the League Secretariat which elaborates on the point of 'overlapping'. On a personal level, it seems evident that the League of Nations was a vehicle for Aghnides to recalibrate his allegiances in a post-Ottoman world and gain a new Greek identity and professional footing. On a more institutional level, Aghnides's reflections on 'amphibious employees' show that it was possible to be unashamedly patriotic and close with one's own government, as long as one strived to align it with the overall mission of the League of Nations and did not openly break with the established bureaucratic norms and rules. This should prompt us to rethink the de facto function of the formal demand for absolute loyalty to the League. It should perhaps be understood as a way of channelling the valuable resource of nationality, conceived of broadly, to serve the internationalist ideals of the organization.

Though we should always be careful with generalizations from any singular case, the chapter has aimed to display how the biography can be used as a 'can opener' that is particularly useful for the study of administrative institutions, such as the League Secretariat, because the temporal and spatial scales of the approach force us to break with the natural inclination of accepting bureaucratic forms and prescriptive rules and ideas prima facie.

4

Prosopography: Unlocking the Social World of International Organizations

Torsten Kahlert

The Secretariat, I found, was a league in miniature.
Never, surely, in the world's history has such
a cosmopolitan group been gathered under one employer.
There were citizens of practical every State which
was a member of the League, as well as seven or eight orphaned Americans.
In the corridors of the one great building which now houses the Secretariat in
Geneva one may hear any language, from Spanish to Greek and Japanese.[1]
– Sarah Wambaugh, 1921

Introduction

The League of Nations Secretariat was the first large-scale experiment in international public administration. Many studies have pointed out the importance of the individuals working in the secretariat, such as the secretaries-general and people from the administrative leadership for instance Dame Rachel Crowdy, Ludwik Rajchman or Arthur Sweetser. Still, the majority of the international staff that populated the secretariat remain in the dark. This lack of interest in the majority of the people who inhabited the secretariat is rooted in the idea that they were merely executive administrators of the political decisions taken by the political leadership of the international organization. However, we now know that they were also important cultural brokers, shapers of policies and carriers of the ideals of these organizations.[2] In this sense they appear as valuable objects to study.

In this chapter, I probe into the broad administrative elite of the League of Nations Secretariat. What were the social and professional characteristics that enabled this particular group of individuals to land a position and have a career as a member of section, a director or an expert in the organization? How did nationality and gender affect individual chances of making a career in the secretariat and how did the group set-up change over time? By approaching the League Secretariat in this way, I want to demonstrate a broader methodological point: by mapping the sociological characteristics of this particular group of actors, it is possible to generate rich analytical insights that can improve our understanding of the political and social qualities of international administrations and their development over time, thus providing a possible model for further research on the social world of international civil services.

The chapter combines archival research with statistical analysis using the LONSEA database.[3] LONSEA contains basic information about people and places associated with international organizations from the interwar period. LONSEA was developed in the research cluster, 'Asia and Europe in a Global Context', based at the University of Heidelberg, and has been publicly available since it went online in 2010. For the statistical analysis an extract of the database containing names, gender, year of birth, nationality and career positions has been transferred to a framework based on the free software environment for statistical computing and graphics called R.[4] The statistical analysis of the group of higher officials will offer a bird's-eye view and description of patterns such as gender, nationality and career trajectories over time.[5] I combine this with a micro-historical perspective that lays out individual lives and careers to illustrate typical as well as exceptional cases.

Institutional Set-Up and General Development of the Secretariat

While the League's council met a number of times a year and the assembly met yearly, the secretariat of the League of Nations was the only permanent institution of the League. It had a complex institutional structure. The founders of the League had made no specifications as to how the secretariat should be organized and the first secretary-general, the Scotsman Eric Drummond, opted for a multinational service, where officials from different member states would work together in a functionally structured organization.

For practical reasons, officials in the lower parts of the tiered hierarchy were usually recruited locally, especially from Switzerland while higher-ranking posts were filled with officials from a broad range of member states.

The most important institutional units were the *sections*. Each section managed one of the League's policy areas. There were sections for political, legal, economic, transport, health, social questions and so on. Each section comprised officials from three divisions. The *divisions* represented the internal hierarchy of the secretariat from directors to messengers. The first division comprised the higher officials, the second or intermediary division the short-hand typists and similar categories, and the third division auxiliary staff from telephonists to lift boys. While the third division was Swiss dominated, the second division officials were predominantly British or French because of the required language knowledge. Only the first division was genuinely diverse in its national composition.[6]

At its height the League's secretariat employed around 700 international civil servants from around 45 different countries. In total, around 4,200 people from 60 different member and non-member states (such as the United States) worked in the League administration. These numbers cover every member of staff from the secretary-general to the gardeners, drivers and bicycling messengers. In this chapter, however, I will focus solely on the group of around 800 officials that belonged to the first division. This group, also known as the 'higher officials', belonged to the highest of three divisions of employees and comprised directors and members of sections as well as translators, experts, senior assistants and précis-writers to name just a few categories.[7]

The following analysis will first outline the general development of the secretariat's personnel. After that I will analyse the national composition of the first division officials over time, the achievements and limits of women in this administrative elite and patterns of post-war careers of League higher officials.

The first characteristic that we note is how relatively stable the League Secretariat was in terms of the number of staff (see Figure 1). After a short, initial recruitment phase, the number of staff evolved rather organically and remained at a relatively high, stable level until the outbreak of the war. The tumultuous political and economic context of the late 1920s and 1930s did not translate into similar fluctuations in the secretariat's size. Even though the League was hit by the effects of the world economic crisis of 1929, it managed to survive the cutbacks. Contrary to what could be expected, the withdrawal of Japan and Germany in 1933 and Italy in 1937 did not cause a massive decline

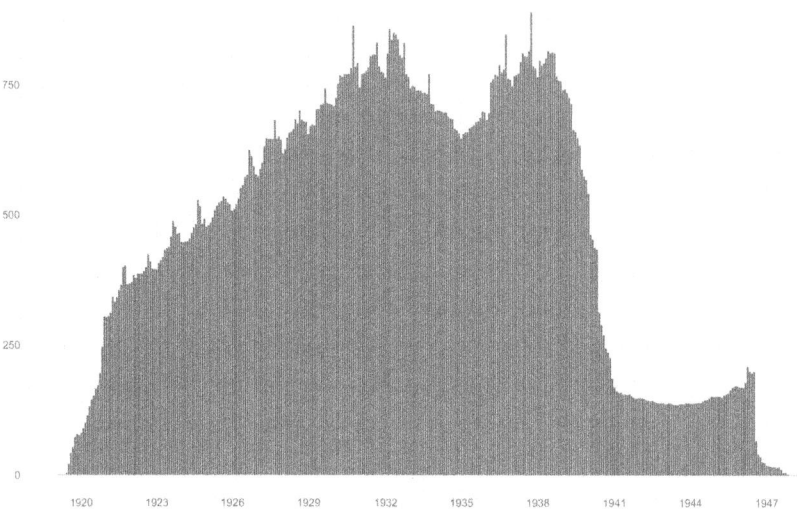

Figure 1 Development of the personnel of the whole secretariat of the League of Nations.

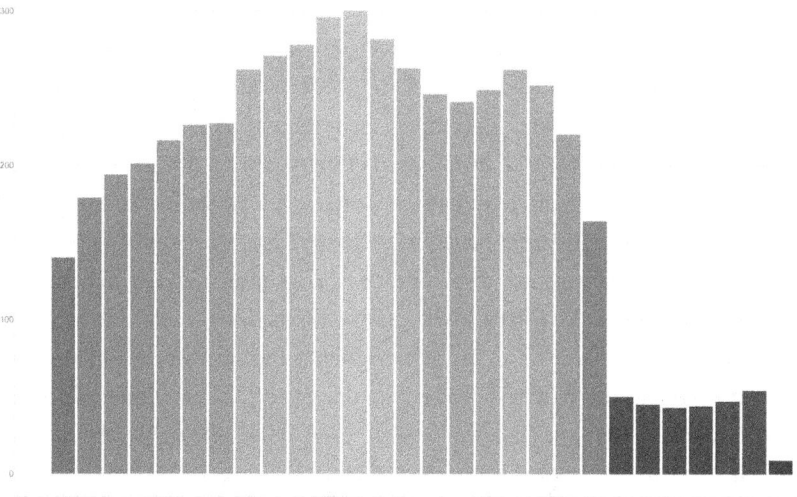

Figure 2 Development of officials of the first division (excluding temporary collaborators).

in staff. Quite the opposite: during the second half of the 1930s, the secretariat expanded again. This is partly explained by the fact that some German, Italian or Japanese officials kept their positions even after their governments had left the organization. That was for example the case for the Italian Pietro Angelo Stoppani, who kept his position as director of the Economic Relations Section until 1939.[8] Likewise, the head of the Publications and Printing Services, the

German Fritz Schnabel, also stayed until 1939 before moving to South America.[9] While Japan was the first of the future Axis Powers to leave the League, the staunch League supporter, Morikatsu Inagaki, stayed in Geneva until 1937.[10]

To sum up, it was only with the outbreak of the Second World War that the League radically declined as more than 80 per cent of the personnel was released from office in 1939–40. As seen in Figure 2, a similar pattern applies to the higher officials of the first division.

National Composition

What role does nationality play in the staffing of international organizations? Why did it play such an important role in the League of Nations Secretariat? The following part will analyse the ways in which 'nationality' was used in the institutional development of the secretariat. (Multi)nationality was, first of all, used by the secretariat's leadership to build up and secure legitimacy. Secondly, and closely related to the issue of legitimacy, it was used by member states to gain insights into and control over the secretariat by having officials inside the organization. Thirdly, it was part of a symbolic and diplomatic game about status and hierarchy in the organization. Last, but not least, it was an individual issue, something that could work to the advantage or disadvantage of a candidate seeking appointments and promotions.

Before diving deeper into these different dimensions by way of a few examples, it is worth mentioning that every member state had at least one official at one point throughout the League's existence. Still, the number of nationalities never reached the number of member states of the League at any one time (see Figure 3) even if it came close during the second half of the 1930s. In the early 1920s only 20 to 25 nations were represented, which was about 30 to 40 per cent of the member states. With the expansion during the 1920s the number of member states with officials in the secretariat would rise to thirty-five and even forty-five member states (or around 80 per cent of the number of member states), a level which was maintained until the beginning of the Second World War. With the suspension of many contracts and the withdrawal of member states from the League by 1940, the representation fell to the level of the early period with around 20 to 25 member states being represented in the secretariat.

Secondly, we note from the statistical analysis that during its existence, the secretariat employed officials from all around the globe. However, in reality the organization was heavily Eurocentric.

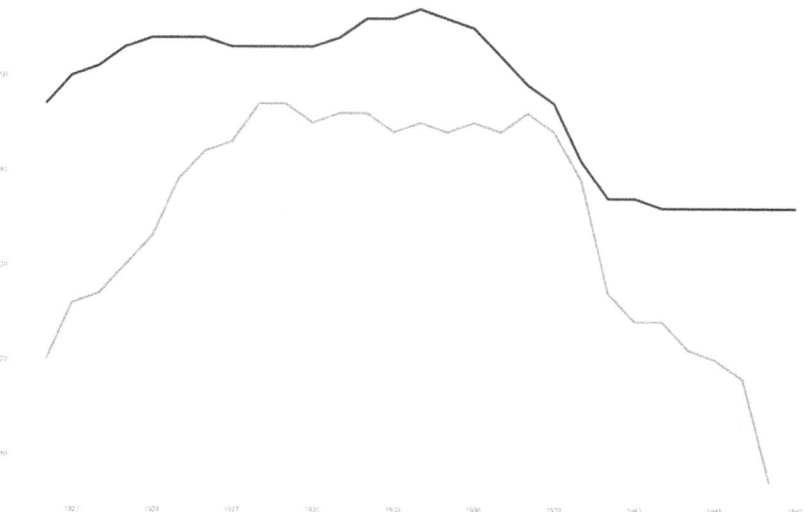

Figure 3 Member states (black line) and nationalities (grey line) in the whole secretariat.

Thus, almost 90 per cent of the personnel were European (see Figure 5) and among the European members of staff, the majority of officials were Western European (see Figure 6).[11] Throughout the period, the British and the French held almost half of all first division posts (48 per cent), while for example officials from South America held less than 2 per cent of similar positions (see Figure 4).

The national and regional distribution was to a large degree the result of the early appointment policy developed by Eric Drummond. He was given quite free hands to appoint staff to the new organization. It had been seen as urgent to set up a basic secretariat, because the first assembly was expected to meet already in the autumn of 1919 and time was running short. However, after the first lists of personnel were published in 1921, criticism against the British-French dominance from other member states was put forward particularly in the assembly, but also through national diplomatic representatives and the press in member states with low levels of representation.[12] Debates on appropriate national composition and representation would become a recurrent issue for the League of Nations Secretariat as well as for the second generation of IOs after the Second World War.[13]

Karen Gram-Skjoldager and Haakon Ikonomou have described how Drummond's appointment policy was used to establish institutional autonomy and how recruitment had to be balanced between the demand of building up an efficient administration and the demands of major and other powers for

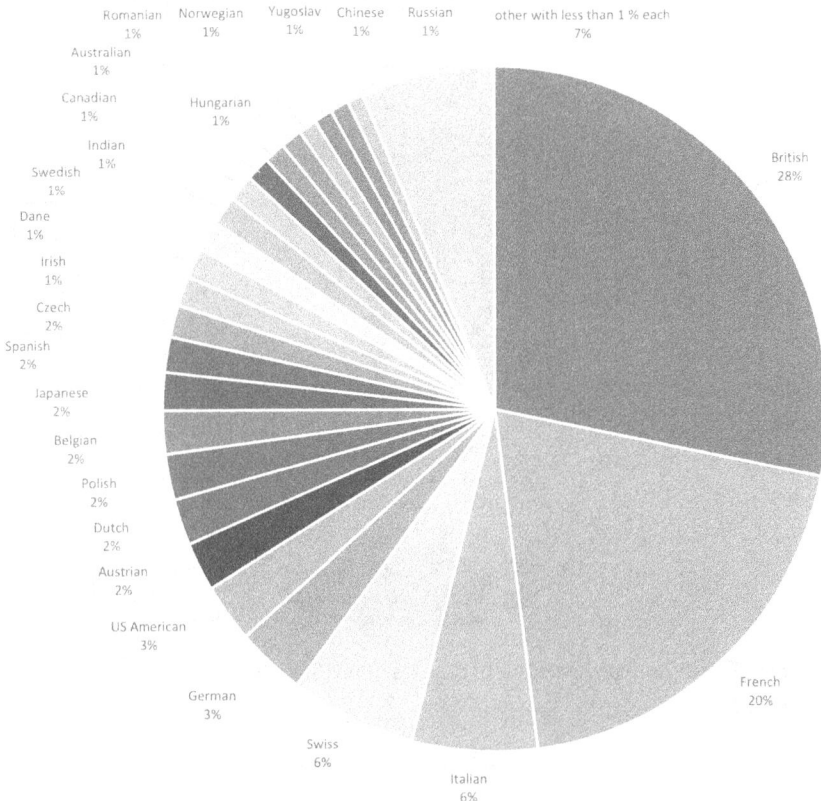

Figure 4 Relative distribution of all nationalities of the first division for the whole period 1919–46.[14]

representation in the secretariat. The composition in this sense reflected the power relations of the member states during the interwar period.[15]

For job candidates, nationality could be a capital with different value, changing because of the changing composition of the secretariat or developments in international relations or the domestic politics of a member state (see Michael Jonas's chapter for the effects of developments in domestic and international politics on German League officials' careers). In appointments and promotions, nationality could play out as more important than skills or experience, even though the appointment policy aimed at taking competence and nationality (and even gender) into consideration when hiring and promoting staff. To make it even more complex, nationality as a qualification was sometimes attached to or overlapped with other criteria such as regions (South America, Scandinavia) or whether the applicant came from neutral state, a state without colonial

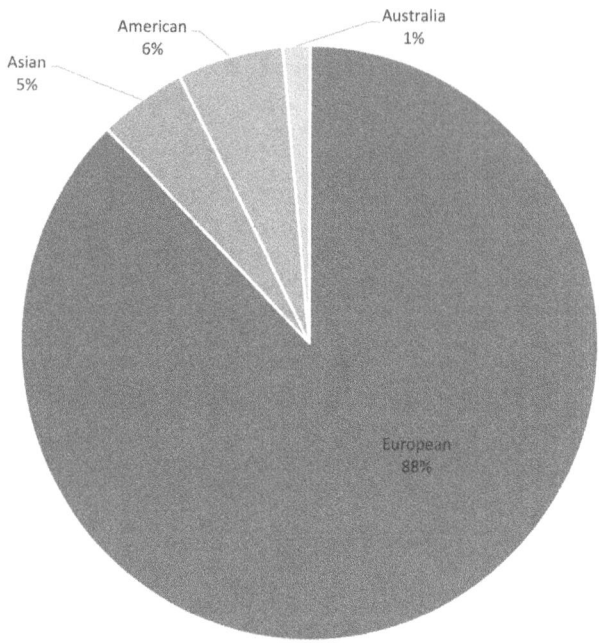

Figure 5 Relative representation of officials in the first division from different continents.

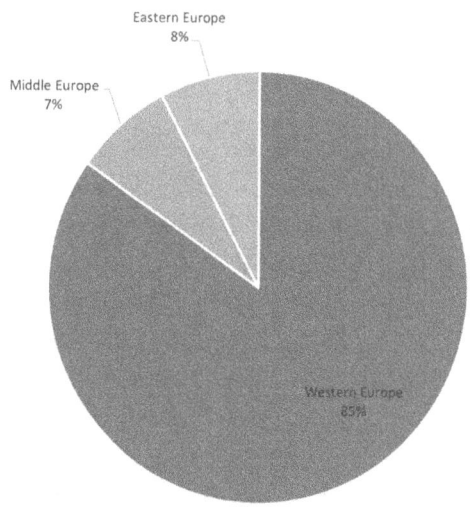

Figure 6 Relative representation of West, Middle and Eastern Europe in the first division.

past, a small or a large member state and so on.[16] Overall, it was impossible to disregard the nationality of a candidate, no matter how cosmopolitan or internationalist he or she thought or felt. Looking at nationality therefore doesn't mean that we should forget about the increasing transnational world since the nineteenth century, where world wars, global trade, migration, communication and so on had changed the lives of many.[17] Transnational lives, such as the ones of the League civil servants, became increasingly prevalent. The leadership of the secretariat used the appointment of staff of certain nationalities to promote the idea of the League in specific countries, as was the case with the appointment of the Swedish diplomat Åke Hammarskjöld, lawyer and son of the former Swedish Prime Minister Hjalmar Hammarskjöld, to the Legal Section.[18] On the other hand nationality also remained an argument to refuse promotion, for instance if a nationality was already well- or over-represented.[19] This was the case even shortly before the dissolution of the League, when Ansgar Rosenborg, who had been in the secretariat from early times on, demanded a promotion, when he became head of the League of Nations Princeton team in 1946. The last Secretary-General Seàn Lester argued that 'the nationality question is not entirely negligible'. As there was still one Swedish chief of section in charge, he had to refuse Rosenborgs request.[20]

Claims for higher positions in the secretariat also related to influence from outside secretariat. This was apparent for instance when the Austrian Chancellor Ignaz Seipel proposed an Austrian candidate for the secretariat in November 1926. He argued that after the assembly in 1926 had resolved to create twenty new posts for members of section (of which he assumed the majority will go to Germans) Austria should at least get one more member of section and would still be under-represented in relation to Austrians' contribution to the budget of the League:

> Though it is impossible to distribute the member-posts of the Secretariat on the basis of the barême [ratio] of contributions, I believe that Austria – contributing to the Budget of the League since the year 1926, 8 units instead of one, and being still 'represented' by only one officer (member B class) should be considered to belong now to the countries, the nationality of which is not adequately represented on the officer-staff of the Secretariat.[21]

The national and regional composition was viewed from the standpoint of international reputation and dignity of a nation state or a region in the world. Therefore, the appointment policy was observed in many member states on the highest political levels.

Political status and power immediately translated into presence of staff. That is illustrated by the representation of the higher officials from four major European powers over time (see Figures 7 to 10). The presence of the British and the French was quite stable throughout the League's existence and reflected the general pattern of the whole secretariat. Britain had the highest number of

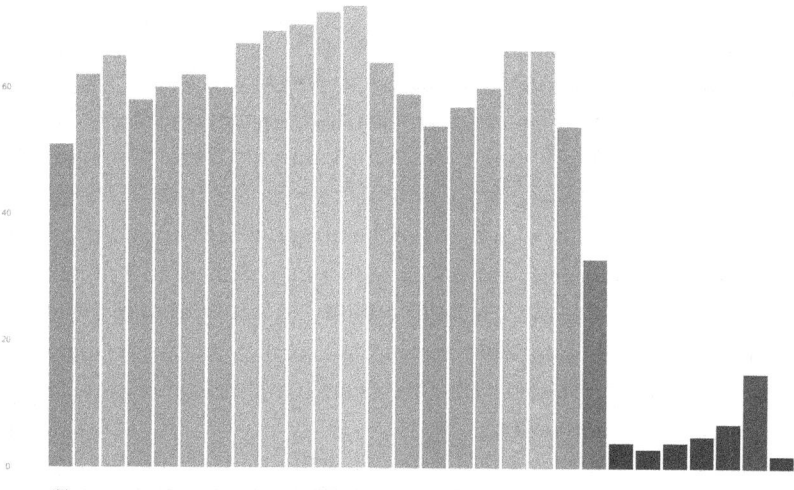

Figure 7 British in the first division.

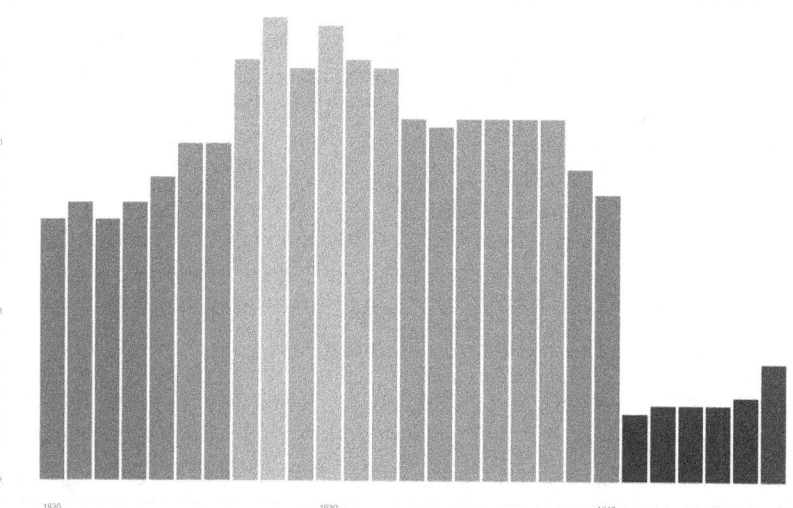

Figure 8 French in the first division.

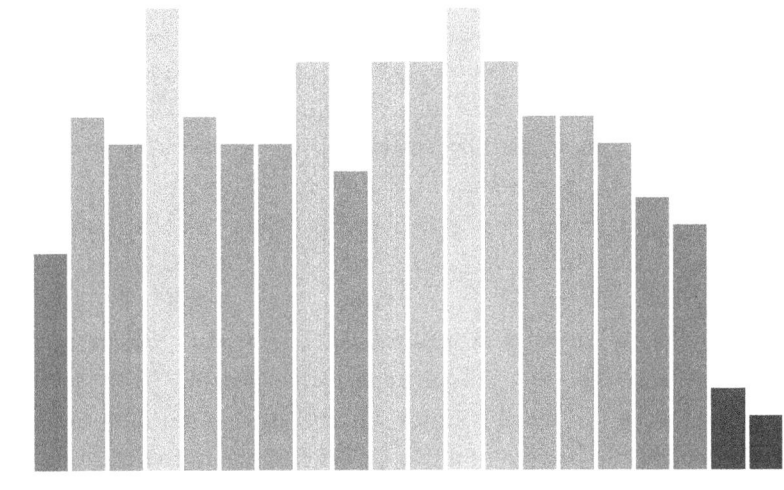

Figure 9 Italians in the first division.

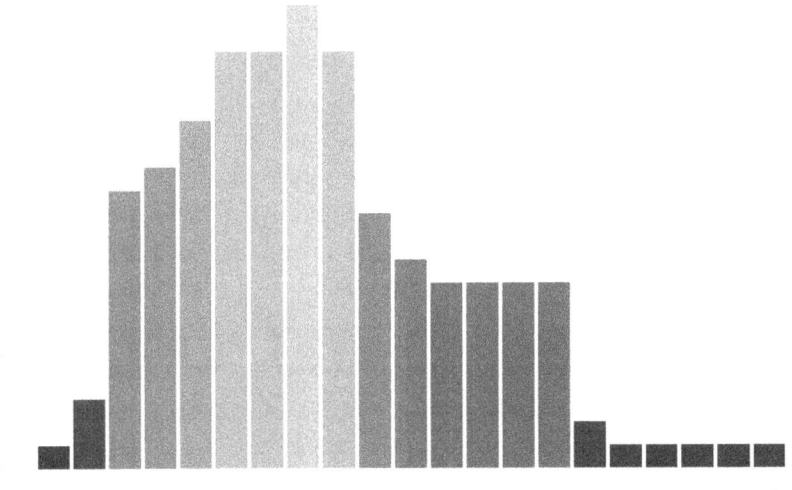

Figure 10 Germans in the first division.

officials (between fifty and seventy-five) in the first division of all member states and its highest relative representation during the early years.

The case of the Germans was different. The German Foreign Ministry and the unit for questions on the League of Nations they had set up in preparation of membership of the organization were closely observing the inner dynamic of the secretariat from early on. They made detailed plans for how many officials they would request when they became member of the League, how they would achieve this and which sections they would try to get into at top level.[22] In 1925, the German ambassador in London wrote to the Foreign Ministry in Berlin pointing out that it might be as important to have someone in a high position on eye level with Eric Drummond and his French deputy Joseph Avenol, as having a seat in the council underlining the importance of the secretariat's leadership in comparison to the council of the League.[23]

The Germans entered the League in 1926. They soon had more officials in the first division than the Italians and as many members of section as the British and they got a position of an under-secretary-general.[24] The request they were refused was a position of a section director, thus again demonstrating the intimate relationship between political power and status and representation within the League (for more on the German League staff, see Michael Jonas's chapter). After their withdrawal from the League, not all officials left the secretariat immediately. In fact, eight officials stayed until the outbreak of the Second World War in the secretariat.

Nationality was not always the deciding factor, even when it came to such a 'politicized' nationality as the German. An example is the appointment of the German Fritz Schnabel as head of the Publications Service in 1927. Initially, Schnabel had been recommended by the German Foreign Ministry together with four other candidates.[25] From the ninety-six candidates who had applied for the post Schnabel made it into the final round. His application was supported by Stanley Unwin, a British publisher, who knew Schnabel personally, from his time in London, when Schnabel studied the British publications market. Unwin's recommendation reached the Secretary-General Drummond via Konni Zilliacus, a British member of the Information Section: 'He is an ideal man for the job. Does it mean he would be in entire charge of the distribution of the official League publications? I hope so, because book propaganda is his specialty. He is a first rate man and a most successful publisher.'[26] None of them mentioned nationality as a reference. The appointments committees recommendation was about skills and experiences and the question of the 'particular character to be given the post and the results expected from it'.[27] Drummond finally decided that 'the particular weakness of the Publications Service had been on the sales side. What they had had particularly in mind in creating the post had been its development'.[28] Schnabel finally landed the position after a long process. His appointment is an example that nationality was not in all cases an issue that played out in the foreground of the appointment process. This might have to do with the particular 'unpolitical' position of the publications departments head and it emphasizes the differences of higher positions in the secretariat. Even though it was not mentioned in the sources, Schnabel, being from a major European power, might still have contributed in the hiring process, on the one hand because of the secretariat's Eurocentrism and on the other hand as a mutual compensation for the refusal to give the Germans a section director's position. Schnabel remained in the secretariat after the Germans had left the League, underlining his internationality and the German government's callback of League civil servants. In 1939 Schnabel consequently left for South America, where he stayed for the rest of his life.

Women in the Secretariat

Article 7 of the Covenant stipulated that '[a]ll positions under or in connection with the League, including the secretariat, shall be open equally to men and women'.[29] That was revolutionary for its time and indeed the gender balance across the whole secretariat was almost equal. However, there were differences (see Figure 11). The first division was dominated by men with 77 per cent male officials, but even here women reached a fairly high level of representation.[30] Every fourth official at the top level of a prestigious political organization being female was exceptional for the time.

Article 7 was a result of intensive lobbying of women's organizations at the Paris Peace Conference[31] and Drummond took note of the new expectations for the organization from the very beginning. When looking for members of section, he mentioned for instance 'the desirability of attaching a woman-lawyer to a section. He believed that it was most likely that she could be found amongst the Scandinavian member states'.[32] While he was unsuccessful in making this particular recruitment, in other cases female officials landed positions in the higher echelons of secretariat.

Myriam Piguet has underscored the point, that even if early recruitments of women were successful and the number quite high, they hit the glass ceiling in various ways and their relative position in the organization declined over time.[33] An example of an early successful recruitment into a high position was Stanislawa Adamowicz. In 1921 Ludwik Rajchman, director of the Health Section, was building up an epidemiological intelligence service. For this service, Rajchman was eager to hire Stanislawa Adamowicz, a highly qualified female Polish statistician. She spoke several languages, had a university degree in

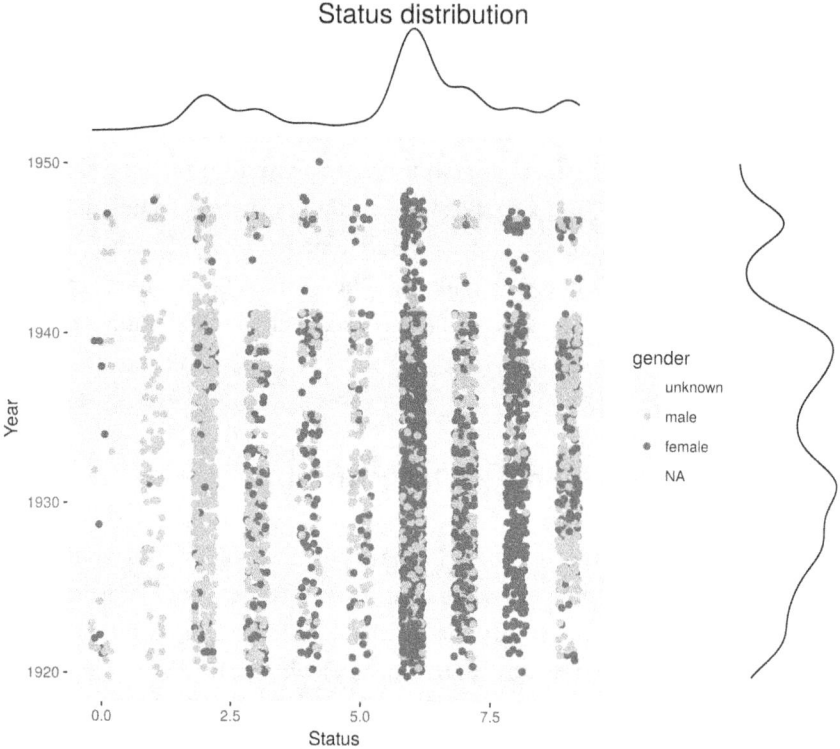

Figure 11 Status distribution of men and women in the whole secretariat.

natural sciences, was assistant editor of *The Epidemiological Review* in Warsaw, and had prepared charts, diagrams and maps for the League of Nations Epidemic Commission.[34] Rajchman probably knew Adamowicz from the epidemiological service in Warsaw so both, strong qualifications and personal networks, seem to have played into his recruitment of her. Once hired, she also proved her worth; even after the American statistician Edgar Sydenstricker arrived in 1923 with plans for him to take over her work, she kept her position.[35] However, eventually Adamowicz returned to her institute Warsaw in 1923 to work for the Polish epidemiological service.[36] Perhaps this was due to rivalry with Sydenstricker; perhaps it had to do with personal reasons. No matter the reason, the shorter and less-successful careers were a shared trait of many female League staff.[37] The presence of female staff varied greatly across the organization. From the beginning, women were most strongly represented in the internal services of the administration of the secretariat such as the stenographic service or the library and here often also in leading positions. Women tended to be less well represented in the political sections such as the Disarmament, Political, Legal or Mandates Sections. The Political Section had one female assistant, the Mandates Section two senior female assistants. The Disarmament Section employed no women at all, except for the secretaries who belonged to the second division. Female representation was stronger in the Social Questions Section and the Intellectual Cooperation Section. Myriam Piguet thus has characterized this as 'the old bourgeois vision of women – naturally organized, kind, attentive and pacifist' that 'was still very much in fashion' and has pointed out that '[w]omen of the first division were assigned to jobs that let them practice their "natural" propensity for nurturing and caretaking, noticeably articulated around what would later be called "humanitarian aid"'.[38] In other words, while the number of all positions was almost equally divided between the gender, the status and subsequently salary and responsibility differed widely.

As has been stated above with one out of four officials women had a substantial presence in the highest division of the secretariat, but only a few of them could actually break the glass ceiling of senior assistants or personal secretaries to get promoted to member of section during their career. One was Gabrielle Radziwill, who started her career in the Information Section as senior assistant, before she was promoted to member of section. In this role, she later moved to the Social Questions and finally the Intellectual Cooperation Section. When Radziwill, a Lithuanian official from the upper echelons of her home country, was promoted to member of section, it was emphasized during the meeting of the appointments committee that it should not be seen as a present or 'personal promotion', but because she was doing the same work with the same responsibilities as male members and she should therefore be treated on equal terms (for more on her career see Emil Seidenfaden's chapter).[39]

Figure 11 shows the status distribution of men (light grey dots) and women (dark grey dots) for the whole secretariat over time.[40] We note that over time the distribution between gender and status was quite stable and resisted in a similar way as the national distribution radical changes once it was set up. The majority of women worked in the parts of the secretariat with a lower status, while men dominated the higher positions.

Career Trajectories

How long did careers in the secretariat last and what would be a typical career? What does the career trajectories tell us about the inner dynamic of the administration? The first thing we note, is that the great majority of officials had only one contract and then left the administration. On average people stayed for around seven years, but the distribution of the career length in the secretariat differed widely. There were people with temporary short-term contracts to assist during the yearly assemblies or for international conferences and there were people who stayed from the beginning to the end, the carriers of the League's secretariat. Next we note that while the majority of officials remained in the section they were hired to, some changed the section.

In general, the secretariat did not develop a clear hierarchy of all positions and how they would relate to each other. This gave the impression of a rather flat hierarchy – an image most probably wanted and propagated as well. While this flat hierarchy was also a result of the aim of reducing complexity to avoid discussions and enviousness about appointments of one or another national to a certain position on the one hand, on the other hand it was a result of the less systematic and more pragmatic development of the secretariat and the specific mixture of different administrative traditions which influenced its development. In consequence the only clear option for promotion as a member of section was from B to A member, to get promoted to one of the rare director or head of section positions, or to move to another section. As vertical promotion was limited, the latter option, to move to another section, served as an additional and equivalent of promotion. The ways people changed sections will enable us to sketch typical and atypical trajectories and also reveal some kind of hidden hierarchy of the sections.

Officials would for example move from the Information Section to the Political Section, such as the Indian journalist Amulya Chandra Chatterjee, who had been director of Reuter's and Associated Press in India before he came to Geneva.[41] The chief and later director of the Disarmament Section, Salvador de Madariaga, had also started his career in the Information Section.[42] De Madariaga was an intellectual, an author and liberal internationalist and he was on the other hand a diplomat.[43] After the war he was one of the founders of the Collège d'Europe, a postgraduate institute, which has become a kind of Oxbridge for EU officials. The US-American Orie Benjamin Gerig, a Mennonite rebel and peace activist, who later became a diplomat in the U.S. State department, moved from the Information to the Mandates Section, to name but just a few examples.[44]

Some officials changed the section more than once. An example is the Austrian Egon Ranshofen-Wertheimer. He was a journalist by training and had served for different newspapers including the Social Democratic newspaper *Vorwärts* in London, before he landed a position in the Information Section in

1930. Because of political pressure he moved for a short period to the Economic and Financial Section in 1933, before he was attached to the Social Questions and Opium Traffic Section, where he stayed until 1940.[45]

Another example is the Dane Ludwig Krabbe, who started his career in 1921 in the Information Section. After ten years of service he moved to the Administrative and Minorities Section for two years, after which he moved to the Political Section as the only Scandinavian ever having served in this section.[46] He left the secretariat in 1939. A last example is the Venezuelan Manual Juan Arocha. Arocha had been Consul at Geneva with special mission to the League and the ILO before he became first liaison officer for Latin America within the Information Section in 1922. In 1924 he became member in the Disarmament Section and one year later member in the Political Section.[47]

While the Information Section served in all of these exceptional cases as the starting point for the career, the Political Section was mostly at the end and peak of a career of people who moved from one section to another. Even though the Uruguayan Julian Nogueria started his career in the Mandates Section, his career also fits this pattern. He was secretary to the president of the Uruguayan Republic during his six months tour in Europe and became secretary to the Delegation of Uruguay during the Paris Peace Conference. After one year in the Mandates Section he became member of section in the Information Section and in 1931 its counsellor. In 1934 he moved to the Political Section, where he stayed until 1940.[48]

The Economic Section was a section in between. Officials started or ended their career here. The English Arthur Elliott Felkin, who served as secretary for the British delegation of the Paris Peace Conference and was after that personal assistant of Arthur Salter, during the period when Salter was general secretary of the Reparation Commission in Paris, entered the secretariat in 1923 in the Economic Section, supposedly thanks to Salter, who led this section during the 1920s.[49] In the 1930s Felkin, who has been described of representing 'the epitome of diplomatic discretion'[50] moved from Economic to the Social Questions Section. He was later appointed Secretary to the Permanent Central Opium Board.

The Czech Valentin Stencek had been working in the Ministry of Finances in Prague before he started in the Economic Section as a member of section and was first appointed as a secretary to the Economic Committee. The director of the Economic Section was in 1921 urgently looking for a specifically skilled diplomat with knowledge of the Austrian finance: 'A young man who has had some experience in banking or public finance or possibly a student of economics would have the required qualifications. Knowledge of German is essential. He should speak English and French.'[51] For this thought a Czechoslovak seemed suitable. The Czech ministry of finance recommended Stencek. Early appointments were often conducted via recommendations of national ministries and personal networks, less on the basis of open and competitive applications processes, a procedure which came under criticism later on. Stencek was married to an English woman and became the longest serving Czech official in the secretariat. In 1937 he was promoted to direct the Internal Administration in the course of the reorganization of the secretariat under the Secretary-General Joseph Avenol and remained in this position until the final dissolution of the secretariat in 1947.[52]

Post-war Careers

At present, there is no systematic analysis of where the League officials went and which jobs they took after the organization was closed down. However, we know enough to say that they continued their careers in many different ways and that a large group went on to work for one of the UN organizations, a fact that shows us that the experiences of these officials were valued even if the League was seen as a failure and the UN tried to minimize its connections to its organizational predecessor.[53]

Having been part of the group of officials which crossed the Atlantic to escape the war in Europe, the so-called League of Nations Princeton team was definitely an advantage for a career in the UN organizational world.[54] We see an example of this when, on 8 April 1946, the last Secretary-General Seàn Lester wrote Ansgar Rosenborg, head of the League's Princeton team, about the procedure of the national repatriation of League officials, whose contracts would end soon with the dissolution of the League. In his letter Lester touched on the question of applications to the UN. For the members of staff at the Princeton Mission, Lester stated that he could transfer applications to the UN collectively, while all other staff would have submitted individual applications.[55] By the end of April, Rosenborg was invited by Trygve Lie to work part-time for a UN statistical commission in New York.[56] Rosenborg was not the only remaining League official during that period who got invitations from UN organizations. William Martin Hill, of English origins, had started his career in 1927 at the age of twenty-two years in the Economic Section. During the war he was part of the League's Princeton team and after the war he was transferred to the UN where he stayed until he retired from a position as assistant secretary-general for Interagency Affairs in 1970. He remained a consultant to the UN even after his retirement.[57] The Princeton team had an advantage in being transferred to the UN. But also some technical experts, who belonged to the small team, which stayed in Geneva during the war, continued in the UN world. An example is Yves Biraud, who had been a member of section of the health organization from 1925 to 1946.[58] During the war Biraud had been the last medical expert of the Health Section in Geneva, a section that secured the League a miniscule level of legitimacy due to the epidemiological data they provided to both belligerent sides.[59] After the war, he held the position of the *Director de la division d'Epidemologie et de la Statistique sanitaires* in the WHO.

Essy Key-Rasmussen, one of the few female higher officials who made it up to a member of section position in the Communications and Transit Section, managed to get a position on her own initiative in the Food and Agriculture Organization of the United Nations (FAO). She is an exceptional example among the group of people who entered the UN world from the League as a solo female who was not part of the privileged Princeton team. In April 1939, Key-Rasmussen had asked for permission to go on a mission to Washington, a request that was turned down by Secretary-General Joseph Avenol.[60] That was probably because she was on the list of people who would not get their contract extended due to the extreme cutbacks on the League's budgets. In 1941, she wrote the League's administration, now from New York, that she was eager to work for the secretariat again. She took classes in Personnel Guidance at Columbia University and was about to complete an MA in June 1942. She was doing this in order to become qualified as Dean of Women at an American College. 'The competence acquired', she added, 'would also be valuable in Europe, in case I return; for the U.S. are far ahead of all other countries in the Personnel Guidance field'.[61] In 1947, she became a member of the secretariat of the FAO, which was based in Washington, DC, at the time.[62]

However, not all officials wished to continue their career in the new multilateral landscape and circulated back into the national political and cultural realm, often through Foreign Ministries or academia.

An example for the latter is Alexander Loveday, director of the Financial Section & Economic Intelligence Service from 1931 to 1939 and after that head of the Princeton team until 1946. He accepted a position in Oxford and would become a fellow at first and later warden at Nuffield College in Oxford.[63] After being an international civil servant from 1919 to 1946, Loveday stands for League officials, who came from and would go back to academia.[64]

To summarize, the experiences of the League's officials were valued, either in academia or in foreign ministries or in the UN world, more than the new world organization would propagate in their tendency of neglecting the close relationship to the first experiment in international administration. Also other officials, who had left the secretariat earlier on, and had been for example in a position in their foreign ministries during the war, re-entered the international civil service after the war. The prominent role Jean Monnet played for the European Integration is but just one example, which also shows that the European history of multilateral organization has roots in the League of Nations, even though Monnet had been in the secretariat only for a few years in its initial phase. Other careers continued in national civil services, often in foreign ministries. The model for that was laid out by the first Secretary-General Eric Drummond himself. He became ambassador in Rome in 1933 but later went back to Great Britain.

Conclusion

The secretariat of the League of Nations was a complex body, a political organization with diplomatic, often academic expert staff, a majority of them with an international mindset and liberal values the League was holding up. Its international civil service with people from many different countries working together was not only new in its scale but also in its practical work. The principal international character and a human composition along functions, not nations, were a model for others who followed. New was also that all positions were open for women too. For all of these features, as for the organization itself, one can argue that the organization failed, because it was dominated by male officials from Western major powers. But as has been shown, that would simplify and undermine the achievements. There were limits for women to rise to higher positions, but for some it was a career option they would never have had in a national environment. The same applies to the nationality question, which was in its tendency shifting more and more to a greater variety and an understanding that an international secretariat should also be composed of officials from all member states. The flexibility of the early appointments policy matured into more controlled pathways in the course of the member states gaining interest into the secretariat.

The UN downplayed the achievements of the League for its own sake. They did not want to be seen in their tradition or too closely attached with the organization which was seen as a failure during and after the Second World War. But the many officials who continued their career in the UN secretariat gives insight to the organizational and institutional knowledge which has been taken over from the League to the UN secretariat and that the experiences of the officials were of high value for the second-generation IOs. It is the historians' task of today to reconstruct these traces. An important group of the carriers of the League were also the carriers of the UN. They, together with the ones who joined them, and even including the non-liberal internationalists, belong to the same history of internationalism and the question of how to organize the world and international cooperation and order.

Part Two

Learning and Norms

5

The Influence of the United States on the Rise of Global Governance in Education: The OEEC and UNESCO in the post–Second World War Period

Maren Elfert and Christian Ydesen

Introduction

After the Second World War, governments embraced multilateralism as a way to secure peace and collaboration among nation states. New international organizations (IOs) were created for specific purposes, and they would become powerful agents of global governance and international politics, building up bureaucracies of specialized knowledge.[1] The new global governance regime that emerged in the post-war period was characterized by bureaucracies forged by dialectical relationships among IOs, governments and an array of communities consisting of experts who derived their authority from new knowledge and scientific instruments generated in the shape of statistics, indicators and comparative studies. The role of the United States that emerged as the major hegemonic world power after the Second World War was instrumental in the formation of this new bureaucracy of global governance.

This chapter focuses on two organizations that played a critical role in these developments: the Organization for European Economic Co-operation (OEEC) and the United Nations Educational, Scientific and Cultural Organization (UNESCO). The OEEC was the precursor of the Organization for Economic Co-operation and Development (OECD) that today is arguably the most influential policy shaper in the global education arena.[2] Established in 1948 in Paris, the OEEC's purpose was to administer the United States–led European Recovery Program (the Marshall Plan) for the reconstruction of Europe. Equally located in Paris, UNESCO had been founded three years earlier, in 1945, as the specialized agency of the United Nations for educational, scientific and cultural affairs, endowed with the mandate of contributing to peace through intellectual cooperation. Despite controversial debates on UNESCO's mandate – some aimed for a broad political mandate, others lobbied for a limited and technical mandate – during the first two decades of its existence, UNESCO represented the global authority for education and carried out global norm-setting functions that led to human rights frameworks such as the *Convention against Discrimination in Education*, adopted by UNESCO in 1960.[3] From the late 1950s onwards, the OEEC also took an interest in education, which continued and expanded after the creation of the OECD in 1961.[4] The United States played a crucial role in the creation of both organizations. While the formation of the OEEC was the consequence of an American initiative, UNESCO was very much a creation of the three Western powers that had won the war: Britain, France and the United States. In the early years of the organization, many UNESCO delegates and staffers, particularly the French, feared that UNESCO would become an agent of 'American cultural imperialism'.[5]

During the first twenty years after the Second World War, education came to be seen as a key catalyst to promoting economic growth and social development in societies. In the United States, governmental bodies, universities, think tanks and philanthropic foundations played influential roles in promoting a rationalist-technocratic approach to education as an investment in economic growth and American dominance in the post–Second World War world order, and they used the OEEC/OECD and UNESCO to spread this approach to Europe and other parts of the world. As we will show, the OEEC was a much more suitable partner for this endeavour than UNESCO.

The guiding question of the chapter is: What was the American influence on the bureaucratic modes of governance developed by the OEEC/OECD and UNESCO? Other connecting questions we are interested in are: What were the tensions within and between these organizations in building their institutional cultures and modes of governance and finding a role for themselves? How did the OECD – an organization created with the purpose of promoting economic development – assume its hegemonic position in the landscape of global governance of education, while UNESCO – which was founded as the specialized agency of the United Nations with a clear mandate for education – experienced a decline in its influence?[6]

To address these questions, we will identify the similarities and differences between UNESCO and the OEEC in terms of (1) the establishment of an institutional culture working for the promotion of a scientific world view, (2) the relationship of the United States with both organizations and (3) the educational activities and modes of governance of both organizations during the 1950s and early 1960s.

The structure of the chapter adheres to these three analytical aspects followed by a concluding discussion weighing the combined explanatory power of the three aspects in light of the research questions. The chapter draws on state-of-the-art research, historical publications and primary source materials harvested from the U.S. National Archives, the Rockefeller Archive Center and the UNESCO and OECD archives in Paris.

The Institutional Promotion of a Scientific World View

Twentieth-century society's unwavering faith in modernization and rationalization 'celebrated the ideals of the Enlightenment: the power of science, the importance of control, and the possibility of achieving progress through [the] application of human will and instrumental reason'.[7] In the context of the Cold War, the Sputnik shock and the fixation with economic growth in the post-Second World War period, the United States was a leading force in the search for new scientific methods for developing and optimizing educational policies and practices.

Through the Marshall Plan, which was accompanied by 'the largest international propaganda operation ever seen in peacetime', the United States exerted considerable influence in post-war Europe.[8] Between 1948 and 1952, this plan funded many 'productivity missions' that brought European managers, trade unionists and technical personnel to the United States 'to study the American way of business'.[9] The OEEC and later the OECD represented key vehicles by which the US government, scientific communities, such as the Research and Development Corporation (known as the RAND Corporation), and philanthropic foundations, such as the Ford Foundation, could spread a scientific-rationalistic approach towards education based on the paradigms of economic growth, productivity and technological advancement.[10]

In 1953, immediately after Marshall Plan funding had expired, the United States provided a grant of 2.5 million dollars to the OEEC for the establishment of the European Productivity Agency (EPA), which was created as a semi-autonomous body within the orbit of the OEEC, with the mandate of boosting European productivity through transferring American technical know-how to

Europe.[11] The EPA represented around 40 per cent of the OEEC's budget.[12] As stated by Boel, '[U]ntil 1957, the European productivity program represented an investment of more than 300 million dollars, approximately two-thirds of which were directly or indirectly financed by the United States.'[13] Alexander King, one of the pioneers of the OEEC and deputy director of the EPA, referred to the 'productivity saga' that guided the OEEC.[14] King had great faith in the 'ability of applied and goal-oriented research to transform modern society' and 'scientists as the key political actors in the future society'.[15] The EPA engaged in a wide range of activities, such as liberalizing trade, improving tax legislation and labour productivity, and promoting modern human resources and business management methods, which spawned business schools throughout Europe.[16] National Productivity Centers were established in some OECD member states that liaised with the EPA.

Such interest in scientifically driven policy innovation went back to wartime research. For example, Alexander King and Ron Gass had been involved in the British government's promotion of scientific and industrial research that began in the context of the First World War. King was 'a social engineer par excellence' and was part of the British scientific community that was highly influential in Britain after the Second World War.[17] Both King and Gass had previously worked in the Department of Scientific and Industrial Research in London. Gass remembered his sense of 'pleasure', when he joined the OEEC/OECD, 'to find that it functioned in very much the same way'.[18]

Nevertheless, while working in the Department of Scientific and Industrial Research, King and Gass felt restricted by the rather 'stiff and … vaguely discouraging' ambiance of a government-sponsored research environment.[19] They were eager to put the scientific and technical work carried out in operational research to use for a greater societal good: reconstructing post-war European society by encouraging interdisciplinary research and exchange in an internationalist climate. In addition to technical and economic issues, they were interested in 'the human, cultural, skill and educational consequences'.[20] The OECD opened up a space for scientists, sociologists and economists to collaborate on innovative policy ideas with a much greater degree of freedom and intellectual exchange than they were used to receiving from government bureaucracies.[21] Many young and idealistic people worked in the OECD: 'We had half the Education division [staffed] with young people. It was glorious, we … believed in something.'[22]

Like the OEEC, UNESCO equally embodied this belief in science and progress. The British scientific community, of which King and Gass were proponents, had pushed for including 'scientific' in UNESCO's name. Some key members of this community assumed leadership positions in the new organization, such as the British scientist Julian Huxley, who was appointed UNESCO's first director general, and Joseph Needham from Cambridge University, who became the first head of UNESCO's science section.[23] Both Huxley and Needham were leading figures in the British scientific community, 'which united scientists ranging from Fabians to Communists who called for … the scientific planning of society'.[24]

Julian Huxley promoted 'scientific humanism' as UNESCO's guiding philosophy.[25] He represented a cosmopolitan world view and believed in a 'world civilization' through the advancement of science and principles of unification. Early debates in UNESCO reflect an ideal of a world community characterized by 'unity in diversity'.[26] To achieve 'unity in diversity', UNESCO engaged in unification projects that promoted universal values, such as human rights and democracy, the debunking of the concept of race[27] and an ambitious project of writing a 'History of Mankind'.[28]

Selcer has examined UNESCO's crucial role in creating a post-war community of scientists who aspired to engineering a peaceful world community in two ways: 'technologically, by changing the material conditions of life, work and production; and intellectually, by changing the way in which men think'.[29] However, this scientific world view also met with strong resistance among UNESCO member states. The most contentious issues were science's secular perspective and an adherence to anthropocentrism. Many maintained that an organization representing such diversity in its membership could not adopt one specific philosophy.[30]

It is therefore fair to say that, although the idea of a scientific world view was deeply engrained in both the OEEC and UNESCO, resistance to it in UNESCO was much greater. The OEEC attracted a tightly knit, like-minded group of scientifically and technologically oriented social scientists who came from a small number of European member states, while UNESCO struggled to find unifying principles for its large and diverse membership. Another crucial difference between the two organizations was that in the OEEC and later in the OECD, given its mandate for economic development, the belief in science was accompanied by a strong economic perspective, whereas this was not the case in UNESCO. UNESCO, which counted many philosophers and educators among its staff, was much more resistant to the emerging economic discourse of the time than the OECD, which attracted mainly economists. In contrast to people like Ron Gass and Alexander King, who came from the British scientific community, several early UNESCO officers had a humanities background and were involved in the political wing of the French Résistance, such as Joseph Rovan and Paul Lengrand, both founders of the French popular education movement *Peuple et Culture*.[31] Others involved in the Résistance who joined UNESCO were René Maheu and Jacques Havet, both trained in philosophy.[32] In his memoirs, Paul Lengrand, who was the main theorist of the concept of lifelong education in UNESCO, described how during his time at UNESCO, apart from his educational work, he re-engaged with Hegel's philosophy, which influenced his writings on lifelong education.[33] However, UNESCO's philosophical disposition did not prevent the organization from becoming a heavy bureaucracy. Lengrand described his struggles to escape the UNESCO bureaucracy by taking leaves for other activities. After he was hired as a consultant to the OECD's Mediterranean Regional Project in Italy, he described how difficult it was for him to reintegrate into the 'physical and moral narrowness of UNESCO's bureaucratic universe'.[34]

In contrast to the OECD, which was guided by a utilitarian approach to education, characterized by faith in numbers, statistics and output, UNESCO's world view was rooted in the humanistic tradition of the Enlightenment, which promoted education not as an extrinsic, but as an intrinsic value for the sake of individual fulfilment and dignity. Many UNESCO officials were worried about the potentially dehumanizing effects of the economistic perspective on education and the use of machines and technology.[35] On the OECD side, there was a conviction that 'the fight for education is too important to be left solely to the educators', as stated by one of the key speakers at the first OECD conference on education in 1961.[36] Although both organizations promoted a modernist ideal of progress, the notion of 'economic growth [as the] sine qua non for human progress' was less pronounced in UNESCO.[37]

The Bureaucratic Influence and Role of the United States

The United States initially viewed UNESCO as a vehicle for exporting Western cultural values to the rest of the world, and the country played a key role in establishing the organization. But fears that the United States would come to dominate UNESCO were unfounded as the relationship between UNESCO and the United States proved complicated and contentious. Since UNESCO's inception, the American government had undermined the role of UNESCO. When Archibald MacLeish, who chaired the American delegation to the 1945 founding conference in London and wrote the preamble to UNESCO's constitution, became aware that his country had opted for other institutions to take over some of UNESCO's potential responsibilities, he sent a letter to the U.S. State Department expressing his frustration: 'I don't like to be made a fool of, and I don't like to make a fool of myself.'[38] Soon, American officials were disillusioned with the lack of UNESCO support to its anti-communist crusade and the war in Korea.[39] Huxley's successor, UNESCO's second director general Jaime Torres Bodet, notoriously frustrated about the gap between the promises of the United States and its actual financial contribution, resigned in 1952.[40] In 1953, Luther H. Evans, who had been a leading member of the U.S. National Commission, took over as UNESCO's third director general.[41] However, he was not backed by his government, and his appointment, 'from the point of view of the U.S. government, was an accident'.[42] Rather, the American strategy was to fill the position of deputy director general with an American citizen. In the early years there was a certain pressure that the big American philanthropic foundations – the Ford, Carnegie and Rockefeller Foundations – could attend UNESCO's General Conferences, and this was approved by the Executive Committee.[43] John Maier from the Paris Office sent regular memos of his observations at UNESCO to the Rockefeller Foundation.[44]

In 1954, after the USSR joined the organization, the United States pressured UNESCO to implement a reform of the Executive Board, which entailed the replacement of individual experts by member-states representatives. The Executive Board, which meets twice a year, monitors the implementation of the decisions taken every two years by the vast General Conference, which involves all UNESCO member states. UNESCO has a 'one country one vote' system, in which the strongest financial contributors have the same voting power as the small island states. This reform allowed governments to have greater control of what was going on in UNESCO, as government officials are subject to tighter accountability to their governments than independent experts.[45] American UNESCO officers were targeted by McCarthyism, and Luther Evans was pressured to terminate the contracts of those who had not appeared before the 'International Organizations Loyalty Board'. When he hesitated to comply, he himself became the object of defamation.[46] Right-wing political groups in the United States were extremely critical of UNESCO's universalism and anti-nationalistic stance. When Cold War tensions rose, the organization was increasingly suspected of being infiltrated by both communism[47] and proponents of 'world government'.[48] As Morel pointed out, '[I]n the early 1950s UNESCO was downright demonized in conservative American circles in the United States.'[49]

In comparison, as UNESCO was a far more global organization than the OEEC, the United States, although influential, found itself compromising with the other nation states that had won the war, in particular France and the UK, which both claimed influence in UNESCO. Not accidentally, Paris became the site of the new organization, and a British national its first director general, although the Americans managed to limit his term to two years as they believed him to be 'soft on communism'.[50] In the late 1950s, in the context of decolonization, more developing countries joined UNESCO as member states. The increasing number of Third World countries challenged the influence of the European and Western countries, and they used their numerical advantage and newly found power in the United Nations to lay claim to their attendant rights and interests.[51]

The ambivalence of the US approach to UNESCO is amply visible in the archival sources. For instance, in June 1956, U.S. Assistant Secretary of State Francis O. Wilcox defended UNESCO before the U.S. House of Representatives Subcommittee on International Organizations:

> It is our view in the Department of State that this organization is properly carrying out the responsibilities entrusted to it by its 75 member states. We do not find that it has violated that provision of its constitution that forbids it to intervene in matters that are within the jurisdiction of its member states. We do not find that it has attempted, either in this country or in other countries, to infiltrate the schools or try to dictate what should be taught or how it should be taught in the schools. Nor do we find that UNESCO in any way constitutes a threat to our freedoms and our way of life, as is sometimes charged.[52]

Apparently, leading US officials still viewed UNESCO as a legitimate and useful forum while other sources indicated frustration within the U.S. Department of Health, Education and Welfare in terms of the inconsistencies vis-à-vis UNESCO. In a letter to the U.S. secretary of state, dated 12 April 1954, Nelson A. Rockefeller described the situation as follows: 'On UNESCO matters … procedures and relationships are less well defined. Furthermore, since there is no interdepartmental committee to deal specifically with education, we find it difficult to secure consistency in policy matters in which both UNESCO and other Specialized Agencies are interested.'[53]

As pointed out by Ydesen, it is fair to speak of an epistemic alliance between some US agencies and UNESCO. For instance, a 'close-orbit forum' existed among UNESCO's education section, the American Council on Education, the U.S. National Commission and the National Education Association, all of which were significantly engaged in shaping and disseminating UNESCO's educational agendas.[54] A good example reflecting the personal nature of the forum is evident in a letter from Lorna McPhee of the UNESCO Governments and National Commission Division to James Quillen, an American historian, who joined UNESCO in 1948 to lead a new UNESCO Education Department: 'The most recent news I have had of you and your wife was from Dr Beeby[55] who was delighted to see you again on his return journey to New Zealand. He now writes that he is very "homesick" for UNESCO and all of us, and I wonder whether you are similarly afflicted?'[56] The epistemic alliance took a very critical stance towards the replacement of individual experts by member-states representatives. Romain Faure, in his analysis of UNESCO's textbook revision programme, notes that participants of key UNESCO seminars particularly emphasized that promoting education for international understanding and textbook revisions were matters 'for *experts* and not for politicians'.[57] But as we have seen, their efforts were to no avail.

The close collaboration with select agencies in the United States did not change the fact that some influential forces in the orbit of the US government consistently worked to limit UNESCO's budget. Goodale argues that the United States played a key role in restricting UNESCO's role in the human rights debates after the Second World War: 'The hidden hand of the United States delegations can be seen working against UNESCO.'[58]

The same ambivalence, however, did not pertain to the relations between the United States and the OEEC. Many activities in the context of the Marshall Plan were channelled through the OEEC and the EPA that had been founded to administer American funds for European reconstruction and – even though the United States was not an actual member – there was no question of which country was the dominant force in the organization. The EPA also collaborated closely with the Ford Foundation, which at the time represented the largest philanthropic organization in the world. As a reaction to the launch of the Soviet satellite 'Sputnik', in 1958, the Office for Scientific and Technical Personnel (OSTP) was established in the OEEC. The purpose of the OSTP was to increase the training of scientific and technical personnel.[59] The U.S. Department of Defense provided half of the budget in support of the development of a new curriculum with a stronger focus on mathematical and scientific subjects.[60]

In 1960 a Study Group on the Economics of Education was set up to examine the economic impact of investment in education, which was underpinned by mostly American studies on the rates of return of education.[61] The Study Group had strong professional connections to the Ford Foundation; for example John Vaizey had received Ford Foundation funding for an Economic Research Institute in Ireland.[62] It is, however, noteworthy that the U.S. Office of Education had not been in contact with the OECD prior to September 1961. In an internal memorandum dated 20 March 1962, Oliver Caldwell, assistant commissioner for International Education, notes that 'we had no records that the Office of Education had previously been involved with the OECD'.[63] A later memorandum from Caldwell dated April 1963 indicates that

> [t]he back-stopping for U.S. participation in these committees [i.e. the OECD committees dealing with education] has been done by an array of Federal agencies, selected in most instances before this broad OECD concern with education developed. Receipt of OECD documents by the Office of Education has been irregular, since they have come either from the Washington Office of the OECD, the National Science Foundation, or the Department of Agriculture rather than from any office of the Department of State. Consequently, the Office of Education has been only peripherally and spasmodically involved in the U.S. participation bearing on these areas.[64]

The somewhat irregular link between the U.S. Office of Education and OECD education activities changed with the first OECD Conference, 'Economic Growth and Investment in Education' held in Washington in October 1961. In terms of the development of an international bureaucracy in education, the importance of the 1961 conference cannot be overestimated. The conference was chaired by Philip Coombs who held the position of director of Research of the Fund for the Advancement of Education at the Ford Foundation from 1952 to 1961.[65] In his opening address, Dean Rusk, U.S. secretary of state, expressed 'great expectations about the possibilities of OECD'.[66] Ron Gass said about the Washington conference: 'That became a very visible event for all the OECD countries because Washington, the Kennedy Administration, the top American economists ... and in the process, the education activities of the OECD within the OECD became sort of ... legitimized by the powerful macroeconomists.'[67]

The Washington conference created momentum for several initiatives, such as the first operational project carried out by the OECD, the Mediterranean Regional Project (MRP) and the establishment of the International Institute for Educational Planning (IIEP) in 1963 with the collaboration of UNESCO, the World Bank, the Ford Foundation and the French government.[68] Philip Coombs, who became the first director of the IIEP, had initially intended to involve the OECD in the project,[69] but 'the OECD was not part of the UN' and 'UNESCO was strongly opposed to that idea'.[70]

After the OEEC transferred to the OECD in 1961 and the United States became a member, the organization remained a 'Club of the Rich'.[71] A 1964 British dispatch described the OECD Development Assistance Committee (DAC) as

[an] essential organ in which, untrammeled by hysterical speeches from the Afro-Asian bloc or subversive maneuvers from behind the Iron and Bamboo curtains, the Western Powers can study the real substance of aid problems in all objectivity and think out a coordinated line to take at New York and Geneva.[72]

Thus, while the United States played an influential role in both organizations, the universalist UNESCO – which reflected geopolitical power shifts and ideological struggles among its heterogeneous membership – was a much more challenging partner than the OEEC/OECD, which was brought into existence to channel American money and ideas and to represent a group of like-minded European countries open to US influence and leadership. As we will show in the next section, the educational activities and modes of governance unfurled by the OEEC/OECD, and supported and encouraged by US funding, were much more in line with US scientific and technical interests than the aspirational humanistic endeavours undertaken by UNESCO.

OEEC/OECD and UNESCO Educational Activities and Modes of Governance in the 1950s and Early 1960s

The OEEC established forms of output-oriented educational governance that derived from military research and a systems analysis approach to education that had been previously applied to military research by the RAND Corporation.[73] These management tools and business approaches geared towards greater productivity and efficiency were pursued by US government circles, and the big American philanthropic foundations in the context of the Cold War push towards social engineering and planning and the belief in scientific-rationalistic methods. In the late 1950s, the Ford Foundation requested that RAND researchers apply systems analysis to education, and the U.S. Office of Education financed a large-scale quantitative study, which came to be known as 'Project Talent', employing systems analysis to 'determine relationships between school characteristics and educational output'.[74] This systems analysis approach was employed in the Mediterranean Regional Project (MRP), which 'aimed at the drawing up of a planning framework for the allocation of resources to education in Greece, Italy, Portugal, Spain, Turkey, and Yugoslavia in relation to the requirements arising out of economic, demographic, and social development up to 1975'.[75] With its labour-force projections, growth rates, rates of return and country studies, the OECD took an output-oriented and comparative approach to educational governance. As Bürgi put it: 'Within the paradigm of planning, researchers analyzed the same phenomena using the same tools and in light of the same standard, enabling them to measure and compare them to thus fit them into a "better-or-worse" schema.[76]

A very different programme was 'fundamental education', UNESCO's first operational flagship programme, which was launched after UNESCO's creation in 1946 and officially lasted until 1958.[77] 'Fundamental education' exemplified UNESCO's universal approach. The organization pursued educational programmes directed towards benefitting the entire population, not only those groups that were instrumental for economic growth, as in the case of the OECD and, at a later stage, other IOs, such as the World Bank.[78] In contrast to the MRP's manpower planning methodology, the programme took a broad community-based education approach that included 'mass education, adult literacy campaigns, popular education, and the provision of primary education'.[79]

Despite this difference in outlook, there was considerable overlap between the activities of the two organizations. Certain initiatives undertaken by the OEEC, such as the MRP, and especially its expansion into Latin America, clearly fell within the mandate of UNESCO. In an internal UNESCO memo on the creation of the OECD addressed to the acting director general, the author Paul Bertrand, head of the division for relations with IOs, refers to the overlap in the two organizations' activities, which 'has created some difficulties in the implementation of some of our programs'.[80] Bertrand explained that, given the limited number of experts available, the same people were sitting around the tables of both organizations and discussing the same questions, which created misunderstandings. He even mentioned a case in which UNESCO deliberately delayed the start of an activity that had been called for by the General Conference so that UNESCO could align its methodology with that of the OECD, working on a similar issue.[81] Some UNESCO staff were very concerned with the activities of the OECD. In a later memo from December 1961, Mr H. Phillips of the UNESCO social science department drily opined that the OEEC had not been slow 'in utilizing our ideas and incorporating them in its own program. They had many more specialists than UNESCO involved in the economics of education and were marching rapidly ahead in this field'.[82] Some UNESCO staff indeed viewed the situation as dire. In 1966, Mr Hans-Heinz Krill de Capello of the UNESCO external relations office noted: 'OECD imitates systematically our work. The situation is very serious, [a] "life or death struggle". Difficulty: OECD Member States are the financing States of UNESCO.'[83]

Regardless of these inter-organizational struggles, governing through comparison was a common denominator in the education programmes of both organizations. Systems analysis was a core feature of the OEEC/OECD methodological toolbox, and comparison was an inherent building block of that approach. The pursuit of comparison soon called for the development of comparable statistics and indicators. In May 1960, an informal meeting of economists and educators was held in the OEEC headquarters at the Chateau de la Muette in Paris. The meeting's proceedings reflected the attention devoted to the perceived need for gathering better statistics on education: 'Several speakers mentioned the usefulness of comparisons, as between countries, of the proportion of gross national product devoted to educational spending and the allocation of funds between the different branches of education.'[84]

UNESCO also invested in instruments that were needed for comparative research and planning. As early as 1947, the organization began gathering cross-national educational statistics.[85] At the Fourth UNESCO General Conference, a clearing house service was established with the purpose of providing member countries with different kinds of comparative information about national education, such as statistics and student performance assessments. In fact, the director general was 'instructed to maintain a clearing house in education' and to 'arrange for educational missions to Member States, at their request and with their financial co-operation, for the purpose of making surveys, advising, and assisting in educational improvement, particularly in war-devastated or less developed regions'.[86] UNESCO's work on statistics involved two main thrusts: statistical standard setting, which led to the adoption of the 1958 *Recommendation Concerning the International Standardization of Educational Statistics*, and the collection of data development and analysis, represented by the five volumes of the *World Survey of Education*, published between 1955 and 1972.[87] In 1961, UNESCO also published a *Manual of Educational Statistics* and, since 1963, has made available its *Statistical Yearbook*. The United States considered the Education Clearing House Service 'among the most valuable in UNESCO's program'[88] and the Ford Foundation commissioned a report about UNESCO's statistical programme.[89]

The UNESCO Institute for Education, created in 1952 in Hamburg, was a cradle of comparative education research.[90] Several conferences were held under its auspices during the 1950s wherein educational researchers discussed such matters as measurement in education in general, evaluation and problems related to examinations in educational systems. The meetings were attended by prominent researchers then dominating the field, such as Swedish psychologist Torsten Husén and American educational psychologist Benjamin Bloom. The attendees shared a common interest in cross-national research within education and attempted to use comparative research to address a range of educational problems. For instance, individual countries were considered too small and homogeneous to be able to explain differences in school performance.[91] These meetings nurtured ideas on how to conduct large comparative international surveys. Supported by the UNESCO Institute for Education, a first such attempt was initiated in the late 1950s with a pilot study called the 'Twelve Country Study'.[92] The project was successful and led to the formation of the International Association for the Evaluation of Educational Achievement (IEA), with, among others, Husén and Danish psychometrician Georg Rasch serving as important contributors.[93] According to Pettersson, the IEA tests set a new standard for international quantitative comparisons in education and contributed to disseminating an ideology based on a 'specific educational language that affected how education was expressed'.[94]

Apart from the clearing house functions, an important pillar of UNESCO's work was standard setting. The *Convention against Discrimination in Education*, adopted by UNESCO in 1960, was a milestone in the establishment of education as a human right. In contrast to the human capital approach of the OEEC, UNESCO supported a human rights approach to education, which was much more idealistic and input oriented.

Another core pillar of UNESCO's early education programmes was its educational initiative for peace programmes launched at the organization's inception.[95] This effort coincided well with UNESCO's aspiration to foster better international understanding across national and cultural borders and promote long-lasting peace throughout the world.[96] UNESCO assumed the role of a clearing house for, among other things, analysing and revising textbooks and providing consulting services to member states as well as continually urging member states to examine their textbooks.[97]

An analysis of both UNESCO's and the OEEC's early educational programmes reveals similarities as well as significant differences in how the two organizations approached their objectives. The efforts of both groups reflected certain trends common to the era, such as the rationalistic-scientific 'planning fervour' noted above, and both pursued educational planning activities in member states: UNESCO with a focus on developing countries and the OEEC with a focus on European member states, although the OEEC's/OECD's MRP targeted poorer European countries and was later expanded to Latin America. Both organizations struggled to find their mandate and identity, embarking on 'adventures' that would not be repeated, of which the operational experiment of the MRP and the overly ambitious fundamental education programme were cases in point. While both organizations were guided by a scientific world view, the limitations of this approach became painfully clear to UNESCO in the fundamental education programme; Watras refers to the scientific underpinnings as a 'tragic flaw' of the programme.[98]

Carnoy has identified the development of three distinct strands of comparative education in the 1950s and 1960s. The first strand focused on the introduction of social scientific methods into comparative education with the aim of improving national education systems by learning from others. The second strand, 'international development education', focused on the promotion of modernization and economic growth in developing countries, and the third strand, pursued by 'educational psychometricians', focused on student achievement and school outcomes.[99] While both UNESCO and the OEEC were involved to varying degrees in all of these strands, UNESCO's approach was more input- and intellectually oriented, characterized by intellectual debates about normative human rights instruments, investments in community education and literacy, and a focus on textbook revisions, peace education and international understanding, while the OEEC's outcome-oriented beginnings already showed clear indications of the 'better-or-worse' schema for which the OECD remains known today.[100]

Concluding Discussion

The literature on governance makes a theoretical distinction between input governance and output governance.[101] As we have shown, despite considerable similarities in the activities of the OEEC/OECD and UNESCO, the tendency to subscribe to different paradigms of governance was already noticeable in the early years of their existence. The OECD was more results-oriented while UNESCO aspired towards universality and unity. Henry et al. cite an OECD official: 'UNESCO's talk is more about core humanistic values …. It's more utopian … It's not that we don't have our dreams, it's simply that a document like that would never go down in the Education Committee. Our paymaster simply expects something different. We're not in the same street as UNESCO.'[102]

Both organizations were created after the Second World War when the United States had become the dominant world power, and both have been greatly influenced and funded by American personalities and institutions. The OEEC was created with the purpose of channelling American funding to Europe and bringing Europe into the orbit of the United States. The organization attracted young scientifically and economically oriented social scientists who were excited by the prospect of contributing to social change and reconstruction in what the British sociologist A. H. Halsey described as the 'buccaneering atmosphere' in the OECD.[103] The educational work of UNESCO, on the other hand, was generally speaking influenced to a high degree by philosophically minded educators rather than economically oriented social scientists. However, given its breadth and its status as the authority for education in the 1950s and 1960s, a wide range of initiatives emerged under the auspices of UNESCO, such as the IEA, which had its beginnings in the UNESCO Institute for Education in Hamburg. The OEEC/OECD also had a much more limited geographical focus, on Europe and later expanding across the Atlantic, but staying a 'Club of the rich', whereas UNESCO's work spanned all world regions, with the focus moving towards the countries of the Third World as many former colonized countries achieved independence and joined UNESCO.

Although the United States greatly contributed to the creation of the UN system, UNESCO was ultimately weakened under US hegemony. Founded as a specialized organization of the UN system, it was a much more cumbersome organization, which could not be easily dominated. With its universal membership and highly bureaucratic governance structures, the organization is a big ship that is difficult to steer in one direction and highly susceptible to what has often been referred to as 'politicization'.[104] UNESCO was not amenable to the influence of the United States and Western interests to the same extent as the OECD, which represents an epistemic community of a tightly knit group of like-minded countries and experts interested in pursuing similar directions and making decisions from within much smaller committee structures. The authority of the OECD builds on its cognitive governance, which is based on the organization's 'embodiment of the values the members hold sacrosanct and which stitch them together as a community'.[105] The OECD's form of governance has often been described as 'soft governance' or 'soft power'. The organization built its influence on what Rubenson has defined as 'bureau-shaping strategies focusing on hegemony over knowledge management, and an extensive interface between national bureaucracies and their counterparts'.[106] Many scholars have pointed to the OECD's 'mechanisms of persuasion' in educational governance.[107] Ron Gass put it as follows: 'Although the OECD has legally binding codes and conventions, it operates mostly according to the "soft power" of peer pressure and persuasion.'[108]

Although the first cross-country comparative research studies started under the auspices of UNESCO, the OECD came to dominate the domain of the large-scale comparative research studies, of which the Programme for International Student Assessment (PISA) is the flagship. After its withdrawal from UNESCO in 1984,[109] the United States focused on educational policy development in the OECD and put pressure on the OECD to develop indicators for education, which led to the Indicators of Education Statistics (INES) programme, from which large-scale assessment surveys such as PISA emerged.[110] According to Klaus Hüfner, conducting this type of comparative research would have been impossible in a heterogeneous organization such as UNESCO and was much easier to carry out in a homogeneous organization such as the OECD. Hüfner also ascribed the rise of comparative research to Cold War tensions: 'That was the race between East and West, that ran through the OECD ... which has set itself up as the one organization that wants to show in the competition of systems that we are always the best.'[111] The 'falling-behind' aspect of comparison was unsuitable for an organization with universal membership that, by its very nature, must avoid competition and advance international understanding.

UNESCO and OEEC represented two organizations established in the post–Second World War American world order, albeit with different bureaucratic set-ups, different purposes and to some extent contrasting agendas of the reconstruction of society and education in the context of the Cold War. Although UNESCO still has a role to play in the context of development agendas such as the Sustainable Development Goals, there is no doubt that UNESCO and the project of the United Nations to which it belongs have been in decline for a while, as the United States and other countries have lost interest in multilateral cooperation. The OECD has found a role for itself with PISA and other large-scale assessment surveys, but critiques of this agenda are mounting, as trust in the scientific-rationalistic world view has been damaged. At a time when the Cold War has become a distant historical period for a new generation and the US-dominated world order begins to crumble, both organizations are in risk of being things of the past.

6

Learning across Institutions: The Officials of the ECSC High Authority and EEC Commission

Katja Seidel

The historiography of European integration tends to present post-war European integration organizations as *sui generis* 'supranational' versions of international organizations, as if these institutions embody a new departure in international life and as if 1945 presented a complete rupture with international organizations of the interwar period.[1] In the academic literature there are very few attempts to consider European integration, and its institutions, as the continuation of early twentieth-century internationalism. Likewise, historians of international organizations hardly ever mention European integration as being part of the story of internationalism.[2] The academic field is therefore compartmentalized into historians specializing in international organizations and those studying European integration and, one could add, into studies on pre-1945 organizations and post-1945 organizations.[3] This narrative had its origin with the founders of the new post-war European administrations such as Jean Monnet at the High Authority of the European Coal and Steel Community (ECSC), who presented these institutions as a new start in international life.[4] In some cases this was because they wanted to gloss over their own problematic more recent past, for example in National Socialism; in others it was because they were imbued by federalist ideals and saw in the European institutions the starting point for a European federalist state, distinct from other intergovernmental international organizations. The High Authority was the first of the European 'supranational' administrations that emerged after the Second World War. However, how 'untainted' by other institutional experiences or indeed personal transnational experiences were the High Authority and the Commission of the European Economic Community (EEC) and their staff? This matters when considering the influence in particular of the first wave of High Authority and commission officials on the institutions' shape, outlook and working methods. Which models influenced them when taking such decisions? Was their rationale for particular decisions rooted in experiences and institutional learning that went back further than 1945? As this volume argues, the period between the 1920s and the 1960s was crucial for the birth of a professional international civil service as well as the emergence of highly stable and institutionalized international secretariats. This chapter aims to contribute to exploring this peak period of internationalism by exploring the administrative roots of European institutions using a biographical method of tracing the careers of a handful of key European civil servants.

It focuses on a small group of individuals, who were involved in setting up the High Authority and the commission in the 1950s. The chapter will pay particular attention to the 'founding fathers' of the High Authority and the commission, the institutions' first presidents Jean Monnet and Walter Hallstein, and what could be considered the heads of the administrations, the secretaries Max Kohnstamm and Emile Noël. It is argued that the secretaries Kohnstamm and Noël, unlike Monnet and Hallstein who had a different vision of the role of the secretariats, developed their secretariats in the tradition of the League of Nations Secretariat, establishing them as the centre or 'engine rooms' of the High Authority and the commission in order to realize their visions of the institutions' shape and missions. These individuals contributed to defining the European administrations' norms, core values and practices. The biographical method applied here aims to recreate the transnational intellectual and institutional spaces these individuals occupied and assesses to what extent they were able to shape and influence these. The chapter thus aims to link their individual careers and preferences with broader institutional developments and turning points in the history of European integration.[5] By tracing their national and transnational experiences and careers in the interwar period, the Second World War and the immediate post-war years, the chapter aims to highlight processes of learning across institutional settings as well as paying attention to the impact of shared war experiences. The research is multi-archival and draws on a broad range of sources, including oral history, European Union archives and personal papers.

First, the chapter briefly explores the career of Monnet during the First World War and subsequently at the League of Nations' secretariat and contrasts it with his time as president of the High Authority (1952–5). Secondly, the chapter considers Kohnstamm, the High Authority's secretary, who challenged some of Monnet's views on the High Authority's organization.[6] Kohnstamm's colleague, Marcel Jaurant-Singer, will also be discussed as his trajectory during and after the Second World War illustrates the range of experiences European civil servants brought with them to the High Authority. The chapter then draws a comparison with the commission and the role of the commission's long-standing executive secretary and then secretary-general, Noël, who, in conjunction with commission president Hallstein, played a crucial role in setting up the commission's administration. Like Kohnstamm, Noël had rather specific ideas for the role his executive secretariat should play in the commission which contrasted with those of President Hallstein.

With its focus on leading staff of the secretariats of the High Authority and the commission, the chapter also contributes to research on international secretariats as a focal point for international organizations. While the High Authority and the commission thought of themselves as distinct from other international organizations, not least due to the executive powers they were invested with and the 'supranational' label they flaunted, this chapter argues that these organizations' secretariats came to embody a certain continuity with other international bureaucracies, both before and after the Second World War.

Jean Monnet's Experience: From Geneva to Luxembourg

Jean Monnet entered the League of Nations Secretariat in 1920 as deputy secretary-general and remained in post until December 1922. While not much is known about Monnet's time in the League Secretariat, his experience there can help explain some of Monnet's views on (international) organization after 1945 as well as his preference for certain working methods.[7] However, it is not the purpose here to draw a straight line from Monnet's time in the League to the High Authority. Rather, it can be argued that his stint in Geneva may have established and solidified certain preferences when it came to organizing, and working with, an international team of staff.

Before joining the League, during the First World War Monnet had been instrumental in organizing joint allied supply committees based in London. Finding a solution to a practical problem – in this case the allies' supply with wheat and other commodities as well as organizing shipping efficiently – became one of Monnet's trademarks. Networks of civil servants were created in this context. For instance Monnet, the British civil servant Arthur Salter and their Italian counterpart, the economist and diplomat Bernardo Attolico, worked together on the Allied Maritime Transport Council created in December 1917 and all three later joined the League Secretariat.[8]

The League Secretariat became the first international civil service in which civil servants did not represent their member states but were meant to act independently, representing the interests of the organization. Secretary-General Eric Drummond insisted that the League Secretariat was to be a 'a truly international civil service – officials who would be solely the servants of the League and in no way representative of or responsible to the Governments of the countries of which they were nationals'.[9] A revolutionary idea at the time, it became the core principle of post-war international organizations, including the High Authority and the commission.

Put off by what he perceived as the nationalistic attitudes of the member states in the League Council, Monnet later sought a more political and independent role for the ECSC High Authority: The members of the High Authority were to combine the role of the League Secretariat and that of the League Council and they were to have independent decision-making powers that were binding for member states. Nominally independent actors from their national governments, the members of the High Authority were nevertheless representatives of their national governments and industry with close links to their capitals and, in an ideal case, able to translate national policies into international compromises. Monnet was not dogmatic when it came to the specific institutional form for international cooperation; instead, he aimed 'to achieve the highest possible degree of autonomy for effective informal and "rational" cooperation'.[10] Rational analysis of problems by experts had become Monnet's mantra. Hence he did not care much about specific institutional structures and staffing policy, which were in his view not immediately important for solving problems.

Monnet's memoirs only contain a few pages on his experience in Geneva and amount to little more than retrospective assessments of an organization later termed a failure and which he judged through the lens of his subsequent international experience. It is also likely that he analysed his experience in Geneva through the lens of his 'Monnet method' of international organization and cooperation, looking in the League Secretariat experience for nuggets of what would later become his preferred style of operation: small teams of well-networked individuals, independent-minded, able to come up with practical solutions to shared problems. He emphasized the importance of the secretariat for making the League work, its expertise in proposing viable solutions to international problems to the council, assisting the council in making the covenant 'real and effective'. For this to happen, it depended on the secretariat's organization that Drummond, Monnet and others were in charge of setting up – and their pioneer spirit.[11]

Fleury writes that there are very few traces of French influence on the organization of the secretariat whose design seems to have been an Anglo-Saxon affair mainly shaped by Drummond.[12] In fact there were not many traces of Monnet participating in the administrative process in the League at all. As a civil servant, Monnet seems to have been rather unusual and displayed what Fleury called 'une forme curieuse d'amateurisme', for example regarding his patchy note writing or irregular attendance at meetings.[13] For students of the High Authority, this observation is interesting as also in Luxembourg Monnet's unpredictability, and his unorthodox working methods caused his collaborators a headache.

At the secretariat, Monnet was in charge of financial and economic issues while Drummond oversaw the administration and the more political problems. Hence Monnet became involved in what is usually seen as the League's most successful cases, the resolution of the Upper Silesia crisis and the Austrian financial crisis in 1921 and 1922, respectively.[14] Solving these problems interested Monnet, and he was able to come up with ingenious solutions such as setting up new types of institutions, for example the independent Arbitral Tribunal whose decisions were final and directly binding on Germany and Poland. This way of working suited him: working with small teams and coming up with original solutions to difficult problems. Monnet's departure from the League in December 1922, after only three and a half years in post, was sudden and has been explained with problems in the family's Brandy business in Cognac to which he returned.

Monnet's short time at the League is only part of the vast international experience he subsequently accumulated in the family business, in banking, or indeed the high-level transatlantic relationships and networks he developed in the interwar period and during the Second World War. Yet the League Secretariat, along with the inter-Allied supplies committees during the First World War, constituted Monnet's first experience with international organization. It arguably provided a model of international administration for the High Authority on which Monnet could draw and from which he, in many cases, consciously deviated.

After the Second World War Monnet first returned to French domestic politics. In 1945 he presented his idea for a national planning commission, the future Commissariat général du Plan (CGP), to Charles de Gaulle, then leader of the French provisional government. A few of Monnet's preferences are visible in this new administration which functioned alongside established ministries.

Monnet was able to keep the CGP independent and circumvent the strict hierarchy of French government organizations. Former collaborator Jacques Van Helmont also underscored how Monnet and his collaborators, among them future European civil servants such as Pierre Uri and Robert Marjolin, were acting outside of official administrative hierarchies and responsibilities.[15] While the plan became a fairly well-organized administration, Monnet usually surrounded himself with a small team of close collaborators who worked day and night and even at weekends.[16]

It was this kind of flexible organization, based on personal relationships, mutual trust, expertise and, crucially, independence from national governments that Monnet tried to impose on the High Authority in the early years. The original Schuman Plan, to a large extent Monnet's creation, had envisaged the High Authority as a powerful organization, acting independently and whose decisions were binding for member states. The term 'supranational' emerged in this context. To Monnet the 'supranationality' of the High Authority was crucial and may have stemmed from his experience at the League Secretariat whose right of initiative was extremely limited and whose independence could only be asserted indirectly through diplomacy and dialogue with member states, confined to providing an 'indirect, moral leadership'.[17] Confronted with the reality of intergovernmental negotiations and in particular the fear of the small member states of Franco-German domination of the new organization, already the negotiations to the ECSC treaty put an end to any illusion of complete independence of the High Authority; Monnet had to accept the addition of a Council of Minister. He also failed to implement the idea of having five members of the High Authority (and not, say, six, one for each member state) to underscore the members' independence from national governments. The compromise was nine, two for the large member states, one each for the smaller ones, which made decision-making in the High Authority rather unwieldy. However, on paper the High Authority had more power and autonomy than the League Secretariat. And Monnet was keen to let people know that the High Authority 'is not just another international "coordinating" organization, but a group endowed with real authority and the intention to exercise it without reference to national governments'.[18]

In terms of the High Authority's administration, Monnet's insistence on flat hierarchies, a flexible recruitment policy and total commitment from staff to the cause they were working for, including unpredictable working hours, soon led to a rebellion among High Authority staff. Monnet tried to insist on short-term contracts to allow a flexible 'hire and fire' policy and to attract the best experts for the job. This was unpopular with staff that sought security and career opportunities in the new institution, in particular if they were to give up their previous employment and uproot their families to live in a foreign country. In the end the question, whether independence of the organization and its staff were better served by short-term contracts or a permanent European civil service, was answered in favour of the latter. The High Authority adopted its Staff Regulations in January 1956, after Monnet had left the organization.

The ECSC's Staff Regulations were inspired by the International Labour Organisation statute[19] and drew on the League's basic premises of the international civil service in that 'les membres du Secrétariat une fois nommés, ne sont plus au service de leur pays d'origine, mais deviennent temporairement et exclusivement membres de la Société des Nations'.[20] This principle of an independent civil service entered the first personnel statute of the ECSC in 1956 in Article 1: 'Les membres du personnel de la Communauté Européenne du Charbon et de l'Acier sont des fonctionnaires supranationaux.'[21]

In the end Monnet's ideal of a flexible but also inherently unstable administration contrasted with leading High Authority officials' vision of the organization as the core of a future European government, something the chapter will turn to next.

Creating a European Administration: The High Authority's Secretariat Staff

While Monnet seems to have been the only member of staff of the High Authority who had a direct experience of the League's secretariat, as far as can be established a large proportion of High Authority staff had transnational careers before entering the High Authority in Luxembourg, often having gained work experience in international administrative settings.[22] Some had used this experience to develop their own ideas on European integration and how the High Authority could become central to help advance such ideas. In addition to experiences in international settings, the Second World War also played a crucial role in sharpening some of these individuals' ideas about the future of Europe and their role in it.

The biography of Marcel Jaurant-Singer may help to illustrate staff's background which links the High Authority firmly with the post-war world of international organizations and, perhaps surprisingly, given the ECSC's explicit inclusion of West Germany as an equal member, the multinational

Allied organizations in occupied Germany, in particular the International Ruhr Authority (IRA). Jaurant-Singer, born in Neuilly near Paris in 1921, had embarked on a degree in Law but in 1942 decided to suspend his studies to follow his father into the French Resistance. In 1943 he was smuggled out of France to Britain where he joined the Special Operations Executives (SOE), a clandestine intelligence initiative dedicated to sabotage German activity in occupied territory. He was trained in radio communication in various sites in Britain and parachuted into France in early 1944 where he carried out his role without ever being discovered by the Germans. In Jaurant-Singer's case, his role in the Resistance opened doors for him which led to a transnational career, rather than that of a lawyer or civil servant in France. Due to the contacts he established during the war, he was first offered a role in the Inter-Allied Reparations Agency (IARA) in Brussels, followed by the IRA in Düsseldorf. The IARA was created by the Paris Conference on Reparations (9–21 December 1945) and was presided by the French economist Jacques Rueff. This international secretariat dealt with distributing 'non-essential' German industrial equipment. What is often forgotten is that these organizations were international secretariats in their own rights, with each signatory nation sending staff, in charge of managing numerous committees and jointly deciding on the distribution of German assets to the Allies.[23] Honorary president of the assembly of the IARA was Paul-Henri Spaak, Belgian Minister of Foreign Affairs, one of the 'founding fathers' of the EU. The aim of the secretariat and the member governments was to organize reparations deliveries from Germany to be distributed among the IARA's members but also to reduce Germany's industrial capacity.[24] From the IARA Jaurant-Singer moved on to the IRA in 1949. The IRA's role was arguably a step towards accommodating Germany's economic needs while still redistributing its assets to its members. It was founded at the London conference on the Ruhr, 28 December 1948, by Belgium, France, Luxembourg, the Netherlands, the UK and the United States. Its role was to supervise the restrictions placed on the German steel production and to ensure a just distribution of German coal, coke and steel to Germany and the six signatory states. The IRA was clearly targeted at preventing another German aggression, even though the language in the founding document of 1948 was more conciliatory, mentioning economic prosperity for all and going as far as calling the IRA a first step towards a united Europe and even as 'an innovation in the international economic field'.[25] Institutionally the IRA was composed of a council and a permanent multinational secretariat, which Jaurant-Singer joined.

One of the attractions of the Schuman Plan for Germany was that it would spell the end for the IRA. According to Jaurant-Singer, after the launch of the Schuman Plan, IRA staff indeed thought 'this is the end'.[26] For them of course it meant losing their jobs. While Jaurant-Singer suggested that Monnet deliberately tried to exclude IRA staff from the treaty negotiations and later the High Authority which was supposed to embody a 'new spirit', one that was not antagonistic to Germany, IRA staff actually joined the High Authority in large numbers. Jaurant-Singer himself had influential backers in Paul Finet, the Belgian trade union member of the High Authority, and the wife of French President Vincent Auriol who wrote to Monnet to recommend Jaurant-Singer, possibly due to their shared experience in the French resistance.[27] In the High Authority Jaurant-Singer joined the secretariat and even headed Monnet's cabinet. Later, as director in the personnel division and with his considerable experience of organizing international secretariats, Jaurant-Singer was tasked with drafting the ECSC personnel statute.

Unlike other High Authority officials, Jaurant-Singer looks back at his experience in the IARA and the IRA as international experiences per se, not distinguishing them from the High Authority as a new type of organization. For Jaurant-Singer all these settings provided him with the international work environment he had come to enjoy in the French resistance and the SOE.[28]

Max Kohnstamm is perhaps the most well-known High Authority civil servant and one of those working very closely with Monnet.[29] He is also one of the High Authority civil servants who already at the time reflected most profoundly on the institution they were creating and the effect it would (or should) have on Europe. Kohnstamm was born into a Dutch family of academics. He studied History and spent a year in 1938/39 in the United States at the American University in Washington, DC. The letters he exchanged with his father, Philip, a professor of Physics, are a testimony of the impression New Deal America had on the young Dutchman.[30] During his year abroad Kohnstamm felt that the United States were building a strong society while Europe was unable to counter the threat of fascism, behaving like a 'rabbit encountering the poacher'.[31] These impressions, together with his experience as a prisoner of the Germans in various prisons and a concentration camp in the Netherlands during the Second World War, shaped his outlook on post-war Europe and European integration.

After the war, Kohnstamm joined the Dutch Foreign Office, became head of its Europe department and, after a visit to war-torn Germany, became one of the first in Dutch government circles to advocate German reconstruction and integration. Even before the Schuman declaration, Kohnstamm advocated

European unity in the form of a European Common market. The Marshall Plan was for him the opportunity to create such an economic union.[32] As a civil servant in the Foreign Ministry, Kohnstamm was involved in preparing the Stikker Plan for market liberalization through tariff reductions in Europe. As the Stikker Plan proved too ambitious for many Western European countries, Kohnstamm embraced the Schuman Plan instead when it was launched in May 1950. Kohnstamm had high hopes for the ECSC, and in particular the High Authority, to become the core of a federal Europe. He participated in the negotiations to the ECSC Treaty, where he became close to Monnet and followed him to Luxembourg as secretary of the High Authority. This was a post he did not find particularly interesting at first, but it offered him the opportunity to remain close to Monnet and this experiment in supranational integration.

However, the two men did not see eye to eye when it came to organizing the High Authority. The numerous letters and notes Kohnstamm wrote to Monnet between 1952 and 1954, when both left the High Authority, are testament to Kohnstamm's tenacity in his attempts to influence the High Authority's organization, so that it would develop into a strong and future-proof institution. In one letter in November 1953, he reproached Monnet: 'Au lieu de faire contribuer la Haute Autorité à la formation d'une administration européenne forte et responsable, vous la réduisez.'[33] Kohnstamm also became one of those who advocated a speedy introduction of staff regulations, to provide civil servants with job security, but also to shield the High Authority from 'national pressure' and thus ensure its independence.[34] The High Authority, in Kohnstamm's view, should establish a proper European civil service, modelled on national examples.[35]

For Kohnstamm, the shape of the administration and its organization was also, if not primarily, a political question; a strong and well-functioning administration would provide the core for a future European government. The secretariat in this sense was behind a development that went contrary to Monnet's wishes, also regarding its own increasingly strong role in the organization. Monnet had wanted to maintain flat hierarchies and the secretariat was not to be interposed between the High Authority members and the administration. It was therefore precisely not conceived as a powerful secretariat general that one finds in many international organizations, such as the League or the UN. However, the secretariat did develop into such a nexus as it subsequently turned into the coordinating body the High Authority would otherwise have lacked.[36] Monnet ended up assigning the secretariat responsibility for coordinating and facilitating the flow of information within the High Authority. Each technical division in the High Authority appointed a secretary who met weekly with Kohnstamm, allowing him to keep an overview of the work going on within the divisions. Kohnstamm also put together the agenda of the High Authority meetings and took the minutes, thus collecting and channelling information. In the end, before he left, Monnet had come to greatly appreciate the secretariat on which he relied to keep him informed on what was going on in the High Authority and in the other institutions of the ECSC.[37]

Kohnstamm also worked for the ECSC to become the driving force behind what he considered to be the necessary next steps in European integration, including an assembly elected by universal suffrage, a European government and an economic programme. He sought to develop the ECSC from a technocratic to a popular and democratic institution, which would be widely supported by the people in the member states. For this he thought the High Authority should be the driver of 'a complete overhaul of the European economy', engineering an 'expansionist economic policy', resulting in an economic boom in the member states which would convince the 'man in the street' of the benefits of European integration.[38] This blue-sky thinking about a European New Deal disregarded completely the limited funds and reach of the ECSC.

Like Monnet, Kohnstamm had set his hopes on the European Political Community (EPC) and the European Defense Community (EDC). When these failed to materialize in 1954, he decided to join Monnet in his new venture, the Action Committee for a United States of Europe whose vice-president Kohnstamm became. The limited possibilities in the High Authority to advance European integration, the 'endless "*Schrott*"' he had to deal with 'day and night', were no long-term perspective for this ambitious European.[39] However, he had played a crucial role in the organizational set-up of the High Authority and creating a more stable and efficient bureaucracy that became in some respects the model for the EEC Commission, in particular regarding the role of its secretariat.

Emile Noël, Executive Secretary of the EEC Commission

When the EEC Commission took up work in Brussels in January 1958, its president, Walter Hallstein, a law professor and former state secretary in the German Foreign Ministry, had already formed precise ideas of the future shape of the administration. With his legalistic approach and experience at the head of a German government department, unlike Monnet Hallstein wanted to create a strong and well-structured administration with departments resembling government 'ministries'. These should be well placed to negotiate on an equal footing with senior civil servants and governments in the member states and, he expected optimistically, might one day become ministries of a European government.[40] However, he agreed with Monnet on one issue: the future secretariat of the commission, while indispensable, was to be weak in its influence and not to be interspersed between the College of Commissioners and the technical departments (or 'ministries'), the directorates-general, which were tasked with devising and managing the EEC's policies. A secretariat-type coordinating unit did not exist in German federal government and thus did not feature high on Hallstein's agenda. Moreover, Hallstein personally wanted to keep the oversight over the administration and the secretary was in his view merely to play a supporting role. He announced this in the first meeting of the College of Commissioners where he proposed to appoint a secretary, but not a secretary-general, a title usually associated with international organizations such as the League or the UN.[41]

This was not a promising start for Emile Noël who would be appointed to the post on 26 March 1958, even though he was delighted about his appointment.[42] Noël, while still only thirty-six years old, could already look back on a remarkable career in the French Resistance and the administration of the Council of Europe. Born in Constantinople (now Istanbul) in 1922 to a Belgian father and a French mother, he grew up in the South of France. During the war, he studied sciences at the elite university Ecole Normale Supérieure and joined the French Resistance in 1942.[43] Even though he did not come from a wealthy family, his activity in the Resistance provided him with a network reaching the highest echelons in post-war French politics. The experience also instilled in him the wish to work for a united Europe. Indeed, the war experience as well as encounters with Resistance leader Georges Rebattet and leader of the French Socialists, Guy Mollet, opened up new opportunities for Noël who had briefly considered becoming a maths teacher.[44]

From 1949, after a brief stint at co-leading a French youth movement, the *Camarades de la Liberté*, Noël's career became entirely dedicated to European integration. Invited by Rebattet, then deputy secretary-general of the European movement, in 1949 Noël briefly worked for this movement. In late 1949 he became secretary to the General Affairs Committee of the Consultative Assembly of the Council of Europe. In 1952 Noël was seconded as director of the secretariat of the Constitutional Committee of the ad hoc assembly in charge of producing the framework and the institutional set-up of the EPC.[45]

Following the rejection of the EDC treaty by the French National Assembly in August 1954, Noël became Mollet's chef de cabinet when the latter took up the presidency of the Consultative Assembly of the Council of Europe; Noël then joined Mollet's cabinet when he became prime minister in 1956. In Mollet's cabinet Noël took charge of the European affairs portfolio.[46] Since 1954 Noël had become close to Monnet and his Action Committee. During the negotiations to the Treaties of Rome, Noël was closely involved with the French negotiation team in Brussels, Maurice Faure and Robert Marjolin. He served as the intermediary between Mollet and Monnet and worked behind the scenes in Paris to ensure the French administration and parliament would accept the Euratom and EEC treaties after the National Assembly had rejected the EDC treaty.[47]

When he was appointed secretary of the commission, Noël was thus far from an unknown quantity. In the weeks before his appointment he met Monnet on an almost daily basis. His diary also records meetings with Marjolin, the French vice-president of the commission, and Mollet. These three men must have been instrumental in securing him the role in the EEC Commission.[48]

Bossuat calls Noël the 'mécanicien de la Commission Hallstein'.[49] It was he who, as Hallstein's right-hand man, ensured the smooth running of the commission's administration. While Hallstein had envisaged the secretariat as a purely auxiliary administrative unit, Noël had his own ideas about what the tasks of the secretariat of the commission should entail and how it should be organized. He also asked to be given the title of executive secretary, instead of secretary.[50] He specified later that when setting up his executive secretariat he drew on his experience at the Council of Europe, as Mollet's deputy director of cabinet and the French secretariat of the Council of Ministers and he looked to the British Cabinet office for inspiration on how to shape his role. His direct experience of French government administration and his admiration for the British civil service therefore set him in contrast with Hallstein's background and expectations and shaped his ideas of the role of the commission's executive secretariat. The executive secretariat, according to him, should fulfil three core functions: 'assurer la bonne marche du Collège [...]; participer à la coordination des services, et notamment assurer la transmission des directives de la Commission, la notification de ses decisions [...]; assurer les relations entre la Commission et les autres institutions'.[51] Accordingly, he set up four divisions within the secretariat: the registry to deal with the College and its weekly meetings, internal relations, relations with other community institutions and a division responsible for putting together the commission's annual general report.

This rather functional set-up somewhat disguised the informal role and powers Noël accumulated over the years. While he received the administrative rank of A1, on a par with the directors general, he became a *primus inter pares*. Firstly, like Kohnstamm, Noël took charge of organizing the commission's services and ensuring their smooth running and efficiency.[52] This was important as the commission as a new organization first had to prove its worth. Secondly, he was able to build a close working relationship with Hallstein and soon earned the president's respect for his organizational skills.[53] He shared Hallstein's view that the commission needed to become a large, competent organization, ready to play its role vis-à-vis the member states but also its sister organizations and competitors, the High Authority and the Euratom Commission. Thirdly, the executive secretariat prepared and managed the weekly meetings of the commission and ensured the College's decisions were communicated to the services and executed. Fourthly, Noël took charge of representing the commission at the other community institutions, in particular the Parliamentary Assembly and the Council of Ministers (together with the responsible commissioner and director general); it also represented the commission in the increasingly important meetings of the Committee of Permanent Representatives of the member states (Coreper) and took charge of the external representation of the commission. Noël himself gave talks to visitor groups in which he was keen to convey a certain image of the EEC and the commission as its motor, namely that of a highly competent, well-functioning and united organization. The commission, he claimed in late 1958, due to its role, set-up and its independence represented the 'common interest' of the community.[54] Like in the High Authority, the executive secretariat became an indispensable coordinating unit, taking over important tasks in communication and the distribution [and control] of information as well as the formation of the institutional memory and the formation of its external image.

Noël also drew on the experience of the High Authority secretariat. He was in frequent contact with Kohnstamm and Kohnstamm's successor, the High Authority's Secretary-General Edmund Wellenstein. Noël's deputy, Winrich Behr, also came from the High Authority's secretariat. Moreover, the three secretaries from the Euratom and EEC Commission and the High Authority contributed to drafting the Statute for the European Civil Service which entered into force in 1962 and met frequently to prepare the merger of the three executives agreed in 1965. But it was Noël who took first prize in 1967: the role and title of secretary-general of the single commission of the European Communities.

What was Noël's influence based on? The first reason why Noël was so influential is usually seen in his personal attributes: his sheer competence, intelligence and work ethic. Noël was also appreciated because he was discrete, well informed and possessed excellent judgement.[55] Secondly, Noël made sure that the executive secretariat became the institutional memory and brain of the commission. He developed an archival system recording all important documents and decisions and he participated in the weekly meetings of the commission, taking notes which were then, under his supervision, condensed by the registrar into the commission's minutes, the procès-verbaux, recording all the important decisions but usually leaving out delicate details of discussions and disagreements between commissioners. Towards the inside and the outside this promoted the idea of a unified College of Commissioners taking joint responsibility for decisions. As advisor to commission presidents, he wrote many background notes for Hallstein and his successors, often including his personal views on certain issues, when the president had asked for his opinion.[56] This allowed him to present his ideas on policy issues. In later years, his knowledge of the commission's past and why certain decisions had been taken became an indispensable source of knowledge for commission presidents and commissioners.[57] Thirdly, the executive secretariat became what could be called the engine room of the commission. While Noël worked long hours himself, the executive secretariat was a twenty-four hours operation with secretariat staff taking shifts to finish work during the night. Noël's network is a final factor explaining his effectiveness and influence behind the scene. For example, as part of the Monnet network he would often meet Monnet in Paris at the weekend, providing him with first-hand information on what was going on in the community. He would also draft positions for Monnet's Action Committee, particularly in the context of the Fouchet Plans in the early 1960s. During the empty chair crisis in 1965/66 he maintained links with the French government.[58]

Noël also understood that the commission could only play an important role in the community if it was trusted by the member states. One way of doing this was to take seriously the adequate representation of each member state in the commission's organization. Comparable to the League and later the UN secretariats, the commission was not free from national influence and ensuring a balance between different nationalities was seen as increasing the legitimacy of commission decisions and policies.[59] Under Noël the executive secretariat became responsible for supervising the so-called geographical balance of posts that was also inscribed into the Staff Regulations for the EEC and Euratom (Article 27).[60]

Noël's hold on the commission's administration was achieved not only through the control and distribution of information but also through the establishment of a network of loyal civil servants. During his first year in post, he set up weekly meetings, first with the assistants of the directors general, then with the directors general themselves. Added to this were, in 1967, the weekly meetings of the chefs de cabinet. The chef de cabinet meetings are seen as particularly important for Noël who was then able to influence policy-making and facilitate compromises.

Noël, though a federalist, did not play a very public role as a militant for political union. Instead, he used his role as executive secretary and later secretary-general to advance European integration. He saw the commission, the institution which he served, as best placed to realize the goal of a united Europe. His role can therefore be seen as administrative and political at the same time. Interviewed in 1987, he insisted on the necessity of a strong, competent and independent commission that 'peut entrer en discussion sans complexe avec les administration nationales et pratiquer avec elles toutes les formes de coopération, d'échanges ou de détachements de fonctionnaires'.[61] Almost thirty years later, Noël was still in complete agreement with Hallstein's vision for a strong commission, which he thought had a political role to play in the community. Noël was not a theorist of European integration; he was a practitioner who sought to advance integration by developing institutions. As such, he did not believe in a big federalist 'coup' but rather put his faith into the gradual development of the EC, which he thought was in a permanent state of negotiation, and in which the role of the commission was crucial: 'A Commission which is strong, united and clear-sighted, which refuses to be dogmatic or glib, will find nothing impossible.'[62]

By the end of the Hallstein period in 1967, Noël had arrived at the centre of the commission and was not merely its 'mechanic'. On a more critical note, in the end Noël's role at the helm of the commission's administration for almost thirty years came to be associated with an administration that was slow to adapt to the accumulation of new responsibilities and the enlargement with new member states which made it ever more difficult to uphold such a personal management style Noël had created. The commission's administration was reformed in the early 2000s when modern management methods were introduced.

Conclusion

'After the Second World War policy makers and advisors had to look back in order to move forward and [...] these continuities constitute a crucial factor for explaining the history of post-war international relations.'⁶³ This chapter studied aspects of institutional continuity through the lens of biography, analysing five individuals as carriers of ideas, values, experiences and institutional practices. These individuals were marked by personal and institutional experiences before, during and after the Second World War. Institutional learning, in terms of adopting, adapting and dismissing ideas, practices and norms, took place from 1920 to the post-war period and contributed to shaping post-war European integration but also other international organizations. Key features of international bureaucracies such as institutional independence and competence as well as an independent career civil service found entry into the High Authority and the EEC Commission even though their founders deemed these organizations 'different' from previous or parallel international experiences.

The High Authority and the commission's secretariats and their secretaries, Kohnstamm and Noël, played a crucial role in putting in place these features. They relied on their ideas of international administration and European integration as well as on their previous experiences in wartime Europe and post-war government to exercise independent leadership and provide direction to the High Authority and the commission. In both cases, the personalities and convictions of the secretaries made a difference: deeply committed to the cause of European integration, they fleshed out a crucial role for themselves, more crucial than Monnet and Hallstein had initially been prepared to grant, and worked hard to ensure the success of their institutions which they deemed the engines for further integration. As non-technical departments, the secretariats had a unique role in these institutions to ensure the smooth running of the High Authority and the commission, thus proving these new organizations' worth to the member states.

Monnet saw in institutions the guarantee for the longevity of ideas. He wrote in his memoirs: 'What we can hand on [to the following generations] are institutions. ... Institutions, adequately structured, can accumulate and transmit the wisdom of successive generations.'⁶⁴ Ironically, his actions at the High Authority could not have been a bigger contrast to this statement. In a sense, the High Authority was his failed attempt to return to nineteenth-century specialized international organizations where experts develop useful solutions to problems of states. He failed because the political and economic stakes were too high, with coal and steel being central to member states' economies at the time and because High Authority members and staff, with their experiences of the interwar economic depression and extreme nationalism and brutality during the Second World War, demanded a stronger and expanding organization to realize their ambitions for a united Europe. In their eyes the High Authority was to be a super-League: a strong supranational institution with minimal interference of member states, able to guarantee economic prosperity and peace.

Monnet was, as far as can be established, the only High Authority official with a direct experience of the League of Nations, the organization that served in many respects as the model for international secretariats. However, the experience of the League and inter-Allied wartime cooperation during the First World War seems to have provided the basis for a consensus for the desirability of pragmatic international cooperation and organizations after 1945. European integration but also other post-war international organizations were 'fed', albeit often indirectly, by interwar experiences Monnet embodied – the United Nations and its general secretariat of course being a more direct heir to the League experiment.[65]

The High Authority and the commission arguably were more immediately shaped by individuals' experiences of the Second World War and the necessities of post-war reconstruction. The answer to the question set out in the introduction whether the Second World War was really a caesura can thus be answered with: yes and no. To an extent the League also lived on in the High Authority, through Monnet, and the practices of international administrations formed there and introduced in the High Authority such as the requirement for complete independence of its staff from the member states and the formation of an international civil service with a career path. In addition, however, the war became a reference point and life-changing experience for many individuals.

As this chapter has shown, careers at the High Authority were, perhaps surprisingly, often the continuation of careers begun in post-war international secretariats such as the IRA in Germany or, in the case of Noël, in the maze of post-war European integration initiatives. These posts themselves may have been the result of a redirection of lives and careers during the Second World War and a more or less conscious reaction to the experiences of war. This resulted in increased mobility, linguistic abilities and networks opening up new avenues for transnational careers. These officials then went on to shape the High Authority and the commission. The impact of the Second World War on these individuals' lives has been considerable. Together with the sentiment of failure associated with the League of Nations, this experience may have given rise to the idea of the European integration institutions as sui generis.

7

Food and Nutrition: Expertise across International Epistemic Communities and Organizations, 1919–63

Amy L. Sayward

Introduction

Issues of food and nutrition became increasingly 'international' problems after the Great War, professionalized by a transnational epistemic community of nutritional scientists and given a global spotlight by the League of Nations and other international organizations. The League's work synthesized the existing nutritional science to establish new international norms – which, in turn, prompted new national standards – and highlighted the central importance of social and economic issues to the League, an idea that carried over to the new United Nations (UN). In fact, the Food and Agriculture Organization of the United Nations (FAO) had its wartime organizational conference (Hot Springs) before any other UN organization.

However, the international nutritionists who had birthed the new organization struggled to learn the new politics of the United Nations and the Cold War. The limits of the FAO's ability to develop the consensus needed to effectively execute its mandate of providing 'freedom from want' were clear in the World Food Board proposals of Director General John Boyd Orr. Its ability to learn from its own history and to navigate global politics, however, was evident in both the reorientation of the FAO agenda towards economic development under Director General Norris Dodd and especially in Director General B. R. Sen's Freedom from Hunger Campaign (FFHC). Nonetheless, the FAO mandate of securing 'freedom from want' remains a distant goal.

Background: The Developing Power of Nutritional Science Moves into the International Institute of Agriculture and the League of Nations Health Organization

In the late nineteenth and early twentieth centuries, a coalition of scientists, doctors, scholars and government bureaucrats gathered at the nexus between agriculture, nutrition and public health. They recognized that the new scientific research on nutrition could greatly benefit humankind – *if* it could be widely disseminated, understood and written into policy, not just nationally but internationally. Their scientific knowledge about how to remedy the evident nutritional and health challenges of all populations vested them with increasing power and prestige in national bureaucracies, which they then sought to wield on the international stage to expand the benefits of their work. In the process, they began to think differently about the role of nutrition and nutritional knowledge; while nutritional science had initially been animated by the goal of determining what was the least the state could feed populations dependent on it (be they soldiers, sailors, prisoners, or children in state custody), the period after the Great War witnessed a paradigm shift in the discussion, which increasingly focused on ideal diets for the health of all, in part to ensure generations of able soldiers for the future.

In the fields of agriculture, nutritional science and public health, the countries of North America and Western Europe had institutionalized higher education and professional training in the late nineteenth century and early twentieth century, which prompted a spate of new research on food and nutrition. Medical training had also moved to an increasingly scientific basis with the introduction of statistics, clinical experiments, microscopy, germ theory, and the application of chemistry and other scientific fields to medical practice. More sophisticated medicine was certainly needed to address the increasingly urgent and dire public health threats raised by urbanization and industrialization. Agriculture had also become increasingly scientific as the same countries invested in higher education facilities (most famously the land-grant college system of the United States), agricultural institutes (such as Britain's Rothamsted) and a broad range of agricultural extension activities in order to become more competitive in the increasingly globalized agricultural markets. As the number of scientists employed in these new universities, research institutions and government agencies reached a critical mass, international scientific communities developed around these professional scientists who frequently had studied abroad to obtain the best training, who belonged to one or more international scientific organizations, who attended conferences overseas, and who subscribed to journals in their own and allied fields that closely followed global developments in their chosen field of inquiry.[1] Following the First World War, these transnational nutritionists increasingly defined both national and international nutrition policy agendas.

One of the key figures defining interwar and post-war international nutrition policy was John Boyd Orr of Scotland, who became the founding director of Scotland's Rowett Research Institution in 1919. Although initially envisioned as a research institute for animal nutrition, Orr shifted quickly to human nutrition. When he provided 1,500 Scottish schoolchildren with a pint of whole milk for the 1926-7 school year, the students showed a marked increase in health, rate of growth and ability to learn. These results helped spark a programme that provided publicly subsidized milk to schoolchildren throughout Scotland and later the entire UK. In 1931, Orr expanded his nutritional studies overseas, heading a collaborative project on the nutritional needs of two East African tribes, which added to a growing body of research that helped break down the belief that different races and nationalities had different nutritional needs. His career highlighted the early twentieth-century trend to apply the emerging scientific information on nutrition to children (and other dependent populations), which then served as a lever for changing social policy and for developing the international implications of such research and policy.[2]

At the same time, two earlier, established international organizations were also exploring the same intersections of food, agriculture and nutrition – understanding that global food markets would have to respond to changing nutritional demands. In 1926, the International Institute of Agriculture (IIA, est. 1905) shifted from primarily collecting crop and market statistics to hosting both the first World Wheat Conference and the first World Forestry Congress (the latter attended by 1,200 delegates from 58 countries). The outgrowth of such international work included the beginning of a world soil map (in conjunction with the International Society of Soil Science) and a set of diplomatic conventions in the 1920s and 1930s that worked towards transnational cooperation in areas such as locust control, marking eggs for international trade and charting livestock heredity. The new League of Nations Health Organization (LNHO, est. 1922) likewise shifted from post-war epidemic control to a number of nutritional inquires during the 1920s. Drawing on its broad membership and supplemental funds from the Rockefeller Foundation's International Health Board, the LNHO also carried out several country-specific studies – e.g. how the nutrition of the poor in Chile affected the death rate of women and children. It also conducted some more general studies, such as guidelines on regulating the manufacture of food products and the physiology of nutrition. But the most significant change came with the advent of the Great Depression; the unprecedented economic disaster centred the global economy and health and expanded the role of the state as the provider of adequate nutrition, which in turn put the spotlight on new nutritional studies by scientists like Orr and led to the significant expansion of the LNHO's nutrition work.[3]

International Organizations Lead Nutritional Discourse in the Great Depression

The Great Depression served as the tipping point in the international nutrition movement. Initial work in countries immediately following the crash acknowledged the importance of nutrition but sought minimal standards – like in previous eras. In early 1931, the British government, for example, created a permanent advisory committee on nutrition to advise the minister of health on practical applications of the most modern knowledge of nutrition, and the British Medical Association followed up with a 1933 report on minimum dietary needs and requirements. Such information helped governments and charitable organizations meet these in the least expensive and most efficient manner. However, international organizations – allied with nutritional scientists (who were producing one thousand research papers per year on vitamins alone in the mid-1930s) – led the way in bringing together the earlier strands of research at the intersections of food, agriculture and nutrition and started to imagine a better future in the midst of the global financial catastrophe – as such, the problem of nutrition became a frequent topic of international discourse and work.[4]

The League of Nations hosted a series of conferences with nutritional experts, the International Institute of Agriculture and the International Labour Organisation from 1931 to 1934 that helped solidify an international epistemic community on nutrition and craft an increasingly coherent international agenda that replaced the previously disjointed and competing research agendas at national schools of public health and research institutions.[5] As a result, nutritional scientists reoriented their studies from minimums to defining the diet needed to maintain and promote overall health. This transition followed earlier nutritional research that had experimentally linked nutrition to success in fighting off infection, tuberculosis and dental decay. An early effort in this direction came from Hazel Steibling of the U.S. Department of Agriculture. She proposed the first set of dietary standards for health that included vitamins and minerals. She also established four levels of diet: a restricted diet for emergency use, two different cost levels of adequate diets and most significantly a 'liberal diet'. In light of Depression-triggered, national agricultural policies of destroying surplus crops and/or subsidizing farmers for not raising crops in surplus, nutritionists began shifting the terms of debate from a starvation-prevention diet to a liberal or optimum diet meant to promote lasting health and seeking to use these diets as leverage to change national policy. The international meetings of the League, IIA and ILO spread these new, optimal nutritional standards and led Australia, Ceylon, China, India, Japan, Kenya, New Zealand, the Philippines, Puerto Rico, Scotland and the United States to begin conducting national nutritional studies to see how their populations compared to these new standards. As such, the leadership of the international organizations had helped to unify national research, making it quantifiable – and therefore translatable – around the globe. In the coming years, the outlines of a seemingly universal problem (inadequate food and nutrition) emerged.[6]

To pull together this work, in 1934 the LNHO called for a general report on nutrition by Drs Etienne Burnet of France and W. R. Aykroyd of Great Britain (who had both conducted nutritional country studies) to synthesize this flurry of new national nutritional work.[7] Published as 'Nutrition and Public Health' in the June 1935 issue of the *Quarterly Bulletin of the Health Organisation*, they sought to translate this research into an ambitious programme of practical action on the national and international levels. Pointing out that scientific research had now largely established what constituted a physiologically sound diet that would promote and maintain health, it called on governments to establish an alliance of politicians, economists, agriculturalists, social workers, businessmen, scientists and doctors to fight the social and economic aspects of the new malnutrition – not nutritional deficiencies that resulted in diseases such as rickets but the lack of sufficient vitamins and minerals as well as proteins to produce optimal physical development and health. After pointing out that even the prodigious agricultural output of the United States was insufficient to meet the needs of all of that country's people for Steibling's liberal diet, Burnet and Aykroyd pointed to the need for a revolution in agricultural production and in dietary customs through education.[8]

They did not stop there but called for a global plan of food production and distribution, since it was clear that food production at the time was 'enormously less than the amount required to provide all mankind with a satisfactory diet'. Even as they recognized the daunting challenges to such a dream, they could imagine doing nothing less, given what they knew and what seemed possible with the advances in agricultural and nutritional science. Additionally, it seemed to be a moment in history ripe for rethinking such fundamental issues. To move these ideas forward and to develop greater capacity to overcome the inevitable obstacles, they proposed creation of an International Institute of Nutrition to maintain and further develop the transnational community of scholars who had coalesced around this set of issues. Although the international institute did not come to fruition, the report attracted considerable attention and prepared public opinion for subsequent work by establishing the 'ideal' diet against which the actual nutritional standards of people around the world would be measured.[9]

Burnet and Aykroyd's report challenged the policy of destroying foodstuffs to raise prices, which struck 'many in the international nutritional community as "iniquitous"' when so many needed that food for their health. Instead, the nutritionists wanted to see an expansion of what had happened, for example, with milk in Great Britain. The British Milk Marketing Board had lowered the price of milk in recognition of the British Medical Association's lament that this most perfectly nutritious food was economically out of reach for the families of the unemployed. As a result, some 3 million British children received a pint of milk a day, subsidizing consumption rather than production. In fact, Orr argued that raising the diet of those British households that earned £1 or less per week would function as a £100 million per year subsidy to agriculture and fisheries as well as industry. The 19th Session of the International Labour Organisation, in June 1935, unanimously approved a resolution that adequate nutrition undergirded workers' well-being and that of their families, making an analogous argument to Orr's, identifying increased food consumption as a way of raising living standards among the agricultural sector.[10]

These Keynesian arguments found a global stage when Stanley M. Bruce (Australian high commissioner in London and the Australian representative on the League's council) and his economic advisor, F. L. McDougall, suggested that the 1935 League Assembly take up the questions raised in Burnet and Aykroyd's report. Despite the pressing issue of how to respond to Italian aggression in Ethiopia, the League Assembly devoted three days' discussion to nutrition, decided unanimously to create an expert commission to study the question from all sides and invited participation from all interested international organizations. Bruce set the tenor of the discussion by proposing a marriage of health and agriculture that would lead countries to commit to providing all their people with a diet adequate for health, which would greatly expand the demand for food, raise commodity prices, increase farmers' purchasing power and thereby stimulate industry. In other words, Bruce wanted to use nutrition as the lever that would raise agriculture, and eventually the entire world economy, out of depression. The League appointed the Mixed Committee on the Problem of Nutrition, which built on the earlier collaborative work of the ILO, IIA and LNHO and met in London in November 1935; it utilized the work of a technical commission consisting of twelve of the globe's leading physiologists and biochemists working on nutrition (including Orr).[11] Its resulting 'optimum diet', published in 1936, crystallized the newer knowledge on nutrition by emphasizing the role of the 'protective foods' in providing the seven known vitamins and four essential minerals. The Mixed Committee expressed its hope that improved nutrition would contribute not only to improved health but 'a solution of national and international agricultural problems and … an improvement in the world economic situation'.[12]

Nutrition professionals throughout the world paid careful attention to the League debate and publications, which helped to coalesce an international consensus that more and better food was needed to fight malnutrition in every country. The *British Medical Journal* opined that the 1935–6 Parliamentary session 'was the first in which the House of Commons recognized national health as a major political issue' and that the country had become finally 'health-conscious'. In October 1936, the prime minister initiated a nutritional survey of all fifty-eight imperial territories and their 55 million people. Adding even more fuel to the fire was the 1936 publication of *Food, Health and Income* by Orr. His research found that at least one-third of the British population did not receive a diet sufficient in protein, vitamins and minerals and that half were deficient in calcium. In other words, rather than focusing almost exclusively on the poor and unemployed, Orr's study found that a significant portion of the British population – even those who were employed and considered safe from malnutrition and deficiency diseases – were in danger of ill health and shortened life expectancy due to a diet insufficient in key vitamins and minerals.[13]

When the League's Mixed Committee on Nutrition issued its final report in 1937, it optimistically stated, 'If the hope which nutrition holds out can be transformed into a reality, entirely new perspectives will be opened up for the improvement of human welfare.' The secretary-general of the League Joseph Avenol (perhaps hoping to emphasize his organization's non-diplomatic work) made a public statement highlighting the need for an improved diet – despite economic challenges – for vulnerable populations, for national evaluations of their prevailing levels of nutrition in the general population and for a broad educational initiative to bring the new knowledge on nutrition to the general public. Recognizing that despite the significant movement that had taken place towards better nutrition 'it has not gone nearly far enough', the Mixed Committee continued its work, spreading nutritional norms and ideas through the creation of critical transnational infrastructure.[14]

Starting in February 1937, the League brought members of national nutritional committees (thirty by 1939) to Geneva at its expense to continue the earlier work of exchanging information and organizing international standards for nutritional work as well as expanding that work to colonial and Pacific areas. Broad consensus developed that a majority of the world's population was undernourished, which was particularly problematic in the case of children. When the representatives of these national committees returned home, they sought to bring their governmental policies into line with emerging global best practices and to bring the new nutritional information to their people.[15]

Questions of health and nutrition – which had initially been low-level technical issues – were increasingly where member states (and non-member states) saw the value of the League. In these areas, the expertise of the Geneva bureaucracy shone. In 1938, as the League contemplated its future and as its diplomatic work lay in shambles, U.S. Secretary of State Cordell Hull wrote to Avenol and asserted that the League's work in 'the development of mutual exchange and discussion of ideas and methods [in the] fields of humanitarian and scientific endeavour' was unprecedented in human history and promised to lay the foundation for real peace. Therefore, Hull pledged continuing US support – both financial and personnel – for this work, despite the fact that his country had never formally joined the League. This support led to the Bruce Committee's suggestion that the League create a new Central Committee for Economic and Social Questions that would be open to non-members and members on the same footing. Although the report was issued just days before the German invasion of Poland, it eventually bore fruit in the creation of the United Nations' Economic and Social Council (ECOSOC).[16]

The Second World War and the Birth of the Food and Agriculture Organization (FAO)

Former deputy secretary-general of the League of Nations F. P. Walters noted that it was 'a painful irony' to see the League's nutrition work used to develop wartime rationing systems, but it was the reality. The British government included John Boyd Orr in the scientific committee on food and nutrition policy advising the cabinet, who used the research of the interwar period to develop its national food system for the duration. Published as *Feeding the People in Wartime* in February 1940, this small book outlined ways to maximize the production of 'protective foods' in the UK and to ensure that their distribution went to the most vulnerable populations. Britain's rationing system therefore ensured expectant and nursing mothers, infants and schoolchildren of an optimum diet (including milk, fruit juice, cod liver oil, eggs and vitamins) regardless of purchasing power. During the war, neonatal, infant, children's and maternal mortality rates fell as did the rate of stillbirths. The US government, preparing for war, similarly established the Food and Nutrition Board under the auspices of the National Research Council of the National Academy of Sciences to advise on issues at the intersection between national defence, food and nutrition. Its 1941 dietary standards drew on the talents of Henry Sebrell, Elmer McCollum and Hazel Steibling, who had worked with the League's Technical Commission on Nutrition, as well as E. W. McHentry from the University of Toronto (who had helped draft his country's standards). The board then subjected the new standards to international peer review before disseminating them.[17]

The war showed that scientifically driven nutritional policy could improve the health of the people and that agriculture could scale up production to meet urgent demands. Additionally, the Combined Food Board (which rationalized and prioritized foodstuff shipping between Britain, Canada and the United States) showed the possibilities of international cooperation in providing adequate food under even the most difficult circumstances. As a result, the LNHO continued meeting during the war, and the *Quarterly Bulletin of the Health Organisation* continued to communicate new research on nutrition, to examine the public health challenges of wartime, and to anticipate the nutritional and health needs of a post-war world.[18]

Some of the people who had been most influential in the League's nutritional movement (especially McDougall, Orr, André Mayer of France and Frank Boudreau of the United States) began working towards the establishment of a new international organization that could coordinate post-war work in agriculture, food and nutrition, echoing the earlier calls of Burnet and Aykroyd. They gained additional impetus from the ideals of the Atlantic Charter and US President Franklin D. Roosevelt's statement that the war was being fought to secure 'freedom from want'. Speaking in 1942, Boudreau stated, 'It will be in the field of nutrition that freedom from want will first find practical expression. For of all human needs our knowledge of man's need for food is by far the most advanced.' Orr echoed these sentiments during his 1942 speaking tour of the United States; he argued that the 'real aim of the war … was the establishment of international conditions under which the great achievements of science could be used in the creation of a golden age of liberty and peace' when 'the primary object of all Governments should be to ensure that a diet fully adequate for health was available to every individual so that he might be able to realize his full capacity for mental and physical fitness'. He went beyond this abstract vision of the future, however, and laid out how this could be built concretely on current wartime activities. The first steps towards this post-war vision would be a continuation and expansion of the work of the Combined Food Board, an extension of provisions from wartime rationing systems that had ensured a good diet even to those unable to afford it, continuation and further development of wartime levels of agricultural production of the protective foods, and development of an international organization to oversee the entire process. Even more than feeding the world, such a system would ensure a better standard of living for farmers who, in turn, would buoy the industrial economy. However, if science was not harnessed to this vision of a positive future, these spokesmen believed that science instead would be used to destroy human civilization in the next world war.[19]

McDougall attained the most direct results from his lobbying. Invited by First Lady Eleanor Roosevelt to a White House dinner, he presented his ideas to the president, who seemed interested and subsequently issued invitations on 31 March 1943 to an international conference on food and agriculture. The resulting Hot Springs Conference, which birthed the Food and Agriculture Organization of the United Nations (FAO), was the first gathering of the wartime allies aimed at building the post-war world, and as such there was significant pessimism about whether it would be successful. But the gathering of international experts looked much like earlier gatherings in Geneva of national nutrition committees and functioned quite smoothly. Not only were many of the people the same, but its modus operandi was also similar; delegates reported on the state of nutrition in their countries and colonies, stressed the new knowledge of nutrition, and expressed optimism at the possibilities offered by a uniting of nutritional and agricultural policy. This shared ideology emerged clearly in a number of the conference's final resolutions, such as 'Freedom from want of food, suitable and adequate for the health and strength of all peoples, can be achieved.' Many of the delegates thought that exactly such a body of international experts was crucial to the success of the proposed FAO.[20]

The Interim Commission on Food and Agriculture established by the Hot Springs Conference included Boudreau, McDougall, Mayer and Steibling. In its first report to Allied governments in 1944, it declared that the modern knowledge of nutrition could be mastered by humans and governments 'to better the lot of the vast majority of people'. It then went on to link such nutritional advances to both agricultural and industrial production and to call on governments to provide their citizens' nutritional needs regardless of income. The Interim Commission concluded with the assertion that '[w]e can now reasonably expect to solve the problem of freedom from want if all will act together'. The technical reports that the Interim Commission produced for the first meeting of the FAO also reflected the commitment to Bruce's marriage of health and agriculture with their focus on nutrition and food management, agricultural production, fisheries, forestry and primary forest products, and statistics. The report on nutrition and food management described 'the urgency of the problems of malnutrition and undernutrition throughout the world' and then pointed to wartime activities that supported its post-war vision, highlighting the British achievements.[21]

Orr Transitions from International Expert to FAO Director General

In many ways, John Boyd Orr had built his reputation as a national and transnational expert who had helped to alter the face of his scientific field through his advocacy connected to the League of Nations. Now he would have an opportunity to see if a new specialized agency of the new United Nations – solely devoted to the issues of food, agriculture and nutrition – could achieve even more. As governments gathered again on 16 October 1945, for the first regular FAO conference at the Château Frontenac in Quebec, Boudreau commented that he had waited 'ten long years' for the birth of the infant FAO, ever since witnessing 'the marriage of health and agriculture' at the League of Nations, 'when Mr. Bruce officiated … and Mr. McDougall was the best man'. But Orr was a reluctant and recalcitrant godfather. The Foreign Office had not invited him to Hot Springs and offered him only an unofficial observer position at Quebec. The Scotsman – irked at the instructions to the delegation to seek an FAO that was primarily a technical clearing house that served member governments as a type of international department of agriculture – seized the opportunity to speak offered by Lester B. Pearson, the Canadian chairman of the conference. In an extemporaneous address to the conference delegates, Orr complained that 'the hungry people of the world [want] bread, and they [are] to be given statistics'. Instead he urged the assembly to scrap the work it had just done and acquire the authority and funds necessary to allow the new FAO to rationalize agricultural production and distribution. It is not surprising that this speech did not endear him to his fellow Anglo-American delegates, who had considered no less than seventeen different candidates to run the new UN agency before being left with Orr. However, they sought to limit his impact by setting the first director general's term at just two years.[22]

Orr quickly took action after taking his oath of office. Following the outline of action that had long served nutritionists on the international stage, he justified significant international action based on the facts. He collated a massive amount of information about the post-war agricultural and nutritional state of the world, published as *World Food Survey*. The picture it painted was indeed bleak. Despite the carnage of the Second World War, global population had grown, and agricultural productivity outside of North America was reeling from wartime destruction. Although some rebound in food production could be expected (and was aided by the FAO-inspired International Emergency Food Committee), even getting back to pre-war levels of food and nutrition would not be sufficient for the majority of the world's population to experience health, as the work of the 1930s had clearly shown. To Orr and others like him, the hungry of the world deserved a radical rethinking of global food and agriculture, and so the post-war world should simply continue and expand the international cooperation and government regulation of food based on nutritional principles that had helped win the war. These ideas were the basis of Orr's draft proposals for a World Food Board.[23]

The World Food Board would primarily manage international buffer stocks of key agricultural commodities to stabilize food prices (1) by storing surpluses that would otherwise depress global food prices and bankrupt farmers and (2) by releasing those surpluses in times of scarcity in order to keep prices in check that would otherwise starve the hungry. This plan was grounded in the conversations that had led to the birth of the International Institute of Agriculture in 1905 and that had buoyed the work of the League of Nations in the midst of the Great Depression. Such support would help farmers – who made up a majority of the world's working population, especially in the colonies and Third World – and thereby stimulate the industrial economy as farmers had a more stable income and therefore greater capacity to invest in improving their agricultural productivity. With this in mind, Orr's World Food Board proposal also called for long-term credits to speed Third World agricultural development. But at the heart of the proposal were the hungry of the world, who would presumably have more and better food consistently within their reach under such a scheme. Although more ambitious than any of the previous League proposals, for Orr and the international nutrition community, this seemed like the logical culmination of the previous decades of their scientific and diplomatic work – the very work that the FAO was established to bring to fruition.[24]

These proposals seemed to confirm Anglo-American apprehensions that the new FAO administration would set an independent agenda very different from the earlier work of the League, ILO and IIA. After seeming to support the 'idea' of the board in the public light of the 1948 Copenhagen meeting of the FAO, Britain and the United States completely derailed it in the subsequent Preparatory Commission, arguing that such work more properly fell under the purview of the developing International Trade Organization.[25] This, coupled with Orr's departure from the FAO's highest office shortly afterwards, seemed to signal the end of the era, to show the hard limits on the power of the new Food and Agriculture Organization, and to indicate the need to rethink and retool its agenda for the newly developing Cold War.

Learning to Live within Limits: The FAO Director Generalships of Norris Dodd and Philip Cardon

The subsequent director generalships of Americans Norris Dodd and Philip Cardon clearly illustrate the limits of FAO power; there would be no supranational system for smoothing out agricultural price fluctuations and promoting optimal nutrition for the people of the world. However, Dodd saw the potential for the FAO to play an important international role when US President Harry S. Truman announced his support for international technical aid and assistance programmes. Indeed, the FAO became a key beneficiary of these Point IV funds through the UN's Expanded Program for Technical Assistance (EPTA), however, as we will see Cardon squandered much of the goodwill that Dodd had built for the organization, showing the tentativeness and fragility of its new power.

Rather than playing the large and independent international role envisioned by Orr for the FAO, Dodd saw the possibility for the organization to become a team player working with other UN entities to promote economic development, the increasingly attractive mission for the UN and its specialized agencies. The FAO's early development efforts largely focused on sending missions to individual countries to aid them with specific challenges – sending 163 missions to 49 countries between 1948 and 1954. The FAO also carried out the types of projects that international organizations were created to do, those projects that stretched across borders that single countries were unable to accomplish individually. These included efforts to control and contain desert locust in the Arabian Peninsula and to slow and stop the spread of rinderpest (a cattle disease) through a vaccination project that stretched across the Middle East, Africa and Asia.[26]

Additionally, under Dodd the FAO collaborated with other UN agencies to leverage resources and expertise effectively. Most prominently, the FAO utilized its expertise in dairy conservation in working with UNICEF, which had more cash resources (due to its private fund raising) in order to improve the health of children and mothers through the production, conservation and distribution of more dairy products in poor countries. Surprisingly enough, this productive partnership was significantly curtailed under the brief Cardon regime (1954–6), when the director general rebuked UNICEF for trespassing on the FAO's area of expertise, promoting a silo mentality that isolated the FAO from effective partnerships. When added to the failure of the desert locust campaign in 1954, much of the goodwill that Dodd had cultivated internationally dissolved, showing the tenuousness of the FAO's efforts to become an effective global power in the very fluid post-war decade.[27] Fortunately for the FAO, Cardon's term in office was cut short (for health reasons), issuing in a creative new vision for how the specialized agency could carry out its mission of promoting both agricultural production and nutrition around the globe.

Redefining the Power of the FAO through the Freedom from Hunger Campaign

When in 1956 Binay Ranjan Sen became the first Third World national to head a UN agency, he clearly illustrated an ability to learn from the organization's history as well as the preceding international advocacy around food and nutrition; but perhaps more importantly, he was able to help the FAO adapt to the new and rapidly shifting circumstances of the 1950s and 1960s. Realizing that FAO's member states placed limits on the organization's direct resources – i.e. its budget – and shied away from ambitious initiatives such as the World Food Board, Sen sought to mobilize additional resources for the organization through his Freedom from Hunger Campaign, which sought to harness the charitable impulses of the world's non-governmental organizations (NGOs) and people in order to fund an ambitious but bottom-up agricultural development initiative. In some ways, this campaign followed in the footsteps of UNICEF, which undertook significant private fundraising around the issue of children's health and which had pivoted from the post-war emergency to Cold War development in 1950. In this way, Sen sought to learn from the other, new UN organizations as they all sought to adjust to shifting global realities and the new 'development' paradigm.[28]

While the pre-war nutritionists had pointed out nutritional shortcomings among almost all of the globe's population, the FAO's new *World Survey* showed that post-war malnutrition was increasingly a problem of the emerging Third World. For example, nutritional levels in Asia and Latin America were below pre-war levels and clearly insufficient for good health and energy levels. As decolonization accelerated and the UN increasingly focused on economic development, Sen wanted to move beyond the earlier technical assistance missions of the Dodd and Cardon administrations and to a grassroots model. Sen envisioned the FFHC as 'a frontal attack on the problems of wide-spread hunger and undernourishment' that would stretch from 1953 until the culminating 1963 World Food Congress. Examples of the type of grassroots agricultural development that the FFHC highlighted and promoted included the promotion of legume production in Nigeria to increase protein levels. Rather than simply sending a technical expert to provide advice, the FFHC provided on-the-ground education to both the farmers who would grow the crop and to the women who would process and cook these legumes. Elsewhere, the campaign promoted cheese production and elementary carts that could be used to transport agricultural products to market. The goal of these projects was to make milk into more durable and profitable cheese and to help small-scale farmers get their products to market. This reduced waste and increased farm income. The range of projects meant that some projects (such as cart construction) could be funded by individuals and local groups, while others (such as the Nigerian educational project) were better scaled for national and even international NGOs such as the British National Federation of Women's Institutes and the Canadian Hunger Foundation.[29]

These FAO-designed agricultural development and nutritional advancement projects also attracted the interest of private businesses, who supplied needed funding beyond the FAO's regular budget. For example, the Outboard Marine Corporation of the United States partnered with the FFHC to increase catches of fish (and therefore increased protein consumption among the local population) in the African nations of Togo and Dahomey (present-day Benin). The corporation provided an initial set of outboard engines (which allowed fishermen to move further out to sea), training for the local mechanics who would repair the engines and an initial inventory of spare parts. On a larger scale, a consortium of fertilizer producers partnered with the FAO to increase fertilization of Asian food crops through a comprehensive programme of education, improved distribution, construction of local fertilizer production facilities, and a series of demonstration projects, funded with 1 million dollars over two years.[30]

Though significant, such joint public-private ventures did not generate sufficient momentum. Although the FFHC shows the ability of the international organization to learn from its own history as well as that of its peers, it also shows the very real limits on the FAO's power and ability to attain its goals. FAO member nations did not provide any additional resources to the organization so that it would have the human and organizational infrastructure to truly bring the FFHC to fruition. Although the idea generated a huge amount of interest and even significant monetary support from the outset, the organization was overmatched as it scrambled to assemble and administer the funded programmes. As a result, the culminating World Food Congress in 1963 had only about a dozen projects to highlight for ten years' effort around the globe. The model and the approach – which focused on sustainability and food self-sufficiency – were ahead of the curve in terms of development thinking, but again the governments who made up the FAO's decision-making body did not welcome the innovation.[31]

The United States – the world's largest agricultural exporter, whose national Department of Agriculture had an annual budget much larger than the FAO's – played a particularly strong deterrent role when it came to building on the momentum and new direction shown in the FFHC. Instead of supporting grassroots agricultural self-sufficiency through the FFHC, the United States launched a competing Food for Peace programme that repackaged its surplus food disposal programme as agricultural development and nutritional support. And when the time came to vote on the leadership of the FAO, the American delegation led the opposition to Sen's continuing in the high office beyond the World Food Congress in 1963. Although it could make an argument that ten years was sufficient for any one person to hold such an office, it is also clear that the United States continued to want to limit the ambitions of the FAO. Shortly after it appointed Sen's successor, Washington also supported the World Food Program, a new organization that was tasked with distributing food surpluses in cases of global emergency.

Conclusion

Many modern international organizations evolved to standardize statistics across borders to advance understanding of global phenomena. So it is not surprising that nutritional scientists sought assistance from the League of Nations and its technical bodies to rationalize various national research agendas, further the field as a whole, and help governments align their own policies with nutritional ideals. During the Second World War, the League and nutritional scientists kept the international spark alive – and showed the practical applications of their theories – so that the work could be rekindled – and indeed expanded – in the post-war era. However, Orr's dreams of reorganizing global agricultural commodity markets along nutritional lines were not realized. Despite having an entire international organization devoted to nutrition and agriculture, the FAO directors general have struggled with severe structural constraints to move their agenda forwards. Although historians can point to significant achievements and innovations across the decades of FAO activity, the world is no closer to 'freedom from want' or 'freedom from hunger' than it was in 1945 or 1963. In many ways, analysing the history of the FAO makes it clearer how important the League's work was in quickly and significantly expanding the field of nutrition in the 1920s and 1930s, setting it up for an independent organization and agenda in the years since.

Part Three

Legitimacy and Legitimization

8

Legitimizing International Bureaucracy: Press and Information Work from the League of Nations to the UN

Emil Eiby Seidenfaden

In future democracies, when public opinion, like a whimsical queen, will be the supreme mistress, and where no one will be able to do anything without her support, we might imagine a diplomacy whose main task will be to popularize, to explain to the public the technical matters around which the major conflicts revolve.[1]

Pierre Comert, Director of the Information Section,
The League of Nations Secretariat, 1921

Since the earliest of their kind, international organizations (IOs) have been obliged to consider their relations to the public. Was the public interested in these institutions? Should they only promote specific causes to clearly defined target groups? Or should promotion serve higher democratic ideas of a 'world public'? Research has *demonstrated* IO publicity to have taken many forms, from the earliest interactions of the Central Commission for Navigation on the Rhine with nineteenth-century print media to more advanced information strategies of the NATO during the Cold War.[2] A small strand of research has dug into the publicity strategies of the League of Nations (1919–45) and its secretariat in Geneva. Yet despite a maturing historiography on the transnational world of interwar Geneva, historians have not yet engaged with the milieu of officials who developed the League's public legitimization strategies and the ways in which they sought to reach the public.[3] Historian Tomoko Akami has discussed the work of the agent in focus in this chapter, the Information Section of the League Secretariat, but focused particularly on its policy in Japan.[4] Arguably, a key to grasping the roots of the public relations of modern international bureaucracies to the public is to study in depth these activities in the League and trace their development into the United Nations.

Based on multi-archival research, this chapter recounts the history of the Information Section 1919–40 and strategies it developed for the League. It examines its set-up, its functions and the messages it disseminated to the publics of member states. Finally, the chapter discusses the legacy of these public legitimization strategies in the planning for the UN, 1940–6.[5]

Jan-Werner Müller has urged historians to employ tools from the Cambridge School to understand processes of what he calls 'public mass justification' in the twentieth century.[6] In this spirit, the research behind the chapter is informed by Quentin Skinner's thinking on how legitimization can be understood as the re-forging of political ideas to serve new controversial ones.[7] *Legitimization* is thus at the heart of the analysis. Arguably, the League, as a new kind of authority in an unstable political atmosphere, faced three tensions in its endeavours to legitimize itself. The first concerned the identity of the *target* of information strategies – did an 'international public' exist, on which the League could base its legitimacy, or was it the League's job to mobilize such a thing? The second tension concerned the *nature* and mandate of the League. Did it have international agency separate from its constituents, the member states? The third concerned what *methods* could be used to promote the League. In what instances could it use 'propaganda' (at the time a word only on the brink of attaining its later derogatory use), and when would it have to make do with 'neutral information'? One of its officials wrote later that a 'taboo' forbidding the section from making propaganda had stunted its efforts to efficiently promote the organization.[8] In private correspondence League officials often used the term 'propaganda', but in official statements they always condemned it.

The chapter argues that between 1919 and 1933, the Information Section came to consider itself to be more than just a press bureau of the League. It sought to reproduce the multinational hierarchy of the whole secretariat, simultaneously using that multinational composition to establish connections to as many 'publics' of the world as possible. Nationality thus had two overlapping meanings; one concerned political representation and reproduced an international hierarchy and one strengthened the League's claim as the enabler of a kind of international democratic accountability. In that same period, the section came to regard the emerging landscape of private organizations in favour of the League as instrumental in promoting its internationalism. The section framed this effort 'cooperative publicity', hinting at an alliance with private elite 'collaborators'.

In 1933, upheavals of international politics resulted in changes inside the secretariat. German representatives in the political bodies of the League forced a change of director in the Information Section. Shortly after, the size and mandate of the section were crippled by the internal budget control organs of the League in collaboration with the new secretary-general, Joseph Avenol.

The chapter shows furthermore that the rhetorical development in the publications of the section mirrored to some extent its organizational rise-and-fall trajectory. Its publications during the first half of the 1920s underscored the enthusiasm with which public opinion supported the League. This established an alliance between the League and its alternative constituency, the public. During 1925–30, publications settled into a cautious tendency of 'legitimization by proxy' the consistent quoting of statesmen who praised the League. The section thus sought to avoid assuming a voice itself in its publications. Later still, in the second half of the 1930s as political crisis erupted and the League's authority was contested, the publications turned 'inwards', both towards a focus on the reliability of the IO bureaucracy and towards its *aesthetics*, constructing symbols that 'mimicked' state power like busts of former secretaries-general and the new impressive *Palais des Nations*.

Finally, the chapter discusses how during the Second World War the section's three leading officials, French Pierre Comert, American Arthur Sweetser and Dutch Adrianus Pelt, contributed to the transfer of experience between the secretariats of the League and the United Nations. What prevailed from the days of the League into the information schemes of the UN was a refocusing of the information policies of the new organization on the employment of new technologies and on less elitist public legitimization strategies.

Connecting to the Public(s): The Information Section 1919–40

The League took publicity seriously. Between the close of the 1920s and 1932 between 17 and 19 per cent of salaries paid to secretariat staff went to officials of the Information Section.[9] The section was part of the original plan for the secretariat worked out by British Secretary-General Eric Drummond and his advisers in 1919, which involved eleven sections. It came to be kept under relatively tight oversight by the secretary-general.

While the Information Section was for most of the League's existence the largest section of the secretariat, both Drummond and the first leadership he appointed always defined its mandate quite vaguely. In 1921 its official duty was 'fully appreciating the meaning of the work carried out by the League and [...] supplying public opinion in the various countries with the most telling account of that work'.[10] Eleven years later, in 1932, it was simply 'responsible for contact between the League and public opinion'.[11] The same kind of vagueness could be found regarding the question of who exactly the target – the public – was. In 1926 the section wrote simply that it strove to explain the League's work 'to people coming from very different countries and classes'.[12]

Yet public opinion was a concept of core importance to the section. It was imagined as a power which would come to determine the rise and fall of regimes. The belief was rooted in the Wilsonian vision of an international diplomacy whose negotiations would take place in full view of the public, inviting its scrutiny. Never again, observers of the time hoped, should a world war be enabled by the secret alliances of the old diplomacies. The Covenant of the League declared treaties to be formally binding only after they had been published by the organization. But this was not enough in the eyes of the secretariat. An educated public was required to keep the hounds of war enchained.

During its first twelve years, the director of the section was the French journalist Pierre Comert, a man who was close enough with his home government to return to serve the French Foreign Ministry in the press department after his resignation from the secretariat in 1932 and at the same time was a dedicated believer in liberal internationalism.[13] He was assisted by Arthur Sweetser, an influential American official who worked in the League for its entire existence. Sweetser's lack of claim to threatening Comert's position, because his government was not a member of the League and therefore unable to pressure for his elevation to director, combined fruitfully with his (Sweetser's) enthusiasm for the League and made for a dynamic early phase of the section.[14] Karen Gram-Skjoldager and Haakon A. Ikonomou have shown how Drummond established the secretariat as an autonomous institution through a cautious balancing of legitimacies – including the consistent demands made by the Great Powers for national representation among its high officials.[15] Yet covering as many of the national publics of the different member states as possible was important to Comert and Sweetser also because they sought to connect the secretariat to a wide spectrum of national 'publics', while giving those of the powerful members, France and Britain, highest priority. In 1932, the multinational composition of the section peaked, with seventeen different nationalities employed.[16]

However, while the constant balancing of national representation was important the council and assembly, the political bodies of the League, resisted the constant growth of the Information Section staff and questioned the idea that this expansion was necessary to mirror the League's composition. Unlimited expansion of one section pushed the expenditure of the secretariat, and in the case of the Information Section there was also the sensitive question of whether the League should spend money on propaganda. The 'Golden Age' of the section was halted in 1933 when the political upheavals of the interwar period affected the secretariat. The rise of French Joseph Avenol to secretary-general instigated German nationalists to demand Pierre Comert's resignation. They could not accept more than one powerful Frenchman in the secretariat and at the same time disliked the liberal Comert.[17] Shortly after, the section was reduced by the assembly, to almost half its size in terms of personnel and a much smaller budget. After one year with Arthur Sweetser as acting director, leadership was given to Adrianus Pelt, a Dutchman. The fact that the Netherlands was a small neutral power and Pelt's knowledge of new technologies like broadcasting led to the Dutchman's ascendancy to the post. The leadership change foreboded a less political and less visible Information Section spending its money on publications, radio and the cinema and disengaging partly from its former semi-intelligence activities and initiation of international conferences, many of which are discussed further below.

To summarize, along the course of two decades – thirteen years under Comert, one under Sweetser and six under Pelt – the Information Section went from employing about a dozen officials in 1920 to over twenty in 1932 and then shrank again to about half that number. The emerging consensus during the 1930s that the League project had failed influenced the evaluation by contemporaries of the work of the section. In 1938, it was criticized for its lack of 'moral courage' by academic Pitman Potter, who would have preferred the League to 'speak up' for itself more confidently.[18] Potter lamented that the section had been 'smashed' as he called it, in 1933, and asserted that some of the Great Powers were 'jealous of this new super-national [sic] organisation' and therefore held back on allowing it to make publicity. While they 'felt compelled' to allow the dissemination of information they were averse to 'propaganda', no matter if it was propaganda for the existence of the League in general or for its actions within specific areas of international cooperation, Potter asserted.[19]

We see that the section's room for manoeuvre was limited by the three tensions of its work: who was the League's public, what was the League and how far could it go in disseminating its messages? Mostly, the section opted for a cautious approach. It refrained from defining its audience but in effect targeted narrowly selected elites which were already in favour of the organization and were expected to speak its cause in their national public debates. It often underscored that the League was 'nothing' outside what agreement could be reached between its member states. Finally, it maintained a 'taboo' of propaganda, partly as a means of self-protection. Thus, to grasp the evolution of the public legitimization strategies of the League it is important to understand that as much as they were informed by the convictions of their instigators, they were equally shaped by tight institutional constraints.

When looking at the activities of the Information Section, the fact of its constant prudence means that we are obliged to consider subtle selections of foci in publications and prioritizations of resources as statements in themselves. Skinner's idea of 'innovating ideologists' or Müller's of 'bureaucrats with visions' enable us to understand the arguments made by the officials to promote the League, even when they were not making them outright.[20] However, although Potter's analysis of a weak Information Section certainly had truth to it, it was granted a large budget and staff, particularly during the first thirteen years, and it utilized a wide array of different channels towards the public. Its three main branches of work were press relations, the use of 'private collaborators', and publications.

The Press

Working with the press was the raison d'être of the Information Section. The work included press services, the preparation of a daily 'review of the press' and the delicate task of disseminating the proceedings of closed diplomatic meetings. At the height of its interactions with the press the section sought to instrumentalize it in more proactive ways as we shall see.

The section oversaw relations with the steadily growing Geneva press corps. After the League had settled in Geneva, the number of resident journalists in the city grew gradually, and it peaked at about one hundred in the closing years of the 1920s, while between 350 and 400 additional reporters arrived for the assembly in September each year.[21] The section accredited journalists to report from League buildings, handled logistics like seating, access to telegraphs, telephones, assistance from telephonists and so on. It organized social events for journalists through the Association of Journalists Accredited to the League of Nations with members from twenty-one countries.[22] It also disseminated communiqués and the like from the private meetings of the council and certain commissions.

In principle, communication between the Information Section and the press went both ways. Officials of the section, predominantly former journalists themselves, stressed in descriptions of their work that informal personal contacts constituted an important part of it and prided themselves in facilitating a new kind of relationship between diplomacy and the press: 'Journalists in Geneva can scarcely feel that they are outsiders standing aloof from the organisation. Rather are they conscious of cooperating in the work.'[23] This idea of engaging the press in the League's cause went hand in hand with the section's initiation of international conferences of press experts and its relations to private pro-League associations which are discussed next.

Collaborating with the Public: Liaison and 'Moral Disarmament'

The section strove to make the interwar landscape of transnational civil society active collaborators of the League by furnishing private associations with information and encouraging them to sponsor pro-League events. It maintained its closest liaison with formally pro-League organizations such as the League of Nations Union in Britain and its equivalents in France, Spain, Italy, and even Germany and the United States which were mostly outside the League. Groups not directly associated with the League were approached as well, such as associations of war veterans, religious movements and the vastly expanding landscape of the interwar women's movements. The section declared in 1933 that it had hitherto assumed that public opinion was 'in a large degree informed through these organisations'.[24]

By all appearances, the section's very first such move to establish 'cooperative publicity', besides that with League of Nations unions, was made towards women's associations. On 23 June 1919 the secretary-general wrote to his deputy, young Jean Monnet, that they should try to secure 'a good woman' as liaison officer for the section with such organizations. They hired an exiled Lithuanian Princess, Gabriele Radziwill. Pierre Comert later also put Radziwill in charge of the coordination of lines of communication between the Information Section and the International Federation for League of Nations Societies (IFLNS), an umbrella organization for national League of Nations societies and an important transnational partner.[25] Princess Radziwill, and later her successor on the job, the Spaniard José Plà, attended the annual congresses of the IFLNS and reported back to the Information Section on the extent to which tendencies 'too radical or extremist' could be detected in the federation.[26] Conversely, representatives of the federation were received in the secretariat from 1921 and had a close 'informal arrangement' with the Information Section involving exchange of information.[27]

The section used the IFLNS, and other groups, as recruitment ground for so-called temporary collaborators. This was a kind of fellowship system, commenced in 1926, through which the section invited people to stay in the secretariat, often during the League's annual assembly, to learn about the League. The collaborators were handpicked by the officials through their own networks giving the impression that public legitimization was imagined working best through informal elite networking. The 'public' came to be constructed not as a broad public of common citizens but as something in between semi-official elites and the broader public. In the beginning, temporary collaborators were primarily other journalists, but the group quickly came to include academics, politicians and public figures of many kinds. In exchange for staying in the secretariat on a stipend, they were expected to use their acquired knowledge to defend the League's cause. The section boasted in 1926 that the arrangement was a success and that the collaborators were able to use their newly acquired League expertise back in their home countries to 'dispel prejudices or errors which often result from ignorance'.[28] This scheme resonated with the section reporting that contacts with 'parliamentarians, skilled journalists, politicians, public officials, people from the financial world, academics, technicians or experts within the fields of work pursued by the League' represented its most promising means to 'secure a more complete collaboration between public opinion and the League of Nations'.[29]

Of equal importance to the section's self-image was the role played by it in 1927, 1932 and 1933 in organizing international conferences for 'press experts' as part of an effort to secure the commitment of the press in maintaining peace. The Information Section discreetly planted the idea of the first of these conferences in the assembly. Officials later highlighted the conference as an example of how the press and the League could bring about peace together. It became conceptualized as part of the League's efforts within so-called moral disarmament the idea that disarmament should extend to include education and cultural bridge-building between different countries.[30] Heidi Tworek has examined these endeavours in some detail as an example of moral disarmament as a multifaceted campaign taken on by the League as a whole. This chapter assumes the outlook of the secretariat and shows how the conferences came about at the initiative of the Information Section specifically. Despite taking obvious pride in them, the section consistently denied having anything to do with their initiation, insisting in correspondence that the conferences were simply 'a baby left on our doorstep'.[31] Yet, twenty-five years later, Arthur Sweetser, in a letter to Pierre Comert, spoke of their cautious manoeuvrings to plant the idea in the assembly without looking like its originator.[32] Seen in this way, the conferences illustrated the organization's ambivalence about propaganda and about its own role in international society. In a piece of promotion material for the conferences in 1928, the section underscored that the League was in no way trying to make propaganda or 'organise a semi-official press' but cited the German Foreign Minister Gustav Stresemann for saying that it was good for the press to cooperate with the League 'for the purpose of conciliation'.[33] The section thus worked continuously to foster advanced liaison with news agencies, journalists' associations and the like to position itself as an authoritative voice in international debates on news and journalism.[34]

From Open Internationalism to an 'Inwards Turn': News and Information

On top of press services and liaison work, the Information Section published news and information material like press releases, a *Monthly Summary* of League events, books, pamphlets and photo collections. Starting from 1932, it broadcasted weekly to overseas countries and even had a few films produced, although this effort was underfunded.

Its printed publications were often neutral in their tone. They rarely promoted the League overtly, but they contained patterns in style, illustrations, language and prioritization of content that served public legitimization. Despite their neutral appearance, they were the target of criticism from the assembly, whose so-called Supervisory Commission introduced a major cutback of the section in 1933. In an announcement on reorganization following the cuts, the commission ordered the section to cease producing pamphlets 'exclusively for the purposes of propaganda'.[35] The commission continued to keep close watch on the section throughout the 1930s. Although it is difficult to trace what specific complaints member states in the assembly raised at any given time, it may be hypothesized that it concerned either the League asserting a role for itself that was felt to go beyond the authority of its members or when publications treated topics that divided Europe at the time, such as minorities protection or the controversial Plebiscite of the Saar Valley. In the overall development, the type of legitimization pursued in the news and information material underwent a transition from some experimenting with overt celebration of the League in the earliest material (1919–21) and towards more indirect but also increasingly professionalized types of legitimization from the mid-1920s up until the last years of the League. From about 1927 publications often attempted to legitimize the League 'by proxy', meaning that it systematically quoted charismatic statesmen who endorsed the League. From 1934 it constructed symbols that mimicked state-like power on behalf of the League, thereby re-forging national symbols to legitimize an *international* authority. This happened for example when an article in the *Monthly Summary* in 1934 compared the League's new buildings to the Palace of Versailles.[36] Such constructions of League symbols and regalia occurred increasingly in its second decade of existence and coincided with what may be called a historical recontextualization of the League. For example, in 1930 the secretariat published a book, *Ten Years of World Cooperation*, in which it insisted that the idea of the League was much older than the Treaty of Versailles. In its final chapter, it discussed its relationship to the public. Public opinion was its lifeblood the book held, because 'the League is the sum of public opinion'.[37]

Publications released by the Information Section constituted, it should be noted, only a fraction of documents released by the League. As part of its obligation to secure an open diplomacy, the League published an abundance of material providing facts and figures about international life. The section thus operated on an ever-growing foundation of information and sought to highlight some and downplay other. This underlines that one of the League's consistent legitimization strategies *was* its neutrality and 'civil-service-ness' in itself. It thus insisted that it could only ever be a conveyer of facts and never a propagandist.

On this foundation, an overall movement through three types of legitimization, each representing small changes in the section's configuration of its three tensions (did the League have independent authority, could it make propaganda, and who or what was the public?), can be summarized in publications 1919–40. During the early 1920s the section actively promoted the League, addressing an assumed liberal public opinion confidently. It then shifted from the mid-1920s towards a more confident reliance (during the optimist Locarno period) on liberal statesmen singing the League's praise. Finally, after the international shocks of the early 1930s it 'turned inwards' focusing on the League's physical settings in Geneva seeking to educate the public about the League's organizational set-up and downplay the League's agency in international life. It thus underlined the responsibility of member states to commit to peace rather than expecting the League to work miracles.

Legacy of the Information Section 1940–5

In 1945 the dormant secretariat, presided over during the war by the Irish Secretary-General Sean Lester, was formally shut down, and the UN took over its responsibilities, its auxiliary organizations, its assets and many of its former employees. Officials of the early UN were not keen on highlighting its ancestry in the 'failed' League. The extent to which experiences from the League were drawn on in the new organization is still under-researched within many of the UN's venues of work, including the United Nations Department of Public Information (UNDPI).[38]

We now study briefly the post-League careers of the three leading League information officials, Comert, Sweetser and Pelt, before zooming in on their part in the transfer of experience to the UN.

Pelt was the only one of the three who stayed solidly in the world of international organizations. After drafting the constitution of independent Libya, as its high commissioner, and serving as advisor to the UN's first secretary-general, Trygve Lie, Pelt directed the *Palais des Nations*, after it had transformed into the UN's European headquarters.[39]

Sweetser never lost his personal interest in the world of international organization. He became initially the director of the Washington Information Office of the UN and maintained an influential role, as Giles Scott-Smith has shown, in fusing British and American ideas in the development of the earliest information agencies under UN auspices. He spent the rest of his career in the United States.[40]

Comert, the section's founder, worked at the *FRANCE* bulletin associated with the Free French government in London during the war. A biographical article hints that he became disillusioned after the war, and if that was the case, he had his reasons, his wife dead shortly after internment in the Nazi concentration camp Ravensbrück.[41] The old internationalist returned to France and became a journalist again, never returning to international organization after having given fourteen years of his life to it. A supplementary explanation for the distance kept by Comert is that, in terms of building a new secretariat, the French had gone into a kind of 'bad standing' among the British and Americans after the ill-reputed secretary-generalship of Joseph Avenol.[42]

To varying degrees, all three men took part in the transition of experience from the League to the UN. From 1942, two networks of former League officials met to evaluate the work of the secretariat with the intent of influencing the new intergovernmental organization expected to emerge after the war. These two networks were in operation in Great Britain and the United States, the power centres of this planning.

In London, a group, consisting of six former officials, headed by Eric Drummond (now the Earl of Perth), published the so-called London report in 1944, a contribution to the Anglo-American debate on international organization and a defence of the League's legacy. The booklet, published under the auspices of the Royal Institute of International Affairs, included an outline for a future Information Section written by Adrianus Pelt, who was one of the members of the group.[43]

During the summer of 1942, shortly after the initiation of the London group, the Carnegie Endowment for International Peace (CEIP) hosted two meetings with a group of former secretariat officials residing in North America, including Alexander Loveday and Arthur Salter, former directors of the Economic Sections of the secretariat. Egon Ranshofen-Wertheimer of the Information Section, who later published a history of the secretariat, was the group's secretary, and Sweetser, who had meanwhile been appointed head of the United Nations Information Office, was also a prominent member.[44]

Although some degree of competition between the two groups took place, a polite and relatively regular correspondence took place between Sweetser, Pelt and Comert, who was with Pelt in London.[45] The London group offered more attention to the question of information policy than did the Carnegie group, and perhaps for that reason it would be Pelt, we shall see, who would become the most important influencer of the specific functions of the UNDPI.

At the San Francisco Conference, which instituted the UN, a Technical Advisory Committee on Information (TACI) to plan for the UN information department was set up. In December 1945, the UN Assembly's Sixth Committee (Administrative and Budgetary) adopted its recommendations for what would become the UNDPI.[46] Members of this advisory committee and of its important sub-committee were Pelt and Belgian Frédéric Blondeel, one of his former League subordinates. Their presence there suggests that League experience was valued, albeit planners of the future organization were not keen on having the League's name mentioned very often in the documents.[47]

How did League experiences shape the new department? Pelt's recommendations in 1944 had restated the League's dogma of neutrality and its 'taboo of propaganda'. On top of that, Pelt expressed three wishes for the future: (1) that a new department should prioritize emerging technologies like broadcasting and motion picture and that it should include fewer journalists and more specialists in mass communication; (2) that it should emphasize international cooperation in 'technical fields' to a higher degree than earlier and (3) that it should be a separate entity from the secretariat with more freedom of expression.[48] While Pelt's former colleagues would probably agree with all these points, it is significant that he did *not* mention informal liaison with powerful individuals and private groups in favour of the League, an effort which had been a mainstay in the work of the Information Section and particularly a hobby horse of Arthur Sweetser.[49] The UNDPI did continue, in a more formalized way, to liaise with private associations but such activities were not important in Pelt's vision for it. Pelt was moving away from an elitist perception of the public towards a vision of communicating with the broader populations of member states. Sweetser, who as we have mentioned was still an influential figure in the British-American information regime during the war, was, by all appearances, on board with this change of priorities. The public as a separate entity from the UN was replacing a notion of the public as a 'collaborator' of the League. Generally, Pelt did not wish for an Information Section that communicated unofficially in any way. In a draft that he sent to Sweetser during the war, he had written that the new section should require from its staff 'a high sense of professional responsibility and an absence of any ambition to play a secondary diplomatic fiddle'.[50]

The UNDPI rose as something quite new. Pelt did not assume a leading role in it, nor did any other official from the old Information Section. Yet most of Pelt's ideas had been realized in the new department. It was put under the direct responsibility of an assistant secretary-general which signified a higher degree of control with its actions. It was granted 12 per cent of the total annual budget of the organization, double the share of the League's section during its last years and roughly equivalent to its first years. We do not have the equivalent numbers for the League for all years, but the UNDPI got a higher budget in actual numbers than the entire League Secretariat altogether.[51] It was a much bigger and more resourceful department, and it was equipped with a multitude of new technologies.

One significant development that none of the League veterans had anticipated was the rise of a focus on culture and education as mainstays of public legitimization in the UN, seen through the emergence of the United Nations Educational, Scientific and Cultural Organization, the UNESCO. This institution was better funded than its predecessors in the League, the Intellectual Cooperation Institute in Paris and the equivalent section in the secretariat, and, more importantly here, it was better funded than the UNDPI.

Conclusion

The Information Section of the League Secretariat 1919–40 developed its public legitimization strategies within the constraints of close political oversight of its work. Its leading officials, Pierre Comert, Arthur Sweetser and Adrianus Pelt, strived to argue the League's cause while respecting, in the organizational set-up of the section, the principle that nation states were the undisputed source of political legitimacy and that a hierarchy between those nation states was inherent in the secretariat. In accordance with the resulting acknowledgement that neutrality was imperative to the section, it increasingly came to communicate, after an early period of more radical internationalist rhetoric, that the League was not 'more than the sum of its parts', to counter accusations that the League was doing nothing about major international crises. It developed an array of ways to subtly legitimize the League without openly speaking its cause, such as quoting extensively pro-League politicians when they endorsed the international organization or later increasingly focusing on the architecture of the League's headquarters in Geneva thus 'mimicking' statehood for the League.

Significantly, the section gradually changed its perception of its target, the public, throughout the League's existence. Originally, it had identified public opinion as consisting primarily of educated people, active in civil society, of middle- to upper-class background, in Europe and the United States. It conceptualized its interaction with this public as 'collaboration' rather than 'dissemination', contributing to an uncertainty as to whether the public was a separate thing from the League in Geneva or if it was entwined with it. It is asserted that this elitist perception of the public was not only the result of convictions of the officials, as is the impression from Akami's work, but resulted equally from the constraints put on the Information Section. It is argued that Akami tends to separate the information policy of the League from the constraints within which it came about when asserting that rather than the rise of nationalism in Europe (and in Japan) it was the League's inherent inability to communicate with the public that led to a 'missed opportunity'.[52] As has been demonstrated however, the Information Section worked constantly to avoid confronting a number of tensions in its work, most notably a taboo of propaganda, and when it was reduced in 1933 it happened partly because even its cautious liaison with elites was seen as going beyond its mandate. To some extent, its officials seem to have been convinced that informal networking, if done discreetly, was the 'safest' way to legitimize the League without risking the label of propagandists. However, this narrow identification of the target of information policy changed after the rise of a more resourceful UN with a broader Great Power backing. Former officials of the League now recommended a bigger and more ambitious public legitimization effort, not anticipating the subsequent sidelining of traditional information policy in the UN by a new focus on culture and education through the UNESCO. The bottom line was that the post-war international public diplomacy would be bigger, more global, and it would aim at the whole public.

9

Between Publicity and Discretion: The International Federation of League of Nations Societies

Anne-Isabelle Richard

Introduction

After the First World War, the 'Old Diplomacy' of secret bilateral treaties and power politics, seen to have caused the war, had to make way for the 'New Diplomacy': multilateral, democratic and proceeding in public view.[1] The League of Nations became the epicentre of this 'New Diplomacy'. As South African statesman and League supporter Jan Smuts pointed out, '[T]he League will never be a great success until there is formed as its main support a powerful international public opinion.'[2] Civil society networks surrounding the League eagerly and explicitly participated to make this happen. In turn, the League informally and more or less hesitantly drew on civil society actors.

Elsewhere in this volume, Karen Gram-Skjoldager and Haakon Ikonomou take up Susan Pedersen's question of how the League worked. In her landmark article, *Back to the League of Nations*, Pedersen also argued that the League 'fed off and promoted popular mobilization', calling for more attention to civil society networks.[3] To answer Pedersen's question and to understand how international public administration operated, this chapters argues that we also need to take civil society actors into account. For the League, both technical and general voluntary societies provided crucial support as well as scrutiny to its work. The International Federation of League of Nations Societies (IFLNS) is ideally suited to analyse the entanglement between the League Secretariat, states and civil society actors.

At the League, 'NGOs' did not have an official status, like they do at the United Nations (UN). However, this did not prevent civil society from playing a significant role. (Partly) because of its unofficial status it complemented the neutral secretariat and the overtly political League Council and Assembly. This was on the one hand due to the activities the IFLNS deployed and how for example states used the IFLNS as an alternative international venue. However, the most important factor for the role the IFLNS played was the actors involved. They moved from civil society organizations to the League Secretariat, from national and international politics to bureaucracies and from being experts to publicists and businesspeople and vice versa. The IFLNS played a central role in this network and could therefore function as an informal liaison as well as a testing ground, in addition to its more straightforward publicity work.

Building on pre-war organizations, in many countries societies were formed that supported the work of the League. In some countries these were unified societies such as the powerful British League of Nations Union[4] or the Dutch Vereeniging voor Volkenbond en Vrede.[5] In other countries, such as France, a considerable number of peace or League societies cooperated in a national federation.[6] At the international level, most of these national societies cooperated in the IFLNS.

The IFLNS saw itself as an 'avant-garde' to the League: it promoted its work; it maintained contact with societies in countries outside the League and investigated new or controversial topics. In this manner the IFLNS combined propaganda and policy work.[7] Aiming to democratize international relations, the IFLNS sought to both shape and represent public opinion through propaganda and education work and 'democratic' oversight of League activities. The IFLNS provided an international platform for actors of all sorts, from liberal internationalists to a wide array of disenfranchised actors. In attempting to channel these sentiments the federation aimed to go beyond popularizing and explaining the League and also to provide a form of political legitimacy to its work. Thus the IFLNS aspired to become an unofficial 'third chamber' to the League.[8]

However, in her above-mentioned article Pedersen also highlighted the dangers of mobilizing public opinion. While public support and scrutiny were hoped to buttress collective security, it became clear that public opinion was not always 'pacific nor [...] easily appeased'.[9] Examining the IFLNS shows how a quest for the democratization of international society brought with it frictions between universal hopes and particularistic ends. At the IFLNS tensions between national and imperial interests, international aspirations and transnational activities came together. At times, the public view required by the New Diplomacy and needed for the federation's propaganda activities clashed with the discretion international relations and policy work often necessitated. Not only the IFLNS struggled with these issues, they applied to many other similar organizations and above all to the League itself.

While the literature has headed Pedersen call for more attention for civil society networks around the League and an increasing number of national League societies is being researched, the IFLNS itself is only starting to be explored.[10] The balancing act between publicity and discretion that characterized League internationalism however benefits from an analysis of the reciprocal relationship between the IFLNS and the League Secretariat. This approach simultaneously highlights the significance of civil society platforms in addition to official channels, as well as stressing the fact that the actors involved defy easy categorization as state, civil society or international agents. It is the networked character and the multitude of roles and contacts that gave these actors relevance and carries their interwar experiences into the post-1945 period. This chapter claims no comprehensiveness; rather than detailing all the activities of the IFLNS, it will touch upon some of the substantive activities of the IFLNS related to 'Information' and Minorities, to illustrate the practice of internationalism the federation developed between the League, the secretariat, states and a global public.[11]

The Organization of IFLNS Internationalism

How were the IFLNS and its national constituents from over thirty countries organized? Building on pre-war peace and women's movements and following inter-Allied contacts during the War, the IFLNS was established in Brussels in 1919 and was fully operational by 1921.[12] The organizational set-up of the federation, and of many other similar organizations, largely mirrored that of the League. It had a general assembly – meeting once a year in a major city – a council, a bureau drawn from the council and a secretariat.[13] There were initially four standing committees, also modelled on the League and International Labour Organization (propaganda and education; national minorities; international labour legislation, social and economic questions; political and legal questions).[14] Theodore Ruyssen, the doyen of the *Association de la Paix pour le Droit* and professor of philosophy in Bordeaux became secretary-general. He retired in 1939 and was succeeded by the young British barrister, LNU activist and later president of European Free Trade Area, Frank Figgures. These careers on either side of the interwar period indicate the longer history and the connections between international civil society and international organizations. In 1923 an 'English-speaking Assistant Secretary-General' was appointed.[15] From the outset there were close personnel ties between the League Secretariat and the IFLNS. In between serving in the League Secretariat Political and Minorities Sections, William O'Molony functioned as the IFLNS English secretary. In 1926 he was succeeded by Captain Lothian Small. From 1927 a germanophone assistant secretary-general was added, first Hermann Kirchhoff, then between 1928 and 1935, Albert von Bodman.

IFLNS leadership positions read as a who's who of interwar internationalists. Figures such as conservative politician and president of the British LNU Lord Robert Cecil (Viscount Cecil of Chelwood), the Belgian socialist and later president of the European Court of Human Rights Henri Rolin or German diplomat Count Johann Heinrich Bernstorff all served as president. They were supported by the bureau that included an expanding group of prominent vice-presidents, a treasurer, until 1935 this was the Belgian lawyer, senator and founder of the Union of International Associations, Henri la Fontaine, a number of auditors and the secretariat. The funding for the IFLNS came for about two-thirds from contributions from member organizations. They, in turn, were often (partly) funded by governments. Another part of the income of the IFLNS came from gifts from private individuals or foundations such as the Americans Theodore Marburg, James J. Forstall or the Carnegie Foundation.[16] All of these actors were also involved with the League in other capacities as well, as national delegates, as experts, as funders etc., creating a tight network.

The number of women in significant posts, chairing committees and bureau sessions, increased with the years and saw a spread across Europe.[17] Particularly the 1930s saw women such as LNU heavyweight Lady Gladstone and future treasurer of the World Federation of United Nations Associations (WFUNA) Christina Bakker-van Bosse represented among the vice-presidents and the honorary members of the council. Although the IFLNS probably did not go much beyond the League in 'only partly fulfil[ing] the hopes of international feminists', it nonetheless provided a parallel track to engage in international relations as a woman.[18]

The IFLNS was explicitly made up of national organizations. Many interwar internationalists (and the IFLNS) conceived of internationalism as building on nationalism. Much like for the League, for the IFLNS international peace and understanding were clear aims, but patriotism was by no means rejected. Although national egoisms had to be overcome, 'love of the fatherland was as honourable as love of humanity'.[19] They often distinguished between 'good patriotism' and 'bad nationalism'.[20] Despite the explicit possibilities to accommodate various forms of patriotism, participating societies could be explicitly nationalistic. This had repercussions for the room for manoeuvre for the federation, since one of its overriding aims was to keep lines of contact open to as many associations as possible. Coupled with a sensitivity to state interests, the international platform the IFLNS provided was often used for national(istic) aims.

Within the IFLNS the British LNU was by far the largest member. The relationship between the organizations was not always smooth, something that also influences the LNU-based historiography on the IFLNS. A continued source of debate between the LNU and the other members of the IFLNS was the location of the IFLNS secretariat. The LNU preferred Geneva, the others Brussels. It was cheaper and signalled the independence of the IFLNS from the League.[21] Until 1934, when the LNU got its way and the secretariat moved to Geneva permanently, it moved to Geneva only in summer in the run up to the League General Assembly to ensure enough close contact.[22] In Geneva it organized many (social) events for League and IFLNS delegates, contributing to the socializing effects of the 'Geneva spirit' and initiating delegates from non-member states into that spirit in preparation of their country joining the League.

The membership of the IFLNS peaked in the early 1930s at about 1.5 million. Associate and corporate membership, which led to dissemination of League ideas in other bodies, such as trade unions or ex-servicemen leagues, would make this number significantly higher.[23] While the IFLNS comprised societies in fifty countries from Argentina to India and Japan and despite the declared universalism and global reach of the IFLNS, most League societies were European.[24] Like the League, the IFLNS sought to balance this situation by reaching out to societies outside the West – while upholding empire.[25] With some success they hoped to stimulate the creation of new associations through a worldwide correspondence and by sending envoys.[26] Despite these efforts, most of the existing non-European societies relied on compatriots residing in Europe to represent them.[27]

The Chinese and Japanese Associations recognized the relevance of the IFLNS early on and managed to set up durable organizations. In 1920 one of the founders of the Japanese League of Nations Association (JLNA), the diplomat Matsui Keishiro explained the importance of the IFLNS to Japanese foreign policy as follows: Firstly, the members of European League societies were important politicians and scholars who could influence public opinion in their respective countries. Secondly, membership of the IFLNS gave Japan the opportunity to 'see what other countries were planning [to discuss at the League of Nations] as well as show Japan's eagerness to contribute to world peace'.[28] Keishiro highlighted how the IFLNS could function as a transmission belt to influence public opinion and to gather information on future policy.

In order to make the federation more global, plans for an annual assembly meeting outside of Europe circulated since the early 1920s. As part of its efforts to use international forums to strengthen their position vis-à-vis Japan, the Chinese society offered to host the annual assembly in the late 1930s.[29] The IFLNS was an obvious choice given its standing but also its links to the International Peace Campaign, which was very strong on and in China.[30] However, given the circumstances in China in 1938–9, the IFLNS relocated the meeting to New York, where the World's Fair took place in 1939–40. The United States were not a member of the League, but the IFLNS hoped that having the congress take place there would strengthen the pro-League and anti-isolationist tendencies among the American public, leading to League membership.[31] In the end, the 1939 assembly never took place.[32] The offers from non-European societies show the importance they accorded to an, unofficial, international platform and to being associated with the federation and by extension the League, also in the late 1930s.

Most League societies were relatively elitist affairs. The British LNU was the only organization that could claim genuine grassroots involvement with at its peak over 400,000 members.[33] Members of League societies often represented an educated public with an interest in foreign affairs. However, pacifist, ex-servicemen and women's rights circles were also well represented. In the later 1930s a number of organizations joined, who, within the framework of the League, sought peace and international cooperation through slightly different means than the IFLNS. The *Comité Fédéral de Coopération Européenne* and the New Commonwealth Society both aimed for European cooperation, while the latter also favoured military force for peace.[34] When in 1937 the International Peace Campaign, led by IFLNS and LNU heavyweight Robert Cecil and French Popular Front minister Pierre Cot, joined the federation, left-wing groups became better represented – with fear of Communist involvement also strengthening.[35] The fact that all of the organizations that joined had a significant overlap in membership facilitated the affiliation. It is noteworthy that these actors, rather than leaving the IFLNS, sought to supplement it with other approaches.

As mentioned before, the individuals involved in the IFLNS constituted a highly networked group; they played multiple, simultaneous roles in 'international society'. They often participated in a number of voluntary organizations, while also engaging in international society as national delegates to the League, (inter)national civil servants, experts, journalists or bankers.³⁶ Organizing IFLNS council meetings in Geneva around the time of the League General Assembly allowed for delegates to attend both. Meetings in Geneva also facilitated attendance by, as well as informal contacts with, League Secretariat members. In turn, other organizations, such as the *Comité Federal de Coopération Européenne*, let their annual conference follow or precede the IFNLS annual conference for the same purpose. This networked character, which facilitated informal contacts and informal diplomacy, added to the impact of the IFLNS.

The Dane Ludvig Krabbe of the Information Section commented about the federation assembly in Geneva in 1930:

> The fact that many of those who took part in the discussion were also delegates to the Assembly of the League […], contributed to creating an impression that one was present less at a manifestation of representatives of public opinion of the various countries, than of a League Assembly in miniature which took place in calmer circumstances […], far from the political passions.³⁷

This qualifies the idea that the IFLNS just represented public opinion. In expressing secretariat opinion, Krabbe drew attention to the position of the IFLNS in between the neutral secretariat and the political turmoil of the assembly. Civil society offered politicians another forum to debate the questions of the times away from the pressure of official representations, thus facilitating discussion.

The observation by Patricia Clavin and Jens-Wilhelm Wessels in relation to the Economic and Financial Sections of the League Secretariat about 'the degree to which internationalism, transnationalism and multi-nationalism coexisted within the same organization' also holds for the IFLNS.³⁸ The IFLNS fashioned itself as a civil society actor participating in the New Diplomacy, who would propagate the League to a general global public and national publics as well as represent those publics, while not shying away from undertaking policy work. The practice of internationalism that the IFLNS came to style nonetheless depended to a large degree on well-connected, high-level actors, who tried to balance openness and discretion while warding off too blatant examples of power politics. In styling itself as the most official and most respectable of the private international organizations surrounding the League, the practice of internationalism of the IFLNS, to which we now turn, was not unlike that of the League Secretariat.

'Cooperative Publicity': The IFLNS and the Information Section

'Cooperative publicity' was the term the American and second in command of the Information Section, Arthur Sweetser, used in 1919 to describe how he envisaged the relationship between the Information Section and private international organizations.[39] The League Secretariat seems to have adopted this approach in other domains as well. The Disarmament Section for example also struggled with the need to publicize its work and the limits it faced in engaging in propaganda itself. Secretary-general of the Inter-Parliamentary Union Christian Lange suggested to Thanassis Aghnides of the Disarmament Section that the secretariat could communicate information to the various peace associations. These could then use this information in their propaganda efforts so that arms limitations 'may be imposed by peoples on Governments' as Aghnides put it in his proposal to Eric Drummond, secretary-general of the League, who sanctioned the idea.[40] This highlights one of the tasks the IFLNS had set itself: educating and activating the global public.

How did the IFLNS go about this? It used a two-pronged strategy, reaching the public directly through propaganda and education activities, and reaching the public through national societies through the sharing of knowledge and best practices. The final aims of the IFLNS with this strategy were a widening of the support base for the League as well as putting pressure on national governments and the League to put questions on their agendas. Many of these activities came out of the propaganda and education committee and can be divided in publications of various kinds (IFLNS Bulletin, pamphlets, posters, slide shows, radio, film, school textbooks) and events. Typical events included lectures by prominent members, campaigns around major events such as the world economic or disarmament conference, the highly publicized annual assemblies and summer schools.

The IFLNS did not undertake this task in isolation. It was one among two hundred international organizations the secretariat had been in contact with by 1934.[41] The Information Section was responsible for most of these contacts and in particular those with the IFLNS (although the IFLNS also maintained close contacts to a number of other sections). Emil Seidenfaden calls the relationship to the IFLNS, the Information Section's 'most ambitious attempt to directly supervise propaganda activities for the League through private collaborators in a way that avoided overstepping the mandate of the neutral secretariat'.[42] The Information Section struggled with balancing between what was perceived as 'neutral information' and 'propaganda' and with how they could reach 'the public' and who that public was. Was it a general global public, an educated global elite, governments, national general or educated publics or all of these?[43] Since press contacts did not suffice – 'a newspaper is more a means of advertisement than of propaganda'[44] – the IFLNS and its members were a means through which the Information Section sought to get in contact with at least an educated global public.[45] These were initially informal contacts as the League 'strove to use unofficial communication, and at times even semi-diplomatic activities, to compensate for its lack of muscle in terms of propaganda and its dogma of neutrality'.[46] The strategy of the Information Section seemed to be that they would provide the IFLNS with neutral information, while the IFLNS and League Associations would transform that into a propaganda effort towards national publics.[47] This section, which focuses on the mechanics of the relationship between the secretariat and the IFLNS, instead of on their interaction (and cooperation) on substantial topics, aims to show that the relationship was a two-way process with information, contacts and attempts at influencing flowing both ways.

In 1921, the Information Section appointed Lithuanian feminist Princess Gabriele Radziwill as liaison officer for the IFLNS. The section followed the activities of the IFLNS closely. While generally not referred to in an active role in the minutes, Radziwill and others attended bureau, council and assembly meetings.[48] According to Radziwill 'much useful work was done at these meetings, mixed with a lot of irresponsible and useless discussion'.[49] Prior to an event, the IFLNS shared the agenda with the Information Section to draw attention to its work and to the topics it thought needed attention. The Information Section in turn circulated the agenda among the secretariat, also to spot and 'prevent, if possible, tendencies too radical or extremist'.[50] Nonetheless, the Information Section also provided the IFLNS and its constituents with information and speakers. Radziwill was for example instrumental in facilitating the yearly summer school the IFLNS organized in Geneva. Many prominent League figures spoke to the students year in, year out. From 1921, representatives of the IFLNS were received by the secretary-general of the League and later also by Albert Thomas of the ILO. From 1923 IFLNS resolutions were presented to the secretary-general and were subsequently included, for information, in the *Journal Officiel* of the League Assembly (as were the communications by many other private international organizations). Apart from their agendas and resolutions, the IFLNS also furnished the Information Section with news about developments and public opinion in various countries and thus made the flow of information a two-way process.[51]

Spanish official Joseph Plà succeeded Radziwill as liaison with the IFLNS in 1931. According to Seidenfaden, he was much less involved in the activities of the IFLNS and acted more as a conveyor of information.[52] This approach corresponded to the official line from 1933. Apart from the ominous developments in the world, this year the Information Section was reorganized leading to significant cuts: to its budget, staff, mandate and concomitantly its activities. This was both a result of the appointment of Frenchman Joseph Avenol as new secretary-general of the League, as well as cuts to the League budget as a result of withdrawals and Great Power displeasure, as Potter put it.[53] The section became more and more a 'mere Press Bureau'.[54] In particular there was less scope for liaison activities, and as a result, the concept of public opinion was more and more matched onto government opinion. By the late 1930s the League legitimization strategies were more geared towards the Great Powers and avoiding problems than to legitimizing itself to the general public.[55] While the scope for the IFNLS could be argued to have increased as a result, it suffered from similar pressures on its resources.

Despite the fact that the section had a smaller mandate and that there was undoubtedly less engagement for fear of attracting criticism, this did not mean that contacts between the section and the IFLNS ceased. An episode relating to the Bombay branch of the League of Nations Union shows a very high level of involvement by the secretariat: the dossier went between the Information Section and its director Pelt, Central Section and its director V. G. Wilson, two deputy secretary-generals, Frank Walters and Pablo de Azcarate, and others for over two years, with both Pelt and Wilson visiting Bombay personally.[56] Support for the League in India was not widespread. Some League of Nations associations existed, but they were scattered across the country.[57] A federation of these associations could lead to more cohesion and more effective activities. The driving force behind this idea was Manjapra Venkatkrishna Venkatsewaran, the secretary of the Bombay branch of the LNU, who also worked for the League's Bombay Office.

A very close association in personnel or other terms between a League Association and the League or a government was not unheard of: as has been pointed out above, there was a lot of overlap in functions and numerous civil servants were prominent members of League Associations, the Delhi branch was located in premises owned by the Indian government, and the Japanese League of Nations Association was closely associated to the Tokyo Office of the League. Deputy Secretary-General Walters saw the advantages of having a close link between the Bombay Office and the LNU, since the League needed 'active connections at the key points scattered over the vast surface of India. The connections of course should primarily be official ones, but the help of active elements outside is desirable and indeed I should think almost indispensable'.[58] Whereas this approach was in line with the informal policy of the Information Section, which continued to draw on informal contacts despite its narrower official post-1933 mandate, in this case there was more to consider. Firstly, there were tensions between the Bombay branch and the others, particularly the Delhi branch, which felt it should lead an Indian Federation.[59] Secondly, there were concerns over the personality of Venkatsewaran. If he had been more 'energetic, fair-minded and reliable', wrote Sudhindra Nath Ghose of the Information Section, the situation could be conceivable. However, he warned of Venkatsewaran's motives for proposing an Indian Federation, effectively under his leadership: this would give him 'greater opportunity for avoiding his routine work'.[60] Like Walters, Pelt appreciated that circumstances in India required more than 'normal' support for the branch but agreed that it was not ideal to have a League official in charge.[61] Finally Professor D. Ghosh agreed to take over in December 1936 – more than two years after the affair had started.[62]

While the League and the Information Section seemed to have been comfortable with an informal arrangement that went beyond the official mandate, the danger of this backfiring and compromising the standing of the League seems to have been too large in this case. This goes a long way to explaining the extraordinary time and effort devoted by high-level League officials in this episode. However, this episode also showcases three other points. Firstly, the importance attached to events and the public outside of Europe as well as the difficulty in reaching those (colonial) publics. Secondly, it portrays once again the networked character of almost all of those involved in the IFLNS. Finally, this episode provides an insight into the relevance of personalities when dealing discretely with publicity. Everyone understood this to be a very delicate balancing act and Venkatsewaran could not be trusted to perform it.

The IFLNS and the League (particularly the Information Section) entertained a close relationship throughout the interwar period. Their contact was indispensable for both sides, and both sides tried to influence and use each other for their own purposes. The answer to the question of how effective the IFLNS propaganda and education work was, depends to a large extend on the issue, the country and the year. Overall, however, the IFLNS was relatively successful in raising awareness about the League and questions of internationalism among an educated elite across Europe (Germany was notoriously difficult as the

Information Section did not cease to point out) and in the 1920s beyond that elite as well. The League became more cautious after 1933 in its contacts with private organizations. However given the political climate, the IFLNS in many respects also adopted a more cautious attitude to remain a trusted interlocutor, as well as to keep societies from countries that had left the League *in* the federation. Already in 1930 Krabbe of the Information Section reported that 'maybe one can even distinguish a certain weakness and excessive prudence in the way the Union treats problems. This became apparent during the discussion concerning the minorities, prudence which leads the Bureau to exclude from the discussion at the next meeting in Hungary any question that relates to that country'.[63] As the League was losing its appeal over the course of the 1930s, so too did the IFLNS among the general public. This did not mean that its more specific campaigns in the 1930s were unsuccessful. The 'excessive prudence' perhaps explains why quite a number of individual activists assumed that the affiliation of other organizations, such as the International Peace Campaign, was a useful, and more outspoken, support act for the IFLNS in the late 1930s.

Policy Work between Publicity and Discretion

If it had been up to Cecil, the driving force behind the always critical British LNU, this chapter could have concluded here after the analysis of the propaganda activities of the IFLNS, which, according to him, were its main aim. Cecil thought the federation concerned itself 'too much with policy and too little with propaganda'.[64] This opinion was perhaps not unexpected given the grassroots character of the LNU which made propaganda work much more feasible. Regardless of the question whether the combination of propaganda and policy was a wise decision and regardless of the feasibility of doing just one, the combination was a difficult balancing act. Where the League also struggled to balance publicity and discretion, the tension between the openness needed to serve the global public and the discretion necessary to be taken seriously as a policy actor played a pivotal role throughout the life of the federation and probably found expression in Krabbe's observation about 'excessive prudence'.[65]

Regarding its work in the policy field, the IFLNS compared its role to that of a legislature; it provided a form of democratic oversight to the League as well as initiating policies. The activities of the IFLNS, and of other non-governmental organizations, can be categorized as agenda-setting, policy formulation and implementation.[66] In practice these activities and the audiences they served often overlapped. The agenda-setting activities of the IFLNS towards the 'public' and national societies have been touched upon above. In turning to activities towards governments and the League the liaison function of the IFLNS, which the Japanese LNA had already pointed out, becomes clear: the IFLNS was used as an alternative platform in what were otherwise often bilateral relations between states/minorities and the League.

Agenda-setting: Influencing Governments and the League

Following the prescripts of the New Diplomacy, lobby work should take place in the public view, like education work. However, in practice, federation activists often operated more 'diplomatically', using informal contacts without publicizing all their activities. Given the networked character of the activists involved, who interacted in many different settings, this was an obvious approach.

The first aim of the federation in its policy work was agenda-setting. Dossiers on the activities of the IFLNS and their assemblies passed through all League sections.[67] This served the purposes of both sides: while the secretariat drew on the information, got a sense of 'public opinion', and hoped to spot and subsequently prevent radical tendencies, the federation hoped to influence decision-making. This could take the form of discussing controversial topics, before the League, or governments, felt ready to discuss these questions. An example is the question of decentralizing the League in 1927. The idea was that regional unions, such as a European or Panamerican union, were a necessary step towards a truly universal League. While this resolution was rejected by the IFLNS assembly at the time, the debate on the topic continued and was formally brought to the League by French Foreign Minister Aristide Briand in 1929.[68] Agenda-setting was not just geared towards the League, national governments were also explicitly targeted. A relatively straightforward example concerned Togoland, where the IFLNS secretariat served as a liaison between the British LNU, which had collected material detailing 'grave charges' against Togoland officials, and the French League for the Rights of Man. They transmitted the documents to Radical *Deputé* Achille Rene-Boisneuf who questioned the French Minister of Colonies after which an investigation was ordered.[69]

States also used the IFLNS to get their causes on the League agenda. Chinese and Japanese examples have already been mentioned. A less well-known example comes from Haiti. Dantes Bellegarde, Haitian delegate to the League, but also a representative of the Haitian League Society, used the IFLNS to protest against the American occupation of Haiti.

Another form of agenda-setting were the contacts with League organizations in countries which were not (yet or no longer) members of the League, such as the US, Japan or Germany. Theses contacts were on the one hand aimed at those states and publics, to draw them into the League, on the other to the League itself, in order to accept them. However, this was also a two-way process, as states tried to set the agenda of the IFLNS and the League. Although Germany did not join the League until 1926, the *Deutsche Liga für Völkerbund* was a member of the federation from 1921. The aim of the *Deutsche Liga* was to fulfil a pioneering role in facilitating German accession to the League. This was geared on the one hand to the sceptical German public, which had lost much of its initial enthusiasm for a League after Versailles, but on the other hand to the League. In 1920 Foreign Minister Walter Simons put it as follows: 'The *Liga* should as a matter of course pursue a different policy from the government and work more actively for the accession of Germany to the League, otherwise she would not have a right to exist. ... We want the League to come to us.'[70] This is a clear example of how the federation had its agenda, but its interlocutors had theirs too. In this case, the goals of these agendas overlapped (the means perhaps less). The IFLNS, driven in particular by the French Federation, called for German accession to the League from 1921, when the *Deutsche Liga* had been admitted.[71] When Germany was finally admitted to the League in 1926, the IFLNS decided to hold its next annual assembly in Berlin. According to Ruyssen this was brilliantly organized by the *Deutsche Liga* and benefited from the cooperation with the German state. Chancellor Marx spoke at the opening and Foreign Minister Gustav Stresemann at the closing ceremony. Ruyssen was convinced that this was a sound basis for the further 'development of the Federation and the education of the general public in the field of international politics'.[72] Membership figures for the *Deutsche Liga* certainly increased significantly in the aftermath of the Berlin assembly.

After Germany left the League, the successor to the *Deutsche Liga* named *Deutsche Gesellschaft für Völkerrecht und Völkerbundfragen* remained a member of the IFLNS until 1938. Both organizations were under the influence of the *Wilhelmsstrasse*. However, the post-1933 organization was quite open in its disagreement with the 'Geneva Spirit' and for example refused to attend the Glasgow assembly of 1936 because the persecution of Jews in Germany was on the agenda.[73] The federation aimed to keep channels open, also to Associations that adopted quite opposite views.

This episode showcases the role the IFLNS played as a channel of contact with non-League member states and as an agenda-setting organization. However, it also highlights the question of the influence of national governments on civil society organizations who used the IFLNS. It thus shows how practices could be appropriated for different purposes: the pursuit of potentially nationalist goals through internationalist civil society means.[74]

Policy Formulation

The next step after agenda-setting was policy formulation, which was similarly geared towards both the League and national governments. The IFLNS used both its personal contacts as well as the more official channel of sending its resolutions to various League bodies as preparation for League discussions. In 1929, parts of a minorities resolution by the Dutch League delegation were adopted by the member states in the League Assembly. This resolution had previously been discussed and accepted at the IFLNS assembly.[75] This successful preliminary work to influence policy formulation led Ruyssen to describe the federation as an avant-garde of the League.[76] Thomas Davies details an example from the Disarmament Conference of where the resolutions adopted by the IFLNS assembly in Budapest in 1931 became the common platform for the global disarmament movement and in turn 'came to dominate the proceedings of the conference from first to last'.[77]

Policy Implementation

This leads to the final point: implementation. When the IFLNS felt that the League failed to live up to its task, it attempted to push the implementation of policies. One of the most far-reaching examples comes from the minorities' question, where the federation set up a procedure in parallel to the League. The League Minority Protection System, administered by the League Secretariat, has been criticized from many quarters but has recently been more positively evaluated in the historiography, arguing that given the highly contentious situation, where minority states were resistant, minorities and their kin states continually argued for change and the great powers above all wanted to avoid being dragged in, the Minorities Section managed to create a system that kept all parties involved, talking and in some cases brought solutions. Eric Colban, the director of the Minorities Section, secured a central role for the secretariat.[78]

The system was based on 'depoliticization through bureaucracy, secrecy and diplomacy' so as 'to resolve inherently political issues without fanfare or complaint'.[79] Nonetheless, it left many unsatisfied and the system was at odds with the precepts of the New Diplomacy. It was predicated on secrecy that kept petitioners in the dark about the outcome of their complaints and thus left the League open for attack as ineffective.

As a result, numerous private organizations entered the minority stage, writing about minority questions, visiting, gathering information, making contacts and engaging in reconciliation work. Some set up committees that received petitions. Willoughby Dickinson, frustrated at the perceived inability of the League to deal efficiently with this question, suggested that the federation set up a minorities committee. The novelty of this committee, set up in 1923, was that the various minorities were engaged in the proceedings, which the League explicitly did not do.[80] Moreover, it also provided a platform for minorities that were not covered by a treaty, such as Germans and Slovenes in Italy. In principle, the committee worked with League Associations that were run by minorities as well as with national League organizations in minority and kin states. After these consultations representatives of the minority and majority groups were heard. The committee avoided appearing to adjudicate but rather sought to facilitate reconciliation or at the very least rapprochement between the parties involved.[81] The outcome of such initiatives depended largely on local circumstances.[82] The federation also published a bulletin *Minorités Nationales*. They were reluctant to publish too much information, often giving more general information or just circulating information among committee members in confidence (which was sometimes leaked to the press nonetheless). For its reconciliation work trips were very important, but also here publicity was by and large avoided. When the IFLNS decided to publish impressions from a carefully planned and executed trip by Bakker-van Bosse to Rumania, Yugoslavia and Italy in 1930, this immediately backfired and the report was used by all sides to add fuel to the fire.[83]

As the IFLNS experienced the benefits of discretion, they became a trusted interlocutor for the Minorities Section. The League had followed the activities of private organizations, and in particular of the IFLNS Committee, closely from the start. As another example of the tight network, William O'Molony, the first Anglophone assistant secretary-general of the IFLNS now member of the Minorities Section, was by 1930 charged to report on the work of the IFLNS. The relationship was reciprocal. The IFLNS for example provided the section with the reports of their trips and checked about possible agenda points at meetings. Given that this system was based on trust, the section occasionally, and only to certain people, gave feedback on why a petition did not succeed or gave advice on how to phrase petitions.[84]

Considering the twin pillars of propaganda and policy work, IFLNS activities in the minority field constituted the most far-reaching policy work. Given the circumstances and with a stronger focus on reconciliation and discretion than on publication, this system worked relatively well, in conjunction with the League Minority Protection System. The IFLNS certainly filled a gap by giving the minority and kin state a role in the process. Nonetheless, with time frustration at the lack of progress increased among the activists, many of whom at one point or another despaired along the lines of Ruyssen who wrote in 1930 that minorities would always be victims.[85] As Dyroff points out however, the measure of success is perhaps best found in the 'contribution to the creation of a climate that facilitated a peaceful exchange of views and search for compromises'.[86] As such, the IFLNS fulfilled its task as liaison between the League and states/minorities.

Conclusion

The IFLNS played a significant role in the network around the League. As one of the principal civil society players in the era of the New Diplomacy, it entered into a reciprocal relationship with the League Secretariat and functioned as a liaison between the supposedly neutral League and the more political states/minorities. While the federation emphasized openness and the importance of public opinion, in practice its strategy was more refined. The propaganda and education work took place largely in public view and was geared to strengthening public opinion in favour of the League. In the work geared towards governments and the League itself publicity was important, but informal contacts and discretion were equally, if not more, important and often more effective.

Part of the reason why the latter approach was more effective was the fact that it could be better controlled. The federation as a platform was easily used for unintended purposes which more often than not did not promote international peace and understanding. Pedersen made this point regarding the League itself: public opinion, despite the best efforts, is not necessarily pacific.[87] In its efforts to maintain contacts between nations and organizations which came to believe in very different things, the IFLNS was, despite itself, sometimes used for unpacific purposes.

In terms of propaganda and education the federation lived up to its aspirations of acting as an avant-garde, although it probably did not manage to create the 'powerful international public opinion' Smuts had had in mind. In its efforts geared towards the League and governments the IFLNS was quite successful in terms of agenda-setting, whereas its endeavours towards policy formulation and implementation were perhaps a little more varied. 'Democratic oversight' also remained mostly an aspiration as the IFLNS exercised 'excessive prudence' and often bowed to state interest. However, being an unofficial organization – more unofficial than today's NGOs with consultative status – the IFLNS had a certain leeway to table topics that were not yet ripe for official discussion. Given the generally high level of the activists, discussion at the IFLNS gave an idea of how certain topics might develop once they reached the official agenda. The fact that its activists were so well connected was the federation's biggest asset, and the one that carried over its experiences to its successor the WFUNA and other international organizations in the post-1945 period.

Civil and official society were intimately entwined in terms of personnel, methods and objectives. The IFLNS mirrored and foreshadowed the League in many ways, in its organization, its efforts to spur the League on; in its successes and its misfortunes. Where, as Zara Steiner put it 'the Geneva System was an [adjunct] to great power politics',[88] the IFLNS operated within and contributed to this system and as such took part in the governing of the world.

Acknowledgements

The author thanks the anonymous referee and Karen Gram-Skoldjager for their insightful suggestions as well as the participants of the workshop 'Organizing the World. International Organizations and the Emergence of International Public Administration, c. 1920-1960' for their comments on an earlier version.

10

An Uneasy Relationship: German Diplomats and Bureaucrats in the League of Nations

Michael Jonas

Scope and Limits of the Analysis

This chapter explores the presence and role of German diplomats, experts and bureaucrats both at and within the League of Nations. Its main interest is to probe into Germany's relationship to the League beyond official foreign and trade policies. The chapter, in other words, focuses on the largely unknown individuals who dealt with and became part of the League as German nationals, mostly in the organization's secretariat. In historiography, German participation in the League has been frequently viewed as exclusively driven by hostility and the overarching strategic aim of undermining an organization allegedly perceived as anti-German. Against such somewhat simplistic assumptions, the chapter will show the breadth of motives, attitudes and modes of behaviour German officials at the League displayed. This, in turn, raises the question to what extent the German involvement in the League – the German challenge in the League – changed the organization's structures, politics and procedures.

The analysis is concentrated on Germany's involvement in the organization, from the preparations around the Treaty of Locarno in late 1925 and the country's admission in early September 1926 to Hitler's exit from the League in mid-October 1933. As institutional continuities and biographical trajectories reach beyond this period, the chapter sets these developments in the broader context of the interwar years. The chapter's main emphasis, however, rests with the Stresemann years, the second half of the 1920s. In line with more recent interpretations, I content that there was much more ambivalence and complexity in the Reich's entanglement with the League, both at the level of official foreign policy-making and – as shown subsequently – with regard to the dimension of German civil service personnel and expert involvement at the League.

The League in Official Foreign Policy-making

Throughout, Germany's official position to the League was ambivalent, at worst hostile, at best pragmatic, and rarely visionary. The fact that Versailles amounted to an enforced peace, barring a defeated and internationally isolated Germany from participating in the creation of a post-war global order, discredited the League experiment for most German observers and resulted in Berlin's initially hostile attitude towards the League. Before the mid-1920s, the League itself was overwhelmingly considered as a power-political extension of French and British hegemony over the European continent – 'an heir and executioner of the treaties of 1919', as Gustav Stresemann expressly conceded in his speech to the General Assembly on 10 September 1926.[1] As Peter Krüger has pointed out, the term 'revisionism' cannot be applied to Berlin's attitude towards Versailles without qualification, as this would reduce Weimar foreign policy to an inflexible appendix of imperial foreign policy prior to the First World War.[2] On closer inspection, Berlin's foreign policy was much more complex, checkered, inconsistent and certainly not consensually built around rejecting the international order created by Versailles and – in extension – the League.

This is particularly true from the mid-1920s when a group of senior diplomats in the Auswärtiges Amt (AA) came to support Gustav Stresemann, the symbolic figurehead and strategic brain behind Germany's new policy of cooperation, engagement and reconciliation ('Verständigungspolitik').[3] First among them were Stresemann's long-standing state secretary, Carl von Schubert, and the AA's chief legal expert, Friedrich Gaus. Along with the head of the Western and Southern Europe department (II), Gerhard Köpke and Karl Ritter, the young but experienced economic and trade expert of the AA, Schubert and Gaus shaped Germany's foreign political and strategic reorientation towards the Western Powers and – by implication – the League on a conceptual and even an everyday basis from the mid-1920s onwards.[4] This is not to say that Stresemann and the moderate, largely liberal wing of diplomats around him, would have wholeheartedly embraced the League and the prospect of German membership from the beginning. Both the foreign minister and the AA's top civil servants perceived the membership question rather as a potential obstacle to their policy initiatives with the Western Powers. This applied even more as hostility towards the League persisted in German public discourse: 'No one here would regard Germany's entry into the League as a German success,' the British ambassador to Berlin, Viscount D'Abernon, reported back to London in early 1925, thereby seconding the hesitant position of the German government.⁵ It was Locarno first and only secondarily – as a component of the international system built by the Locarno Treaties – membership in the League. Only after the process leading up to Locarno had made apparent that the country's membership was to assume the character of an equal joining equals, did Stresemann and the liberal diplomats move forward. The AA was well aware that the League effectively needed German membership for a number of reasons: in security-political and systemic terms, Germany naturally complemented the organization's far-reaching European security conceptions, 'thus completing the League'.⁶ Additionally, the secretariat around Secretary-General Eric Drummond was keenly interested in the country's substantial contribution to the League's precarious budget and the inclusion of German expertise in a number of scientific fields.⁷

Even before accession was being contemplated, though, the League had necessitated the establishment of institutions on Berlin's part. Within the AA, Gaus's legal department ('Rechtsabteilung') initially dealt with affairs related to the League, as they were subsumed under the overall header of managing the conditions and impositions of the Versailles Treaty. However, from 1923 onwards, the Foreign Office thought it necessary to centralize and coordinate League affairs in a separate sub-department ('Sonderreferat Völkerbund'). As departmental head, Bernhard Wilhelm von Bülow was brought in. Having headed a sub-commission on the war-guilt question at Versailles, Bülow had left the AA in protest against the treaty and spent the early 1920s continuing to push an anti-League agenda in the German public discourse. His 1923 book on the League, however, *Der Versailler Völkerbund: Eine vorläufige Bilanz*, became the standard political reference work in Germany, betraying its author's attitude towards the League as that of a 'lapsed idealist' – a species found frequently in German political discourse after 1918.⁸ As opposed to the liberal Schubert, Bülow's relationship to the League was less accommodating and, once the ground was shifting from 1930 onwards, more confrontational in forcing through Germany's revisionist goals. It was symptomatic for the changing tides in Weimar foreign policy that Bülow succeeded the alleged 'appeaser' Schubert when the latter's career within the ministry came to an effective end after Stresemann's death in 1929.⁹

The German accession to the League also changed the AA's presence in Geneva. Before admission in 1926, the AA received its regular information about League affairs through its consulate in Geneva. This relative backwater of a consular posting had been developed into a well-informed listening post headed by Gottfried Aschmann, an astute, if often sceptical, observer of the League, who ceaselessly reported on virtually everything that Geneva and the organization had to offer. Equally important as the consular presence was the politico-diplomatic German presence through the delegations at the yearly League Assemblies. Here, Stresemann, Schubert and Gaus formed the representative backbone of the German delegation at Geneva from 1926 to 1929, not Bülow.[10] They were accompanied by a group of high-profile politicians, members of parliament and industrialists. The inclusion of non-diplomats in Germany's representation in Geneva raised the German profile, as parliamentarians and other public figures appeared more capable of free speech and spontaneous rhetorical improvisation than the professional diplomats did.[11] The participation of politicians at Geneva also served to strengthen the delegations' political legitimacy as they spanned the breadth of Weimar politics. Members thus counted such diverse characters as Rudolf Breitscheid, leftist-liberal, social-democratic former Prussian minister of the interior; the theologian Ludwig Kaas for the Catholic Centre Party ('Zentrum'); and Johann Heinrich von Bernstorff, a radical liberal diplomat of the Wilhelmine Empire with strong (democratic) convictions, former ambassador to Washington and since 1922 head of the German 'Liga für Völkerbund'. The latter had been established in December 1918 and became, once it had been admitted to the International Federation of League of Nations Societies in June 1921, 'a substitute for an active policy working towards admission [to the League]', at least in official German policy.[12] Its main purpose was twofold: cooperatively preparing the groundwork for an eventual inclusion of Germany in the League both at home and in the international arena, while seconding Weimar's overarching strategic premise of revising or at least readjusting the Versailles order as it existed. The Liga's 'national internationalism' mirrored the ambivalence of German perceptions of the League almost exactly, even among advocates of the organization, of which Bernstorff was certainly one of the most prominent.[13]

Germans in the League Apparatus

Basics of Personnel Planning: Prerequisites, Posts and Recruitment

Having outlined how the League affected the AA's institutional structures and created new forms of diplomatic and political representation, we now turn to the presence of German bureaucrats, civil servants and experts in the League of Nations. My analysis here is largely exploratory, highlighting a number of biographical trajectories that – taken together – aptly mirror the divergent paths through Germany's and the League's history in the Age of the World Wars.

As admission had become a concrete prospect, Berlin started lobbying for a strong German presence within the League. Germany's admission to the League Council as one of five of its permanent members had already been conceded by Drummond – and indeed France and Britain – early on. Through the consulate in Geneva, feelers were extended to the secretariat, often to the secretary-general personally, in order to prepare the ground for both German personnel demands and influence within the secretariat. Drummond, whose interest in the integration of Germany into the League had been constant, treated the German demands carefully and with utmost diplomatic sensitivity, even visiting Berlin in early 1926 in order to hammer out the modalities of the country's accession.[14] Based on the frequent flow of incoming information and on Bülow's own systematic assessment of the League, his section drew up a complex analytical table, breaking down the representation of the League's different member states within the organization's secretariat.[15] As expected, the table pointedly identified the relative overrepresentation of especially Britain and France, even more if one focused on the more prominent positions in the League's civil service.[16] On that comparative basis, the AA came up with two lists covering Germany's maximal and minimal expectations as to the German presence in the League, not necessarily aimed at creating parity but at assuring a substantial influence on the everyday affairs of the secretariat. Maximally, Berlin intended to attract an under-secretary-general's post already hinted at by Drummond and the Western Powers, one or two director's positions, preferably for the Economic and Financial and/or the Transit Sections, one or two 'Chefs de Services' ('Dirigenten' in the AA's hierarchy), and 18 to 20 'Membres de Section'. With demands also for around thirty office workers such as interpreters and secretaries, the German claims spanned a minimum figure of forty-one civil servants and a maximum number of fifty-nine.[17] Even if the number of staff that Germany was granted did end up within this bracket, there was a pronounced German discontent with the outcome. This dissatisfaction rested on the fundamental misconception on the part of the AA that it effectively had the right to decide *which* German staff was employed by the League. Drummond, however, insisted on his – and the secretariat's – prerogative to choose the personnel of his administration – and to do so irrespective of nationality.[18]

Berlin was also more specifically frustrated with the secretary-general's insistence on not being able to provide Germany with a director's post. This was partly because the eleven sections of the secretariat had all already been successfully filled, but it also owed itself to the fact that for directors, as for other administrative jobs, Berlin demanded posts in sections of the organization from which it had to be excluded on grounds of obvious partisanship. This applied in particular to the administrative commissions and Minorities Section, which dealt, among other issues, with the highly sensitive question of the Free City of Danzig and the Saar. One eventually ended up with an under-secretary's post and a number of senior civil service employments in various sections, but apparently nothing to rival the British or French presence. That outcome was, in any case, more than the nationalist press referred to when scandalizing the 'three little posts' Germany had to allegedly settle for.[19]

Harry Kessler and Ludwig Quidde: Two Cases of Rejection

Once the intended membership of Germany in the League had become public, in some rare cases even before that, the AA received a significant number of applications at all levels of qualification and desired employment profile. Despite Drummond's insistence on choosing his own staff, there was quite a sizable room for manoeuvre on the part of the AA, as the secretariat obviously required suggestions and pre-screened applications by the member states. How did Berlin then go about choosing the personnel that was to be recommended to the League? In this context, it might be useful to look, firstly, at who was not wanted and thus excluded from finding employment in Geneva. Programmatically, Bülow had stated that his preference was for as few non-diplomats as possible in the secretariat. He believed that diplomats would be best qualified for the job and wanted to avoid upsetting the AA's career structures by having a large number of 'outsiders' returning from Geneva and applying for admission to the German diplomatic service.[20] With this, so it seems, went the suspicion that allowing outsiders into the AA would also mean allowing less reliability and more party politics into the Foreign Service, hence eroding the diplomats traditional esprit de corps.

One category of outside applicants in particular was rejected by the AA: the pacifist wing on the left of German politics. A natural candidate for a high-profile position within the League was undoubtedly the arch-liberal Harry Kessler, especially as he functioned as a delegation member both at Geneva and in separate missions for the AA. A convinced internationalist, Kessler had been a fierce advocate for the pacifist cause from the early 1920s and a renowned advocate for a somewhat different type of supranational institution building and global governance.[21] His candidacy, however, failed before it had even been announced. The reservations were mutual as he considered Stresemann and his old boys' network deeply corrupt. In the same vein, Kessler's utopian idealism would have certainly collided with the power-political realities of the League's everyday routine.

Another renowned pacifist, who desired to be commissioned at the League, was the leftist-liberal historian Ludwig Quidde, recipient of the Nobel Peace Prize for 1927 (along with Ferdinand Buisson). He had functioned for some years as president of the pacifist umbrella organization Deutsches Friedenskartell, when inquiring with Bülow in mid-1926 whether the AA could not have him placed onto a civil service post in Geneva, preferably in the Information Section. In Bülow's assessment, this was not only rather difficult, as Quidde was too much of a generalist, but obviously also politically undesirable on the part of the German Foreign Office. However, he managed to spin his rejection of Quidde's intentions diplomatically by letting the potential applicant know that the League was not interested in known pacifists, no matter how great their international esteem, because Geneva would have discovered that an overt association with pacifism would make the League somewhat 'unpopular in Germany'.[22] This clearly was a pretext, to an extent even a farce, as Quidde himself did not belong to the radical pacifist wing of the German peace movement and would have been undoubtedly qualified for the civil service of the League, especially on the grounds of his earlier publication 'Völkerbund und Demokratie' and his continued involvement in international disarmament debates.[23] Quidde did not let Bülow and the AA that easily off the hook and continued to pester the respective heads of the 'Referat Völkerbund', from 1928 to 1931, without success. Germany's foremost pacifist died, stripped of his citizenship, in 1941 as an exile in Geneva.

Assessing the German Presence in the League: Employment at Different Levels, Areas of Conflict

Between 1924 and 1932, with a significant emphasis on the second half of the 1920s, Bülow's sub-department carefully registered a total of 593 applications. The extensive table included criteria such as age, qualification, previous employment and, if applicable, the sponsor of the application.[24] The comparatively high number of applications, an average of a little less than 100 per annum, points to a rather robust presence, even a certain popularity of the League in German public discourse for which the general historiographical accounts usually do not allow. This is also evident in correspondence with the federation of technically specialized civil servants in which the organization communicated some of its members' expectations to join the League, if possibilities existed. At about the same time, the Reich Union of German Industry approached the AA in order to point to the enormous interest the country's industry had in Geneva's economic and trade policies, requiring German expertise to join the organization at committee and civil service levels as soon as possible.[25] Even the so-called colonies of diaspora Germans in and around Geneva registered the possibilities of their home country's League membership eagerly, accompanied by the expectation of future employment opportunities.[26]

In the face of the limited amount of posts in Geneva, only a minority of the applicants qualified for further recommendation to the League and received employment subsequently. Over the roughly seven-year period of German membership in the League, from 8 September 1926 to 14 October 1933, the organization employed eighty German nationals, some of them as permanent civil servants on regular tenures, others – especially the clerical staff at midlevel – on renewable short-term contracts.[27] There were nonetheless a sizable number of employees within the higher civil service and at clerical level whose employment extended over several years, in some cases even beyond the watershed of Hitler's exit from the League. The same applied to Germany's constant presence in the broad cosmos of commission work in and around the League. A list of these activities with German participants extends to about three dozen names – among them, some of the renowned figures of German public life such as the eminent Kiel-based international jurist Walther Schücking and Albert Einstein as the German member of the International Committee on Intellectual Cooperation.[28]

With the first appointments to the League in place in early 1927, the German focus shifted from getting Germans into the secretariat to boosting the position and status of the German civil servants in the secretariat. A case in point is the second major appointment – after Albert Dufour-Féronce as under-secretary-general – of Cécil von Renthe-Fink as member of the Political Section. Renthe-Fink was an experienced career diplomat of the AA and joint secretary-general of the International Elbe Commission – and hence rather senior for the post he received.[29] This created difficulties, as his planned salary did not meet his seniority and expectation. Drummond, who had anticipated a junior civil servant, settled the emerging dispute by increasing Renthe-Fink's commencing salary from 19,000 to 23,000 Swiss francs, well below the 25,000 francs Renthe-Fink had demanded, but eventually enough to pacify the AA.[30] A few years later, Renthe-Fink's salary and position within the section became sensitive again, as his French colleague Eugène Vigier was designated for a quiet promotion and a salary increase. This supposedly deliberate act in order to satisfy French demands was immediately scandalized, first by Renthe-Fink himself, who saw the national interest of Germany and the equilibrium among the great powers in the secretariat affected, then by the AA and the German press. The objectively disadvantaged Renthe-Fink considered his symbolically enacted resignation from the League in order to defend the 'rights of German civil servants' in Geneva, but neither Drummond nor the AA would allow for this.[31] While Renthe-Fink was among those senior German civil servants who left Vienna right after Hitler's exit from the League in mid-October 1933, Germany's sudden departure did not necessarily preclude permanent employees of the League from continuing to work for the organization.[32] The majority of higher civil servants, especially those placed on administrative leave for the period of their employment in Geneva, were promptly recalled.[33] For those, with no German civil service background to fall back on, the AA actively sought employment with German institutions or on the job market.[34] If a particular civil servant preferred to remain with the League, however, the German Foreign Office tended to arrive quickly at its wit's end.

A Diverse German Presence: Albert Dufour-Féronce, Max Beer and Otto Olsen

To illustrate the breadth and divergence of German professional biographies at the League let us now turn to three German League officials with three very different backgrounds and career trajectories. In Albert Dufour-Féronce, we see the rather typical example of a German diplomat at the League, chosen and commissioned by the AA as under-secretary-general between 1926/7 and 1932. Max Beer – the second example – represents the 'outsider as insider' whose relationship to the organization remained ambivalent throughout, before turning more accommodating post-1933.[35] Finally, Otto Olsen, a scientist in an emerging expert culture, as the third case covers the segment of permanently employed civil servants at the League and its sub-organizations, who were recruited on their expertise skills.

Albert Dufour-Féronce, Under-Secretary-General

Dufour's position was the highest price Berlin managed to extract from the League, one out of three under-secretaries in Drummond's administration. He was employed from 1 January 1927 until late October 1932. Dufour had won the position through a fiercely competitive, but also stage-managed, process. As soon as it became known that German was granted an under-secretary position, a wide range of names surfaced in the corridors of the Wilhelmstraße and the German press, with high-profile liberal candidates from politics or diplomacy featuring prominently. Soon, however, the field narrowed to rather subaltern candidates from the diplomatic corps, typically embassy counsellors like Clemens von Brentano, Dufour or the head of the Southeastern Europe section in the AA, Julius von Zech-Burkersroda. A list with these names was forwarded to Drummond. On that basis and a talk with Dufour, the secretary-general opted for Dufour, the embassy counsellor of Germany's legation in London, who happened to be a close friend of Schubert during the latter's tenure in Britain in the early 1920s and generally agreeable to British political circles.[36] The appointment was greeted with unanimous enthusiasm, both in London and by the press in Geneva and Berlin.[37]

Despite the advance praise and heightened expectations in London, Geneva and Berlin, Dufour turned out to be a relative failure throughout his tenure with the League. With an attitude towards his employer, which was at best ambivalent, he attempted in vain to foster an overhaul of the secretariat in the German interest, as he saw it. His analytical skills, however, appear to have been less developed, with most of his reporting excessively minute and unnecessarily verbose. This 'analytical flabbiness' necessitated seconding the German under-secretary with more capable junior staff, such as the junior diplomat Werner von Schmieden.[38] Despite going perpetually through enormous troubles, Dufour failed to leave a mark or even to establish a position for himself. At heart, it seems, he lacked an understanding of the complex workings of the League. Just as with Renthe-Fink, Dufour alienated his immediate international colleagues, especially the French and Italians, by complaining about his allegedly inferior status. His grievances and relentless objections are somewhat puzzling, given that Drummond had gone to extraordinary lengths to accommodate some of the more eccentric wishes of his new under-secretary, among them salary issue and the 'import' of his former secretaries at the London embassy as League civil servants.[39] Usually not getting his way, Dufour channelled his frustrations in an unfiltered manner back to Berlin, complaining about the practical injustices of everyday life at the League and not least about his miserably monotonous duties, especially as director of the section on intellectual cooperation.[40] Reviewing the German performance along with Stresemann, Schubert resumed that the 'wholly unhappy' Dufour was apparently not a man of the bigger picture, a hard, but essentially eclectic labourer, whose passion for detail – and for bearing grudges – would make him miss the forest for the trees.⁴¹

Dufour's grievances and general pessimism as to the League's development did not resonate with the AA, which increasingly resorted to bypassing him. On noticing this, he complained bitterly about a 'Berliner System', allegedly built by Bülow's successor, Ernst von Weizsäcker, and the 'Referat'. A 'Fronde', consisting of Beer, Renthe-Fink and Hans Völckers, Aschmann's successor as general consul in Geneva, would have emerged which happily circumnavigated the existing hierarchies and threatened to undermine the German presence at the secretariat.⁴² By then, it had been obvious for some time that the under-secretary would not emerge as the 'pivot' of activity and potential League reform that Bülow, Schubert and not least Stresemann had hoped for.⁴³ In that, they were unwittingly seconded by Dufour's superior, Secretary-General Drummond, who thought his colleague less than satisfactory and indicated early on that he was not going to renew his under-secretary's contract.⁴⁴ Dufour's compensation for the loss of his high-profile position with the secretariat was the legation in Belgrade, from where he retired in 1933.⁴⁵

Max Beer, Member of the Information Section

Beer was one of the most sought-after German additions to the civil service of the secretariat and could have – in all probability – played an important role in the future of the organization, if circumstances and issues of character and temper would not have cut his tenure short. The Vienna-born German-Jewish journalist worked from 1920 as the chief correspondent in Geneva for both *Wolffs Telegraphisches Bureau* (WTB) and the centrist-liberal *Kölnische Zeitung*, the country's by then biggest nationwide daily. Already during the First World War, Beer had lived and worked in Switzerland. During his period as League correspondent for the *Kölnische*, he established himself as one of the key players of the local community in and around the Geneva sociotope and one of the chief interpreters of the League in Germany. His attitude towards the organization was sceptical, even hostile, with the gist of his articles in the German press vilifying the League for its inconsistencies, especially in its treatment of Germany. This nationalist, continually critical angle of his reporting was in turn criticized by the liberal and socialist press, partly with anti-Semitic overtones.⁴⁶ Somewhat inverted, one could justifiably claim that exactly these qualities recommended Beer to the AA as the only serious candidate for a member's post in the secretariat's Information Section. His long-standing presence in Geneva and renowned ability to sway the League's milieu combined with his robust, articulate nationalist position made him into Berlin's uniquely favoured candidate.[47] The AA even went as far as to portray Beer publically as the potential link between the secretariat and Berlin, which Dufour was forced to deny in Geneva. The German journalist's employment was with the secretariat's Information Section, after all, not with the Wilhelmstraße.[48]

The actual procedure of attracting Beer to the post, however, was difficult and protracted. First feelers were extended already in late 1925, right after Locarno. Beer was acutely aware of his importance and complicated the appointment process with a number of at times eccentric requirements, one of them was the decoration with either a title – preferably that of a professor – or a formal senior civil service post with the AA. Both seemed impossible, as he apparently lacked the nominal qualification and experience for both.[49] Furthermore, Beer began to use his excellent connections to senior members of the League's secretariat, especially to the director of the Information Section, Pierre Comert, to facilitate his employment. This two-track diplomacy did not necessarily ease the situation for the AA, as the journalist always seemed at least a step ahead of developments and rather successfully played off one party against the other. Besides the demand of being able to use his League employment as a future stepping stone for a German civil service career, preferably in the diplomatic corps, Beer also insisted with Drummond and Comert that, if entering the Information Section, he would do so without any immediate hierarchical control from above. The only people he was willing to consider loosely as his superiors were the secretary-general and Comert, but none of the other, usually more senior members of the section. Comert even seems to have gone as far as to assure him of becoming his deputy, on a par with the American Arthur Sweetser, an offer that Drummond saw himself forced to revoke.[50] These assurances were to cause the first substantial crisis within the secretariat in relation to Beer's appointment. His relations to his counterparts in the Geneva administration never really recovered from that crisis.

The crises around Beer continued after his employment. On discovering on August 1, 1927, that Sweetser unofficially bore the title of 'assistant director' of the Information Section, the conflict heated up again. From the autumn 1929 onwards, Beer filed multiple complaints within the secretariat, involving numerous talks with Comert and even Drummond, and to the AA, threatening resignation and making his own situation into a symbol-political epitome of the German position in the League.[51] In the latter, the clumsy Dufour, who constantly sponsored Beer's eccentricities, assisted, so that the AA was forced to deescalate and contain Comert's irritation about the Germans' behaviour at the secretariat.⁵² Beer, however, was unwilling to concede and continued to lobby for his own advancement and 'equal status', even accepting that Drummond's reputation began to be severely affected by 'this very embarrassing Beer-Sweetser affair'.⁵³ At the same time, he rarely missed an opportunity to seek his exit from the League, repeatedly inquiring about the allegedly agreed fallback positions either within the AA or the Reich government's civil service. The AA was unwilling to commit and tried to keep the journalist in office as long as possible, even when Beer claimed that further employment would have become an impossibility due to his severed relationships to Comert and Drummond.⁵⁴

Eventually, everyone in both Berlin and Geneva was aware that Beer's resignation was not only due to his alleged mistreatment by the secretariat or the 'dilatory behavior' of Comert and Drummond, but also due to the 'complicated and checkered character' of Beer himself.⁵⁵ Once released from his duties, Beer attempted in vain to be incorporated into the German civil service system, either as a member of the AA's press department or as a senior civil servant for the Reich government. The AA had manoeuvred itself into serious difficulties in this respect, as the initial negotiations with Beer, dating back to 1926 and 1927, conveyed the impression that his transition after the League tenure into the AA – or indeed an equivalent post – was intended. The contract the AA had drafted for him stipulated such a legal obligation clearly but had apparently remained unsigned.⁵⁶ In the face of Beer's impossible, even damaging behaviour, Berlin gradually pulled back and attempted to pacify the justifiably outraged journalist with alternatives to an admission to the German civil service, among them, ironically enough, a rapprochement with Comert and the revocation of his resignation.⁵⁷ From mid-1930 onwards, he received an allowance from the AA, 'for advisory services' on press and League issues. However, this was gradually reduced and with the general transition towards a more National Socialist course within the Foreign Office, the German diplomatic elite increasingly distanced itself from Beer. As a bitter follow-up to his stint with the secretariat, he published an essayist account of the League in 1932, in which he castigated the apparent disconnect between the League's self-professed ideals and its bleak power-political reality.⁵⁸

Beer eventually took up his old work as a correspondent in Geneva but was dismissed 'on racial grounds' in 1933. Now, Beer exiled first to France and eventually to the United States, where he became a founding figure of the press corps of the United Nations after the Second World War. On his death in 1965, the obituaries published in his honour recognized a stringency and consistency of internationalist engagement that unwittingly levelled out the complexity of Beer's biography.[59] He was, in essence, an internationally, even transnationally based nationalist who – more or less forcibly – migrated to an internationalist position from the early 1930s onwards. Ironically, his professional biography, connecting the League's secretariat (1927–31) and the UN (ca. 1945–50), marks him out as a transitional figure of internationalism much like his old rival of the late 1920s, the more consistently internationalist Arthur Sweetser.[60]

Otto Olsen, Member of the Health Section

The long-standing and distinguished career of Otto Olsen mirrors another variant of interwar internationalism, the technocratic 'Internationale', which found apt structural accommodation within the League and its manifold organizations.[61] Iris Borowy has seized upon Olsen and some of his fellow practitioners in and around the Health Section of the secretariat for an extremely useful collective biographical probing into the internationalization and globalization of health discourses.[62] An epidemiologist of German-Danish origins, assistant of Martin Hahn at the Berlin Hygienic Institute, Olsen was apparently only second choice. When the League of Nations Health Organisation (LNHO) attempted to recruit German expertise, their initial intention was to attract the renowned epidemiologist Heinz Zeiss, who had headed the German Red Cross programmes in the Soviet Union and Eastern Europe. Zeiss, a fervent nationalist and opponent of the League, who early on joined the NSDAP, turned down the offer of joining the LNHO after long deliberations with the AA in 1924/25 on how to relate to the League with German membership still not a definite prospect.[63] After Zeiss's refusal, the AA came up with Olsen as an alternative. Olsen's appointment as a member to the LNHO, commencing from 1 October 1925, anticipated the German admission by a year and turned out to be not only uncontroversial but also one of the most successful stints of any German national at the League.[64] Until the discontinuation of his contract in 1940, Olsen was centrally placed in the LNHO administration and constantly developing his expertise across different fields. His most significant contribution appears to have been numerous pioneering studies on the development of global housing that – taken together – were among the first systematic assessments problematizing the link between poverty, social medicine and housing. Olsen was also, as Borowy has pointed out, 'the only German [within the LNHO, MJ] who was able to extract himself from the grip of the Auswärtiges Amt for longer periods of time'.[65]

His independence from the AA was also reflected in his effective refusal to return home after the German exit from the League. Everything that the AA offered to him to make him come back, Olsen calmly turned down by hinting at his stable position in the League's secretariat and the excellent professional prospects at the LNHO.[66] His problems got more severe, however, from the moment that the gradually disintegrating League could not afford his services anymore. In 1940, the secretariat saw itself eventually forced to discontinue Olsen's employment. He nonetheless did not return to Germany but appears to have stayed on in Geneva. Borowy has found another mention of him in UN reporting, with Olsen seemingly employed as an interpreter for the organization in New York at one point in the 1950s. Besides that, his post-war whereabouts are mysterious. Despite his pioneering contributions, Olsen's biography nonetheless is not the straightforward, almost ideally conceived career of an internationalist in the emerging global health networks. After 1933, with his contract at the LNHO downgraded and prospects for continued employment increasingly bleak, he cultivated frequent relations to German diplomacy, especially the consulate in Geneva, feeding regular reports on League affairs to Berlin. This, however, seems to have been authorized by his LNHO superiors, presumably in order for the League to sustain some sort of back channel to the AA and the Reich government. In 1937, Olsen even joined the NSDAP, probably in order to facilitate his return to Germany.[67]

Olsen's autonomy and relative success in Geneva most likely derived from the fact that he was not a career diplomat, but a scientific expert. For the AA, it was therefore impossible to exercise the same cautious, indirect control as with many other members of the League and its organizations. This resulted in a quite a different commitment to and involvement in the League. Olsen's fifteen years with the League are therefore testament to how expert internationalism continued to evolve, as political cooperation was increasingly hit by paralysis and eventual failure.

Concluding Remarks

A certain diversity rather than uniformity defined Germany's conceptions of the League and Berlin's personnel policies towards the secretariat and the organization as a whole. This, however, applies most forcefully to the brief window between the mid-1920s and around 1930, the period associated with

Stresemann and his 'Verständigungspolitik'. After the country had become a constitutive, probably the most significant element of Europe's post-war security architecture, Germany's admission to the League would have to be considered as the epitome of Stresemann's policy. There certainly was a pointed revisionist potential throughout, but the gist of Weimar's attitude towards and involvement in the League during the Stresemann years did not aim at disrupting and ruining the organization, but much rather at an accommodating reform and fostering what the 'idealists' in the German camp would have labelled an evolution towards a supposedly 'true' League of Nations.[68] The at times aversive behaviour, the manifold ill-tempered protests, even the occasional sabotage were more akin to the role of an 'opposition in a parliamentary democracy which is being brought into government for the first time after years of futile opposition'. In government, however, such a party is usually confronted with a 'civil service that has been exclusively selected according to the needs and wishes of earlier governments', having hence fully internalized their institutional and political interests.[69] If seen against such a comparative backdrop, the transition, indeed the fundamental clear-out Berlin insisted on, appears to follow a certain systemic logic.

Bearing the overall political framework in mind, it would also have to be stated that the concrete implementation of Berlin's League policies often seemed deficient. The personnel choices with regard to the top level of German civil servants in the secretariat were undeniably less than visionary and certainly not 'really first-class'.[70] The majority of the effectively commissioned civil servants, illustrated above through the case studies of Albert Dufour-Féronce – as under-secretary-general – and Cécil von Renthe-Fink, originated with the German diplomatic corps. Their ideological and political disposition towards the League was at best ambivalent, often hostile, frustrated or plain pessimistic – and rarely ever 'progressive', let alone internationalist, in exactly the way in which Geneva was conceived.[71] Underneath that top level, however, one could find a comprehensive biographical collective of practising internationalists of the calibre of Otto Olsen, the health and – later on – housing expert in the LNHO, and Max Beer, Germany's foremost journalist observer and critic of the League. The same would have to be said for the wider institutional environment of the League, beyond the confines of the secretariat and hence outside the actual focus of this analytical probing. Here, German experts and bureaucrats participated frequently and influentially in League deliberations and policy-making. Occasionally, German League policy – and not least the personnel employed in the secretariat – was even capable of a certain visionary force. Most succinctly, Stresemann captured this in his last public speech on 9 September 1929 to the League's assembly. Pushing for greater integration, the German foreign minister asked, almost prophetically pointing to the continent's future economic integration: 'Where is in Europe the [common] European coin, the European stamp?'[72] Few of the contemporaries present that day could have imagined that within less than five years an internationally unbound, aggressively revisionist and increasingly expansionist German state would have left the League, while working towards its dissolution and the destabilization of the European security system.

Part Four

Leadership and Administration

11

Secretaries-General and Crisis Management: Trygve Lie and Dag Hammarskjöld at the United Nations

Ellen J. Ravndal

Introduction

During the first few years after an intergovernmental organization's (IGO) foundation, important precedents will be established through the interplay between formal and informal institutional rules and expectations, individual personalities and the changing political context. During this initial period, the everyday decisions of staff working in the International Public Administration (IPA) will have important consequences for defining the autonomous powers of the IPA. Bob Reinalda has suggested the term 'frontierspersons' to describe the crucial role of the first executive head in establishing international organizations.[1] This chapter examines the practices of crisis management of the first two United Nations (UN) secretaries-general: Trygve Lie (1946–53) and Dag Hammarskjöld (1953–61). By crisis management I refer to attempts (successful or not) at managing peace and security situations by UN actors and through UN forums. Crisis management is often considered the primary purpose of the UN. Through this focus on crisis management the chapter addresses the questions of how and why the office of UN secretary-general developed into a powerful actor in international politics, what types of power the office possesses and what the limits of this power are.

In focusing on Lie and Hammarskjöld jointly, the chapter contributes a new perspective to existing literature where Hammarskjöld's role has frequently been celebrated, while Lie's has been largely overlooked. The UN's first two secretaries-general were both from Scandinavian countries, and they shared a belief in the importance of social justice and democracy. They had both served in government or the civil service during the 1930s–1940s when their home countries established welfare state systems. They also shared an interest in outdoor activities such as hiking and skiing. But their personalities and socio-economic backgrounds were starkly different. Whereas Lie came from a Norwegian working-class background and often came across as blunt, direct and sometimes blundering, Hammarskjöld grew up in an upper-class family with a long tradition of service to the Swedish state and presented a much more sophisticated and intellectual image compared to Lie.

Despite their differences, both Lie and Hammarskjöld believed firmly in the principles of the UN and sought to use their office to defend and strengthen the organization, but they used different tactics to reach their shared goal. They agreed that the UN secretary-general held an important responsibility and must occupy a central position in UN crisis management and sought to consolidate and expand the office's powers. The combined result of their efforts was that the office of UN secretary-general, within fifteen years of the organization's foundation, had been established as a central node in the UN's apparatus for maintaining peace and security and as a position with widely autonomous rights and responsibilities as a crisis manager. Based on a shared vision and commitment to the ideals of the UN, both acted decisively in the face of crisis. Hammarskjöld, as the second, could build on and refine the basis Lie had built, and he contributed a legacy of justifications linked to the ideal of the International Civil Service that remains of vital importance to understanding the position of the UN secretary-general today.

The analysis of this chapter proceeds in four parts. First I examine in more detail what crisis management is and what mandate the UN secretary-general, at the time of the establishment of the UN, had been given for activities in this area. The next two sections analyse the tenures of Lie and Hammarskjöld in turn. Each section focuses on three key crises: for Lie, the crisis in Palestine and the First Arab-Israeli War (1947–9), the Berlin Blockade (1948–9), and the outbreak of the Korean War (1950); and for Hammarskjöld, the situation of the American airmen in China (1954–5), the Suez Crisis (1956), and the Congo (1960–1). The chapter concludes with an assessment of each secretary-general's contribution to developing the UN secretary-general's autonomous role in crisis management.

The UN Secretary-General and Crisis Management

The United Nations was established in 1945 'to save succeeding generations from the scourge of war',[2] and most observers then and now consider the maintenance of international peace and security as the organization's primary purpose. To this end the founders of the UN established a new and more powerful Security Council in place of the earlier council of the League of Nations and also explicitly tasked the secretary-general with a share of this responsibility. The UN Charter (article 7(1)) designated the secretariat (and secretary-general) as one of six principal organs of the UN, thereby giving the secretary-general equal responsibility for pursuing the UN's purpose. Furthermore, article 99 mandates that the UN secretary-general 'may bring to the attention of the Security Council any matter which in his opinion may threaten the maintenance of international peace and security'. Although the exact implications of this responsibility remained unclear, the UN Preparatory Commission recognized that it conferred on the secretary-general 'a quite special right which goes beyond any power previously accorded to the head of an international organization'.[3] Discussions during the Charter drafting process and the election of the first secretary-general further revealed an expectation that the UN secretary-general would play some sort of political role, but it was always a vague and ambiguous idea. This ambiguity would contribute to the role's flexibility and allowed the first two holders of the post room for manoeuvre to expand their autonomous powers of crisis management.[4]

In the peace and security field the Security Council and the secretary-general are often consumed by trying to deal with pressing matters of the day, the latest headlines and most urgent crises. In the literature these activities are variously referred to as 'conflict management', 'conflict prevention', 'conflict resolution', 'crisis diplomacy', or similar. Some of the crisis situations are ongoing armed conflicts between or within member states, while others are tense situations which could escalate to armed conflict. For this reason I have chosen to use the term 'crisis management'[5] to refer to the activities of the secretary-general to prevent a crisis or conflict situation from breaking out, to limit and prevent escalation of the crisis, to seek solutions or settlements of ongoing conflicts, and to implement and monitor agreements.

There are several levels to any UN crisis management situation. The political scientist Robert Putnam famously suggested that all international diplomacy is a two-level game, where agreement must be reached both at the international level and at the domestic level of the two negotiating states.[6] Crisis management at the UN is more complex and agreement must be found on multiple levels to reach a successful outcome. There is a 'level' in New York where agreement must be reached among the UN member states, first, that something should be done and, second, on a recommended course of action. A second level involves negotiations with the parties to the actual crisis situation. During Lie's and Hammarskjöld's terms in office these were mostly government actors, but increasingly this can also mean non-state actors. Third, all the domestic- (internal-) level games of all the state (and non-state) actors involved further complicate the picture. Unless a government has the support of its domestic constituents, it cannot commit resources to the solution of an international crisis. Finally, from the perspective of the UN secretary-general, it is also necessary to keep in mind internal secretariat relations. If the secretary-general loses the support of the secretariat staff, as Lie did over his handling of the McCarthy process, they will find it more difficult to execute their job and navigate to find a solution at the other levels of the game. Finding a mutually acceptable solution to a crisis is therefore an inherently difficult and complex process.

Crisis management can entail a number of different activities, many of which the secretary-general can also use for other purposes. Peter Wallensteen has identified three phases of a crisis and suggested that different diplomatic activities are necessary during each of them.[7] The first phase, he argues, is *agenda diplomacy*, where the objective is to focus attention on the situation and secure consent from the parties and the international community that negotiation is necessary. During the second phase, called *agreement diplomacy*, negotiations take place, and the UN secretary-general may serve as a third-party mediator. Finally, once there is an agreement, the third phase is that of *implementation diplomacy* which largely corresponds to current UN peacebuilding activities.[8]

Taking into account all three phases of a crisis, the secretary-general may have to employ several different tools in the pursuit of crisis management. One key role of the secretary-general is to find and disseminate *information*. The secretary-general may appoint fact-finding commissions, on their own initiative or at the request of the Security Council or General Assembly,[9] and regularly presents reports to the Security Council on ongoing crisis situations. Beyond providing information, the secretary-general may engage in different *mediation* activities between the parties to the conflict and among the UN member states in New York. Mediation includes a range of strategies where a third party seeks to help the parties to a conflict reach agreement. *Communication-facilitation strategies* fall at the low end of intervention and see the mediator in a passive role as a channel of communication and facilitating cooperation, but without exercising much control over the process.[10] The role as a channel of communication is a traditional role of diplomacy, and it was also one the League of Nations secretary-general served on occasion.[11] A more involved mediation role involves *procedural strategies* where the mediator exerts more formal control over the process of mediation. This can include organizing talks, providing a meeting space, setting the agenda, and controlling communications to the media and the distribution of information to the parties.[12] At the highest end of mediator intervention, employing so-called *directive strategies*, the mediator provides incentives or issues ultimatums to the parties and seeks to directly 'change the way issues are framed, and the behavior associated with them'.[13] Such mediation may be difficult for the secretary-general to engage in alone because the office does not possess sufficient material resources to threaten or induce parties to agreement. But as the example of Hammarskjöld's cooperation with the United States during the Suez crisis showed, a coalition of the secretary-general with one or more member states may be able to employ this strategy.[14] Today such coalitions are often called the 'groups of friends' approach.[15]

Although the secretary-general largely lacks the resources necessary to use material power to threaten or induce parties to agreement, the office is not without authority. The secretary-general enjoys high levels of moral authority within the UN context.[16] The basis for this authority comes from the secretary-general's position within the UN and in relation to the UN Charter. More than anyone else within the UN, the secretary-general represents the UN overall – he can be described as a 'guardian of the UN Charter'.[17] On the basis of this authority, the secretary-general can urge UN member states to act either in informal behind-the-scenes meetings or using the public stage. Appealing to the media and the public to put pressure on states is often called using the 'bully pulpit'.[18] Finally, the secretary-general can play a central role in the third phase of a crisis during so-called *implementation* diplomacy. Just because the parties have reached an agreement, or the Security Council or the General Assembly has passed a resolution recommending a certain course of action, this does not mean the crisis is over. At that point the difficult work of implementing the agreement starts. The secretary-general will often be tasked by the Security Council or the General Assembly to follow up on resolutions. As examples in this chapter show, this follow-up process may even involve seeking agreement from the actual parties to the crisis as focus shifts from New York to the field. During Lie's and Hammarskjöld's tenures, peacekeeping was developed as an innovative tool of crisis management for the implementation of agreements.

Today, in the twenty-first century, the UN secretary-general's role in crisis management is widely accepted and relied upon by the UN membership. This role has developed over time, and as this chapter shows, important foundations for this role were established during Lie's and Hammarskjöld's tenures as they each grappled with different crisis situations. In the process, both contributed to consolidating and expanding the autonomous powers of the UN secretary-general and, by extension, the International Public Administration.

Trygve Lie, 1946–53

Trygve Lie was sworn in as UN secretary-general on 2 February 1946 during the first General Assembly session in London and was immediately thrown into challenging crisis situations. While the first General Assembly session was still ongoing, signs of the Cold War became visible in intense arguments in the Security Council. On 5 March Winston Churchill held his famous speech declaring that the 'iron curtain' had fallen. Lie was determined that the UN should become a success. Remembering his experiences of fleeing his home country to live in exile during the Second World War, Lie put his hopes and faith in the power of the UN to prevent another world war like it. But the tensions between the Soviet Union and the United States and their respective allies would make this an increasingly difficult task. In Lie's own words: 'The hard realities of world politics intruded. Like gusts of wind warning of future storms to come, they blew in the door of the new-built house of peace before the workmen had finished.'[19] From the beginning, Lie was convinced that the secretary-general would have to play a central role if the UN was to succeed in its task to maintain international peace and security. During his tenure he would often be required to play a part in the management of crises large and small. This section looks closer at three of them: the situation known as the 'Palestine Problem' and the first Arab-Israeli war in 1947–9, the Berlin Blockade in 1948–9, and the outbreak of the Korean War in June 1950.

The 'Palestine Problem' – the question of the future administration of the British mandate of Palestine where Zionists sought to establish an independent Jewish state against the opposition of the local Arab population and the regional Arab states – first entered the UN's agenda in February 1947 when Britain asked the UN to help propose a solution. Over the summer of 1947, the United Nations Special Committee on Palestine (UNSCOP) toured the Palestine mandate and Jewish refugee camps in Europe, before giving a majority recommendation to divide the territory into two independent states, one Jewish and one Arab, with Jerusalem to remain an international territory. On 29 November 1947 the General Assembly endorsed this recommendation and adopted the partition plan. However, on the ground local actors had their own ideas. Fighting had already broken out and escalated over the coming months. On 14 May 1948 the

Jewish state of Israel declared itself independent, only to be invaded the next day by the armies of the neighbouring Arab states.[20]

Throughout 1948, Secretary-General Lie sought to urge the UN member states to take forceful action to implement the partition plan. Already in December 1947, Lie had suggested that an international UN force should be established to maintain order in the Palestine mandate and help the UN commission implement the partition plan.[21] The question gained new relevance when the crisis escalated to that of an international war. The Security Council had appointed the Swedish Count Folke Bernadotte as a mediator and tasked him with bringing armistices to the region. The first truce started on 11 June and the mediator recruited what essentially became the UN's first peacekeeping mission, UNTSO, to monitor compliance with the cease-fire agreement. Lie's suggestion in this context was to make a public proposal that the UN secretariat could establish a UN armed guard, a small force of 1000–5000 men, largely from the smaller member states, that could be at the disposal of the Security Council, the General Assembly, and the Trusteeship Council when they needed support to guard UN premises and operate in conflict situations. In 1949 the General Assembly eventually adopted a scaled-down version of the plan, what became the UN Field Support.[22]

While the conflict in Palestine was still ongoing, a new crisis broke out in Berlin in June 1948 when the Soviet Union closed off access to the Western occupation zones ostensibly in retaliation against the introduction of a new currency. Britain, France and the United States responded by setting up an airlift to bring supplies into the city, but the situation remained tense and there was a risk of escalation into military conflict between East and West.[23] At first this issue was not on the UN agenda because the founders of the UN had decided that the post-war peace settlement would be handled outside the UN. In late June, Lie offered his services as a negotiator and suggested that he could use article 99 to place the blockade on the Security Council agenda, but Britain and the United States responded that 'any action by the Secretary-General would not be appreciated at the present stage'.[24] However, when the blockade dragged out without an immediate solution likely, the three Western states themselves referred the issue to the Security Council in late September 1948. Initially, Secretary-General Lie held back while the Security Council delegated to the six 'neutral' council members, under the leadership of the Argentinian representative and that month's council president, Juan Atilio Bramuglia, to negotiate a solution.

When the Soviet Union vetoed the 'neutral's' proposal, Lie decided to take on a more active role in seeking a solution to the blockade. His first initiative was to offer the use of two assistant secretaries-general, one American and one Soviet, to negotiate a solution to the underlying currency issue. He wrote to his daughter that he remained optimistic for a solution: 'At the moment I'm in the middle of conversations … to see if I can do something useful.'[25] But the proposal was once again rejected by the Western states, who told Lie to leave the negotiations to Bramuglia and the neutrals.[26] Next, the secretary-general decided to adopt a more public strategy. On 13 November he issued a joint public appeal with Herbert Evatt of Australia, then serving as president of the General Assembly. The two urged immediate conversations to solve the Berlin blockade and resumption of negotiations for the general peace settlement and also offered their services to assist in these goals. This statement unleashed a storm of criticism. The Western states, again, were the most negative, while Council President Bramuglia and many smaller states welcomed the initiative as a reflection of 'the universal desire for lasting peace'.[27] Ultimately, Lie's initiatives public or private did not bring about a solution of the Berlin blockade, but the argument can be made that they were 'a necessary failure' to buy time and defuse tension which prepared the way for direct negotiations on a more realistic basis.[28] While the various UN initiatives played out, the Soviet Union and the United States started direct negotiations in secret, using their UN delegations in New York.[29] The Berlin blockade thus demonstrated 'the value of proximity' – that diplomatic staff are present in New York and regularly interact with each other[30] – which might be seen as an important part of the UN's overall capacity for crisis management.

With hindsight, the third crisis situation – the outbreak of the Korean War in June 1950 – was the most dangerous crisis of Lie's tenure as UN secretary-general. In the early hours on 25 June 1950 (Korean time), the armed forces of North Korea crossed the 38th parallel into South Korea. Lie was outraged. 'My God, Jack, that's against the Charter of the United Nations!' was his response when John D. Hickerson of the US delegation told him the news.[31] Lie asked the UN commission in Korea to send a report and started to plan for a Security Council meeting to be held the next day. At the council meeting in the afternoon on 25 June (New York time), Lie spoke first. It was neither 'necessary [n]or expected' that the secretary-general would speak first, because it had never happened before.[32] Lie later considered this a case of invoking article 99, but most legal scholars today dispute this interpretation because the United States had asked for the council meeting to be called.[33] Nonetheless, the secretary-general played a crucial role in mobilizing UN support for South Korea. He encouraged states to vote in favour of the resolution and, once the resolution passed, took it upon himself to send telegrams to all UN member states asking them to communicate offers of help to South Korea back to him. Lie also drafted a Security Council resolution to establish a coordination committee for the UN operation in Korea.[34]

In all this, Lie saw himself as an executive of the Security Council. He wrote in his memoirs that he had chosen to take on such a public role 'because the response of the Security Council would be more certain and more in the spirit of the Organization as a whole were the Secretary-General to take the lead'.[35] The outbreak of the Korean War was one of the few times during his tenure when Lie's actions were broadly welcomed by the majority of the member states. The United States was happy to allow Lie to take public action because they believed 'it was a good idea to use the United Nations umbrella as much as possible'.[36] The secretary-general's actions to mobilize support for a strong UN response to the Korean War meant that he became a focal point and symbol of the organization's unity in this trying time. In a further display of this unity, the General Assembly extended Lie's term in office in November 1950.[37] However, Lie's strong stand in support of the US-led UN intervention in Korea, which the supporters of that intervention welcomed, was strongly resented by those opposed to the intervention. From November 1950 onward, the Soviet Union refused to recognize Lie as the legitimate secretary-general and instead boycotted his office. This made Lie's position untenable, and in November 1952 he became the first and hitherto only secretary-general to have resigned from office.

Overall, Lie's tenure as secretary-general saw the formation of many important precedents for the autonomous powers of the UN secretary-general. Lie secured recognition for the right of the secretary-general to make statements in the Security Council, to appoint independent investigative committees, to mediate between parties to a conflict and to urge UN members to action. The membership also accepted that the secretary-general could draft Security Council resolutions, delegate his rights to his representatives, and that he had a role to play in coordinating the response of UN member states and different UN organs to a crisis situation. Lie operated behind the scenes in informal meetings with member-state representatives but was not afraid to take his views public and use his 'bully pulpit' to seek to rally public support for his ideas.[38] Although the majority of Lie's initiatives met with opposition or inaction from the member states, they did not directly challenge his right to take such initiatives. In this way, Lie's trial-and-error approach secured acceptance for many procedural norms which amounted to an expansion of the secretary-general's space for autonomous political action. Lie's successors have been able to build on this foundation to refine and expand the secretary-general's toolbox for crisis management.

Dag Hammarskjöld, 1953–61

Following Lie's resignation from office, in March 1953 the Security Council offered the job to Dag Hammarskjöld of Sweden. Lie welcomed his successor to Idlewild airport with the famous warning that he was taking on 'the most impossible job in the world'.[39] The permanent members of the Security Council had appointed Hammarskjöld based on his 'reputation as a skilled administrator with no apparent political ambition', in the hope that he would be a less activist and interfering secretary-general than Lie had been.[40] At first it looked as if they might have gotten their wish, as Hammarskjöld focused on re-establishing trust inside the secretariat where morale had reached a low point during the McCarthy process and kept a generally low profile in diplomatic matters. But the council had misjudged Hammarskjöld, who soon proved himself equally as determined as Lie to play an independent role in crisis management.

Hammarskjöld's reputation as a diplomat has become legendary since his untimely and mysterious death in September 1961, and his approach to crisis management is often held up as a model for later secretaries-general. Kofi Annan, the UN's seventh secretary-general, once said in a lecture that 'there can be no better rule of thumb for a Secretary-General, as he approaches each new challenge or crisis, than to ask himself, "how would Hammarskjöld have handled this?"'[41] Already during his tenure, diplomats, secretariat officials and journalists in New York referred to the 'leave it to Dag' approach to difficult problems.[42] Some of Hammarskjöld's interventions in crisis management have become textbook examples of the genre. This section looks closer at three of them: the situation of the American airmen in China (1954–5) which debuted the 'Peking formula' for 'quiet diplomacy', the Suez Crisis (1956) with the establishment of the principles of UN peacekeeping, and the Congo (1960–1).

In the aftermath of the Korean War, one unresolved issue was the fate of a group of American airmen who had been shot down during the war and had ended up in Chinese prisons. The Communist government of China claimed they were spies and, on 24 November 1954, convicted them to between four years and life in prison. The United States disputed this, claiming that the airmen were prisoners of war and should be released as part of the Korean armistice agreement. Relations between the Chinese and American governments were very tense at this time. The United States continued to support the Nationalist Chinese government on the island of Taiwan and refused to recognize the government of the People's Republic of China or to grant them UN membership.[43] In this context, the United States decided to refer the issue to the UN, and the General Assembly on

10 December 1954 passed a resolution asking Secretary-General Hammarskjöld to seek the release of the airmen.[44] Hammarskjöld's actions have since been the subject of much analysis. He decided to seek a meeting directly with the Chinese government in Beijing, and to get there he cleverly sought to distance himself from the General Assembly resolution. China was not a member of the UN and was therefore not bound by the organization's resolutions. Furthermore, to base his mission squarely on the assembly resolution would have conveyed the impression that Hammarskjöld was acting as an agent of the United States, and this would not be a good basis for establishing friendly relations with the Beijing government. Instead, Hammarskjöld in his initial letter to Zhou Enlai in December 1954 and during their meetings in Beijing in early January 1955 emphasized his position and responsibility directly under the UN Charter.[45]

In contrast to Lie's open relationship with the press, Hammarskjöld throughout was careful not to reveal any details to the press. This behind-the-scenes approach is what has given it the label 'quiet' or 'private' diplomacy. Such behind-the-scenes diplomacy was of course not a new invention by Hammarskjöld – indeed the first secretary-general of the League of Nations, Sir Eric Drummond, had also achieved some successes with quiet diplomacy[46] – but Hammarskjöld seemed to 'sum up in his person the virtues of this sort of activity; here is the quiet diplomat *par excellence*'.[47] Hammarskjöld is credited with having perfected the art of quiet diplomacy, and indeed this first high-stakes application of it did eventually lead to success. Timed to coincide with Hammarskjöld's fiftieth birthday, China announced the release of the last airmen on 1 August 1955.[48] Further underlining the quiet and private character of Hammarskjöld's approach, he did not take public credit for the airmen's release or even protest when V. K. Krishna Menon from India publicly claimed credit for the successful outcome or when the press credited negotiations between the United States and China.[49] It is hard to believe Lie would have let the same occurrence slide by without public comment, but this underlines their different personalities and approach to the media and the public.

A second high-profile crisis where Hammarskjöld has later been credited with innovation in the techniques of crisis management is the Suez crisis of October–November 1956. On 29 October 1956 Israeli forces invaded Egypt and pushed towards the Suez Canal. Unknown to Hammarskjöld, the United States and the public, this was the first stage of a coordinated plan between Britain, France and Israel with the aim of removing Gamal Abdel Nasser from power and returning the Suez Canal to international ownership.[50] The secret collusion soon became obvious, however, when Britain and France issued an ultimatum to Israel and

Egypt and started moving its troops into position for an invasion. Britain and France had massively misjudged the situation and their own capabilities. Before their troops had even reached Egypt, the UN General Assembly passed several resolutions and created the (second) first UN peacekeeping force, the United Nations Emergency Force (UNEF). Hammarskjöld's role in these events has been widely praised.

The crisis had started when Nasser nationalized the Suez Canal on 26 July to secure funds to build the Aswan dam. Over the next few months negotiations sought a solution acceptable both to Egypt and to other states with an interest in the canal. In early October Hammarskjöld chaired several meetings with representatives of Britain, Egypt and France, which resulted in agreement on six principles on the use of the canal which the Security Council adopted on 13 October.[51] But despite this apparent diplomatic solution, Britain, France and Israel proceeded with their military plans, leading to the next phase of the crisis and the eventual creation of UNEF. Hammarskjöld, at first, was hesitant when Lester Pearson of Canada suggested the creation of a UN military force on 1 November during General Assembly discussions. Over the coming days Hammarskjöld and Pearson held several meetings, accompanied by Andrew Cordier and Ralph Bunche from the UN secretariat to explore the implications of and practical viability of Pearson's idea.[52] In his notes Hammarskjöld wrote, 'Mr. Pearson still had no clear idea at all about what kind of arrangements might be possible ... His main hope was to gain the tactical advantage of having put forward something positive which might help the British off the hook.'[53] Thus while the initial idea of peacekeeping force came from Pearson, Hammarskjöld and his staff had to work out what this would mean in practice. Hammarskjöld himself formulated what became the basic principles of UN peacekeeping: its limited nature, the importance of impartiality, force can only be used in self-defence, no troops from the permanent five, and the need for consent from the host country and parties to the conflict.[54] For the practical details of organization, troops, supplies etc., Hammarskjöld relied on the experience and expertise of Bunche, who had been instrumental in setting up UNTSO in 1948, and General E. L. M. Burns, the commander of UNTSO.[55]

The final major crisis of Hammarskjöld's tenure would also become the last of his life, as the secretary-general, and fifteen others lost their lives when their plane crashed in mysterious circumstances near Ndola in what was then Northern Rhodesia (today Zambia) in September 1961. Where the Suez crisis earlier had been connected to the end of empire as Britain and France struggled to accept their new position in the world, the crisis in the former

Belgian colony of the Congo was an example of the problems that could emerge during decolonization processes.[56] After seven years in office, Hammarskjöld's reputation as an efficient and talented diplomat, negotiator and problem-solver was already established before the events of the Congo occurred. His independent approach to crisis management and firm and eloquent defence of the position of the UN secretary-general would reach its high point during the Congo crisis.

On 13 July 1960 Hammarskjöld became the first secretary-general to explicitly invoke article 99 when he called a meeting of the UN Security Council in response to a plea for help from the Congolese government.[57] Over the next fourteen months, Hammarskjöld established and oversaw the UN's largest and most complex peacekeeping mission to date, the Opération des nations unies au Congo (ONUC). The mission had a mandate from the Security Council, but the resolution was unclear on the details. As Henning Melber notes, while this 'provided space for maneuvering – at times deliberately used by Hammarskjöld at his discretion – it also created the risk that, in the absence of clarity, at different moments all of the parties involved would become critical of what the Secretariat did'.[58] In seeking to manage the crisis in the Congo, Hammarskjöld was under pressure from Belgium, Britain, France and the United States, as well as the white settler minority regimes in Southern Africa,[59] but it was his difficult relationship with the Soviet Union and its leader Nikita Khrushchev that would create the headlines.

At the General Assembly in September 1960, Khrushchev proposed that the office of UN secretary-general should be replaced by a 'troika' of three secretaries-general: one each from the Western bloc, the Eastern bloc and the non-aligned movement.[60] In response, Hammarskjöld delivered an eloquent defence of the principles of the International Civil Service: '[T]his is a question not of a man but of an institution ... I would rather see that office break on strict adherence to the principle of independence, impartiality, and objectivity than drift on the basis of compromise.'[61] Hammarskjöld linked his position both to the UN Charter and as a servant of the smaller member states and peoples of the world. A few days later he was forced to once again defend his position and make clear that he would not resign but 'remain in my post during the term of office as a servant of the Organization in the interest of all those other nations as long as they wish me to do so'.[62] This speech was met by several minutes' standing ovation. Hammarskjöld's defence of his position in the face of Soviet opposition thus strengthened his authority and support, while also serving to clarify the moral position of the office.[63]

Overall, later scholars and practitioners have celebrated the contribution of Hammarskjöld to the development of the office of UN secretary-general, to peacekeeping and to the UN's crisis diplomacy. Hammarskjöld's approach was innovative in his emphasis on travel diplomacy, building trust and personal relationships with world leaders, the importance of early action or what has come to be known as preventive diplomacy, and his skills in building coalitions of interested members states.[64] Although Lie had also delegated his authority to his representatives on occasion, Hammarskjöld refined the technique of appointing special representatives.[65] Both Lie and Hammarskjöld maintained good relationships with the UN press corps, but Hammarskjöld seems to have had a more nuanced strategy for when to use the media and public statements and when to rely on a behind-the-scenes approach and let others be the public face for an initiative. Not least, Hammarskjöld did a better job than Lie in defending his actions and providing generalized justifications for them. Compared to Lie the man of action, Hammarskjöld comes across as a more intellectual and refined diplomat. He also, perhaps by luck had some early success with his initiatives, whereas most of Lie's proposals had been ignored or resented. Nonetheless, Lie's actions had built important precedents. Even though the member states may have declined to follow Lie's advice, they accepted that as secretary-general he was entitled and obligated to give such advice.[66] Already during Lie's tenure the member states accepted that the secretary-general occupied a central position in the organization's crisis management team. Hammarskjöld was therefore able to walk into this position Lie had carved out and spend his time refining and confirming the approach.

Conclusion

As this chapter has shown, both Lie and Hammarskjöld played important roles in developing the powers of the UN secretary-general office. In the context of Cold War tensions, unresolved legacies of the Second World War, the end of Western empires and decolonization, both UN secretaries-general sought to chart a path through various crises that would allow for a consolidation and expansion of their office's powers. Lie was a man of action who immediately poured his heart and soul into the organization and pushed to the limits the secretary-general's room for manoeuvre in crisis management. Where Lie acted, sometimes rashly or bluntly, Hammarskjöld later refined and provided general justifications for those actions. Both Lie and Hammarskjöld were activist secretaries-general. Both were intent on establishing a firm basis in formal and informal institutional rules and practices for the secretary-general to act in matters of peace and security. Both were deeply committed to the project of the UN and sought as best they could to ensure that the secretary-general had a meaningful role to play in the organization. Lie was the first and created a number of important precedents for the office and its relationship with the Security Council, but Hammarskjöld did a better job of defending the position of the secretary-general and providing general justifications and legitimations for the expanded role of the UN secretary-general. In this way, they both helped to build the foundations for the office as a crisis manager, and they should therefore both be credited for establishing the power and authority of the UN secretary-general in matters of peace and security.

12

Leadership Styles and Organizing Principles in NATO: Ismay, Spaak and Wörner

Linda Risso

The secretary-general is the representative and principal spokesperson of the North Atlantic Treaty Organization (NATO). He – at the time of writing all secretaries-general have been men – is traditionally a European diplomat who presides over the work of the North Atlantic Council at the NATO headquarters in Brussels. The role of secretary-general was instituted early on in the history of the alliance to promote political dialogue and cooperation among the member nations. It reflected the overall post-war trend towards structured international cooperation and multilateralism.[1] The secretary-general traditionally promotes transatlantic unity and internal cohesion among the member states by promoting diplomatic dialogue and fostering compromises. He is also the alliance's principal spokesperson and its most recognizable face. In the post–Cold War years, as NATO enlarged to the East, the alliance launched partnership agreements with nations on its periphery, and it engaged militarily out of area. Consequently, the secretary-general has become an ambassador for the alliance across the world. In an era of digital information, the secretary-general's speeches and public appearances are powerful strategic communication tools. Crucially, the secretary-general is the chairman of the council and in this role he promotes political cohesions, mediates in case of tensions and promotes a shared strategic vision.

NATO is a unique organization in so far as it has a dual military and civil structure which is deeply connected yet operationally separated. The military side of the alliance is led by the Supreme Allied Commander Europe (SACEUR), traditionally an American general, whose headquarters are now based in Mons in southern Belgium. The secretary-general and SACEUR work closely together and provide political and military leadership in their respective spheres.[2] As argued below, the evaluation of the leadership style and effectiveness of the secretary-general must therefore take into account the working relationship and personal affinity with the SACEUR.

As discussed at length elsewhere, the history of NATO tends to adopt a crisis-led approach whereby historians and analysts focus on great moments of crisis.[3] In these circumstances, as it is obvious, the secretary-general and SACEUR are described without fail as operating under serious political and organizational constraints. This approach prevents us from gaining an understanding of how the role is shaped over time by weekly meetings and a continuous process of negotiation and diplomatic exchange. For this reason, a long-term historical approach that considers the sustained development of the role of the secretary-general and of SACEUR within the development of NATO's structures and mission is essential to be able to evaluate the issue of leadership.

The examination of the role and impact of NATO's secretary-general is challenging as the alliance is an intergovernmental organization whose own action revolves around its members' national interests. As a political mediator within the council, the secretary-general's leadership is often exercised behind closed doors and in informal discussions. As mentioned above, this topic has not yet attracted the attention it deserves but there are some helpful exceptions. Among the most helpful contributions is Robert Jordan's *Political Leadership in NATO*, which examines the tenure of several secretaries-general between 1952 and 1971. Jordan underlines that secretaries-general were all skilled diplomats, who had to be sensitive towards national interests while operating within often difficult institutional constraints.[4] Ryan Hendrickson's *Diplomacy and War at NATO* is probably the only attempt to date to offer a sustained evaluation of the role of leadership within NATO since its inception.[5] Hendrickson's focus is primarily on the post–Cold War era and on the personal commitment of the secretaries-general to ensure a future for NATO after the collapse of the Soviet Union and the increased attempts by the European Union to become a credible security actor. Both Jordan's and Hendrickson's offer valuable information and insights. Their research also has the not negligible advantage of making extensive use of interviews with a wide range of diplomats, international civil servants and security experts. While providing useful information and interesting insights, these works tend to perpetuate the idea of individual leadership primarily as a personal endeavour. In these works, the secretaries-general are pigeon-holed into stereotypes: the leader, the technocrat, the bureaucrat. The question of the extent to which each of them was able to shape the institutional role so that their successor could exert a greater leadership role remains open, in the study of NATO as well – more broadly, in the study of international organizations.[6] To offer this kind of analysis, it is essential to examine the action of each secretary-general within the opportunities and constrains imposed on him. It is then necessary to evaluate how his personal charisma, skills and experience, as well as his ability to build trust and form strong networks allow each secretary-general to overcome pre-existing constraints and to capitalize on the opportunities when they present themselves. As other authors in this volume discuss, it is essential to evaluate the role of each secretary-general within the institutional perspective taking into account the nature of the organization they lead, pre-existing institutional constraints, resources, opportunities and obstacles. In the words of Michael Schechter, it is essential to merge the analysis of personal and idiosyncratic qualities of each leader with the systemic and institutional frameworks in which he must operate.[7] The recent work of Karen Gram-Skjoldager on the League of Nations shows the potential of examining how the institutional framework and identity of international organizations are produced through the institutionalization of recruitment and working practices, which ultimately contribute to the creation of a recognizable institutional culture in which leadership can be exerted.[8]

It would be impossible to make justice to the impact of each secretary-general and to examine their leadership styles in a short chapter. In order to give the reader a sense of the potential that further research would yield, this chapter focuses on three secretaries-general. It evaluates their leadership style and systemic factors that shaped their effectiveness as leaders. The case studies are Lord Ismay, the first secretary-general (1952–7), who was given almost complete freedom in laying the foundation of his own office soon after the foundation of the alliance itself. His successor, Paul-Henri Spaak (1957–61), had to navigate the complex aftermath of the Suez Crisis and of the publication of the Three Wise Men Report, which redefined the role of the secretary-general. Finally, Manfred Wörner (1988–94) oversaw the end of the Cold War and led the alliance in a new phase of its history including the first operational engagement in the Balkans. The inclusion of Wörner as a case study allows the reader to gain a glimpse of how the role of secretary-general changed over the course of the Cold War and how the basis laid by the early secretaries-general kept hold for the following decades.

Lord Ismay

The role of the secretary-general was established at the Lisbon Council meeting of February 1952 along with the creation of the North Atlantic Council (NAC). This is when the Council of Deputies was replaced by permanent representatives of senior diplomatic rank to ensure continuous contact among the members and to allow for substantial groundwork to be carried out on a weekly basis. The secretary-general was to direct the work of the international staff, to assist the council by chairing its meetings and by overseeing all appropriate follow-up action. The international staff and the secretary-general ensured continuity of service and support for the members of the alliance.[9]

The decision of who should be appointed as the first secretary-general was not an easy one. The ideal candidate needed to have extensive political expertise, to be respected in military circles, and to share the vision of the founding members regarding the future of collective defence. Yet he should not be so ambitious and politically driven to make the secretary-general a political leader in his own right thus challenging the authority of the nation states. It took the allies a few attempts before being able to find the suitable candidate, willing to take up the post.[10]

When Ismay was offered the role, he negotiated a few changes to ensure that he would be able to carry out his functions effectively. Ismay, for example, argued that the permanent representatives should be respected figures in their own countries so as to allow the council to make substantial progress in the day-to-day work. Most importantly, Ismay obtained the right to appoint his own team and to decide the size of the international staff. He argued that if he did not have sole control over appointments things would soon grind to a halt as nations would compete to have their men close to the secretary-general. Desperate to appoint a secretary-general as swiftly as possible, the member nations agreed to his requests.[11] It could therefore be argued that Ismay shaped the role of secretary-general even before taking up his post.

It could be argued that Ismay laid the foundation of NATO administrative framework with hardly any precedent to guide him. The most obvious reference point would have been the work of Eric Drummond at the League of Nations. Drummond had been an effective secretary-general and had created an extensive administrative machinery to support the numerous agencies linked to the League. Drummond had also published extensively on the nature of the international civil service.[12] Yet there is no evidence in Ismay's private papers nor in the records of his conversations with his collaborators that he ever referred to Drummond for inspiration. Instead, archival documents suggest that the model Ismay looked at his own past experience in the Foreign Office. This is evident in the way in which he structured the secretariat and the role of his private secretary, which reflects the same functions and structures of the Foreign Office. The style of memorandums and record keeping also mirror what Ismay learnt during his time as secretary for Commonwealth Relations.[13]

Ismay was aware of the fragility of the political context he was navigating and was determined not to undermine the precarious balance by imposing his own views. In interviews and private conversations, he talked of himself as 'servant of the Council' and described his function 'stewardship'.[14] Yet this does not mean that he did not work behind the scenes. The examination of NATO documents along with Ismay's private papers reveals that he established some simple, yet unbending, rules. No permanent representative could walk out of meetings, and if somebody was not present, the decision under discussion was to be postponed until everybody was in the room.

Unfortunately, we do not have official records for the Restricted Sessions. These are meetings called at short notice to discuss confidential matters, in which permanent representatives can take one or possibly two advisers. We know even less about the numerous informal meetings that took place on a daily basis in the offices of the headquarters. Informal meetings are crucial to get the pulse of the alliance. They allow the permanent representatives to inform their respective governments of the mood of the council and of the direction in which things are moving before decisions made. Possible disagreements or potential disputes can be solved before they reach a formal stage in the NAC. In an article he wrote for the *NATO Letter*, Ismay recalled that he found informal meetings extremely helpful and that they increased in number over the years, from seventeen in 1952 to sixty-six in 1956.[15]

As the first secretary-general, Ismay laid the basis for the administrative framework at the core of the international staff. He appointed two assistants: a private secretary, Peter Scott from the Foreign Office, and a deputy private secretary, Gilles de Boisgelin from the Quay d'Orsay. Ismay was aware of the need to make sure that the two official languages of the alliance were represented at the top of the international staff and to mitigate the overly 'Anglo-Saxon' outlook of his team. Ismay also appointed three assistant secretaries-general, each at the head of one of the three principal branches of NATO: politics, economics and production.[16] He also created the post of deputy secretary-general (DSG) to give smaller nations the chance to be in the top echelon of the alliance.[17]

As the head of the international staff, Ismay was keen to instil the need for impartiality and commitment into his team. He believed that 'every single member of the Staff regarded himself, not as a national of his own country but as a member of an international team dedicated to the cause of world peace.'[18] As an experienced military leader, he knew that such ethos could not be imposed but had to be embraced voluntarily by his staff. To encourage this process, he worked actively to create a vibrant esprit de corps. He launched the NATO Staff Association to bring members of the international staff together. Other initiatives included sponsored language courses, sport clubs, holiday camps for employees' children and social events designed to help people get to know each other socially.[19] Smaller – yet symbolic – steps helped create a sense of community and shared ethos, one of them was the way in which members of international staff were expected to dress. Ismay recalled: 'I used to get very angry with my flock if they did not wear NATO ties on all important occasions.'[20]

While Ismay managed to lay the foundation of the bureaucratic framework to support the council, his action on other fronts was far less successful. Political cohesion was – and still is – essential for the credibility of NATO as a defensive alliance. If the alliance is divided, it is difficult to imagine it having the resolve necessary to carry out a full-scale military response or stand firmly behind the use of nuclear weapons.[21]

Despite his efforts to foster political dialogue, however, five months after his appointment, Ismay was faced with criticism that the council was breaking down because of the excessive use of bilateral contacts and the tendency of the key member nations, particularly France and Britain, to make unilateral decisions. In an internal memorandum to the secretary of state, Livingston T. Merchant spoke of a 'serious situation' which was characterized by 'an extremely disquieting sense of depression and concern among the members of the Council' about the perceived American disengagement and lack of leadership. In Merchant view this was due to the problems connected with Lord Ismay's caution and the fact that 'his Deputy, Van Vredenburch, lapses increasingly into cynical discouragement'.[22] At the same time, the smaller countries complained about not being kept informed of what was discussed by the bigger members at the Geneva summit of 1955. At this point in the history of NATO, there was nothing Ismay could do other than reiterating the need to cooperate and to share information with the alliance's partners. He had no tools to force the members to follow suit.

The Suez crisis exposed the fragile political consensus within the council.[23] The crisis was a blow to Ismay both as the secretary-general as well as a British civil servant. Neither he nor – more worryingly – Christopher Steel, the UK permanent representative, had been informed by London about the planned military action. Great embarrassment was palpable at the emergency council meeting called the day after the invasion. According to his biographer, Ismay was close to resigning but was persuaded otherwise at the last minute.[24]

The Suez crisis showed that any general principle about political consultation and alignment of foreign policies clashed with the reality of international life, particularly given that many NATO members had competing interests beyond the European theatre. The Three Wise Men Report, which was published soon after the Suez crisis, condemned the narrow use of political consultation and enhanced the role of the secretary-general to ensure he could intervene at an earlier stage when differences emerged. The secretary-general was given the right – and in fact the duty – to bring to the council attention matters that threatened the solidarity or effectiveness of the alliance. He was to prepare progress reports for ministers about the state of political consultation with the analysis of key political problems and the examination of the extent to which members cooperated. The Political Affairs Division was strengthened through the creation of the Committee of Political Advisers. Most crucially, the Report conferred onto the secretary-general new powers to ensure that frictions between members could be de-escalated at an early stage. The secretary-general could help proactively solve dispute by initiating a process of mediation, enquiry, consultation or arbitration. This means that secretary-general was allowed considerable degree of discretion. He could decide independently when and how to act and, crucially, which members should assist him in resolving the disputes amicably. The Three Wise Men Report effectively raised the status of the secretary-general within the council. The member states became more like colleagues less than his masters. Yet it should not be forgotten that the member states continued to retain full control over their policies, budgets and right of action and the secretary-general could not force any decision on to the members or on to the council.[25]

The Report was too late for Ismay to make a difference. He retired in April 1957, a few months after the approval of the Three Wise Men Report. The appointment of Spaak as Ismay's successor was a sign of new phase in the history of the alliance. Spaak was a politician, an ardent federalist and had been appointed precisely because at that point the alliance wanted a strong voice. Yet Spaak could have not been in a position to act as he did, had not Ismay established precise features and boundaries for the secretary-general's role. After his retirement, Ismay jokingly characterized himself as the wet nurse and Spaak as the governess.[26]

Paul Henri Spaak

Like Lord Ismay, Spaak brought a wealth of experience in international affairs to the role, having served as Belgian prime minister and foreign minister. However, while Ismay's record dated back to the war years and focused primarily on the close Anglo-American bond, Spaak's won experience reflected the post-war transatlantic as well as European enthusiasm for close political and economic cooperation on federalist lines. Spaak was a fervent internationalist and had been president of the United Nations' General Assembly. He had also played a pivotal role in the foundation of the Council of Europe, presided over the Common Assembly of the European Coal and Steel Community, and helped lay the foundations of the Common Market.[27]

Not surprisingly given his background, Spaak had strong views about the direction in which the role of NATO secretary-general should develop. In contrast to Ismay, Spaak sought to exercise stronger leadership within the council in an open and more direct way. As a tireless advocate for European unity and transatlantic cooperation, Spaak argued for a strong NATO that would bring together its members' defences as well as economies. He envisioned the expansion of NATO's scope to include a broad coordination of policies outside the purely military and strategic domains and he stressed 'the necessity for giving the organization of the Atlantic Alliance a political and also an economic basis'.[28]

Spaak attempted to take full advantage of the new avenues opened to him by the Three Wise Men Report. Yet he was navigating a difficult political context. There is no doubt that the Suez Crisis had showed the limits of the alliance's political consultation mechanisms and had created tensions between the American Administration on the one hand and the British and French on the other. Thus, Spaak had a strong argument in favour of strengthening political consultation but at the same time he had to be mindful of existing divisions and national sensitivities.

Spaak pinned his strategy to advance political consultation on the narrative of an existing Atlantic community of nations with a common heritage. He argued that political consultation would be improved by abandoning the unanimity rule and by creating permanent committees for consultation on specific geographical areas of the world beyond the NATO's remit. Of course, Spaak knew that such radical proposals would not be approved immediately. However, he believed in the value of stating a strategy for the long course that would eventually prove to be the solution to new emerging problems.[29]

However, Spaak's enthusiasm and determination had the opposite effect to what he had hoped. Member nations feared his overly pro-integration stand and felt that their national interests were under attack. Despite his repeated attempts, Spaak failed to make progress and felt discouraged. He spoke of a situation that had 'become less satisfactory, causing considerable uneasiness'.[30] As he had expected, the foreign ministers eventually rejected the idea of adding any permanent consultative organs to the already complicated bureaucratic apparatus.

De Gaulle's approach to NATO and to transatlantic cooperation further impeded Spaak's attempt to lead NATO effectively. When the French president expressed his concerns about the United States' predominance in nuclear weapons, he did not address the matter in the council but spoke directly with the United States and Britain. He called for a triumvirate of the NATO nuclear powers to discuss the matter behind closed doors, thus showing disregard towards the council and the secretary-general. As it is well known, De Gaulle was uncompromising and adopted a confrontational approach towards the alliance, which further jeopardized NATO's internal stability and political cohesion. De Gaulle mistrusted the United States and the British and developed France's own nuclear capabilities to ensure an independent and effective French security policy.[31]

In this fraught context, Spaak tried to assert his voice and to identify himself as NATO's principal spokesperson. Yet the member states were reluctant to support him in his attempt to widen his portfolio. The alliance was still in its infancy and the national governments were suspicious of any change that could undermine their independence and prevent any attempt that could allow the secretary-general to speak to their own populations over their heads. Throughout the Cold War, the national governments kept a tight control over the secretaries-general's press conferences and speeches and, more generally, over all the work carried out by the alliance in the fields of information and press.[32]

Spaak's relationship with SACEUR was also less than ideal. His confidence with military issues varied and he could not claim the same clout nor the same degree of expertise as his predecessor. Spaak was eventually overshadowed by SACEUR General Lauris Norstad, who was a strong, charismatic military leader. Norstad had worked well with Ismay, whom he respected as a military leader in his own right. Spaak and Norstad never achieved a similar level of cooperation and the secretary-general often felt ignored and side-lined. Despite his strong Atlanticism, Spaak also was never able to establish conducive working relations with the US permanent representative W. Randolph Burgess.[33]

In these circumstances, it became increasingly difficult for Spaak to promote political cohesion within the council and to give NATO a stronger voice. Sensing that his relationship with the key member states and military leaders was becoming strained, Spaak resigned in January 1961. His memoirs speak of his disappointment about his time at NATO and express doubts about the future of the alliance.[34]

Spaak's personal enthusiasm and political passion clashed with the political sensitivities of the member states. The alliance was still in the early phases of its formation and national governments were cautious about institutional centralization. There was no institutional framework to support Spaak's attempt to achieve better coordination of the members policies and to enhance political consultation. The suggestions brought forward by the Three Wise Men Report were not supported by institutional reforms that could indeed give the secretary-general new tools to force the hand of the national governments.

Manfred Wörner

The appointment of Manfred Wörner preceded the Fall of the Berlin Wall and the collapse of the Warsaw Pact of a few months. The end of the Cold War brought a radical strategic shift for Western Europe and North America. The very survival of NATO came under discussion. Wörner was pivotal in ensuring the survival of NATO at a time in which the alliance's own survival was challenged. He is instrumental in putting forward a new vision for NATO's future in the new post–Cold War security environment. The military engagement in Bosnia and Herzegovina, which he strongly supported, paved the way for the first out-of-area operations and for the creation of new notions of security that included crisis management, peacekeeping, human rights protection and cooperative security.

Manfred Wörner became NATO's seventh secretary-general in July 1988. He came to NATO with strong defense credentials having served as West Germany's defence minister for six years. Before that he had been a leading voice on defence issues for the Christian Democratic Union (CDU) and had chaired the Bundestag's Defense Committee. Wörner therefore joined NATO with recognized expertise in defence and security matters and with a strong network of contacts on both sides of the Atlantic. Crucially, he was respected in both political and military circles.[35]

In order to understand the leadership role of Wörner at the time, it is important to recall the fast pace of events: in November 1989, crowds crossed the border dividing Berlin. The German Democratic Republic fell soon after that. A few months later, the Warsaw Pact was disbanded. In December of that year, Mikhail Gorbachev, the secretary of the Communist Party of the Soviet Union and leader of the USSR, resigned and declared his office extinct. In little bit more than one year, the security, political and economic outlook of Europe had radically changed.

As far as NATO was concerned, the fall of the Warsaw Pact brought into question whether NATO should be disbanded, too. After all, it no longer had an enemy and it had lost its own raison d'être. The years 1989–1991 proved to be truly transformative for the alliance, which emerged with a new strategic concept and a new vision of its geopolitical role. NATO redefined its own mission by focusing on the need to stabilize Europe as a whole and by engaging with the ex-Warsaw Pact countries to ensure disarmament and peaceful transition to democracy. NATO worked closely with the European Union to strengthen diplomatic relations with Central and Eastern European (CEE) countries. Both organizations saw the economic prosperity and progress towards democracy of the CEE countries as essential preconditions for Western Europe's own stability and security.[36]

Wörner was essential in ensuring NATO's survival and adaptation. He was actively engaged with the debate about the future of the alliance. He released interviews, press conferences, speeches and articles at a hectic pace. He stressed the political role of the alliance as a motor for peaceful change and as vehicle to engage with the people of Central and Eastern Europe.[37] Crucially, Wörner engaged both with the Western policymakers and public as well as with ex-Soviet leaders. He was acutely aware of maintaining support among the alliance while engaging proactively with the East.

Possibly the most symbolic step was Wörner's invitation to the Soviet Foreign Minister Eduard Shevardnadze to visit the NATO headquarters on 19 December 1989. It was a tangible sign of the radical change that had taken place and of the determination of the secretary-general to show NATO's commitment to support the peaceful process of change that was underway in the East. Wörner himself visited Moscow in July 1990 and was in Prague, Warsaw and Budapest over the next few months. Pictures of Wörner strolling on the Red Square appeared on most NATO national newspapers and became symbols of the new geopolitical environment as well as signs of Wörner's personal commitment to lead the change.[38]

In 1990–1, the NATO headquarters hosted a hectic series of high-level exchanges by senior political and military officials.[39] In an historic moment, in

March 1991, the president of Czechoslovakia, Václav Havel, was invited to give a speech to the North Atlantic Council at the NATO headquarters, the first foreign leader to do so. As a undisputable measure of how far NATO had changed, in the autumn of 1991, special courses at the NATO Defense College in Rome and the SHAPE School in Oberammergau were opened to military personnel of the Soviet Union and of Central and Eastern Europe.[40]

The real work of Wörner was directed towards the political leaders of the member nations. They had to be convinced of the continued need to have NATO and to revise its strategic scope so as to allow the alliance to respond to the new geopolitical challenges. To ensure this geostrategic shift, Wörner organized countless bilateral meetings and special sessions of the NATO Council. The results can be monitored through four key steps: the NATO Summit Declaration of May 1989, which was released before the Fall of the Berlin Wall; the Message from Turnberry (7–8 June 1990); the London Declaration (5–6 July 1990); and the Rome Summit of November 1991. In all cases, what strikes the reader is the non-confrontational, positive tone and the enthusiasm for the changes that were taking place in Europe at the time. The NATO Summit Declaration of May 1989, for example, was released for the fortieth anniversary of NATO. At the time President Bush and Mikhail Gorbachev had good working relations and the declaration underlined the optimism of those months.[41] A few months later, after the Fall of the Berlin Wall, the allies renewed their determination to contribute to the transition to peace and democracy.[42]

There is no doubt that Wörner was the first secretary-general to perceive the alliance as a political actor in its own right, not simply as a sum of its parts. Wörner built the case for the pivotal role that NATO should play in ensuring a peaceful transition to democracy in Central Europe. In Wörner's own words, 'NATO is ultimately seeking to convert a confrontational relationship into a cooperative one.'[43] To the question as to why should NATO take up this role, why not a new organization, why not the European Union, Wörner replied consistently that NATO was the only alliance with a specific security and defence remit and the only one that linked both sides of the Atlantic in a binding treaty. In his speeches and bilateral meetings, Wörner placed emphasis on the fact that, contrary to the EU, NATO includes Canada and the United States and that the best outcome for the security and prosperity of Europe would be for NATO and the EU to work closely together.[44]

At the Rome Summit, NATO released its new strategic concept. Significantly, following Wörner's pressure, the document was declassified and immediately made available to the public (not the military guidance). Deterrence and security of NATO members were still at the core of the alliance's mission as critical tools of collective defence. In addition, the document put forward a new vision to strengthen Europe's security through partnership and cooperation with countries on NATO's periphery. The beginning of the idea is that Europe can be peaceful and prosper only if the nations on its borders are stable, well governed and peaceful (cooperative security). Wörner also argued strongly in favour of NATO's enlargement and as a way to support the CEE countries' progress towards democracy. Although published after his death, the key document that laid the basis for the 1999 and 2004 enlargements had been spearheaded by Wörner.[45]

Wörner was indefatigable and he oversaw the very first involvement of NATO out of area. NATO's involvement in Balkans started in February 1992, in support of a UN peace-keeping mission. It was the first step towards a new role as a security actor in human rights protection, crisis management and peace-keeping functions. Throughout 1993, the role of NATO forces in Bosnia gradually grew. In February 1994, NATO fighters operating under Operation Deny Flight shot down four Serb jets over Banja Luka, the first combat engagement in NATO's history.

At the time, Wörner faced an alliance deeply torn over how to handle the Balkan crisis and pushed forward his vision of an engagement long before consensus among the allies had been reached. He was personally committed both because of the humanitarian crisis on NATO's doorstep as well as a means to show how NATO could fulfil its new role in the post–Cold War era. He remained personally committed to this cause until his death in August 1994. Colleagues working at the NATO headquarters at the time remember how Wörner continued to release interviews and to contribute to the debate from his hospital bed in Aachen. On one occasion, when the council was about to vote on expanding the mission in the Balkans, Wörner left his hospital bed against doctors' orders to speak at the council and persuade the allies to support the decision.[46]

Since the beginning, the task of persuading the allies to intervene had not been an easy one for Wörner. In 1992 and for most of 1993, President George W. Bush resisted direct military involvement and only supported UN-sponsored humanitarian assistance. Washington saw the Balkans primarily as a European problem. In the words of Secretary of State James Baker, the United States did not 'have a dog in this fight'.[47] In May 1993 Secretary of State Warren Christopher stressed that the United States was not willing of taking the lead. At the time, the European Union seemed equally unable to formulate a common position on the Balkan question.

The lack of American leadership and the endless European discussions left room for Wörner to articulate a NATO-wide response. This took the form of the so-called Dual-Key Arrangements between NATO and the United Nations. UN peacekeeping forces (Protection Force, UNPROFOR) in the region were coming increasingly under fire. The UN and NATO agreed a joint decision-making process for approving military action to protect UN peacekeeping troops: before NATO could intervene militarily, both organizations would have to turn their metaphorical 'key' and agree that military action was warranted. This arrangement allowed NATO's members the safety of UN-approved mandate. It also defined a clear and limited role for NATO forces. The national governments' concern that without UN approval, military operations would escalate beyond members' control was quelled. Wörner worked tirelessly behind the scenes to reach the Dual Key agreement, as testified by several members of the international staff that supported him in his endeavor.[48]

In evaluating Wörner's impact as secretary-general, it is essential to take into consideration his personal charisma, his commitment to ensuring a future for the alliance and his ability to forge conducing and effective working relations with political leaders, military commanders and international civil servants. However, all these qualities would have not been sufficient hadn't the political context allowed it. Wörner led NATO at a time of great change in which a new security environment allowed him to take the lead while national leaders and EU policymakers were still looking for answers. He had the opportunity to shape the role of the secretary-general in ensuring that he was involved in all decisions about the future of the alliance and that he was also involved in any strategic and operational decision taken during his time as secretary-general. He shaped the role and opened the way to a new, more visible and vocal role for his successors.

Conclusion

The examination of the role of the NATO secretary-general shows that the way in which Ismay and Spaak defined the role shaped the action of their successors for following decades. The secretary-general's key role is to be the Chairman of the North Atlantic Council and as such to foster political agreement and a shared vision of common defence and security strategies among fully sovereign member nations. As such, the room for manoeuvre and independent action is limited and well codified. At times of great change, when the alliance is divided, member nations stand firm in their right to pursue independent defence and security policies. Faced with a divided alliance, the secretaries-general refrain from seeking major policy changes that would widen the internal rifts within the council. They try to foster consensus by arguing for the least divisive – and often less innovative – position. Following the example of Ismay – and mindful of the obstacles encountered by Spaak – their successors tried to be humble servants of the council, too. The post–Cold War era opened new avenues of influence but ultimately the institutional framework of the alliance did not change. Beyond the more visible presence of the secretary-general in the media, their actual role within the council and their ability to shape the discussion remain limited. Yet, contrary to his hopes, Manfred Wörner ultimately failed in reshaping the role of the secretary-general in the long term. His time at NATO was an exception and did not become the rule. Wörner navigated a new security context in which the whole perception of what NATO was and what it aimed to achieved were still being defined. He benefited from a fluid political debate in which the United States was still evaluating the options and in which all member nations were willing to consider new avenues of influence and new security scenarios. In this new space, Wörner could lead effectively. Yet as NATO became operational in the Balkans, the nations reasserted their voice and the window of opportunity closed. Today, the national governments retain the right to make their own decisions about defence and security policies. There is no institutional framework or tool that the secretary-general can deploy to force the hands of the members. In this sense, very little has changed since the time of Lord Ismay.

13

The Making of the International Civil Servant c. 1920–60: Establishing the Profession

Karen Gram-Skjoldager and Haakon A. Ikonomou

Introduction

The creation of the League of Nations not only created new multilateral forms of diplomacy; it also created an entirely new professional figure on the international stage: the international civil servant.

Taking the League as its starting point, this chapter shows how early formative decisions of the post–First World War period established key principles that came to define international civil service throughout the twentieth century. The chapter investigates how principles such as international loyalty, impartiality, confidentiality and diplomatic immunity that define the profession today came into being; it traces how these ideas developed through the interwar years; how they were affected by the Second World War and how they were continued (or discontinued), transformed and reinterpreted in the UN and the wider context of multilateralism during the early Cold War. In doing so, we hope to offer a first coherent historicization of the coming into being, characteristics and role of this understudied and critically important international figure.[1]

For the last decade, the League of Nations has gained an increasingly important place in the flora of international history. In this process, the organization has gone from being understood as a stage upon which states and statesmen acted out and articulated their interests to being studied in its own right as an institution that was much more than the sum of its member-state parts. Even more significantly, historians have taken their cue from Susan Pedersen – one of the pioneers in this refocusing of efforts – and her seminal 2007 article 'Back to the League of Nations', and asked not why it failed, but how it worked.[2] This, much more constructive, question has opened up for a flood of groundbreaking works. Since the 2010s, it is fair to say that we have a flourishing historiography of international organizations and several classic interpretations of their importance and development in the nineteenth, twentieth and twenty-first centuries.³

The renewed interest of historians in the League has partly coincided with the 'transnational turn' in international history. In its most basic sense, this is history that seeks to transcend the 'box' of the nation state by studying phenomena, people, goods, ideas and interactions that cross (national) borders. This has prompted several works that study the nexus between transnationally organized networks of legal, colonial, economic or technical expertise, social movements or interest groups. In these accounts, the League features as a hub that ties these together and thus plays a role in the production of knowledge regimes and practices that shape specific realms of global governance, be it minority rights, health work, disarmament or standardization of road networks.⁴

What is still missing, however, is a comprehensive analysis of the development and role of the international civil servant who appeared as a new professional figure alongside the activists, experts and intellectuals that rose to prominence in the varied transnational terrain around the League of Nations. Looking at scholarship on the League, the most clear-cut 'administrative' focus comes from what can be labelled the first generation of work, mostly produced by former League officials themselves. Written mainly in the 1940s and 1950s, these works have a clear tendency of seeking to find redeeming features of an organization that by then was known as a failure and is clearly aimed for future IOs, with normative assessments about what could be done better next time around.⁵ Self-evidently, since it was written while the League gave the *baton* to the United Nations, there is little reflection on the longer trajectory and significance of the international civil servant as a pervasive figure on the global stage.

The 'second generation' of literature by contrast was dominated by the 'soft realism' so prominent in international history writing generally in the 1960s, 1970s and 1980s. Here the focus was predominantly on the figure of the secretary-general as a diplomat. While this perspective would produce valuable work on the secretaries-general across the Second World War, connecting the experiences of the League and the UN, the analysis was state-centric in the sense that the secretary-general could only act in accordance with or coordinate with the interests of greater powers.⁶ These works, moreover, seldom went below the rank of secretary-general to understand the new caste of international civil servants who were dedicated to and worked on behalf of the organization, ensured its continuity and represented it internationally as well as in their countries of origin. Thus, a fundamental part of Pedersen's question of 'how it works' remains unanswered.

Our contribution to this question is to investigate some of the basic features of the international civil servant from the 1920s until the immediate post-war period. Specifically, we use Staff Regulations within the League of Nations and the Standard of Conduct of the United Nations along with other office circulars and regulations as a starting point to flesh out the norms, rules and expectations that went into the production and professionalization of the international civil servant. The chapter places this process within the context of the establishment of the secretariat as a functional institution with recognized powers and responsibilities and the broader fluctuations of international politics to understand how administrative ideals and political and ideological pressures combined in moulding the international civil servant as a professional figure.

Inspirations and Precedents

'[I]nternational administration is administration pure and simple', writes the former League of Nations official Egon Ranshofen-Wertheimer in his meticulous work on the League Secretariat before he continues:

> The manner in which these processes are actually organized is not the consequence of some mysterious quality inherent in international administration but is due to a conscious choice from among a number of precedents supplied by existing highly developed and differentiated national administrative systems.[7]

In other words, since administration is 'generic in character – applicable wherever organized activities are carried out in a continuing matter'[8] and since functioning public administrations were already in place, the League Secretariat did not have to *invent* international public administration but could rather adapt existing organizational principles to a new setting. Like a newly established country (say Czechoslovakia), the League could 'make its selection from among the existing patterns or could decide upon a combination of different types of public administrative experiences'.[9]

However, it is also true that Sir Eric Drummond – the first secretary-general of the League of Nations – had the task of adopting familiar principles of administration to a context, which posed *specific and distinctly unfamiliar challenges*. Here we will focus on three. First, the League Secretariat political position and external relations were fundamentally different from that of a national public administration. The secretariat was not part of an executive branch of government and was not subjected to permanent control of a legislative branch. On the contrary, it was 'the only permanent element' of the organization and 'its policy-shaping organs [were] not legislatures but diplomatic bodies' as Ranshofen-Wertheimer put it.[10] Second, the secretariat had a multinational make-up. As Austen Chamberlain noted in a 1930 speech entitled 'Civil Servant Traditions and the League of Nations':

> [In the League] you must form your Secretariat not merely of competent people but of competent people fairly evenly distributed over the 47 or 50 nations who comprise the League. All must be reasonably represented in the different grades of the Secretariat, and out of these people, drawn from so many different countries, trained in so many different traditions, you must make one international Secretariat acting under and for that common entity which is the League of Nations.[11]

Some existing administrations had similarities to this – the Austro-Hungarian civil administration with its multi-ethnic make-up, for instance. Here civil servants were not forced to renounce their (proto-)national identity but required to serve the administration faithfully and conduct themselves in German. However, the civil service of Austria-Hungary was not an international administration but a multinational administration within a sovereign state. Allegiances and loyalties had grown over centuries, not overnight. Existing international public unions did not offer any workable models to import either as they usually had a very small staff, often dominated by one or a few nationalities. The inter-Allied war agencies during their First World War would be a more obvious predecessor with their national contingents of experts sorted around a functional division of labour.[12] We shall return to this later.

The third characteristic worth mentioning here is that the League Secretariat dealt purely with international and transnational issues. In this way, it set itself apart from national central administrations, but also the international public unions and inter-Allied agencies which dealt with only one or a very limited range of technical issues. The League Secretariat, by contrast, spanned a multitude of areas, some of them strongly politically charged, reaching from security and disarmament to trade, humanitarianism and epidemiology. In this way, it resembled the European Foreign Services at the time (or how they would develop in the interwar period). The wide span of policy issues and the size of the administration required to deal with them were probably the reasons why we do not find any traces of Drummond drawing inspiration from the river commissions and international public unions of the nineteenth century when it came to developing the organizational blueprint and career structures of the secretariat.[13]

Though Drummond himself never revealed his sources of inspiration in composing and managing the secretariat we may observe that many of the choices he made emulated the British Civil Service tradition and particularly closely resembled the British Foreign Service which he came from. He had entered the Foreign Office (FO) in 1900 as a clerk and slowly progressed to a series of successful private secretaryships, ending with Foreign Secretaries Edward Grey (1915–16) and Arthur J. Balfour (1916–18).[14]

The inspiration from the Foreign Service was also noted by Chamberlain, in his 1930 speech, which claimed that Drummond had carried to the League 'the traditions of our British Civil Service', adding: 'He brought to his first colleagues and to the establishment of the League organisation all that he could of that spirit of loyalty, impartiality and detachment which are the foundation of the reputation which our Service has built up.'[15]

The Foreign Service and the League Secretariat

Before diving deeper into Drummond's relationship with and inspirations from the Foreign Service, we first need to consider some early and critically important decisions taken by him in the spring of 1919 on the fundamental form and function of the secretariat.

Immediately after the First World War, several key British civil servants such as Cabinet Secretary Sir Maurice Hankey and James A. Salter, a former member of the Chartering Committee of the Allied Maritime Transport Council during the war, wished to model the new secretariat on the international conference system that had emerged before the war and the inter-Allied committees. This implied that the League Secretariat would be organized around national contingents of diplomats and technical experts appointed by and paid for by the each member state.[16] Drummond by contrast decided to set up a genuinely international secretariat organized around functional dividing lines with staff from many different national backgrounds working on the same policy issue and based on unambiguous loyalty to the organization – rather than national delegations and short-term secondments from national foreign services. An organizational set-up of this kind and size was something fundamentally new.[17]

When interviewed about his decision to introduce this organizational model five years later, Drummond gave two reasons for picking it. Firstly, he believed that preparatory work for the conferences that had been held before the First World War had not been sufficiently professional.

> It seemed to us that it would be of great value if an expert and impartial organization existed which, before discussion by the national representatives took place, could draw up objective statements of the problems to be discussed, and indicate those points on which it seemed that the Government were generally in accord. If this could be done, we held that discussion by the Government representatives would be automatically limited to matters where divergence of view really existed – and all who have had experience of international affairs know how much this increases the chances of reaching a definite and successful result.[18]

Secondly, he wanted to secure that these results were then executed in a loyal and neutral manner: '[W]e maintained that the execution of decisions should be entrusted to people who, being the servants of all the States Members of the League, could be relied upon to carry them out with complete freedom from national bias.'[19]

However, once these fundamental institutional innovations had been made, Drummond seems to have modelled the secretariat on the organizational principle of the Foreign Office. If we imagine the foreign secretary as the executive authority 'outside' the secretariat, i.e. the League Council, then the secretary-general of the League resembled the role of the permanent under-secretary (PUS) as it developed in the 1900s.[20] Beneath the secretary-general of the League of Nations came the under-secretaries-general of the League Secretariat, who had both administrative responsibilities (often scattered across several functionally defined sections) and 'representative' roles, as they held semi-ambassadorial positions within the secretariat for the major powers. These resembled the assistant under-secretaries of the FO, under the PUS, who supervised the remaining departments. 'It was not uncommon', writes Steiner of these, 'for each to direct two or more geographic areas as well as an administrative department depending on seniority and past experience'.[21] Moreover, the assistant under-secretaries would often represent certain parties, direction or people in the political sphere within the FO. Under the League's under-secretaries-general came the directors, who each directed a specific section, and whom would either already be, or grow to be, experts within their given field, serve for longer stints, and shape minority, health, transport, intellectual, etc., policies profoundly. These held many of the same qualities as the Foreign Office senior clerks – '[t]he real experts', as Steiner called them – who headed 'only one department and frequently stayed there for eight to twelve years. All the business of the department passed through their hands and they built up a fund of detailed knowledge during their years of service'.[22]

In fact, several of the early choices Drummond made on behalf of the League Secretariat resembled reforms introduced to the FO during his years in the Foreign Service before the First World War. The League's in-house Staffing Committee (introduced in 1921 and renamed the Appointments Committee in 1922) had similarities to the FO's 'Board of Selection', which replaced the private secretary to the foreign secretary as a means of screening prospective candidates in 1905.[23]

Likewise, the League Secretariat's pride and joy, the centralized registry, separate clerical divisions and pools of efficient and multilingual précis writers, translators and stenographers[24] seemed to build on the 1906 reform of the FO, which was the first step of many which turned clerks into policy advisers engaged in the policy-making process and handing their recommendations higher up the food chain until it, potentially, reached the foreign secretary. This was, in part, achieved by removing clerical work – such as copying, printing, distributing and indexing – from the 'first division clerks' of the FO, who were in fact diplomatic staff, and giving this to a new and centralized registry staff, together with an entirely new filing and registry system.[25] Thus, decision-making power was pushed 'down the food-chain' and a large number of issues never reached a higher level of authority. This was certainly the case within the League Secretariat too, where members of sections – working under directors of sections – were involved in serious policy-making.

While the template for the secretariat's organizational structure was drawn from the Foreign Office, it was also clear that in other important regards, the rules and procedures for a national administrative body were not directly applicable to the new international administration. This was the case not least for questions of budgetary planning and oversight which would necessarily be more volatile than if the secretariat had been a national administrative body. Therefore, one of the first things the director of the secretariat's newly established Financial Section did was to contact a handful of international technical unions and industrial federations to enquire about a wide range of questions as for instance how they assessed their expenses and planned their budgets, their methods for collecting revenues and auditing their accounts and pension and insurance provisions for their permanent staff.[26]

National Composition

It was a precondition for Drummond's genuinely international secretariat that it had considerable institutional autonomy from the outset. However, Drummond's attempts to create institutional autonomy were, from the very beginning, balanced with an acute sensitivity to state interests. Looking at the staffing practices of the Appointments Committee in the 1920s, we observe an omnipresent concern for national representation in the secretariat in all staff appointments. Despite the lack of clearly explicated principles, the human make-up of the secretariat came to reproduce European power hierarchies and a particular civilizational order: the great powers held a de facto monopoly of the top positions in the secretariat, small and middle powers were scrambling for the mid-range positions, and staff from Western Europe was systematically preferred over staff from Eastern and South-eastern Europe, as was European staff over non-European staff. This fundamentally hierarchical nature of the secretariat is important to keep in mind when considering the relatively flat and flexible mode of organization that had been adopted from the Foreign Office.

There were, of course, variations over time: From the day the commission on the League of Nations in Paris informally decided that a British head of the League had to be balanced by a French deputy in the same organization and a French head of the ILO, great power balance was an integral part of the secretariat staffing. Greater diversity, particularly non-Western representation, was pushed through in the assembly in the 1920s and came naturally as the number of member states expanded. A greater presence of small powers at the top only came through the tumultuous reforms of the 1930s and as several major powers withdrew from the League or became rather more disinterested in the League institutions.[27]

The Interwar Years: Professionalization and Fractured Loyalties

After the secretariat had found its shape and been staffed, a process of professionalization and formal clarification of the role of the international civil servant began.

Already in the early 1920s, when struggles over national representation and balances played out, Drummond had put certain formal rules and structures in place to strengthen the independence, loyalty and neutrality of his civil service. He had, in other words, attempted to integrate the multinational mode of organization with his internationalist ideals of a neutral, independent civil service working for the common interests among the League's member states. In response to the assembly's attempt to influence appointments in the secretariat he had created the 'Appointments Committee' mentioned above, which ensured that all appointments and promotions were discussed between him and group of high-ranking officials thus giving him broad institutional backing in the secretariat against any outside pressures.[28]

In 1922, a set of staff regulations was published that set out the principles for being a loyal, professional international civil servant. The regulations opened by pointing out that:

> The officials of the Secretariat of the League of Nations are international officials, responsible in the execution of their duties to the Secretary-General alone. They may not seek or receive instructions from any other authority.[29]

The regulations went on to spell out what this loyalty to the organization entailed: League officials, according to the staff regulations, could not hold any kind of political office or have side jobs without the secretary-general's consent. They were not allowed to receive any honours or decorations while serving in the secretariat. They could not publish or lecture on matters relating to the League without the secretary-general's permission and they were to maintain strict secrecy on all confidential matters relating to the League.[30]

In 1926, Drummond took another step to consolidate the international civil servant as an independent professional figure, when the League reached a formal agreement with the Swiss federal government fleshing out the League Covenant's provision that League Officials should enjoy diplomatic immunities and privileges (Article VII, 4).[31] As in most other matters relating to the secretariat, the covenant's provisions on diplomatic privileges and immunities were underspecified and shortly after his arrival in Geneva in 1920, Drummond got to work on the matter. In 1921, an 'initial and provisional' modus vivendi was reached and in 1926 a formal agreement on the League and the ILO's diplomatic presence in Geneva was concluded.[32]

The essential principle of the agreement was to give the League and its officials the same status and prerogatives as the diplomatic missions in Berne. The League premises and archives were declared inviolable, as were the homes of the secretary-general, the deputy and under-secretaries-general and League directors who were all considered equal to the heads of missions. All League officials above a certain pay grade were granted immunity from civil as well as criminal jurisdiction and all League officials enjoyed tax exemptions. The highest-ranking personnel also had complete customs exemption, enjoyed freedom from luggage searches on entering and leaving Switzerland, and were allowed to mark their cars with CD (Corps Diplomatique).[33]

Despite its construction of the League official as a fully fledged diplomatic agent, the agreement still left the League staff in a somewhat precarious legal position. The problem was that the bilateral agreement between Switzerland and the League did not bind member states in their dealings with League officials. This turned out to be a problem during the Second World War when France and Spain did not always respect the diplomatic status of League staff trying to make their way out of Europe.[34]

A further step in the professionalization of the League's civil servants was taken by the Committees of Thirteen in 1930–1. At this point, the secretariat had reached a level of maturity that created new problems: it was becoming increasingly clear that many League officials were staying in the secretariat for many years, developing proper long-term international careers. The secretariat's system of seven-year contracts and a moderate pension's scheme that only secured one year's salary at the end of employment did not support this type of career, and discontent with the system among League officials was growing. Most member states were sympathetic to the League staff's wishes to develop a system of proper long-term contracts and the majority of the New Committee of Thirteen recommended a de facto system of tenure for League officials and a new pension scheme that allowed for League staff to retire and live on their League pensions in old age. However, two major member states did not support these planes: Germany and Italy believed that the secretariat had grown too independent and influential and were now sliding essentially towards Hankey's initial proposal for the League Secretariat, pushing for shorter contracts and national secondments – much like the system that Drummond had rejected when he created the secretariat in 1919. The aim was clear: to enhance member state control over the secretariat.

The Italian and German position in the Committee of Thirteen was part of broader development where Drummond's ideas of a secretariat of loyal civil servants came under increasing pressure as the number of authoritarian and totalitarian regimes with little ideological sympathy for the League's liberal internationalist project grew. From the late 1920s, German and Italian members of staff in particular had started taking directions from their Foreign Ministries, and leaks from the secretariat back to Berlin and Rome became increasingly common.[35] In the case of the Committee of Thirteen, the German-Italian opposition meant that the majority recommendations of the Committee of Thirteen were not formally adopted by the 1930–2 League Assemblies. Still, the recommendations and their reception were a clear signal that among the majority of member states there was solid political backing for the idea of a genuinely international, independent civil service.[36]

The increasingly critical Italian and German attitude towards the League was also what lay behind the introduction of an oath of loyalty in 1932 in which all new members swore

> to exercise in all loyalty, discretion and conscience the functions that have been entrusted to me as an official of the Secretariat of the League of nations, to discharge my functions and to regulate my conduct with the interests of the League alone in view and not to seek or receive instructions from any Government or other authority external to the Secretariat of the League of Nations.[37]

While the new oath could be read as a new form of supranational allegiance, it was in reality primarily introduced as a disciplinary measure which enabled the secretary-general to dismiss an official 'in the case of flagrant violation of international duties'[38] as a former League official put it – something that was becoming increasingly relevant.

During the 1930s the world economic crisis and growing political tensions crippled the secretariat even further, and the League's civil service was given a final, devastating moral blow when, in the summer of 1940, the French Secretary-General Joseph Avenol responded to the news of the German invasion of France by claiming that the only viable option for the League now was to become an exclusively 'European' League that should 'work hand in hand with Hitler in order to achieve the unity of Europe' – something that involved expelling Britain from the continent and all British members of staff from the secretariat.[39]

Legacies

In the summer of 1940, Avenol was ousted from the secretariat and the Irishman Seán Lester took over the post as secretary-general. This re-established the traditional, close ties between the (now severely diminished) secretariat and the British Foreign Office. A new and previously unseen relationship also emerged with the rising American superpower when the secretariat's Economic and Financial Section was transferred to Princeton.[40] This last part traces the legacies of the secretariat into the post-war years by looking at how organizational principles and civil servant norms transposed to the United Nations (UN). As we shall see, the specific model of balancing autonomy and legitimacy, internationality and national considerations identified above was, in large parts, continued. However, there were qualitative differences too. Some were the result of learning by the mistakes of the League; others were prompted by the fact that the United States now took on the role as the undisputed guardian of a new multilateral order. Others still were the product of the new geopolitical tensions of the Cold War, emerging particularly from 1948 onwards.

The United Nations Charter was produced and ratified in what Glenda Sluga termed 'the apogee of internationalism' and was to some extent echoing the U.S. Constitution. The Charter 'signalled the shifting moral and political center of the new world order, from Europe to America, and to a new era of political democracy and equality in America's image'.[41] In this context of bustling internationalism and changing of the guards, the United Nations formalized most of the incrementally developed norms and principles of international civil service that the League had produced. Article 100 of Chapter XV of the Charter, for instance, restated that the staff had to be loyal to the organization and that member states had to respect the UN's international nature.[42] In this continuation lay the perhaps biggest change, too: what had so far been practised and articulated internally in the League Secretariat was now elevated to the constitutional level of the UN and enshrined in the Charter (and other treaties).[43] The international civil servant was now a solemnly recognized professional feature of post-war multilateralism.

The experiences of international administration made in the League made their way into the post-war setting not least due to representatives of the secretariat themselves. In a series of meetings in London during the Second World War, Drummond and other leading League officials drew up the so-called London Report to convey the institutional know-how of the League Secretariat to subsequent IOs.[44] The report was picked up by the International Civil Service Advisory Board (ICSAB), set up in 1949 to develop a Standard of Conduct for international civil servants. The board was chaired by long-term League official Thanassis Aghnides (whose early career in the League is explored in Chapter 3 of this volume).[45] Significantly, he had been one of the co-authors of the London report, and thus the direct link between League experiences and UN formulations of its own civil servant principles. The fruit of ICSAB's labours was the 'Report on Standards of Conduct in the International Civil Service (1st Ed. 1954)' which came to serve as a handbook for international civil servants in the UN and its many special agencies (such as the ILO, the WHO and UNESCO).

The principles of independence from member states and international representation (i.e. a broad geographical dispersion in personnel) articulated in the Standards of Conduct[46] were adopted and emulated by other post-war international and regional organizations such as the Organisation for European Economic Cooperation (OEEC) and the European Coal and Steel Community (ECSC). In this way, the influence of the interwar experiment in international administration was prolific and deep.

More concretely, several previously established norms and procedures were adopted by the UN as part of the way international civil service was practised. This was the case when an independent Selection Board *within* the secretariat was created that would 'be advisory to the Executive Head, who would retain his independent authority for the final choice', and when a competitive examination for recruitments to certain parts of the administration was established.[47] Equally, the principle of legitimacy through the integration of state interests was continued and further formalized: the selection of staff was to be based on efficiency and competence as well as a 'wide geographical distribution of the staff' (more important in political parts of the UN machinery than in the small specialized agencies).[48] Also, the norm that promotions should be sought within the institution first and from other international organizations second, before hiring from the outside, while allowing a 'reasonable inflow of fresh talent', which had been established in the League Secretariat in the 1920s, was firmly re-established.[49]

Last, but not least, the flexibility and room of manoeuvre, which had been key to the League Secretariat's staffing practices, were continued. ICSAB's report on recruitment methods held the 'firm conviction that the fixing of any rigid quota for geographical distribution would be extremely harmful to an international secretariat'.[50] Apart from flexibility, this would dissuade member states from 'demanding' a post filled by someone of their nationality with reference to an established quota. The principle was, in other words, key to the UN secretariat's autonomy.

In addition to its political and legal dimension, the 'Standard of Conduct' also had a moral dimension. The text was printed as a small handbook and given to every official when they were appointed, as the legal and moral codex of the profession. Indeed, for the man responsible for the wording, Thanassis Aghnides, the 'Standards of Conduct' was meant to 'give, the moral tone to the organization', as it was 'much more than a literal or mechanical knowledge of which I speak. It is a deep understanding and acceptance, both intellectually and spiritually, of the basic purposes and high demands which the Charter places on all of us'.⁵¹ In sum, there was a qualitative shift from the fragile understanding that unravelled in the 1930s. Indeed, variations of these obligations were proliferated across multiple international organisations as professional ideals that were considered relatively undisputed. The international civil servant's role and norms were articulated and recognized as legitimate.⁵²

There was at least one obvious reason, owing in large part to the (initially) determined US leadership, for this formalization of the international civil servant's role: the sheer size of the UN system. In 1946, the UN – at that point in London – had a temporary staff of 300. Over the course of a few months another 2,900 people were hired. By 1964, the staff of the UN secretariat proper had grown to 3,400.⁵³ At that point one of its agencies, UNESCO, employed twice as many as the entire League Secretariat ever did.⁵⁴ The entire staff of the UN and all its agencies was under the authority of the secretary-general.⁵⁵ This basic fact was a driver of uniformity.

Central traits of the administrative logic of the League were thus continued, and further strengthened, and the 'Standards of Conduct' – which fully articulated these principles – remained relatively unchanged until 2001. It got its last major update in 2013 and is an important document for international civil servants to this day.⁵⁶

Yet the creeping Cold War challenged some of these principles, just as the tumultuous 1930s had challenged the League Secretariat's fragile structures. Even though the UN secretary-general's political role was strengthened, most noticeably with the right to bring before the Security Council issues that he considered a threat to international peace and security (Article 99), his ability to safeguard the secretariat itself from political pressures was not increased in practice. Particularly the two first UN secretaries-general, Trygve Lie (1946–52) and Dag Hammarskjöld (1953–61), faced immense pressures. The communist states kept an attentive eye on appointments in the UN system and, as Bob Reinalda writes, '[t]he primary responsibility of their own people was to their states and their communist beliefs. The UN could hardly ignore the lists [of proposed staff] submitted for its attention'.⁵⁷ Perhaps even more harrowing, during the years of McCarthyism, the US government interfered directly in the UN's organization and staffing. At its peak, in 1952–3, the US government conducted several highly publicized investigations of the political reliability of the American candidates.⁵⁸ The secretariat had become just another Cold War arena. Though these tensions would pass, they revealed what is a systemic tension in international administrations: the balance between being accepted as legitimate by member state and being autonomous from the same.

Much like the League Secretariat which was only briefly mentioned in the covenant, the UN secretariat's structure was barely articulated in the UN Charter. Chapter XV of the Charter – containing only five articles (97–101) – gave few substantive pointers about how the UN secretariat should operate. Yet it had much more experience – good and bad – to draw upon. It is a fair to say that the UN secretariat was one of the clearest continuations from the League of Nations, even as most politicians and officials were eager to distance themselves from the legacies when setting up the new world organization.

Conclusion

In this chapter we have shown how the early history of international civil service was the result of two juxtaposing trends. On the one hand, and at a formal level, the first secretary-general of the League of Nations, Sir Eric Drummond's conception of a politically neutral secretariat recruited internationally and loyal only to the organization was a radically new and daring idea. This ideal was developed and consolidated during the 1920s and 1930s, which saw a rapid professionalization as rules about pensions, recruitments and promotions, loyalty and diplomatic immunities. These developments solidified the role of the international civil servant and created the formal preconditions for the career official that could work in IOs until old age.

The professional matrix developed in the interwar years carried over into the post-war period, largely owing to former League officials who described, evaluated and promoted what they considered the key lessons in international public administration. At the creation of the UN the formal status and role of international civil service were further strengthened and clarified as the rules, rights and obligations that had developed as internal rules and principles in the League Secretariat were enshrined at the highest legal level in the Charter of the UN.

On the other hand, it is also evident that while Drummond's vision of the secretariat was radically new in terms of its insistency on international autonomy, loyalty and multinationality, it was also deeply inspired by his Foreign Office training and characterized by a profound sensitivity to member-state interests and power balances. From the early 1930s, these national rifts and concerns increasingly came to shape the notion of international civil service. As the League was buffeted by the ideological rifts and power clashes that rapidly escalated in Europe and beyond, we note an increasing polarization around the question of the 'internationality' of officials, as imperial Japan, fascist Italy and pre- and post-national socialist Germany pushed for a 're-nationalization' of loyalties and thus a reversal of the fundamental principles set down by Drummond. This trend continued into the post-war years when the enhanced position of the principles of international loyalty and autonomy in the UN Charter was immediately challenged by the United States and the USSR as the tensions of the Cold War increased.

Notes

Chapter 1

1 Jarle Trondal et al., *Unpacking International Organisations. The Dynamics of Compound Bureaucracies* (Manchester: Manchester University Press 2010), 6–7; Akira Iriye, *Global Community. The Role of International Organizations in the Making of the Contemporary World* (Berkeley: University of California Press, 2004).

2 Alexandru Grigorescu: 'Transparency of Intergovernmental Organizations: The Roles of Member States, International Bureaucracies and Nongovernmental Organizations', *International Studies Quarterly* 51, no. 3 (2007): 625–48, here 625.

3 Patrick Finney, 'Introduction: What Is International History?', in *Palgrave Advances in International History*, ed. Patrick Finney (Houndmills: Palgrave Macmillan, 2005), 1–35.

4 Iriye, *Global Community*; Daniel Gorman, *The Emergence of International Society in the 1920s* (Cambridge: Cambridge University Press, 2012); Davide Rodogno, Shaloma Gauthier and Francesca Piana, 'What Does Transnational History Tell Us about a World with International Organizations? The Historians' Point of View', in *Routledge Handbook of International Organization*, ed. Bob Reinalda (London and New York: Routledge, 2013), 94–105.

5 Paul Weindling (ed.), *International Health Organisations and Movements, 1918–1939* (Cambridge: Cambridge University Press, 1995); Vincent Lagendijk, *Electrifying Europe: The Power of Europe in the Construction of Electricity Networks* (Amsterdam: Aksant, 2008); Johan Schot and Vincent Lagendijk, 'Technocratic Internationalism in the Interwar Years: Building Europe on Motorways and Electricity Networks', *Journal of Modern European History* 6, no. 2 (2008): 196–217; Mark Mazower, *Governing the World: The History of an Idea, 1815 to the Present* (London: Penguin, 2012); Patricia Clavin, *Securing the World Economy: The Reinvention of the League of Nations, 1920–1946* (Oxford: Oxford University Press, 2013); Wolfram Kaiser and Johan Schot, *Writing the Rules for Europe: Experts, Cartels, and International Organizations (Making Europe)* (Basingstoke: Palgrave Macmillan, 2014); Susan Pedersen, *The Guardians: The League of Nations and the Crisis of Empire* (Oxford: Oxford University Press, 2015); Sandrine Kott and Martin Lengwiler, 'Experts internationaux et politiques sociales', *Revue d'histoire de la protection sociale* 10, no. 1 (2017): 9–21; Quinn Slobodian, *Globalists: The End of Empire and the Birth of Neoliberalism* (Harvard: Harvard University Press, 2018).

6 Clavin, *Securing the World Economy*.

7 Kaiser and Schot, *Writing the Rules for Europe*; Kiran Klaus Patel and Wolfram Kaiser (eds.), 'Continuity and Change in European Cooperation during the Twentieth Century', *Contemporary European History* 27, no. 2 (2018): 165–82.
8 Internationalism is an elusive concept and one that is rarely defined in the literature that deals with it. Glenda Sluga, *Internationalism in the Age of Nationalism* (Philadelphia: University of Pennsylvania Press, 2013), Glenda and Patricia Clavin (eds.), *Internationalisms: A Twentieth-century History* (Cambridge: Cambridge University Press, 2016)). In our definition here we draw on Daniel Laqua, *The Age of Internationalism and Belgium, 1880–1930: Peace, Progress and Prestige* (Manchester: Manchester University Press, 2013), 3–5 and Kjell Goldmann, *The Logic of Internationalism: Coercion and Accommodation* (London: CRC Press, 1994).
9 Daniel Laqua (ed.), *Internationalism Reconfigured: Transnational Ideas and Movements between the World Wars* (London: Bloomsbury/I.B. Tauris, 2011); Sluga, *Internationalism in the Age of Nationalism*; Kaiser and Schot, *Writing the Rules for Europe*; Jessica Reinisch, 'Agents of Internationalism', *Contemporary European History* 25, no. 2 (2016) (special issue).
10 See particularly Sluga *Internationalism in the Age of Nationalism*.
11 Sluga and Clavin, *Internationalisms*.
12 Martin H. Geyer and Johannes Paulmann (eds.), *The Mechanics of Internationalism: Culture, Society, and Politics from the 1840s to the First World War* (Oxford University Press, 2001).
13 Madeleine Herren, *Hintertüren zur Macht Internationalismus und modernisierungsorientierte Außenpolitik in Belgien, der Schweiz und den USA 1865–1914* (Munich: Oldenbourg Verlag, 2000), 2, Geyer and Paulmann, *The Mechanics of Internationalism*, 3–4.
14 A sub-field where this is particularly evident is global health: Paul Weindling, 'Philanthropy and World Health: The Rockefeller Foundation and the League of Nations Health Organisation', *Minerva* 35 (1997): 269–81; Sunil S. Amrith, *Decolonizing International Health India and Southeast Asia, 1930–65* (London: Palgrave, 2006); Iris Borowy, *Coming to Terms with World Health: The League of Nations Health Organisation 1921–1946* (Frankfurt: Peter Lang, 2009); Sunil S. Amrith and Patricia Clavin, 'Feeding the World: Connecting Europe and Asia, 1930–1945', *Past and Present*, Supplement 8 (2013): 29–50; Thomas Zimmer, *Welt ohne Krankheit: Geschichte der Internationalen Gesundheitspolitik 1940–1970* (Göttingen: Wallstein, 2017); Klaas Dykmann, *Internationale Organisationen und ihre Zivilisierungsbestrebungen. Die Geschichte der Weltgesundheitsorganisation* (Zürich: LIT, 2017).
15 Pedersen, *The Guardians* is a clear exception.
16 Bob Reinalda, *Routledge History of International Organizations: From 1815 to the Present Day* (London and New York: Routledge, 2009); Bob Reinalda, 'The History

of International Organization(s), *Oxford Research Encyclopedia, International Studies* (Oxford: Oxford University Press, 2019); Benjamin Auberer, 'Digesting the League of Nations: Planning the International Secretariat of the Future, 1941–1944', *New Global Studies* 10, no. 3 (2016): 393–426. Karen Gram-Skjoldager and Haakon A. Ikonomou, 'The Construction of the League of Nations Secretariat. Formative Practices of Autonomy and Legitimacy in International Organisations', *The International History Review* 41, no. 2 (2019): 257–79; Karen Gram-Skjoldager and Haakon A. Ikonomou, 'Making Sense of the League of Nations – Historiographical and Conceptual Reflections on Early International Public Administration', *European History Quarterly* 49, no. 3 (2019): 420–44.

17 Katja Seidel, *The Process of Politics in Europe: The Rise of European Elites and Supranational Institutions* (London: I.B. Tauris, 2010); Emmanuel Mourlon-Druol, 'Less Than a Permanent Secretariat, More Than an Ad Hoc Preparatory Group: A Prosopography of the Personal Representatives of the G7 Summits (1975–1991)', in *International Summitry and Global Governance: The Rise of the G7 and the European Council, 1974–1991*, ed. Emmanuel Mourlon-Druol and Federico Romero (Basingstoke: Routledge, 2014), 64–98; Elisabetta Tollardo, *Fascist Italy and the League of Nations, 1922–1935* (London: Palgrave Macmillan, 2016); Vera Fritz, *Juges et avocats généraux de la Cour de Justice de l'Union européenne (1952–1972). Une approche biographique de l'histoire d'une révolution juridique* (Frankfurt am Main: Vittorio Klostermann, 2018); Benjamin Auberer, '"From the Australian Bush to the International Jungle". Internationale Karrieren und der Völkerbund' (PhD diss., University of Heidelberg, Heidelberg, 2018); Torsten Kahlert, 'Pioneers in International Administration: A Prosopography of the Directors of the League of Nations Secretariat', *New Global Studies* 13, no. 2 (2019): 190–227.

18 Linda Risso, '"I Am the Servant of the Council": Lord Ismay and the Making of the NATO International Staff"', *Contemporary European History* 28, no. 3 (2019): 342–57.

19 The term *Sattelzeit* is borrowed from Reinhard Koselleck, 'Einleitung', *Geschichtliche Grundbegriffe: Historisches Lexikon zur politisch-sozialen Sprache in Deutschland*, vol. 1 (*A-D*), ed. Otto Brunner, Werner Conze and Reinhard Koselleck (Stuttgart: Ernst Klett Verlag, 1972), xv.

20 Preamble of the Covenant of the League of Nations: http://avalon.law.yale.edu/20th_century/leagcov.asp (accessed 9 April 2020).

21 F. S. Northedge, *The League of Nations: Its Life and Times, 1920–1946* (Leicester: Holmes & Meier, 1988).

22 Egon F. Ranshofen-Wertheimer, *The International Secretariat. A Great Experiment in International Administration* (Washington: The Carnegie Endowment for International Peace, 1945), 242, 358.

23 Ranshofen-Wertheimer, *International Secretariat*, 81.

24 The Carnegie Endowment for International Peace, *Exploratory Conference on the Experience of the League of Nations Secretariat*, New York City, 30 August

1942 (Washington: The Carnegie Endowment for International Peace, 1942); The Carnegie Endowment for International Peace, *Conference on Experience in International Administration*, Washington, 30 January 1943 (Washington: The Carnegie Endowment for International Peace, 1943).
25 Mazower, *Governing*, 148–53.
26 Amy Sayward, *The United Nations in International History* (London: Bloomsbury, 2017).
27 Melvyn L. Leffler and Odd Arne Westad, *The Cambridge History of the Cold War*, vol. 1–2 (Cambridge: Cambridge University Press, 2010); Mazower, *Governing*.
28 For example Giuliano Garavini, *After Empires. European Integration, Decolonization, and the Challenge from the Global South 1957–1986* (Oxford: Oxford University Press, 2012); Steven Jensen, *The Making of International Human Rights: The 1960s, Decolonization, and the Reconstruction of Global Values* (Cambridge: Cambridge University Press, 2016); Miguel Bandeira Jerónimo and José Pedro Monteiro (eds.), *Internationalism, Imperialism and the Formation of the Contemporary World* (London: Palgrave Macmillan, 2017); Alanna O'Malley, *The Diplomacy of Decolonisation: America, Britain and the United Nations during the Congo Crisis 1960–1964* (Manchester: Manchester University Press, 2018).
29 Alan S. Milward, *The Reconstruction of Western Europe 1945–51* (London: Methuen, 1984); Michael J. Hogan, *The Marshall Plan: America, Britain, and the Reconstruction of Western Europe, 1947–1952* (Cambridge: Cambridge University Press, 1987).
30 Matthieu Leimgruber and Matthias Schmelzer, 'Introduction: Writing Histories of the OECD', in *The OECD and the International Political Economy since 1948*, ed. Matthieu Leimgruber and Matthias Schmelzer (London: Palgrave Macmillan, 2017), 1–22.
31 Robert S. Jordan, *The NATO International Staff/Secretariat, 1952–57* (London: Oxford University Press, 1967).
32 Dirk Spierenburg and Raymond Poidevin, *The History of the High Authority of the European Coal and Steel Community* (London, Weidenfeld & Nicolson, 1994); Seidel, *Process of Politics*; Morten Rasmussen, 'Legal History of the EU: Building a European Constitution?', in *Oxford Encyclopedia of European Union Politics*, ed. Derek Beach and Finn Laursen, 1–19 (Oxford: Oxford University Press, 2019). https://oxfordre.com/politics/view/10.1093/acrefore/9780190228637.001.0001/acrefore-9780190228637-e-1064.
33 Jürgen Kocka, 'Comparison and Beyond', *History and Theory* 42, no. 1 (2003): 39–44; Jürgen Kocka and Heinz-Gerhard Haupt (eds.), *Comparative and Transnational History: Central European Approaches and New Perspectives* (New York: Berghahn Books, 2009).
34 Niall Ferguson, Charles S. Maier, Erez Manela, Daniel J. Sargent (eds.), *The Shock of the Global. The 1970s in Perspective* (Harvard: Harvard University Press, 2011).

35 Jonas Brendebach, Martin Herzer and Heidi Tworek (eds.), *International Organizations and the Media in the Nineteenth and Twentieth Centuries. Exorbitant Expectations* (Oxon/New York: Routledge, 2018); Heidi Tworek, 'Peace through Truth? The Press and Moral Disarmament through the League of Nations', *Medien & Zeit* 25, no. 4 (2010): 16–28; Tomoko Akami, 'Beyond the Formula of the Age of Reason. Experts, Social Sciences, and the Phonic Public in International Politics', in *The League of Nations – Perspectives from the Present*, ed. Haakon A. Ikonomou and Karen Gram-Skjoldager (Aarhus University Press; Århus: Aarhus Universitetsforlag, 2019), 161–72; Thomas R. Davies, 'A "Great Experiment" of the League of Nations Era: International Nongovernmental Organizations, Global Governance, and Democracy beyond the State', *Global Governance* 18 (2012): 405–23; Emil Seidenfaden, 'Message from Geneva: The Public Legitimization Strategies of the League of Nations and Their Legacy, 1919–1946' (PhD diss., Aarhus University, Aarhus, 2019).
36 A point that is amply demonstrated in Brendenbach, Herzer and Tworek: *International Organizations*.
37 For more on this, see Laurien Crump and Simon Godard, 'Reassessing Communist International Organisations: A Comparative Analysis of COMECON and the Warsaw Pact in Relation to their Cold War Competitors', *Contemporary European History* 27, no. 1 (2018): 85–109: https://paneur1970s.eui.eu/project-description/ (accessed 6 April 2020).
38 Daniel Laqua, *Wouter Van Acker and Christophe Verbruggen, International Organizations and Global Civil Society: Histories of the Union of International Associations* (New York: Bloomsbury, 2019); Thomas Davies, *NGOs: A New History of Transnational Civil Society* (Oxford: Oxford University Press, 2014).
39 Pedersen, *The Guardians*.

Chapter 2

1 *IO BIO, Biographical Dictionary of Secretaries-General of International Organizations*, edited by Bob Reinalda, Kent J. Kille and Jaci L. Eisenberg: http://www.ru.nl/fm/iobio (accessed 8 August 2020). Entries can be found in alphabetical order by executive head.
2 M. C. Horowitz, 'Leaders, Leadership, and International Security', in *The Oxford Handbook of International Security*, ed. A. Gheciu and W. C. Wohlforth (Oxford: Oxford University Press, 2018), 246–58.
3 See D. L. Byman and K. M. Pollack, 'Let Us Now Praise Great Men: Bringing the Statesman Back In', *International Security* 25, no. 4 (2001): 108.
4 K. N. Waltz, *Theory of International Politics* (New York: McGraw-Hill, 1979), 111.

5   E. B. Haas, *Beyond the Nation-state: Functionalism and International Organization* (Stanford, CA: Stanford University Press, 1964); R. W. Cox, 'The Executive Head: An Essay on Leadership in International Organization', *International Organization* 23, no. 2 (1969): 205–30; M. G. Schechter, 'Confronting the Challenges of Political Leadership in International Organizations', in *Comparative Political Leadership*, ed. L. Helms (Houndmills: Palgrave Macmillan, 2012), 249–71. N. Hall and N. Woods, 'Theorizing the Role of Executive Heads in International Organizations', *European Journal of International Relations* 24, no. 4 (2017).
6   Author instructions and databases are available at the *IO BIO* website.
7   T. G. Weiss et al., *UN Voices: The Struggle for Development and Social Justice* (Bloomington, IL: Indiana University Press, 2005).
8   R. Biermann and J. Koops (ed.), *The Palgrave Handbook of Inter-organizational Relations in World Politics* (London: Palgrave, 2017).
9   B. Reinalda and K. J. Kille, 'The Evolvement of International Secretariats, Executive Heads and Leadership in Inter-organizational Relations', in *Palgrave Handbook of Inter-organizational Relations in World Politics*, ed. R. Biermann and J. Koops (London: Palgrave Macmillan, 2017), 217–42.
10 J. ter Meulen, *Der Gedanke der Internationalen Organisation in seiner Entwicklung 1300–1800* (The Hague: Martinus Nijhoff, 1917), 195–7.
11 B. Reinalda, 'The Evolution of International Organization as Institutional Forms and Historical Processes to 1945', in *The International Studies Encyclopedia*, vol. III, ed. R. A. Denmark (Chichester: Wiley-Blackwell, 2010), 1903–21.
12 J. Siotis, *Essai sur le secrétariat international* (Geneva: Librairie Droz 1963), 27–8.
13 E. B. Haas, *When Knowledge Is Power: Three Models of Change in International Organizations* (Berkeley, CA: University of California Press, 1990), 3–4; K. Thelen, 'How Institutions Evolve: Insights from Comparative Historical Analysis', in *Comparative Historical Analysis in the Social Sciences*, ed. J. Mahoney and D. Rueschemeyer (Cambridge: Cambridge University Press, 2003), 228.
14 J. Klabbers, *Advanced Introduction to the Law of International Organizations* (Cheltenham: Edward Elgar, 2015), 71–2.
15 R. M. Spaulding, 'Revolutionary France and the Transformation of the Rhine', *Central European History* 44 (2011): 216.
16 G. J. Mangone, *A Short History of International Organization* (New York: McGraw-Hill, 1954), 69.
17 J.-M. Woehrling, 'L'administration de la Commission centrale pour la navigation du Rhin', *Revue Française d'administration publique* 126 (2008): 345–58; R. M. Spaulding, 'The Central Commission for the Navigation of the Rhine and European Media, 1815–1848', in *International Organizations and the Media in the Nineteenth and Twentieth Centuries: Exorbitant Expectations*, ed. J. Brendebach, M. Herzer and H. Tworek (London: Routledge, 2018), 17–37.
18 See Constantin Ardeleanu's *IO BIO* entry.
19 Reinalda, 'The Evolution', 1909–10.

20 I. L. Claude Jr., *Swords into Plowshares: The Problems and Progress of International Organization* (London: University of London Press, 1966), 32.
21 See Simone Fari and Gabriele Balbi's *IO BIO* entry.
22 Bureau international des administrations télégraphiques, *Rapport de Gestion*, 1899, Personnel.
23 G. Moynier, *Les bureaux internationaux des unions universelles* (Geneva and Paris: Cherbuliez and Fischbacher, 1892), 22.
24 Mangone, *Short History*, 82.
25 F. S. L. Lyons, *Internationalism in Europe 1815–1914* (Leiden: A.W. Sijthoff, 1963), 100.
26 C. N. Murphy, *International Organization and Industrial Change: Global Governance since 1850* (Cambridge: Polity Press, 1994), 113.
27 For example F. P. Walters, *A History of the League of Nations* (Oxford: Oxford University Press, 1952), 75; J. Mathiason, *Invisible Governance: International Secretariats in Global Politics* (Bloomfield: Kumarian, 2007), 25.
28 L. S. Woolf, *International Government* (New York: Brentano's, 1916), 116.
29 Woolf, *International Government*, 167.
30 J. A. Salter, *Allied Shipping Control: An Experiment in International Administration* (Oxford: Clarendon Press, 1921), 252.
31 See Karen Gram-Skjoldager's *IO BIO* entry.
32 M. D. Dubin, 'Transgovernmental Processes in the League of Nations', *International Organization* 37, no. 3 (1983): 473–5.
33 Quoted in S. Aster, *Power, Policy and Personality: The Life and Times of Lord Salter, 1881–1975* (Lexington, KY: Aster, 2015), 88.
34 Quoted in Dubin, 'Transgovernmental Processes', 472.
35 E. F. Ranshofen-Wertheimer, *The International Secretariat: A Great Experiment in International Administration* (Washington DC: Carnegie Endowment for International Peace, 1945), 81.
36 Dubin, 'Transgovernmental Processes', 483.
37 See Martyn Housden's *IO BIO* entry.
38 See Francesca Piana's *IO BIO* entry.
39 See Marta Balinska's *IO BIO* entry.
40 Reinalda and Kille, 'The Evolvement', 223–6.
41 International Regulations, Article 14 and Staff Regulations, Article 3.
42 Ranshofen-Wertheimer, *The International Secretariat*, 245.
43 S. F. Martin, *International Migration: Evolving Trends from the Early Twentieth Century to the Present* (Cambridge: Cambridge University Press, 2014), 62.
44 Articles of Agreement IMF, Sec. 4.c, Articles of Agreement IBRD, Sec. 5.c.
45 Article 59.
46 A. W. Rovine, *The First Fifty Years: The Secretary-General in World Politics 1920–1970* (Leiden: Sijthoff, 1970), 203–4.

47 Rovine, *The First Fifty Years*, 207.
48 S. D. Bailey, *The Secretariat of the United Nations* (New York: Carnegie Endowment for International Peace, 1962), 23.
49 See Ellen Ravndal and Jim Muldoon's *IO BIO* entry.
50 Constitution, 2014, Article 20, Explanation.
51 Article 148.
52 Article 127–2.2.
53 See Michael Schechter's *IO BIO* entry.
54 See Chloé Maurel's *IO BIO* entry.
55 See Auriane Guilbaud's *IO BIO* entry.
56 See Michael Schechter's *IO BIO* entry.
57 See Chloé Maurel's *IO BIO* entry.
58 See David Webster's *IO BIO* entry.
59 See Francine McKenzie's *IO BIO* entry.
60 See Jeroen Corduwener and Bob Reinalda's *IO BIO* entry.
61 See Michael Schechter's *IO BIO* entry.
62 See Michael Schechter's *IO BIO* entry.
63 D. Williams, *The Specialized Agencies and the United Nations: The System in Crisis* (London: Hurst & Company, 1990), 19.
64 Williams, *The Specialized Agencies*, 21–2.

Chapter 3

1 Karen Gram-Skjoldager and Haakon A. Ikonomou, 'The Construction of the League of Nations Secretariat. Formative Practices of Autonomy and Legitimacy in International Organisations', *International History Review* 41, no. 2 (2019): 257–79.
2 Chapter 13 '*The Making of the International Civil Servant c.1920-60 – Establishing the Profession*', x–x.
3 It is beyond the scope of this chapter to delve into the details of Aghnides's role in the creation of the Standard of Conduct for the UN. The question is touched upon in Haakon A. Ikonomou, 'Thanassis Aghnides og skabelsen af den international Embedsmand', *Baggrund* (2019): https://baggrund.com/2019/09/02/thanassis-aghnides-og-skabelsen-af-den-internationale-embedsmand/ (accessed 8 April 2020); Gram-Skjoldager and Ikonomou, 'The Construction of the League of Nations Secretariat'; Benjamin Auberer, 'Digesting the League of Nations: Planning the International Secretariat of the Future, 1941–1944', *New Global Studies* 10, no. 3 (2016): 393–426. It will be discussed in greater detail in Haakon A. Ikonomou, *The International Bureaucrat in the Twentieth Century – A Transnational Biography of Thanassis Aghnides* (London: Palgrave Macmillan, forthcoming 2021).

4 For the transnational biography, see Florian Kreutzer and Silke Roth, 'Einleitung zu Transnationale Karrieren: Biographien, Lebensführung und Mobilität', in *Transnationale Karrieren*, ed. Florian Kreutzer (Wiesbaden, 2006), 7–33; Ann-Christina Knudsen and Karen Gram-Skjoldager (eds.), *Living Political Biography – Narrating 20th Century European Lives* (Aarhus: Aarhus University Press, 2012); Angela Woollacott, Angela, Desley Deacon and Penny Russell (eds.), *Transnational Lives. Biographies of Global Modernity, 1700–Present* (New York: Palgrave, 2010); Sarah Panter, Johannes Paulmann and Margit Szöllösi-Janze (eds.), *Mobility and Biography* [=Jahrbuch für Europäische Geschichte/European History Yearbook 16 (2015)]. For three very interesting examples of biographical approaches applied to the League (and beyond): Madeleine Herren, Isabella Löhr (eds.), *Lives beyond Borders. Toward a Social History of Cosmopolitans and Globalization, 1880–1960*, Comparativ 23/6 (2013); Benjamin Auberer, ''From the Australian Bush to the International Jungle'. Internationale Karrieren und der Völkerbund', PhD diss. (Heidelberg: Universität Heidelberg, 2018).

5 See for instance: Susan Pedersen, *The Guardians: The League of Nations and the Crisis of Empire* (Oxford: Oxford University Press, 2015); Davide Rodogno, 'The American Red Cross and the International Committee of the Red Cross: Humanitarian Politics and Policies in Asia Minor and Greece (1922–1923)', *First World War Studies* 5, no. 1 (2014): 83–99; Keith David Watenpaugh, *Bread from Stones: The Middle East and the Making of Modern Humanitarianism* (Berkeley: University of California Press, 2015); Philippe Bourmaud, Chantal Verdeil and Norig Neveu (eds.), *Experts et expertises dans les mandats de la Société des Nations: figures, champs et outils* (Paris: Presses de l'INALCO, 2020).

6 For a review essay on this, see Simon Jackson, 'From Beirut to Berlin (via Geneva): The New International History, Middle East Studies and the League of Nations', *Contemporary European History*, 27, no. 4: 708–26. Two publications that add a fresh take on the imperial powers, the collapse of the Ottoman Empire, the Mandate System and (post-)First World War Middle East from an Ottoman Studies and Migration Studies perspective, respectively: Michael Provence, *The Last Ottoman Generation and the Making of the Modern Middle East* (Cambridge: Cambridge University Press, 2017); Stacy Fahrenthold, *Between the Ottomans and the Entente. The First World War in the Syrian and Lebanese Diaspora, 1908–1925* (Oxford: Oxford University Press, 2019).

7 To my knowledge, there are no published works focusing on Thanassis Aghnides, not even in Greek, though he is present in several publications on the League of Nations. Two notable examples are Lena Divani, **Η 'ύπουλος θωπεία'** Ελλάδα και ξένοι, 1821–1940 (Athens: Εκδόσεις Καστανιώτη, 2014) and Marit Fosse and John Fox, *Sean Lester. The Guardian of a Small Flickering Light* (London: Hamilton Books, 2016).

8 These reflections are based on the ongoing research which will appear in a much extended and altered version in an edited volume provisionally entitled *Global Biographies*, edited together by Gunvor Simonsen (University of Copenhagen), Laura Almagor (University of Sheffield) and myself: https://cemes.ku.dk/activities/2019/global-biographies-a-writers-workshop/ (accessed 6 December 2019).
9 Oscar Handlin, *Truth in History* (Harvard: Harvard University Press, 1979), 276. Borrowed from David Nasaw 'Introduction – AHR Roundtable: Historians and Biography', *The American Historical Review* 114, no. 3 (June 2009): 573–8.
10 Sarah Panter, Johannes Paulmann and Margit Szöllösi-Janze, 'Mobility and Biography. Methodological Challenges and Perspectives', in *Mobility and Biography* [=Jahrbuch für Europäische Geschichte/European History Yearbook 16 (2015)], ed. Sarah Panter, (De Gruyter: Oldenbur) 1–14, 4.
11 Sebastian Conrad, *What Is Global History?* (Princeton: Princeton University Press, 2016), 136; Akira Iriye, *Global and Transnational History. Past, Present, Future* (London: Palgrave Macmillan, 2012).
12 Sidsel Eriksen 'Biografier som lakmuspapir. Overvejelser omkring den socialhistoriske biografi', *Historisk Tidsskrift*, 16: https://tidsskrift.dk/historisktidsskrift/article/view/53756 (accessed 6 December 2019).
13 'Any occurrence', writes Sebastian Conrad, 'can be interpreted within different and multiple time frames.' Conrad, *What Is Global History?* 146.
14 David Runciman, 'What Time Frame Makes Sense for Thinking about Crises?' in *Critical Theories of Crisis in Europe from Weimar to the Euro*, ed. Poul F. Kjær and Niklas Olsen (London: Rowman & Littlefield, 2016), 3–17.
15 William McGrew, *Educating across Cultures. Anatolia College in Turkey and Greece* (Lanham: Rowman & Littlefield, 2015), xvi.
16 Benjamin Fortna, *Imperial Classroom: Islam, the State, and Education in the Late Ottoman Empire* (Oxford: Oxford University Press, 2002).
17 Aude Aylin De Tapia, 'Orthodox Christians and Muslims of Cappadocia: Intercommunal Relations in an Ottoman Rural Context (1839–1923)' (Istanbul: Boğaziçi University, 2016). On the mobility and 'success' of Orthodox and Greek-speaking Cappadocians.
18 League of Nations Archives, Geneva [henceforth, LONA], Private papers of Thanassis Aghnides, Folder 1 [henceforth, P1], Curriculum Vitae.
19 LONA, P1, Thanassis Aghnides. Notice Biographique.
20 Recorded interview with Rika Aghnides. Conducted by Markos A. Bouketsidis-Skourtelis, 14 September 2019.
21 'Water Faucet: Miniature Aerating Plant Makes Tap Water Foamy and Splashless' *Life*, 5 August 1946; Nicholas P. Aghnides, *Mohammedan Theories of Finance. Studies in History, Economics, and Public Law. Columbia University* (New York: Long, Green and co., 1916).

22 Archives nationales [France] – Pierrefitte sur Seine – FACULTE DE DROIT – Fiches individuelles de scolarité des étudiants nés avant 1905, AJ/16/1806. AARNOUG – ALLEZAUD. An indication of this is his slipping grades.
23 Thanassis Aghnides, 'Vladimir Rosing and Greek Music', *The Musical Times*, 1 June 1918.
24 Michael Llewellyn Smith, ''Venizelos' Diplomacy, 1910–1923: From Balkan Alliance to Greek-Turkish Settlement', in *Eleftherios Venizelos. The Trials of Statesmanship*, ed. Paschalis M. Kitromilides (Edinburgh: Edinburgh University Press, 2008), 134–92.
25 Thanassis Aghnides, 'Greek Art Itself Again', *The New World*, n.d.
26 Smith, 'Venizelos' Diplomacy', 137–8.
27 LONA, P273, 'Interview with Thanassis Aghnides' (Geneva: Centre de Reserches sur les institutions internationales, 1966), 3.
28 See Thanassis Aghnides, *La Méditerranée orientale: revue-bi-mensuelle politique, historique, scientifique*, 1917–18.
29 LONA, [Personnel Files] S699-700, 'My Dear Drummond', British Delegation, Paris, 4 July 1919, H. Nicolson.
30 This paragraph builds largely on Karen Gram-Skjoldager and Haakon A. Ikonomou, 'Making Sense of the League of Nations – Historiographical and Conceptual Reflections on Early International Public Administration', *European History Quarterly* 49, no. 3 (2019): 420–44.
31 Particularly, international law, in which many career diplomats had training, was a central educational expertise that would shape the professional culture of the League, the role of its employees and how global governance was articulated and practised. Martti Koskenniemi, 'History of International Law, World War I to World War II', in *Max Plank Encyclopedia of Public International Law*, ed. Rüdiger Wolfrum, online edition (Oxford: Oxford University Press, 2011). The rest were two political scientists, one economist, three with other backgrounds (army, theology and classics), while two are unknown. Five out of five directors were diplomats, three of them also holding a law degree. Karen Gram-Skjoldager, Haakon A. Ikonomou, and Torsten Kahlert, 'Scandinavians and the League of Nations Secretariat, 1919–1946', *Scandinavian Journal of History* 44, no. 4 (2019): 453–83.
32 Mark Mazower, 'Minorities and the League of Nations in Interwar Europe', *Daedalus* 126, no. 2 (1997): 47–63, 50–1.
33 Gram-Skjoldager and Ikonomou, 'Making Sense of the League of Nations', 435–6.
34 Gram-Skjoldager, Ikonomou and Kahlert, 'Scandinavians in the League of Nations'; Susan Pedersen, 'Back to the League', *The American History Review* 112, no. 4 (2007): 1091–117; LONA, [Section Files] S956, Minutes: 1st Appointment Committee Meeting [henceforth AC-Meeting], 19 January 1928; S954-1, Minutes, 10th AC-Meeting, 03 August 1922.
35 LONA, P1, 22 September 1919, Dear Politis (Mr. Minister), from Aghnides; LONA, P1, 23 July 1919, My dear Nicolson, from Eric Drummond.

36 Haakon A. Ikonomou, '"He Used to Give Me Turkish Lessons in Constantinople": How to Get a Job in the League Secretariat', in *The League of Nations: Perspectives from the Present*, ed. Haakon A. Ikonomou and Karen Gram-Skjoldager (Aarhus: Aarhus University Press, 2019).
37 Michael Goebel, *Anti-imperial Metropolis: Interwar Paris and the Seeds of Third World Nationalism* (Cambridge: Cambridge University Press, 2015).
38 Volker Prott, *The Politics of Self-determination. Remaking Territories and National Identities in Europe, 1917–1923* (Oxford: Oxford University Press, 2016), 83–112, 180–211.
39 For a diplomatic history analysis of the population exchange, see Onur Yildirim, *Diplomacy and Displacement Reconsidering the Turco-Greek Exchange of Populations, 1922–1934* (London: Routledge, 2006); for legal-historical analysis of population transfers, see Umut Özsu, *Formalizing Displacement: International Law and Population Transfers* (Oxford: Oxford University Press, 2015).
40 Mads Drange, 'Supervisor, Facilitator and Arbitrator. A Study of the Minority Department in the League of Nations Involvement in the Forced Population Exchange between Greece and Turkey in 1923', MA diss. (Oslo: University of Oslo, 2017).
41 LONA, S954, 03 August 1922, Monnet's Office.
42 LONA, S699, 22 November 1928, Memorandum, Eric Drummond. Due to the contested nature of the many similar disputes in Eastern Europe, these also fell to him, as he was of a 'neutral' nationality, without any evident vested interests. 'Convention Between Greece and Bulgaria Respecting Reciprocal Emigration', 27 November 1919, in *AJIL* 14, Supplement, Official Documents (1920): 356–60. See Leonard V. Smith, *Sovereignty at the Paris Peace Conference of 1919* (Oxford: Oxford University Press, 2018), 179–4.
43 A part of the Political Section's role is explained in the following memorandum: LONA, S699, 22 November 1928, Thanassis Aghnides. Memorandum, Eric Drummond. The coordination between the various sections is explored in LONA, Directors' Meeting, 25 February 1924, the treaties of Lausanne. Note by the secretary-general and Memorandum by Dr Van Hamel. Geneva.
44 This is based on an overview of the correspondence of Aghnides regarding this matter in his Personal Archives kept by the League of Nations Archives in Geneva and the digital Venizelos Archives.
45 Venizelos Archives [henceforth, VA], 23 January 1923, League of Nations, Geneva. To Michalopoulos, from Aghnides (translation from Greek).
46 VA, 18 October 1922, League of Nations, Geneva. To Venizelos, from Aghnides (translation from Greek).
47 VA, 17 November 1922, League of Nations, Geneva. To Venizelos, from Aghnides (translation from Greek).
48 Smith, 'Venizelos' Diplomacy'.
49 Aghnides forwarded his correspondence with Venizelos, including English translations, and that statesman's recommendation, to William McGrew, with

explanatory notes, 29 September and 25 October 1977, Anatolia College Archives [henceforth ACA]. McGrew, *Educating Across Cultures*, 190–1, 445. William McGrew has been so kind as to forward his correspondence with Aghnides to me. For this I am thankful.
50. McGrew, *Educating across Cultures*, 190–1.
51. William McGrew's Archives [henceforth, WMA], 25 October 1977 Aghnides to McGrew.
52. John O. Iatrides, 'Missionary Educators and the Asia Minor Disaster: Anatolia College's Move to Greece', *Journal of Modern Greek Studies* 4, no. 2 (October 1986): 143–57.
53. LONA, [Registry Files] R1600, 19 June 1924, Voyage de M. Aghnides en Grèce, 25 June 1924. He also helped set up the official Greek League of Nations Associations at the University of Athens while on his brief visit.
54. LONA, R1600, 19 June 1924, Voyage de M. Aghnides en Grèce, 25 June 1924.
55. LONA, P1, 22 November 1928, Memorandum regarding Aghnides, by director Sugimura (Political Section). In this memorandum director Sugimura goes quite far in saying that Aghnides is overburdened with responsibilities due to the above-mentioned situation.
56. LONA, P1, 22 September 1919, Dear Politis (Mr. Minister), from Aghnides.
57. VA, 2 February 1923, League of Nations, Geneva, to Michalopoulos, from Aghnides (translation from Greek). He mentioned Rachel Crowdy as an example of these 'not so important' officials.
58. VA, 2 February 1923, League of Nations, Geneva, To Michalopoulos, from Aghnides (translation from Greek).
59. VA, 7 February 1923, League of Nations, Geneva, Mr. Minister, from Aghnides (translation from Greek).
60. LONA, P1, 4 May 1924, Bern, To Aghnides.
61. This would increasingly be the case with the Italian officials of the League Secretariat. Elisabetta Tollardo, *Fascist Italy and the League of Nations, 1922–1935* (London: Palgrave Macmillan, 2016).
62. LONA, P1, 22 April 1926, to Aghnides, from the foreign minister [Loukas Kanakaris-Roufos].

Chapter 4

1. Sarah Wambaugh, 'League Work from Inside', *The New York Times*, 14 August 1921.
2. Patricia Clavin, *Securing the World Economy: The Reinvention of the League of Nations, 1920–1946* (Oxford: Oxford University Press, 2013); Amy L. Sayward, *The United Nations in International History* (London: Bloomsbury Academic, 2017).

3   The database can be found at http://www.lonsea.de (accessed 8 August 2020). I would like to thank Madeleine Herren and her team for providing a copy of the database LONSEA.
4   https://www.r-project.org/ (accessed 8 August 2020). The code for some of the calculations is publicly available via github: (digitaltxtlab/LONSEA_DB). For the data cleaning, openrefine (http://openrefine.org/, accessed 8 August 2020) and Microsoft Excel have been used. Some calculations were done with Excel. Visualizations were done using Excel, R studio and shiny app, a visualization tool based on R. I would like to thank Kristoffer Neilbo and Adam Finnemann for setting up the virtual environment and assistance in the statistical calculations.
5   A similar prosopographical study by the author of this article focused only on the section directors: Torsten Kahlert, 'Pioneers in International Administration: A Prosopography of the Directors of the League of Nations Secretariat,' *New Global Studies* 13, no. 2 (2019): 190–227.
6   For a detailed account on the structure of the secretariat see Egon Ranshofen-Wertheimer, *The International Secretariat: A Great Experiment in International Administration* (Washington: Carnegie Endowment for International Peace, 1945).
7   The category of the so-called 'Temporary Collaborators' was excluded from the set, because they usually stayed only for periods of not more than three months and were not actual employees of the secretariat. See Emil Seidenfaden's chapter for more detailed information.
8   Elisabetta Tollardo, *Fascist Italy and the League of Nations, 1922–1935* (London: Palgrave Macmillan, 2016).
9   LONA, PF Fritz Schnabel. Schnabel went to South America in 1939 to study the publishing market and henceforth lived in Argentina until he died in 1948.
10 Entry LONSEA Morikatsu Inagaki. Inagaki was also active after the Second World War as an internationalist, for example against the 'Bomb'. He was also the leader of the World Federal Government movement in Japan. See Lawrence S. Wittner, *The Struggle against the Bomb* (Stanford University Press, 1993), 51f, 168.
11 The question, how international the secretariat actually was, has been tackled also by Klaas Dykmann, 'How International Was the Secretariat of the League of Nations?,' *The International History Review* 37, no. 4 (8 August 2015): 721–44.
12 Critique concerning the composition of the secretariat was put forward by South American, Asian and also smaller European member states. The publication of complete lists of appointed personnel was first demanded by the Japanese representative Tanetarō Megata. European representatives demanded more competition in the selection process. For references see Thomas Fischer, *Die Souveränität der Schwachen: Lateinamerika und der Völkerbund, 1920–1936* (Wiesbaden: Steiner, 2012), 191.
13 Karen Gram-Skjoldager and Haakon A. Ikonomou, 'The Construction of the League of Nations Secretariat. Formative Practices of Autonomy and Legitimacy in International Organizations,' *The International History Review*, 21 December 2017, 1–23.

14 Other nationalities with less than 1 per cent of first division officials were Luxembourgish, Finish, Greek, Lithuanian, New Zealander, Argentine, Portuguese, Turkish, Uruguayan, Chilean, Latvian, Iranian, South African, stateless, Venezuelan, Albanian, Bulgarian, Columbian, Panamanian, Brazilian, Cuban, Dominican, Estonian, Mexican, Thai, three officials with multiple nationality.
15 Gram-Skjoldager / Ikonomou, Construction, 1–23.
16 LONA, Appointments Committee, Box S954, Minutes of the Seventh Meeting of the Appointments Committee, held on 6 June and the Tenth Meeting, held on 3 August 1922.
17 Out of many publications of this research field, Jürgen Osterhammel, *The Transformation of the World. A Global History of the Nineteenth Century* (Princeton: Princeton University Press, 2014).
18 For more details on the recruitment of Hammarsköld and the Scandinavians in the secretariat see Karen Gram-Skjoldager, Haakon A. Ikonomou, and Torsten Kahlert, 'Scandinavians and the League of Nations Secretariat, 1919–1946', *Scandinavian Journal of History* 44, no. 4 (8 August 2019): 454–83.
19 LONA, Appointments Committee, Box S954, Minutes of the Seventh Meeting of the Appointments Committee, held on 6 June 1923.
20 Ibid.
21 LONA, Appointments Committee, Box S955, 18 November 1926 letter from Ignaz Seipel to Eric Drummond.
22 Akten Auswärtiges Amt Berlin, R96860, Organisation des Sekretariats, 1923–8, Bd. 2.
23 Akten des Auswärtigen Amtes, R96802, Personal. Deutsche Vertreter im Generalsekretariat 1922–5, Bd.1.
24 See the lists of personnel from 1928 in LONA, Liste du Personnel au Secretariat 1920–38. Under-secretary-general became Albert Dufour-Féronce, the former German ambassador in London. See also LONA, Personnel File: Dufour-Féronce.
25 This was the normal procedure, as the German Foreign Minister Gustav Stresemann wanted all higher posts to be controlled by the Foreign Ministry. See Akten Auswärtiges Amt Berlin, R96854, Bewerbungen allgemeines, memo Gustav Stresemann 21 October 1926.
26 LONA, Personnel File: Schnabel, Memo of Zilliacus to Secretary General, 11 December 1926.
27 LONA, Appointments Committee, 19 February 1927.
28 LONA, Appointments Committee, 5 March 1927.
29 'The Covenant of the League of Nations' (including Amendments adopted to December 1924), Avalon Project, Yale Law School: https://avalon.law.yale.edu/20th_century/leagcov.asp (accessed 6 April 2020).
30 For the larger second division (2406 employees), the distribution was almost the other way around: 35 per cent male vs 65 per cent female employees. The second division comprised all the secretaries and short-hand typists, which were almost all women.

31 Carol Ann Miller, 'Lobbying the League' (unpublished PhD thesis, University of Oxford, 1992).
32 LONA Personnel File: Hammarskjöld, note by Joost van Hamel, 23 July 1919.
33 Myriam Piguet, 'Gender Distribution in the League of Nations,' in *The League of Nations. Perspectives from the Present*, ed. Haakon A. Ikonomou and Karen Gram-Skjoldager (Aarhus: Aarhus University Press, 2019), 62–71.
34 LONA Personnel File: Adamowicz, Rajchman to Miss Dudgeon, 27 February 1921.
35 LONA Personnel File: Adamowicz, Sydenstricker to Rajchman, 12 February 1923.
36 For more on her biography and career see Iwona Dadej, *Beruf und Berufung transnational. Deusche und polnische Akademikerinnen in der Zwischenkriegszeit* (Osnabrück: fibre, 2019); Katharina Kreuder-Sonnen, *Wie man Mikroben auf Reisen schickt: zirkulierendes bakteriologisches Wissen und die polnische Medizin 1885–1939*, Historische Wissensforschung 9 (Tübingen: Mohr Siebeck, 2018).
37 Piguet, 'Gender Distribution'. See also Madeleine Herren, 'Gender and International Relations through the Lens of the League of Nations (1919–1945)' in *Women, Diplomacy and International Politics since 1500*, ed. Glenda Sluga and Carolyn James (London: Routledge, 2016), 182–201.
38 Piguet, 'Gender Distribution', 69.
39 LONA, Personnel File Radziwill and Appointments Committee, Box S955, Memo by Pierre Comert, Chairman of the Appointments Committee, 26 November 1926.
40 The graph has been processed in different discrete steps. First, all 150 job categories of the secretariat have been ordered into a hierarchical status list between one as highest and nine as lowest job category. This list has been related with the LONSEA data of job categories, gender and time so that it becomes possible to visualize continuity and changes over time in the gender and status distribution over time.
41 LONA, Personnel File: Chatterjee.
42 LONA, Personnel File: Madariaga.
43 Thomas Nitzsche, *Salvador de Madariaga: Liberaler – Spanier – Weltbürger. Der Weg eines politischen Intellektuellen durch das Europa des 20. Jahrhunderts* (Baden-Baden: Nomos, 2009).
44 LONA, Personnel File: Gerig.
45 LONA, Personnel File Ranshofen Wertheimer. See also Tamara Rachbauer, *Egon Ranshofen-Wertheimer: Chronologie eines bewegten Lebens* (München: GRIN, 2008).
46 LONA, Personnel File Krabbe. See also Gram-Skjoldager, Ikonomou and Kahlert, 'Scandinavians'.
47 LONA, Personnel File: Arocha.
48 LONA, Personnel File: Nogueria.
49 LONA, Personnel File: Felkin.
50 William B McAllister, *Drug Diplomacy in the Twentieth Century an International History*, 2000.

51 LONA, Personnel File: Stencek. Letter from Frank Horsfall Nixon to Vilem Pospisil, 13 April 1921.
52 LONA, Personnel File: Stencek.
53 Torsten Kahlert '"The League Is Dead, Long Live the United Nations". The Liquidation of the League and the Transfer of Assets to the UN', in *The League of Nations. Perspectives from the Present*, ed. Haakon A. Ikonomou and Karen Gram-Skjoldager (Aarhus: Aarhus University Press, 2019), 254–64.
54 An investigation of the transfer of personnel from the League of Nations Secretariat (especially the Princeton team) to the UN secretariat is still missing, but there are first accounts. See for example the chapters of Haakon A. Ikonomou on the biography of Thanassis Aghnides and the chapter of Emil Seidenfaden on the leadership staff of the Information Section in this volume.
55 LONA, Personnel File: Rosenborg, Lester to Rosenborg, 8 April 1946.
56 LONA, Personnel File: Rosenborg, Telegram from Rosenborg to Lester, 23 April 1946.
57 *The New York Times*, 19 May 1976, p. 36.
58 LONA, Personnel File: Biraud.
59 Iris Borowy, 'Maneuvering for Space. International Health Work of the League of Nations during World War II', in *Shifting Boundaries of Public Health: Europe in the Twentieth Century*, ed. Susan Gross Solomon, Lion Murard, and Patrick Zylberman (Rochester: University of Rochester Press, 2008), 91ff.
60 LONA, Personnel File: Key-Rasmussen/Lehmann, Avenol to Lehmann, 14 April 1939.
61 LONA, Personnel File: Key-Rasmussen/Lehmann, Lehmann to Stencek, 4 February 1941.
62 LONA, Personnel File: Key-Rasmussen/Lehmann, Stencek to Key-Rasmussen, 29 August 1947.
63 Nuffield college was a rather new college. It had been founded in 1937. It offered a postgraduate education with a specialization in social and political sciences, economics and industrial relations.
64 That reintegration of British officials was rather typical is supported by Katharina Erdmenger, *Diener zweier Herren? Briten im Sekretariat des Völkerbundes 1919–1933* (Baden Baden: Nomos, 1998).

Chapter 5

1 D. D. Avant, M. Finnemore and S. K. Sell (eds.), *Who Governs the Globe?* Cambridge, UK; New York: Cambridge University Press, 2010.
2 R. Gorur, 'Seeing like PISA: A Cautionary Tale about the Performativity of International Assessments', *European Educational Research Journal* 15, no. 5

(2016): 598–616; S. Sellar and B. Lingard, 'The OECD and the Expansion of PISA: New Global Modes of Governance in Education', *British Educational Research Journal* 40, no. 6 (2014): 917–36.

3   M. Elfert, *UNESCO's Utopia of Lifelong Learning: An Intellectual History. Routledge Research in Education Series* (New York: Routledge, 2018); K. Hüfner, 'The Human Rights Approach to Education in International Organisations', *European Journal of Education* 46, no. 1 (2011): 117–26.

4   R. Bürgi, 'Engineering the Free World: The Emergence of the OECD as an Actor in Education Policy, 1957-1972', in *The OECD and the International Political Economy since 1948*, ed. M. Leimgruber and M. Schmelzer (Cham: Springer International Publishing, 2017a), 285–309.

5   C. S. Asher, 'The Development of UNESCO's Program', *International Organization* 4, no. 1 (1950): 12–26, 19.

6   Elfert, *UNESCO's Utopia of Lifelong Learning*.

7   N. Gilman, *Mandarins of the Future. Modernization Theory in Cold War America* (Baltimore and London: The Johns Hopkins University Press, 2003), 7–8.

8   D. W. Ellwood, 'The Marshall Plan and the Politics of Growth', in *OECD Historical Series: Explorations in OEEC History*, ed. R. T. Griffiths (Paris: OECD, 1997), 99–107, 101.

9   T. Judt, *Postwar. A History of Europe since 1945* (New York: Penguin Books, 2005), 93.

10 Bürgi, 'Engineering the free world', 285–309; R. Bürgi, *Die OECD und die Bildungsplanung der freien Welt. Denkstile und Netzwerke einer internationalen Bildungsexpertise*. Promotion 7. (Opladen, Berlin & Toronto: Verlag Barbara Budrich, 2017b); M. Elfert, 'The OECD, American Power, and the Rise of the "Economics of Education"', in *The OECD's Historical Rise in Education: The Formation of a Global Governing Complex*, ed. C. Ydesen (New York: Palgrave Macmillan, 2019), 39–61.

11 B. Boel, *The European Productivity Agency and Transatlantic Relations, 1953–1961* (Copenhagen: Museum Tusculanum Press, 2003), 49; (Boel, *The European Productivity Agency*, 49; Bürgi 2019).

12 Bürgi, 'Engineering the Free World', 288.

13 Boel, *The European Productivity Agency*, 115.

14 A. King, *Let the Cat Turn Around. One Man's Traverse of the Twentieth Century* (London: CPTM, 2006).

15 K. Eide, '30 Years of Educational Collaboration in the OECD. International Congress "Planning and Management of Educational Development"', Mexico, 26–30 March 1990', 1990. Cited by Bürgi, *Die OECD*, 74.

16 R. Bürgi, 'Learning Productivity: The EPA – An Educational Enterprise', in *The OECD and the Rise of the Economic Paradigm in Education*, ed. C. Ydesen (New York: Palgrave Macmillan, 2019), 17–37; King, *Let the Cat Turn Around*, 233.

17 Bürgi, 'Learning productivity'.
18 R. Gass, 'The OECD as a "culture", as seen by an "old timer"', *@tmosphere* (2002 October), 10.
19 King, *Let the Cat Turn Around*, 198.
20 Ibid., 203.
21 Ron Gass, personal communication, 22 August 2017. Ron Gass joined the OEEC in 1958 and worked for the OECD until his retirement in 1989. He was the first director of the OECD's Centre for Educational Research and Innovation (CERI).
22 Louis Emmerij, personal communication, 29 December 2018. Louis Emmerij was hired by Ron Gass to work on the Mediterranean Regional Project (MRP) in the early 1960s. In 1986, he was appointed president of the OECD's Development Centre. Between 1971 and 1976, he headed the World Employment Programme at the International Labour Organization.
23 Elfert, *UNESCO's Utopia of Lifelong Learning*.
24 P. Selcer, 'Patterns of Science: Developing Knowledge for a World Community at UNESCO' (University of Pennsylvania Dissertation, paper 323, 2011), 161.
25 Elfert, *UNESCO's Utopia of Lifelong Learning*; G. Sluga, 'UNESCO and the (one) World of Julian Huxley', *Journal of World History* 21, no. 3 (2010): 393–418.
26 W. H. C. Laves and C. A. Thomson, *UNESCO: Purpose, Progress, Prospects* (Bloomington: Indiana University Press, 1957).
27 S. Gil-Riaño, 'Perturbed by "race": Antiracism, Science, and Education in UNESCO during the Cold War', in *UNESCO without Borders: Educational Campaigns for International Understanding*, ed. A. Kulnazarova and C. Ydesen (London: Routledge Press, 2016), 203–19.
28 P. Duedahl, 'Selling Mankind: UNESCO and the Invention of Global History', *Journal of World History* 22, no. 1 (2011): 101–33.
29 Selcer, 'Patterns of science', iv.
30 Elfert, *UNESCO's Utopia of Lifelong Learning*; J. P. Sewell, *UNESCO and World Politics* (Princeton, NJ: Princeton University Press, 1975).
31 Elfert, *UNESCO's Utopia of Lifelong Learning*.
32 Both René Maheu and Jacques Havet joined UNESCO in 1946. Havet was the head of UNESCO's Philosophy and Humanistic Studies division. Between 1947 and 1948, he coordinated the *Comité sur les principes philosophiques des droits de l'homme* ('Committee on the problem of the philosophical basis for an international declaration of the Rights of Man'), an inquiry among philosophers and influential thinkers into the origins and philosophic bases of human rights (Goodale, 2017). Maheu held the position of director general of the organization from 1962 to 1974.
33 P. Lengrand, *Le métier de vivre*, in Collection Histoires de vie, Série Histoire de vie d'acteurs (Paris: Peuple et Culture – Éducation permanente, 1994); Elfert, *UNESCO's Utopia of Lifelong Learning*.
34 Ibid., 105. All translations are made by the authors unless otherwise stated.

35 Elfert, *UNESCO's Utopia of Lifelong Learning*.
36 Organisation for Economic Co-operation and Development (OECD), *Policy Conference on Economic Growth and Investment in Education. Washington 16th–20th October 1961* (Paris: OECD Publishing, 1961), 35.
37 R. Mahon, 'In Conversation with Ron Gass: The OECD and the Crisis of Progress', *Global Social Policy* 15, no. 2 (2015): 113–24, 116.
38 R. H. Winnick, *Letters of Archibald MacLeish: 1907 to 1982* (Boston: Houghton Mifflin Company, 1983), 339.
39 G. Archibald, *Les États-Unis et l'UNESCO 1944–1963* (Paris: Publications de la Sorbonne, 1993).
40 I. Düssel and C. Ydesen, 'Jaime Torres Bodet and the Struggle over History Writing of the Americas: The Mexican Experience', in *UNESCO without Borders: Educational Campaigns for International Understanding. Routledge Research in Education Series*, ed. A. Kulnazarova and C. Ydesen (Oxford, UK: Routledge, 2016a), 197–221; Archibald, *Les États-Unis*.
41 Laves and Thomson, *UNESCO: Purpose, Progress, Prospects*.
42 Sewell, *UNESCO and World Politics*, 161. One of the reasons why the US government did not support Evans's appointment was that the president of the United States, Dwight D. Eisenhower, was a Republican, while Evans was a Democrat (Archibald 1993: 154).
43 Rockefeller Foundation. 'Memo "JM". UNESCO General Conference. Paris – second week. 17 November to 22 November 1952. Rockefeller Foundation Records. Field offices, RG6, SG1. Series 2: Post-war, sub-series 01: Post-war correspondence. FA# 395, Box 69, Folder 667 (General – Unesco), 1952–1958'. Rockefeller Archive Center, 1952.
44 Ibid.
45 Archibald, *Les États-Unis*.
46 Ibid.
47 C. Dorn and K. Ghodsee, 'Cold War Politicization of Literacy: Communism, UNESCO and the World Bank', *Diplomatic History* 36, no. 2 (2012): 373–98.
48 R. J. Hart, 'Battling minds: Conservatives, progressives, and UNESCO in postwar United States', in *UNESCO without Borders: Educational Campaigns for International Understanding. Routledge Research in Education Series*, ed. A. Kulnazarova and C. Ydesen (Oxford, UK: Routledge, 2016), 35–52.
49 C. Morel, 'Le rêve d'un "gouvernement mondial" des années 1920 aux années 1950. L'exemple de l'Unesco', *Histoire@Politique* 10 (2010): 1–18, 10.
50 Elfert, *UNESCO's Utopia of Lifelong Learning*, 17. Citing Weindling 2010.
51 M. Schmelzer, 'A Club of the Rich to Help the Poor? The OECD, "development", and the Hegemony of Donor Countries', in *International Organizations and Development, 1945–1990. Palgrave Macmillan Transnational History Series*, ed. M. Frey, S. Kunkel and C. R. Unger (London: Palgrave Macmillan, 2014), 171–95.

52 U.S. National Commission. 'Newsletter, 13 July 1956, Vol. III No. 11'. Washington, DC: US National Archives, 1956, 2.
53 U.S. Department of Health, Education and Welfare. 'Letter to the Secretary of State from Nelson A. Rockefeller, 12 April 1954. RG 12 Records of the Office of Education. Office of the Commissioner 1939–1980. Education Missions Advisory Board, 1952–54. Box 37'. Washington, DC: US National Archives, 1954.
54 C. Ydesen, 'Debating International Understanding in the Western World: The American Approach to UNESCO's Educational Campaigns, 1946–54', in *UNESCO without Borders: Educational Campaigns for International Understanding. Routledge Research in Education Series*, ed. A. Kulnazarova and C. Ydesen (Oxford, UK: Routledge, 2016), 239–55.
55 Dr Clarence Edward Beeby served as UNESCO's first assistant director general for education.
56 Ydesen, 'Debating International', 246.
57 R. Faure, 'Connections in the History of Textbook Revision, 1947–1952', *Education Inquiry* 2, no. 1 (2011): 21–35, 31.
58 M. Goodale, 'UNESCO and the United Nations Rights of Man Declaration: History, Historiography, Ideology', *Humanity: An International Journal of Human Rights, Humanitarianism, and Development* 8, no. 1 (2017): 29–47, 43.
59 King, *Let the Cat Turn Around*; G. S. Papadopoulos, *Education 1960–1990. The OECD Perspective. OECD Historical Series* (Paris: Organisation for Economic Co-operation and Development, 1994).
60 R. Bürgi, 'Systemic Management of Schools: The OECD's Professionalisation and Dissemination of Output Governance in the 1960s', *Paedagogica Historica* 52, no. 4 (2016): 408–22.
61 T. W. Schultz, *The Economic Value of Education* (New York: Columbia University Press, 1963); G. S. Becker, *Human Capital: A Theoretical and Empirical Analysis, With Special Reference to Education* (New York: National Bureau of Economic Research, 1964).
62 P. Murray, '"Can I write to you about Ireland?": John Vaizey, the Ford Foundation and Irish Educational Policy Change, 1959–1962 [document study]', *Irish Educational Studies* 31, no. 1 (2012): 67–75.
63 Office Files of the Commissioner of Education, 'Memo to Mr. Francis Keppel regarding relation of OECD activities to Office of Education, RG 12, Entry No. A1122. Box 531' (Washington, DC: U.S. National Archives, 1963).
64 Ibid.
65 In 1961 Philip Coombs became the first secretary of state for Educational and Cultural Affairs in the administration of President John F. Kennedy. Coombs represents like no other the intersections and entanglements between the US government, philanthropic foundations and the newly created IOs.

66 M. Schmelzer, *The Hegemony of Growth. The OECD and the Making of the Economic Growth Paradigm* (Cambridge: Cambridge University Press, 2016), 39–40.
67 Ron Gass, personal communication, 22 August 2017.
68 G. Benveniste, 'Creation of the International Institute for Educational Planning', *Educational Planning* 16, no. 3 (2007): 1–9.
69 Bürgi, *Die OECD*.
70 Benveniste, 'Creation of the International', 3.
71 Schmelzer, 'A Club of the Rich'.
72 Cited in M. Leimgruber and M. Schmelzer, 'From the Marshall Plan to global governance: Historical transformations of the OEEC/OECD, 1948 to present', in *The OECD and the International Political Economy since 1948*, ed. M. Leimgruber and M. Schmelzer (Cham: Springer International Publishing, 2017), 23–61, 44.
73 Bürgi, 'Systemic Management of Schools'.
74 J. A. Kershaw and N. M. Roland, *Systems Analysis and Education* (Santa Monica, CA: RAND Corporation, 1959), iii–iv.
75 R. Lyons, 'The OECD Mediterranean Regional Project', *The American Economist* 8, no. 2 (1964/65): 11–22, 12.
76 Bürgi, 'Systemic Management of Schools', 416.
77 Boel, *The European Productivity Agency*.
78 Elfert, *UNESCO's Utopia of Lifelong Learning*, 97.
79 UNESCO, 'Fundamental Education. Description and Programme', in *Monographs on Fundamental Education, I* (Paris: UNESCO, 1949b), 12.
80 UNESCO, 'Relations avec l'O.E.C.E. À M. Malcolm S. Adiseshiah, Director General. De Paul Bertrand, Chef de la Division des relations avec les Organisations internationales. ODG/RIO/Memo.24.903' (Paris: UNESCO Archives, 1961, 29 September), 6.
81 UNESCO, 'Relations avec l'O.E.C.E.'.
82 Cited in C. Ydesen and S. Grek, 'Securing Organisational Survival – A Historical inquiry into the Configurations and Positions of the OECD's Work in Education during the 1960s', *Paedagogica Historica* 56, no. 3 (2019): 412–27, 421–22.
83 Cited in Ydesen and Grek, 'Securing Organisational Survival', 12.
84 OEEC, *Investment in Education and Economic Growth* (Paris: OEEC, 1960a), 5.
85 K. Mundy, 'Educational Multilateralism in a Changing World Order: UNESCO and the Limits of the Possible', *International Journal of Educational Development* 19 (1999): 27–52.
86 UNESCO, 'Records of the General Conference of the United Nations Educational, Scientific and Cultural Organization, Fourth session, Paris 1949', Resolutions, November 1949a, 14.
87 UNESCO, *50 Years for Education* (Paris: UNESCO, 1997).
88 U.S. Office of Education, 'Proposed Programme and Budget – 1961–1962, Part II, dated 15 September 1960, RG 12 Records of the Office of Education, Office of the

Commissioner 1939–1980, Education Missions Advisory Board, 1952–54, Box 37' (Washington, DC: US National Archives, 1960).

89 C. A. Anderson, *A Critique of the UNESCO Statistical Program*. Ford Foundation, Series I: Subject Files, FA# 608, Box 7 (Rockefeller Archive Center, 1959).

90 M. Elfert, 'Six Decades of Educational Multilateralism in a Globalising World: The History of the UNESCO Institute in Hamburg', *International Review of Education* 59, no. 2 (2013): 263–87; G. Landsheere, 'IEA and UNESCO: A History of Working Co-Operation'. Paper on the accompanying CD to the UNESCO publication *50 Years for Education*. Paris: UNESCO, 1997.

91 J. Landahl, 'Small-Scale Community, Large-Scale Assessment: IEA as a Transnational Network', Conference paper presented at the European Conference for Educational Research (ECER) in Copenhagen, Denmark, 22–25 August 2017.

92 J. Keeves, 'IEA – From the Beginning in 1958 to 1990', in *IEA 1958–2008: 50 Years of Experiences and Memories*, ed. C. Papanastasiou, T. Plomp and E. C. Papanastasiou (Amsterdam: The International Association for the Evaluation of Educational Achievement, 2011), 3–40; Landsheere, 'IEA and UNESCO'. The 12-country study ran between 1959 and 1962, and included Belgium, England, Finland, France, the Federal Republic of Germany, Israel, Poland, Scotland, Sweden, Switzerland, the United States and Yugoslavia. According to Landsheere (1997), some 10,000 children of age 13:0 to 13:11, speaking eight different languages, were tested in reading comprehension, mathematics, science, geography and non-verbal ability.

93 Keeves, 'IEA'.

94 D. Pettersson, 'The Development of the IEA: The Rise of Large-Scale Testing', in *Transnational Policy Flows in European Education. The Making and Governing of Knowledge in the Education Policy Field. Oxford Studies in Comparative Education*, ed. A. Nordin and D. Sundberg (Oxford, UK: Symposium Books, 2014), 105–22, 114.

95 The education for peace components were *International Textbook Revision* (1946), *Atoms for Peace* (1946), *Education for Living in a World Community* (1947), *Education in Great Issues Related to Peace and Advancement* (1953), and *Major Project on the Mutual Appreciation of Eastern and Western Cultural Values* (1956) (UNESCO 1965).

96 A. Kulnazarova and C. Ydesen, 'The Nature and Methodology of UNESCO's Educational Campaigns', in *UNESCO without Borders: Educational Campaigns for International Understanding. Routledge Research in Education Series*, ed. A. Kulnazarova and C. Ydesen (Oxford, UK: Routledge, 2016), 1–14.

97 I. Düssel and C. Ydesen, 'UNESCO and the Improvement of History Textbooks in Mexico, 1945–1960', in *The History of UNESCO: Global Actions and Impacts*, ed. P. Duedahl (New York: Palgrave Macmillan, 2016b), 231–56; Laves and Thomson, *UNESCO: Purpose, Progress, Prospects*.

98 J. Watras, 'Was Fundamental Education Another Form of Colonialism?' *International Review of Education* 53, no. 1 (2007): 55–72, 71.
99 M. Carnoy, *Transforming Comparative Education: Fifty Years of Theory Building at Stanford* (Stanford, CA: Stanford University Press, 2019), 4.
100 Bürgi, 'Systemic Management of Schools', 416.
101 F. Fukuyama, 'What Is Governance? Commentary', *Governance* 26, no. 3 (2013): 347–68; F. W. Scharpf, *Governing in Europe: Effective and Democratic?* (Oxford, UK: Oxford University Press, 1999).
102 M. B. Henry, B. Lingard, F. Rizvi and S. Taylor, *The OECD, Globalisation and Education Policy* (Oxford, UK: Pergamon, 2001), 119.
103 Cited in Bürgi, 'Engineering the Free World', 299.
104 Elfert, *UNESCO's Utopia of Lifelong Learning*, 220.
105 R. Woodward, 'The Organisation for Economic Cooperation and Development (OECD)', in *Global Institutions Series* (New York: Routledge, 2009), 6.
106 K. Rubenson, 'OECD Education Policies and World Hegemony', in *The OECD and Transnational Governance*, ed. R. Mahon and S. McBride (Vancouver: UBC Press, 2008), 241–59, 244.
107 Henry et al., *The OECD*, 2.
108 R. Gass, 'Speaking Truth to Power. Reflections on the Future of the OECD', *OECD Observer* (January 2013), para. 3.
109 The United States returned to UNESCO in 2002, but officially left UNESCO again on 31 December 2018.
110 A. P. Jakobi, *International Organizations and Lifelong Learning: From Global Agendas to Policy Diffusion* (London: Palgrave Macmillan, 2009); Ron Gass, personal communication, 22 August 2017.
111 Klaus Hüfner, personal communication, 4 July 2014. Klaus Hüfner, Professor Emeritus, Freie Universität Berlin, worked in the OECD/CERI in the early 1970s, has served on many UNESCO committees and boards and has written several books about UNESCO and the UN system.

Chapter 6

1 The author of this chapter is also guilty of this charge: Katja Seidel, *The Process of Politics in Europe: The Rise of European Elites and Supranational Institutions* (London: I.B. Tauris, 2010); David Coombes, *Politics and Bureaucracy in the European Community* (London: Allen and Unwin, 1969); Spierenburg, Poidevin, *The History of the High Authority of the European Coal and Steel Community* (London: Weidenfeld & Nicolson, 1994).

2   Mark Mazower, *Governing the World: The History of an Idea. 1815 to the Present* (New York: Penguin, 2012); Glenda Sluga, *Internationalism in the Age of Nationalism* (Philadelphia: University of Pennsylvania Press, 2013).
3   For an exception see Wolfram Kaiser and Kiran Klaus Patel, 'Continuity and Change in European Cooperation during the Twentieth Century', *Contemporary European History* 27, no. 2 (2018): 165–82. It is more common to study the continuities between the League of Nations and the United Nations; see e.g. Benjamin Auberer, 'Digesting the League of Nations: Planning the International Secretariat of the Future, 1941–1944', *New Global Studies* 10, no. 3 (2016): 393–426.
4   Cf. e.g. Jean Monnet, *Memoirs* (London: Third Millennium, 2015, reprint); François Duchêne, *Jean Monnet. The First Statesman of Interdependence* (New York, London: W. W. Norton, 1994).
5   For the method cf. e.g. Ann-Christina Knudsen and Karen Gram-Skjoldager (eds.), *Living Political Biography – Narrating 20th Century Political Lives* (Aarhus: Aarhus Universitetsforlag, 2012).
6   Seidel, *Process of Politics*, chapter 2. Katja Seidel, 'Gestalten statt Verwalten: Der Beitrag von Europabeamten zur europaeischen Integration', *Historische Mitteilungen* 18 (2005): 136–49.
7   In June 1940, Monnet gave the order to destroy his archives at the League. The surviving material on his time as deputy secretary-general is therefore patchy. See Antoine Fleury, 'Jean Monnet au Secretariat de la Société des Nations', in *Jean Monnet, L'Europe et les Chemins de la Paix*, ed. Gérard Bossuat, Andreas Wilkens (Paris: Publications de la Sorbonne, 1999), 31–41.
8   Duchêne, *Jean Monnet*, 36–8.
9   Drummond quoted in: Karen Gram-Skjoldager and Haakon A. Ikonomou, 'The Construction of the League of Nations Secretariat. Formative Practices of Autonomy and Legitimacy in International Organisations', *The International History Review* 41, no. 2 (2019): 257–79, 261.
10 Wolfram Kaiser, 'Transnational Practices Governing European Integration: Executive Autonomy and Neo-Corporatist Concertation in the Steel Sector', *Contemporary European History* 27, no. 2 (2018): 239–57, 243.
11 Monnet, *Memoirs*, 81.
12 Fleury, 'Monnet', 37.
13 Ibid., 40.
14 Cf. Lubor Jilek, 'Role de Jean Monnet dans les règlements d'Autriche et de Haute-Silésie', in *Jean Monnet, L'Europe et les Chemins de la Paix*, ed. Gerard Bossuat and Andreas Wilkens (Paris: Publications de la Sorbonne, 1999), 43–61.
15 Historical Archives of the European Union, Florence (HAEU), INT 530, François Duchêne with Jacques van Helmont, Paris, 24 April 1988, pp. 7–8. Frances Lynch,

France and the International Economy: From Vichy to the Treaty of Rome (London: Routledge, 1997), 82–3.
16 HAEU, INT 530, p. 23.
17 Gram-Skjoldager and Ikonomou, 'The Construction', 27.
18 Stanley Cleveland cited in Jacob Krumrey, *The Symbolic Politics of European Integration: Staging Europe* (Basingstoke: Palgrave Macmillan, 2018), 22.
19 Interview Marcel Jaurant-Singer with the author, Paris, 22 January 2005.
20 Dieter Rogalla, *Dienstrecht der Europäischen Gemeinschaften* (Köln, Berlin: Heymann, 1981), 2.
21 HAEU, CEAB 01 No 1347, Texte définitif adopté le 28 Janvier 1956, Statut du personnel de la communauté, p. 16.
22 Seidel, *Process of Politics*, chapter 2.
23 Fonds de l'Agence interalliée des réparations (Interallied Reparation Agency, IARA): https://francearchives.fr/findingaid/901597d8eed485e0aa18fb1851146a385 64cc380 (accessed 8 August 2020).
24 Foreign Relations of the United States (FRUS), 1947, Council of Foreign Ministers; Germany and Austria, vol. II, Document 171, Report of the Deputies for Germany to the Council of Foreign Ministers, Statement of the Representatives of the Inter-Allied Reparations Agency, 3 April 1947.
25 FRUS, 1948, Germany and Austria, vol. II, Document 370, 740.00119 Control (Germany)/12-2848 Communiqué of the London Conference on the Ruhr, 28 December 1948.
26 Interview Jaurant-Singer.
27 FJM, AMH 4/3/197 and AMH 4/3/190, Personnes susceptibles d'occuper un poste de direction dans l'une ou l'autre division', liste par Finet.
28 Interview Jaurant-Singer.
29 Anjo Harryvan and Jan van der Harst, *Max Kohnstamm: A European's Life and Work* (Baden-Baden: Nomos, 2011); Katja Seidel, 'Gestalten statt Verwalten'.
30 *Still No War. A Correspondence between Two Dutchmen – Son Max and Father, Philip Kohnstamm, 1938–1939*, ed. Dolph Kohnstamm (London: Athena Press, 2003), 15.
31 Interview Max Kohnstamm with the author, Fenffe, 26 April 2004.
32 Annemarie van Heerikhuizen, 'Max Kohnstamm's New Europe', in *European Identity and the Second World War*, ed. Menno Spiering and Michael Wintle (Basingstoke: Palgrave Macmillan, 2011), 165.
33 HAEU, Fonds Max Kohnstamm 1, M. Kohnstamm, Note pour Monsieur Monnet (III), 21 November 1953.
34 Fondation Jean Monnet, Lausanne (FJM), AMH 6/4/31, M. Kohnstamm, Note pour Monsieur Monnet, 22 October 1953.
35 FJM, AMH 6/4/29, M. Kohnstamm, Note pour Monsieur Monnet, 14 October 1953.

36 Seidel, *Process of Politics*, 20. Cf. also HAEU, MK28, Dagboek – 24, Strasbourg, 14 January 1954.
37 Seidel, *Process of Politics*, 20–1.
38 FJM, AMH 6/4/14, Letter Kohnstamm to Monnet, 1 August 1953.
39 HAEU, Fonds MK 1, M. Kohnstamm to J. van Helmont, 23 February 1954. Emphasis added.
40 Seidel, *Process of Politics*, 69.
41 HAEU, BAC 209/1980 No 1, PV of the EEC Commission, 1st session, Val Duchesse, 16 January 1958.
42 HAEU, MK 13, Letter Noël to Kohnstamm, Strasbourg, 28 March 1958.
43 HAEU, EN 1254, CV Emile Noël, 17 June 1945; for a short overview over Noël's life and career until 1958 see Catherine Previti Allaire, 'A propos des archives Emile Noël: aux origines d'une carrière européenne (1922–1958)', *Journal of European Integration History* 10, no. 2 (2004): 77–92.
44 Gérard Bossuat, *Emile Noël, premier secrétaire général de la Commission européenne* (Brussels: Bruylant, 2011), 16.
45 For example HAEU EN372, Report, Conseil de l'Europe, 17 September 1952 Assemblée consultative, Commission spéciale pour la Communauté Politique Européenne, première session.
46 Bossuat, *Noël*, 26–7.
47 Previti Allaire, 'A propos', 88; also Monnet, *Memoires*, 417.
48 See the entries in Noël's diary, HAEU, EN 2122 1958.
49 Bossuat, *Noël*.
50 Bundesarchiv, Koblenz (BAK), N 1266/1071, Note Karl-Heinz Narjes to President Hallstein, 2 April 1958.
51 Interview with Emile Noël, *Courrier du personnel*, no 488 (September 1987): 16.
52 Bossuat, *Noël*, 39.
53 Ibid., 90–2.
54 HAEU, EN 300, Visite d'information d'un group de banquiers français a la Communauté Européenne, Brussels, 14 November 1958.
55 See the testimonial in Gérard Bossuat, 'Emile Noël, a Loyal Servant of the Community of Europe', in *The European Commission, 1958–1972: History and Memories*, ed. Michel Dumoulin (Luxembourg: Office for Official Publications of the European Communities, 2007), 205–18.
56 Bossuat, *Noël*, 54.
57 Klaus Meyer, 'Emile Noël's Contribution to Europe', in *The Construction of Europe. Essays in Honour of Emile Noël*, ed. Stephen Martin (Dordrecht: Kluwer, 1994), 253–67, 264.
58 Bossuat, 'Loyal Servant', 211–12.
59 Gram-Skjoldager and Ikonomou, 'The Construction', 270.

60 Regulation No 31 (EEC), 11 (EAEC), laying down the Staff Regulations of Officials and the Conditions of Employment of Other Servants of the European Economic Community and the European Atomic Energy Community (OJ 45, 14 June 1962, p. 1385).
61 Interview with Emile Noël, *Courrier du personnel*, no. 488 (September 1987): 28.
62 Emile Noël, 'Crises and Progress: The Bricks and Mortar of Europe', in *A Tribute to Emile Noël. Secretary-General of the European Commission from 1958 to 1987* (Luxembourg: Office for Official Publications of the European Communities, 1990), 53–8, 54–5.
63 Patel and Kaiser, 'Continuity and Change', 166.
64 Monnet cited in Duchêne, *Jean Monnet*, 238–9.
65 Auberer, 'Digesting the League of Nations', 393–426.

Chapter 7

1 A brief cross section of this immense literature on institutionalization and internationalization in medicine, health and agriculture includes J. Harwood, *Technology's Dilemma: Agricultural Colleges between Science and Practice in Germany, 1860–1934* (Oxford: Peter Lang, 2005); J. F. M. Clark, 'Bugs in the System: Insects, Agricultural Science, and Professional Aspirations in Britain, 1890–1920', *Agricultural History* 75 (Winter 2001): 83–114; D. H. Yaalon and S. Berkowicz (eds.), *History of Soil Science: International Perspectives* (Reiskirchen, Germany: Catena Verlag, 1997); H. C. Knoblauch, E. M. Law, and W. P. Meyer, *State Agricultural Experiment Stations: A History of Research Policy and Procedure* (Washington, DC: Department of Agriculture, May 1962); E. Jensen, *Danish Agriculture, Its Economic Development: A Description and Economic Analysis Centering on the Free Trade Epoch, 1870*–1930 (Copenhagen: J. H. Schultz Forlag 1937); C. S. Orwin and E. H. Whetham, *History of British Agriculture, 1846–1914* (Newton Abbot, UK: David and Charles, 1971); Sir E. J. Russell, 'Rothamsted and Its Experiment Station', *Agricultural History* 16, no. 1 (October 1942): 161–83.
2 D. Smith, 'The Agricultural Research Association, the Development Fund, and the Origins of the Rowett Research Institute', *Agricultural History Review* 46, no. 1 (1998): 47–63; Lord Boyd Orr, *As I Recall* (London: MacGibbon and Kee, 1966), 118; J. Barona, 'International Organisations and the Development of a Physiology of Nutrition during the 1930s', *Food and History* 6, no. 1 (2008): 139, 153–4.
3 For the LNHO, see P. Weindling: 'Philanthropy and World Health: The Rockefeller Foundation and the League of Nations Health Organisation', *Minerva* 35 (1997): 269–81; F. P. Walters, *A History of the League of Nations*, 2 vols. (Oxford: Oxford University Press, 1952), 1:164, 265, 390, 2:585, 752; H. R. G. Greaves, *The League Committees and World Order: A Study of the Permanent Expert Committees of the*

League of Nations as an Instrument of International Government (Oxford: Oxford University Press, 1931; reprint, New York: AMS, 1979), 96; and J. Barona, 'Nutrition and Health: The International Context during the Inter-war Crisis', *Social History of Medicine* 21 (2008): 87–105. For IIA work, see A. Hobson, *The International Institute of Agriculture: An Historical and Critical Analysis of Its Organization, Activities, and Policies of Administration* (Berkeley: University of California Press, 1931); L. Tosi, *Alle Origini delle FAO: Le relazioni tra l'Instituto Internazionale de Agricoltura e la Società delle Nazioni* (Milan: Franco Angeli, 1989).

4   'Advisory Committee on Nutrition', *British Medical Journal* 1, no. 3654 (1931): 108; 'The Nutrition Question: An Agreed Report', *British Medical Journal* 1, no. 3828 (1934): 900; 'Research on Nutrition', *British Medical Journal* 1, no. 3885 (1935): 1274; J. L. Barona, *The Problem of Nutrition: Experimental Science, Public Health and Economy in Europe, 1914–1945* (Peter Lang, 2010), 21–3, 26.

5   Stiebling's 1933 diet took into account vitamins A and C as well as calcium, phosphorus and iron. See Barona, 'International Organisations', 145–7, 152–3, 161–4; E. Burnet and W. R. Aykroyd, 'Nutrition and Public Health', *Quarterly Bulletin of the Health Organisation* 4, no. 2 (1935): 368, 457–8; 'The Most Suitable Methods of Detecting Malnutrition due to the Economic Depression: Conference Held at Berlin from December 5th to 7th, 1932', *Quarterly Bulletin of the Health Organisation* 2 (1933): 116–29; Weindling, 'Philanthropy and World Health', 275–8; Technical Commission of the Health Committee, *The Problem of Nutrition*, vol. II: *Report on the Physiological Bases of Nutrition* (League of Nations, 1936), 4.

6   The Rome Experts Conference in September 1932 and the Berlin Conference in December 1932 prompted two meetings of LNHO and ILO experts in sanitary administration and social insurance. See E. Burnet, 'General Principles Governing the Prevention of Tuberculosis', *Bulletin of the Health Organisation* 1 (1932): 489–663; Burnet and Aykroyd, 'Nutrition and Public Health', 367, 453–4; Orr, *As I Recall*, 118; Robert McCarrison, 'Nutrition and National Health', *British Medical Journal* 1, no. 3921 (1936): 430; L. B. Pett, C. A. Morrell, and F. W. Hanley, 'The Development of Dietary Standards', *Canadian Journal of Public Health* 36 (June 1945): 233; Barona, *Problem of Nutrition*, 24, 30–1; N. Cullather, 'The Foreign Policy of the Calorie', *American Historical Review* 112, no. 2 (2007): 337–64; F. Trentmann, 'Coping with Shortage: The Problem of Food Security and Global Visions of Coordination, c.1890s–1950', in *Food and Conflict in Europe in the Age of the Two World Wars*, ed. F. Trentmann and F. Just (Palgrave, 2006), 39.

7   'The Nutrition Report', *British Medical Journal* 2, no. 3805 (1933): 1084; British Medical Association, 'Committee on Nutrition', *British Medical Journal* 25 (1933): supplement; Technical Commission of the Health Committee, *Problem of Nutrition*, 2:4.

8   Burnet and Aykroyd, 'Nutrition and Public Health', 326–474.

9   Ibid., 367. See also *Nutrition*, 11–12; and Stuart J. Cowell, 'The Physiological Bases of Nutrition', *British Medical Journal* 2, no. 3999 (1937): 407–9.

10 Burnet and Aykroyd, 'Nutrition and Public Health', 367. See also Helen M. Jardine, 'The Nutrition Report', *British Medical Journal* 1, no. 3816 (1934): 356; 'The Nutrition Question: An Agreed Report', 900–1; 'Nutrition an International Problem', *British Medical Journal* 2, no. 3899 (1935): 588–9; Walters, *History of the League of Nations*, 2:522–3, 753; R. Schickele, *Agricultural Policy: Farm Programs and National Welfare* (McGraw-Hill, 1954); Orr, *As I Recall*, 112, 115; and Barona, *Problem of Nutrition*, 31.

11 W. Way, *A New Idea Each Morning: How Food and Agriculture Came Together in One International* Organisation (Canberra: Australian National University E Press, 2013), 153–74; A. E. Harper, 'Origin of Recommended Dietary Allowances: An Historic Overview', *American Journal of Clinical Nutrition* 41, January issue (1985): 141–2; Walters, *History of the League of Nations*, 2:754; F. L. McDougall, 'Food and Welfare', *Geneva Studies* 9, November issue (1938): 9–10, 14–15, 26–7, 35, 41, 45–9, 52, 54–6; W. C. Waite and J. D. Black, 'Nutrition and Agricultural Policy', *Annals of the American Academy of Political and Social Science* 188, November issue (1936): 219–27; Technical Commission of the Health Committee, *Problem of Nutrition*, 2:5; 'Nutrition an International Problem', 588–9; Orr, *As I Recall*, 119; A. L. S. Staples, *The Birth of Development: How the World Bank, Food and Agriculture Organization, and World Health Organization Changed the World, 1945–1965* (Kent, Ohio: Kent State University Press, 2006), 73. For ILO work specifically, see F. G. Boudreau, 'Nutrition in War and Peace', *Milbank Quarterly* 83, no. 4 (2005): 610; International Labour Office, *Workers' Nutrition and Social Policy* (Geneva: International Labour Office, 1936).

12 Mixed Committee, *Nutrition: Final Report of the Mixed Committee of the League of Nations on the Relation of Nutrition to Health, Agriculture and Economic Policy* (Geneva: League of Nations, 1937), 5. See also League of Nations, *The Problem of Nutrition*, vol. III: *Nutrition in Various Countries* (Geneva: League of Nations, 1936); International Institute of Agriculture, *The Problem of Nutrition*, vol. IV: *Statistics of Food Production, Consumption and Prices* (Geneva: League of Nations, 1936); and Barona, 'International Organisations', 142–4.

13 'Health Matters in Parliament', *British Medical Journal* 2, no. 3956 (1936): 874. See also United Nations Interim Commission on Food and Agriculture, *Five Technical Reports on Food and Agriculture: Nutrition and Food Management* (Washington, DC: UNICFA, 1945), 14; E. W. H. Cruickshank, *Food and Nutrition: The Physiological Bases of Human Nutrition* (Edinburgh: E & S Livingston, 1946), 24; J. Boyd Orr, *Food, Health and Income: Report on a Survey of Adequacy of Diet in Relation to Income* (London: Macmillan, 1936).

14 Mixed Committee, *Nutrition*, 31, 33. See also ibid., 15–17, 35–8, 52, 60, 296–322; Cowell, 'Physiological Bases of Nutrition', 407; Walters, *History of the League of Nations*, 2:754–55; McDougall, 'Food and Welfare', 14, 31, 44; and Technical Commission of the Health Committee, *Problem of Nutrition*, 2:10.

15 Harper, 'Origin of Recommended Dietary Allowances', 143, 145; League of Nations, *Problem of Nutrition*, vol. II; Mixed Committee, *Nutrition*; 'Report by the Technical Commission on Nutrition on the Work of Its Third Session', *Quarterly Bulletin of the Health Organisation* 7 (1938): 461–82; U.S. Department of Agriculture, *Yearbook: Food and Life* (Washington, DC: U.S. Department of Agriculture, 1939); Canadian Council on Nutrition, 'The Canadian Dietary Standard', *National Health Review* 8 (1940): 1–9; Pett, Morrell, and Hanley, 'The Development of Dietary Standards', 232–9; 'National Nutrition Conference', *British Medical Journal* 1, no. 407 (1939): 226; 'Nutrition in Its Wider Aspects', *British Medical Journal* 4086 (1939): 221–2; 'Food and a Fit Nation', *British Medical Journal* 2, no. 4112 (1939): 861–2; and Barona, 'International Organisations', 153.

16 As quoted in Walters, *History of the League of Nations*, 2:760. See also ibid., 2:760–62.

17 Ibid., 2:755. See also Ministry of Health, *On the State of the Public Health during Six Years of War: Report of the Chief Medical Officer of the Ministry of Health, 1939–45* (London: HMSO, 1946), 1–2, 6, 92–4, 115; Orr and Lubbock, *Feeding the People in War-time*. For US nutrition work, see Harper, 'Origin of Recommended Dietary Allowances', 145–6; 'Recommended Allowances for the Various Dietary Essentials', *Journal of the American Dietetic Association* 17 (1941): 565–7; and Lydia J. Roberts, 'Scientific Basis for the Recommended Dietary Allowances', *New York State Journal of Medicine* 44 (1944): 59–60.

18 See Staples, *Birth of Development*, 75–6; F. G. Boudreau, 'International Health Work', in *Pioneers in World Order: An American Appraisal of the League of Nations*, ed. H. Eager Davis (New York: Columbia University Press, 1944), 203–5; Y. M. Biraud, 'Health in Europe: A Survey of the Epidemic and Nutritional Situation', *Quarterly Bulletin of the Health Organisation* 10, no. 4 (1943/44): 557–699; 'Famine Disease and Its Treatment in Internment Camps', *Quarterly Bulletin of the Health Organisation* 10, no. 4 (1943/44): 722–72.

19 As quoted in Karl Evang, *Norway's Food in Peace and War* (Washington, DC, 1942), 4; 'Food and a Fit Nation', 861; Sir John Boyd Orr, 'The Role of Food in Post-war Reconstruction', *International Labour Review* 47, no. 3 (March 1943): 1. See also Orr, 'Role of Food in Post-war Reconstruction', 1–18; Orr, *As I Recall*, 157–59, 161; Staples, *Birth of Development*, 75–76; Boudreau, 'Nutrition in War and Peace', 611; and Ministry of Health, *On the State of the Public Health during Six Years of War*, 7–8.

20 As quoted in J. F. Booth, 'Our Hungry World', *Behind the Headlines* 8 (1948): 6. See also P. Lamartine Yates, *So Bold an Aim: Ten Years of International Co-operation toward Freedom from Want* (Rome: FAO, 1955), 49–50; S. Howson and D. Moggridge, eds., *The Wartime Diaries of Lionel Robbins and James Meade, 1943–45* (London: Macmillan, 1990), 9, 13, 16–18, 34–6; Staples, *Birth of Development*, 76–7; Orr, *As I Recall*, 158; Cruickshank, *Food and Nutrition*, 11, 18–19, 307–9; UNICFA, *Five Technical Reports: Nutrition and Food Management*, 12–13.

21 *First Report to the Governments of the United Nations by the Interim Commission on Food and Agriculture* (Washington, DC: UNICFA, 1944), 10–11; UNICFA, *Five Technical Reports: Nutrition and Food Management*, 11. See also *First Report*, 3; UNICFA, *Five Technical Reports*, 17, 31, 38–9, 54–5.

22 Boudreau comments, proceedings of the fourth plenary meeting, 18 October 1945, Record Group 59, Decimal File 1945–49, 501.SA, box 2292, U.S. National Archives, College Park, Maryland; Orr, *As I Recall*, 161. See also Staples, *Birth of Development*, 78–9.

23 Proceedings of the first plenary session of the Special Meeting on Urgent Food Problems, 20 May 1946, and proceedings of the sixth plenary session of the Special Meeting on Urgent Food Problems, 27 May 1946, both RG 59, Decimal File 1945–49, 501.SA, box 2307, U.S. National Archives, College Park, Maryland; D. J. Shaw, *World Food Security: A History since 1945* (Palgrave Macmillan, 2007), 15–31.

24 'Proposals for a World Food Board', FAO memorandum to member nations for submission to the Second FAO Session in Copenhagen, 2 September 1946, Treasury Files 236/92, Public Record Office, Kew, UK; S. Marchisio and A. Di Blase, *The Food and Agriculture Organization (FAO)* (Dordrecht, Netherlands: International Organization and the Evolution of World Society Series, M. Nijhoff, 1991), 16–17.

25 Staples, *Birth of Development*, 82–96; A. L. S. Staples, 'To Win the Peace: The Food and Agriculture Organization, Sir John Boyd Orr, and the World Food Board Proposals', *Peace & Change* 28, October issue (2003): 495–523; R. Jachertz, 'Bretton Woods, the International Trade Organization, and the Food and Agriculture Organization', in *Global Perspectives on the Bretton Woods Conference and the Post-war World Order*, ed. G. Scott-Smith and J. S. Rofe (London: Palgrave, 2017), 287–90.

26 Staples, *Birth of Development*, 96–104; 'Food, Farming, and Peace', Dodd address at Bunker Hill, 19 July 1948, Dodd papers, box 1, folder 7, Hoover Institution on War, Revolution and Peace, Stanford, California.

27 'FAO/UNICEF Cooperation: Past and Future', FAO memorandum, April 1954, attached to Cardon letter to Pate, 29 April 1954, Record Group 1.3, series A2, Food and Agriculture Organization Archive, Rome, Italy; this series contains other letters in which Cardon resisted partnerships with other organizations on significant issues.

28 B. R. Sen, *Towards a Newer World* (Dublin: Tycooly, 1982); A. L. Sayward, *The United Nations in International History* (London: Bloomsbury, 2017), 58–9, 85–94; R. Jolly, *UNICEF (United Nations Children's Fund): Global Governance That Works* (London: Routledge, 2010).

29 Sen introductory statement to plenary of 1959 Conference, as quoted in Staples, *Birth of Development*, 105. See also ibid., 105–21, and 239n6 for a list of NGO participants; Sen, *Towards a Newer World*, 144–63, 279; R. Jachertz, '"To Keep Food out of Politics": The UN Food and Agriculture Organization, 1945–1965', in

International Organizations and Development, 1945–1990, ed. M. Frey, S. Kunkel, and C. R. Unger (London: Palgrave Macmillan, 2014), 75–100.
30 Staples, *Birth of Development*, 113, 116; minutes of working group on FFHC fertilizer programme, 17 June 1960, RG 12, box 2, folder 1, FAO Archive.
31 Staples, *Birth of Development*; Sen, *Toward a Newer World*, 131–8; M. J. Bunch, 'All Roads Lead to Rome: Canada, the Freedom from Hunger Campaign, and the Rise of NGOs, 1962–1980', PhD thesis (University of Waterloo, 2007), and accompanying website, freedomfromhungerproject.weebly.com; Shaw, *World Food Security*, 77–84.

Chapter 8

1 Pierre Comert, 'Article by M. Comert', attached to note by the secretary-general 29 March 1921, *Minutes of the Directors' Meetings (MDM), 1921–1922*, LONA.
2 Robert Mark Spaulding, 'The Central Commission for Navigation on the Rhine and European Media 1815–1848', in *International Organizations and the Media in the Nineteenth and Twentieth Centuries – Exorbitant Expectations*, ed. Jonas Brendebach, Martin Herzer and Heidi Tworek (London: Routledge, 2018), 17–38; Linda Risso, *Propaganda and Intelligence in the Cold War: The NATO Information Service* (New York: Routledge, 2014).
3 In the field of media and communication studies, a project was launched in 2017 at the Universität Bremen directed by Professor Stefanie Averbeck-Lietz, 'The Transnational Communication History of the League of Nations, 1920–1938'. The project focuses specifically on the interplay between journalism and communication in the period and the ambivalent understanding of the term 'open diplomacy': https://www.uni-bremen.de/en/zemki/research/research-projects/transnational-communication-history-of-the-league-of-nations-in-the-inter-war-period-1920-1938/ (accessed 14 March 2020).
4 Tomoko Akami, 'The Limits of Peace Propaganda: The Information Section of the League of Nations and Its Tokyo Office', in *International Organizations in the Making of the Contemporary World*, ed. Jonas Brendebach, Martin Herzer, Heidi Tworek (Berkeley: University of California Press, 2002), 70–90. For a recent study of the impact of public opinion on diplomacy – a question the present chapter does not engage with – see Daniel Hucker, *Public Opinion and Twentieth Century Diplomacy – A Global Perspective* (London: Bloomsbury, 2020).
5 The research draws on material from the League of Nations Archives in Geneva and from the Library of Congress. In Geneva, a combination of correspondence, personnel files and 'registry files' of the League Secretariat is operationalized to grasp the long-term development of the Information Section which, unfortunately,

does not have its own section files. To compensate, material from the private papers in the Library of Congress of one of its most influential officials, Arthur Sweetser, has been consulted as well. Finally, a selection of the information material released by the Information Section throughout its existence has been consulted, taken from five 'moments' (1920–1, 1927, 1930, 1934 and 1937–8) throughout the interwar period to build a progressive understanding of the messages it disseminated. See Emil Eiby Seidenfaden, *Message from Geneva: The Public Legitimization Strategies of the League of Nations and their Legacy, 1919–1946* (Aarhus University, PhD thesis, 2019).

6   Jan Werner-Müller, 'European Intellectual History as Contemporary History', *Journal of Contemporary History* 45 (2011): 574–90, 588.

7   Quentin Skinner, *Visions of Politics Vol 1: Regarding Method* (Cambridge: Cambridge University Press, 2002), 146, 148.

8   Egon Ranshofen-Wertheimer, *The International Secretariat – A Great Experiment in International Administration* (Washington, DC: Carnegie Endowment for International Peace, 1945), 203.

9   Years 1921, 1922 and 1929–33: 'General Budget of the League of Nations', *Official Journal of the League of Nations (O.J.)*, vol. 1, no. 7 (October 1920), LONA, 453; '— Fourth Fiscal Period 1922', *O.J.*, vol. 2, no. 9 (November 1921), 1034; '— Eleventh Financial Period (1929)', *O.J.*, vol. 9 (1928), 1789; '— Twelfth Financial Period', *O.J.*, vol. 10, no. 10 (October 1929), 1326; '— Thirteenth Financial Period (1931)', *O.J.*, vol. 11, no. 10 (October 1930), 1174; '— Fourteenth Financial Period (1932)', *O.J.*, vol. 12, no. 10 (October 1931), 1909; '— Fifteenth Financial Period (1933)', *O.J.*, vol. 13 (1932), 1602. LONA. Years 1923–8: League of Nations, 'Budget for the Fifth Fiscal Period (1923):' C.713.M.425.1922.X; League of Nations, '— Sixth Financial Period (1924):' C.668.M.268.1923.X; League of Nations, '— Seventh Financial Period (1925):' C.618.M.217.1924.X; League of Nations, '— Eighth Financial Period (1926):' C.619.M.201.1925.X; League of Nations, '— Ninth Financial Period (1927):' C.581.M.220.1926.X: https://search.un.org/ (accessed 2 November 2017). All data from Schedule B: Salaries, Wages and Allowances of the Secretariat.

10 'Report on the Information Section', 6 April1921, in Secretariat de la Société des Nations – Commission d'enquete, *CE/1-27*, 1921, LONA, 2.

11 League of Nations, *A.10.1933.X: Technical Concentration of the Activities of the League of Nations and Rationalisation of the Services of the Secretariat and the International Labour Office, Report by the Supervisory Commission to the Assembly July 20th, 1933*, LONA, 8.

12 Information Section, 'Report of the Information Section to the 8th Assembly, 1927', September 1926, *File Concerning Report of the Information Section to the 8th Assembly*, 1927, 62097, R1354, LONA, 1; Akami, 'Limits of Peace Propaganda', 73.

13 For example Manigand, 99.

14 See Seidenfaden, *Message from Geneva*, 47.
15 Karen Gram-Skjoldager and Haakon Ikonomou, 'The Construction of the League of Nations Secretariat. Formative Practices of Autonomy and Legitimacy in International Organizations', *The International History Review* (2017): 1–23.
16 Raw data on staff of the secretariat courtesy of the League of Nations Search Engine project: Madeleine Herren et al., LONSEA – League of Nations Search Engine, Heidelberg/Basel, 2010–17: http://www.lonsea.de/
17 Salvador de Madariaga, *Morning without Noon* (Farnborough: Saxon House, 1973), 279.
18 Pitman B. Potter, 'League Publicity: Cause or Effect of League Failure?', *The Public Opinion Quarterly* 2, no. 10 (1938): 399–412, 410.
19 Ibid., 406. When Potter wrote 'revision' he was referring to revision of the Treaty of Versailles and other parts of the Paris settlements after the First World War.
20 Müller, *European Intellectual History*, 588.
21 Secretariat of the League of Nations, *Ten Years of World Co-operation* (London: Hazel, Watson and Viney, 1930), 406–07, Unknown author, 'Memorandum on the work of the Information Section 1930–1931', nd., 1932, *Section Reorganization [...], 1926–1940*, P191, Adrianus Pelt Papers (PP henceforth), LONA, 2; Ranshofen-Wertheimer, *The International Secretariat*, 209.
22 Information Section of the League of Nations Secretariat, *The League of Nations and the Press* (Geneva, 1928), 40.
23 Ibid., 26.
24 Committee to examine the organization of the Information Section, Annex to 'Commission de Controle – Réorganisation de la Section d'Information. Note du Secrétaire general', 21 September 1933, *Section Reorganization*, P191, PP, LONA, 3.
25 Drummond, letter to Jean Monnet, 23 June 1919, *Propaganda among Women's Organisations [...]*, 992, R1332, LONA; see also Thomas R. Davies, 'Internationalism in a Divided World: The Experience of the International Federation of League of Nations Societies', 37, no. 2 (2012): 227–52. 'Cooperative publicity' was used by Arthur Sweetser to describe relations between the section and private pro-League groups. E.g. Sweetser, 'League of Nations publicity', 27 May 1919, *Memo Defining Activities of the Publicity Section*, 272, R1332, LONA, 2.
26 Pelt, 'Information Section – Liste des associations privée avec lesquelles la Section d'information est en rapport et analyse de chacune de ces liaisons', nd., 1933, *Committees (Liaison Committee)*, P191, PP, LONA, 8.
27 Theodore Ruyssen, 'La propagande pour la Société des Nations', in *Les Origines et l'œuvre de la Société des Nations 2nd vol.*, ed. Peter Munch (Copenhague: Rask-Ørstedfonden/Nordisk Forlag, 1924), 237.
28 Information Section, 'Report of the Information Section to the 8th Assembly, 1927', 18.
29 Ibid., 16.

30 See also: Heidi Tworek, 'Peace through Truth – The Press and Moral Disarmament through the League of Nations', *Medien & Zeit* 25, no. 4 (2010): 16–28.
31 For example Pelt, letter to Rey G. Howard, 24 December 1925, *Press & Communication*, P192, PP, LONA.
32 Sweetser, letter to Pierre Comert, 23 October 1952, *Miscellaneous: General*, Box 28, Arthur Sweetser Papers, Library of Congress, Washington DC (A.S.P, L.O.C henceforth). See Seidenfaden, *Message from Geneva*, 67–8.
33 Information Section, *The League of Nations and the Press*, 43, 49.
34 See also: Tworek, 'The Creation of European News: News Agency Cooperation in Interwar Europe', *Journalism Studies* 14, no. 5 (2013): 730–42, 734.
35 League of Nations, *A.10.1933.X: Technical Concentration*, 8.
36 Information Section, *The League of Nations and the Press*, 47, Information Section, *The Monthly Summary of the League of Nations*, vol. XIV, no. 5, May 1934, LONA, 127.
37 Secretariat, *Ten Years of World Co-operation*, 414.
38 Giles Scott-Smith has cast light on the ancestry of the UNDPI in one of the first UN agencies, the United Nations Information Office (UNIO), which rose out of the Inter-Allied Information Committee (IAIC). Giles Scott-Smith, 'Competing Internationalisms: The United States, Britain and the Formation of the United Nations Information Organization during World War II', *International Journal for History, Culture and Modernity* 1, no. 6 (2018). A central player in the UNIO was from an early stage Arthur Sweetser, whose wartime activity has also been illuminated by Madeleine Herren and Isabella Löhr, Herren, Löhr, 'Being International in Times of War: Arthur Sweetser and the shifting of the League of Nations to the United Nations', *European Review of History* 25, no. 3–4 (2018): 535–52.
39 Front matter document, nd., S852 (Adrian Pelt, Personnel File), LONA.
40 L.O.C, *Arthur Sweetser Papers – A Finding Aid to the Collection in the Library of Congress* (Washington DC, Manuscript Division – L.O.C, 2013): http://hdl.loc.gov/loc.mss/eadmss.ms013059 (accessed 14 June 2017); Scott-Smith, 'Competing Internationalisms'.
41 Susan Sweetser Clifford, *One Shining Hour*, 1990, Private publication. 122.
42 As suggested by Benjamin Auberer, 'Digesting the League of Nations Secretariat: Planning the International Secretariat of the Future 1941–1944', *New Global Studies* 10, no. 3 (2016): 393–426, 409.
43 Lord Perth (Eric Drummond) et al., *The International Secretariat of the Future – Lessons from Experience by a Group of Former Officials of the League of Nations* (London: RIIA, Oxford, 1944); Auberer, *Digesting the League*.
44 *Proceedings of the Exploratory Conference of the Experience of the League of Nations Secretariat*, Box 244, *CEIP Records*, Rare Books and Manuscript Library (RBM), Columbia University Libraries (CUL); Philip Jessup, letter to Arthur Sweetser, 17

August 1942, Box 210–211, *CEIP Records*, RBM, CUL. Scott-Smith, 'Competing Internationalisms'.
45 Pelt, letter to Sweetser, 10 March 1943, *General League Correspondence: Adrian Pelt*, Box 34, A.S.P, L.O.C.
46 Technical Advisory Committee on Information, 'Draft Recommendations for Submission to the Preparatory Commission […]', 20 December 1945, Nineteenth Meeting of Committee Six: Administrative and Budgetary, Box 69, *Liquidation of League*, A.S.P, L.O.C.
47 Sub-committee of the Technical Advisory Committee on Information, 'Report to the Secretary-General', 11 February 1946, Box 69, *Liquidation of League*, A.S.P, L.O.C.
48 Adriaan Pelt, 'Suggestions by A. Pelt for the Organization of a Secretariat Information Section', in Lord Perth (Eric Drummond) et al., *The International Secretariat of the Future*, 61–4.
49 See also: Madeleine Herren, Isabella Löhr, 'Gipfeltreffen im Schatten der Weltpolitik: Arthur Sweetser und die Mediendiplomatie des Völkerbunds', *Zeitschrift für Geschichtswissenschaft* 62, no. 5 (2014), 411–24.
50 Pelt, letter to Sweetser, 10 March 1943, 3.
51 Robert H. Cory, 'Forging a Public Information Policy for the United Nations', *International Organization* 7, no. 2 (1953), 229–42, 230; Brendebach, Herzer and Tworek, 'Introduction', in Brendebach, Herzer, Tworek (ed.), 12; Information Section, Budget 1939, nd., 1938, *1939 Budget of the Information Section*, 33022, R5189, LONA.
52 For example Akami, 'Limits of Peace Propaganda', 86.

Chapter 9

1 Arno J. Mayer, *Political Origins of the New Diplomacy 1917–1918* (New Haven: Yale University Press, 1959), 58.
2 Jan Smuts, *The League of Nations. A Practical Suggestion* (1918), 36.
3 Susan Pedersen, 'Back to the League of Nations', *American Historical Review* 112, no. 4 (2007): 1091–117, 1096–7; see also Susan Pedersen, *The Guardians. The League of Nations and the Crisis of Empire* (Oxford: Oxford University Press, 2015), 8.
4 Helen McCarthy, *The British People and the League of Nations: Democracy, Citizenship and Internationalism, c. 1918–45* (Manchester: Manchester University Press, 2011); Donald S. Birn, *The League of Nations Union, 1918–1945* (Oxford: Clarendon Press, 1981); Gaynor Johnson, *Lord Robert Cecil. Politician and Internationalist* (Farnham: Ashgate, 2013).

5 Remco van Diepen, *Voor Volkenbond en vrede: Nederland en het streven naar een nieuwe wereldorde, 1919-1946* (Amsterdam: Bert Bakker, 1999); Anne-Isabelle Richard, 'Between the League of Nations and Europe. Multiple Internationalisms and Interwar Dutch Civil Society', in *Shaping the International Relations of the Netherlands 1815-2000. A Small Country on the Global Scene*, ed. Ruud van Dijk, et al. (Abingdon: Routlegde, 2018), 97-116.

6 Jean-Michel Guieu, *Le rameau et le glaive: les militants français pour la Société des Nations* (Paris: Presses de Sciences Po, 2008); Christian Birebent, *Militants de la paix et de la SDN* (Paris: L'Harmattan, 2007).

7 Théodore Ruyssen, 'Un année bien remplie', *Bulletin Union International des Associations pour la Société des Nations* (henceforth: *Bulletin*) 8, no. 1 (1929): 9.

8 Jan Smuts, 13 February 1919, Peace Conference Commission on the League of Nations. Felix Morley, *The Society of Nations* (Washington, DC: Brookings Institution, 1932): 116.

9 Pedersen, 'Back to the League', 1096-7.

10 For national societies beyond those cited above see for example: Kuniyuki Terada, *Actors in International Cooperation in Pre-war Japan. The Discourse on International Migration and the League of Nations Association of Japan* (Baden-Baden: Nomos, 2018); Tomoko Akami, 'Experts and the Japanese Association of the League of Nations in the International Context, 1919-1925', in *The League of Nations, Histories, Legacies and Impact*, ed. Joy Damousi and Patricia O'Brien (Melbourne: Melbourne University Press, 2018), 158-78. On the IFLNS see Anne-Isabelle Richard, 'Competition and Complementarity: Civil Society Networks and the Question of Decentralising the League of Nations', *Journal of Global History* 7, no. 2 (2012): 233-56; Jean Michel Guieu, 'La SDN et ses organisations de soutien dans les années 1920. Entre promotion de l'esprit de genève et volonté d'influence', *Relations Internationales* 151, no. 3 (2012): 11-23; Thomas R. Davies, 'Internationalism in a Divided World: The Experience of the International Federation of the League of Nations Societies, 1919-1939', *Peace&Change* 37, no. 2 (2012): 227-52.

11 Glenda Sluga, *Internationalism in the Age of Nationalism* (Philadelphia 2013).

12 *League of Nations Journal and Monthly Report*, February 1919, 72.

13 'Session d'automne du Bureau', *Bulletin* 12, no. 5 (1933): 321.

14 League of Nations Archives, Geneva (henceforth LoNA), International Federation of League of Nations Societies (henceforth: IFLNS), P102, Interview Ruyssen, Brussels, February 1931.

15 LoNA, IFLNS, P102, Note: Appointment of an English-speaking Assistant Secretary-General, 18 December 1923. Early English translations make the need for an Anglophone secretary clear, *Bulletin*, 1, no. 3 (1922): cf. 16 and 28-9.

16 *Bulletin*, 8, no. 5 (1929): 3 and 10, no 4 (1931): 7; 10, no. 5 (1931): 38.

17 LoNA, P102, Listes des personnalités féminines membres d'Associations pour la Société des Nations.

18 Susan Pedersen, 'Metaphors of the Schoolroom: Women Working the Mandates System of the League of Nations', *History Workshop Journal* 66, no. 1 (2008): 188–207.
19 LoNA, IFLNS, P93, Assembly files, General Assembly Lyon 1924, M.W.F. Treub.
20 Anne-Isabelle Richard, 'Huizinga, Intellectual Cooperation and the Spirit of Europe, 1933–1945', in *Europe in Crisis. Intellectuals and the European Idea, 1917–1957*, ed. Mark Hewitson and Matthew D'Auria (Oxford: Berghahn, 2012), 243–57, in particular 245, John Breuilly, *Nationalism and the State* (Manchester: Manchester University Press 1993), 8; Patricia Clavin and Glenda Sluga, 'Rethinking the History of Internationalism', in ibid., *Internationalisms. A Twentieth Century History* (Cambridge: Cambridge University Press, 2017), 3–16, 10.
21 Ruyssen, 'Les Associations pour la Société des Nations et leur Associations Internationales', *Bulletin* 5, no. 1 (1926): 2–14, 13.
22 'Session d'automne du Bureau', *Bulletin* 12, no. 5 (1933): 321. 'Conference de Prague, Modification des statuts', *Bulletin* 1, no. 4 (1922): 8.
23 'Discours du Vicomte Cecil of Chelwood, Président de l'Union', *Bulletin* 8, no. 1 (1929): 30.
24 LoNA, IFLNS, P102, Interview with Ruyssen, Brussels, February 1931.
25 See also Mark Mazower, *No Enchanted Palace: The End of Empire and the Ideological Origins of the United Nations* (Princeton, NJ: Princeton University Press, 2009).
26 *Bulletin*, 'Assemblée', 7 (1928): 25.
27 *Bulletin*, 14, no. 3 (1935): 165.
28 Cited in Terada, *Actors*, 109: 'Kokusai renmei Kyokai ni kansuru Matsui no iken [Ambassador Matsui's Opinion about the League of Nations Societies], Japan Centre for Asian Historical Records: B04013930300,42.
29 *Bulletin* 4, no. 4 (1925): 28; 13, no. 3 (1934): 119; 16, no. 4 (1937): 164–7. See also Tsuchida Akio, 'China's "Public Diplomacy" toward the United States before Pearl Harbor', *Journal of American–East Asian Relations* 17, no. 1 (2010): 35–55.
30 Ke Ren, 'The International Peace Campaign, China, and Transnational Activism at the Outset of World War II', in *The Routledge History of World Peace since 1750*, ed. Christian Philip Peterson, William M. Knoblauch, and Michael Loadenthal (Abingdon: Routledge 2019), 359–70.
31 LoNA, IFLNS, P113, Circulars, Circular 170, 20 January 1939.
32 Ibid., Circular 173, 17 April 1939, Circular 176, 29 August 1939.
33 McCarthy, *The British People*, 4.
34 *Bulletin* 9, no. 5 (1930): 17; 13, no. 4 (1934): 191; 16, no. 5 (1937): 239–41. Richard, 'Competition', Christoph Ploß, *Die 'New Commonwealth Society'. Ein Ideen-Laboratorium für den supranationalen europäischen Integrationsprozess* (Stuttgart: Franz Steiner Verlag, 2017).
35 *Bulletin* 16, no. 5 (1937): 239–41, Ren, 'The International Peace Campaign'.

36 On these networks see Patricia Clavin, 'Defining Transnationalism', *Contemporary European History* 14, no. 4 (2005): 421–39.
37 LoNA, R3303, Report Krabbe, 14th General Assembly, Geneva 5–9 June 1930.
38 Patricia Clavin and Jens-Wilhelm Wessels, 'Transnationalism and the League of Nations: Understanding the Work of Its Economic and Financial Organisation', *Contemporary European History* 14, no. 4 (2005): 465–92, 467.
39 Sweetser, 'League of Nations publicity', 27 May 1919, 2, quoted in Emil Seidenfaden, *Message from Geneva. The Public Legitimization Strategies of the League of Nations and Their Legacy, 1919-1946* (Unpublished PhD thesis, University of Aarhus 2019), 71.
40 I am grateful to Haakon Ikonomou for drawing my attention to this reference. LoNA, R217, Aghnides-Drummond 3 April 1922, LoNA, R217, Aghnides-Drummond, 13 April 1922. Cited in Haakon A. Ikonomou 'The Administrative Anatomy of Failure: The League of Nations Disarmament Section, 1919–1925', *Contemporary European History*, under review, 2019.
41 LoNA, PP, P191, Committees, Liaison Committee, Information Section, 'Memo on Liaison with International Organisations', 21 September 1933, 3. Quoted in Seidenfaden, *Message*, 72.
42 Ibid., 81.
43 Ibid., 74.
44 Report on the Information Section, 16 April 1921, 12 cited in Seidenfaden, *Message*, 76.
45 See also Jonas Brendebach, Martin Herzer, Heidi Tworek (eds.), *International Organizations and the Media in the Nineteenth and Twentieth Centuries. Exorbitant Expectations* (Abingdon: Routledge, 2018).
46 Seidenfaden, *Message*, 75, 92.
47 Ibid., 71, 75, 76.
48 For an overview see the delegates' lists in the IFLNS Bulletin.
49 LoNA R3302, Radziwill, Twelfth annual meeting of the League of Nations Unions [*sic*], 30 June–7 July 1928, The Hague, 30 July 1928.
50 Pelt, 'Information Section – Liste des associations privées, 1933', 8, cited in Seidenfaden, *Message*, 79.
51 For example: LoNA, R5172, Small-Pelt, 17 January 1939.
52 Seidenfaden, *Message*, 157.
53 Pitman B. Potter, 'League Publicity: Cause or Effect of League Failure?', *The Public Opinion Quarterly* 2, no. 10 (1938): 399–412, 406–7.
54 Seidenfaden, *Message*, 138.
55 Ibid., 158.
56 LoNA, R5172, Bombay. Joseph McQuade, *Terrorism, Law and Sovereignty in India and the League of Nations 1897–1945* (Unpublished PhD diss. Cambridge, 2017) 146.
57 On the League in India see ibid.

58 LoNA, R5172, Bombay, Walters-Pelt, 27 December 1934.
59 Ibid., Sen-Ghose, 3 April 1935.
60 Ibid., Ghose-Pelt, 8 January 1935.
61 Ibid., Pelt-Ram, 6 January 1937.
62 Ibid., Ram-Venkatsewaran, 7 January 1937, Ghosh-Ram, 11 December 1936.
63 LoNA, R3303, Report Krabbe, 14th General Assembly, Geneva 5–9 June 1930.
64 British Library, Add Mss 51111, Cecil Papers, Cecil-Drummond, 27 April 1929.
65 LoNA, R3303, Report Krabbe, 14th General Assembly, Geneva 5–9 June 1930.
66 Peter Willetts, 'From "Consultative Arrangements" to "Partnership": The Changing Status of NGOs in Diplomacy at the UN', *Global Governance* 6, no. 2 (2000): 191–212, 196–7. See also Davies, 'A "Great Experiment"', 410.
67 For example the files in LoNA, Information Section, R5177, R5178, R5179, International Federation of League of Nations Societies.
68 LoNA, IFLNS, P93, XIst Plenary Congress Berlin, 26–31 May 1927, Richard, 'Competition'.
69 *Bulletin*, News from societies, France, 16.
70 Cited in Jost Dülfer, 'Vom Internationalismus zum Expansionismus. Die Deutsche Liga für Völkerbund', in *Internationale Beziehungen im 19. und 20. Jahrhundert: Festschrift für Winfried Baumgart zum 65. Geburtstag*, ed. Wolfgang Elz and Sönke Neitzel (Paderborn: Schöningh, 2003), 251–66, 255.
71 Guieu, *Le Rameau*, 69–70.
72 Ruyssen, 'Avant-Propos', *Bulletin* 6, Assemblée, (1927): 2–3.
73 Dülffer, 'Vom Internationalismus'.
74 Jürgen C. Heß, 'Europagedanke und nationaler Revisionismus: Überlegungen zu ihrer Verknüpfung in der Weimarer Republik am Beispiel Wilhelm Heiles', *Historische Zeitschrift* 225, no. JG (1977): 572–622.
75 'Les Associations pour la Société des Nations et leur Union Internationale, *Bulletin* 8, no. 1 (1929): 13–14; IISH, VvVeV, 15.
76 Ruyssen, 'Une année bien rempli', *Bulletin* 8, no. 1 (1929): 9.
77 Thomas Davies, *The Possibilities of Transnational Activism. The Campaign for Disarmament between the Two World Wars* (Leiden: Brill, 2008), 94, 101; Philip Noel-Baker, *The First World Disarmament Conference, 1932–1934, and Why It Failed* (Oxford: Pergamon Press, 1979), 75, cited in Davies, 'Internationalism', 242–3.
78 Mark Mazower, 'Minorities and the League of Nations in Interwar Europe', *Daedalus*, 126, no. 2 (1997): 47–63; Martin Scheuermann, *Minderheitenschutz contra Konfliktverhütung? Die Minderheitenpolitik des Völkerbundes in den zwanziger Jahren* (Marburg, Herder Institut, 2000); Stefan Dyroff, 'Avant-garde or supplement? Advisory bodies of transnational associations as alternatives to the League's Minority Protection System, 1919–1939', *Diplomacy and Statecraft* 24, no. 2 (2013): 192–208; Thomas Smejkal, *Protection in Practice. The Minorities Section of the League of Nations Secretariat, 1919–1934* (Unpublished Senior Thesis, Columbia University 2010).

79 Ibid., 57, 26.
80 Dyroff, 'Avant-garde', Daniel Gorman, 'Ecumenical Internationalism: Willoughby Dickinson, the League of Nations and the World Alliance for Promoting International Friendship through the Churches', *Journal of Contemporary History* 45, no. 1 (2010): 51–73.
81 Ruyssen, 'L'activité de l'Union Internationale des Associations pour la S.D.N. en matière des minorités nationales', *Bulletin* 18, no. 1 (1939): 39–53, 45.
82 Dyroff, 'Avant-garde'.
83 *Bulletin* 9, no. 1–2 (1930): 62–9; Christina Bakker-van Bosse, 'Voyage dans les Balkans', *Minorities Nationales* 3 (1930): 1–9; 'Minderheiten in Sudost-Europa', *Neue Zürcher Zeitung* 9, 11, 13 February 1930; Dyroff, 'Avant-garde', 198.
84 See Dyroff, 'Avant-garde', for examples.
85 Cited in ibid., 201. Ruyssen-E. Bovet, 26 February 1930, Ruyssen II (1928–31) Private Archives of the Bovet Family Lausanne.
86 Dyroff, 'Avant-garde', 203.
87 Pedersen, 'Back to the League', 1097.
88 Zara Steiner, *The Lights That Failed. European International History 1919–1933* (Oxford: Oxford University Press, 2005), 299.

Chapter 10

1 Cit. in 'Rede des Reichsaußenministers Gustav Stresemann zum deutschen Beitritt zum Völkerbund am 10.9.1926', in *Gustav Stresemann: Vermächtnis. Der Nachlaß in drei Bänden*, ed. Henry Bernhard, vol. 2 (Berlin: Ullstein, 1932), 591–5. All translations are mine [MJ].
2 Peter Krüger, *Die Außenpolitik der Republik von Weimar* (Darmstadt: WBG, 1993), 213–18, against earlier research, e.g. Jürgen Spenz, *Die diplomatische Vorgeschichte des Beitritts Deutschlands zum Völkerbund 1924–1926. Ein Beitrag zur Außenpolitik der Weimarer Republik* (Göttingen: Musterschmidt, 1966), 13–19. Rather similar in their line of argument Marshall M. Lee and Wolfgang Michalka, *German Foreign Policy 1917–1933: Continuity or Break?* (Leamington Spa: Berg, 1987), 73–111.
3 The only systematic study of this relationship remains the unpublished PhD of Marshall M. Lee from 1974. Marshall M. Lee, 'Failure in Geneva: The German Foreign Ministry and the League of Nations, 1926–1933' (Phd diss., Madison: University of Wisconsin, 1974); for a condensed version see Marshall M. Lee, 'The German Attempt to Reform the League. The Failure of German League of Nations Policy 1930–1932', *Francia* 5 (1977): 473–90.
4 Krüger, *Außenpolitik*, 210–11; Peter Krüger, 'Die "Westpolitik" in der Weimarer Republik', in *Deutschland und der Westen: Vorträge und Diskussionsbeiträge des*

Symposions zu Ehren von Gordon A. Craig, ed. Henning Köhler (Berlin: Colloquium Verlag, 1984), 105–30.

5   Cit. in Joachim Wintzer, *Deutschland und der Völkerbund 1918–1926* (Paderborn: Schöningh, 2006), 455.

6   Wintzer, *Deutschland und der Völkerbund*, 189, who cites a note of Manley O. Hudson, the US adviser of the League's legal department, to Drummond, 20 August 1920.

7   Symptomatic for this: Politisches Archiv, Auswärtiges Amt (PA/AA), R 96802, Nasse to AA, 26 May 1922.

8   Bernhard Wilhelm von Bülow, *Der Versailler Völkerbund: Eine vorläufige Bilanz* (Berlin: Kohlhammer, 1923); Wintzer, *Deutschland und der Völkerbund*, 14–15, 133, 305–10; Krüger, *Außenpolitik*, 355 (cit.); Hermann Graml, *Bernhard von Bülow und die deutsche Außenpolitik. Hybris und Augenmaß im Auswärtigen Amt* (München: Oldenbourg, 2012), 65–7.

9   Martin Kröger, 'Carl von Schubert. Eine biographische Skizze', in *Carl von Schubert (1882–1947). Sein Beitrag zur internationalen Politik in der Ära der Weimarer Republik (Ausgewählte Dokumente)*, ed. Peter Krüger (Berlin: Duncker & Humblot, 2017), 9–31, here 27–9. A biography of Bülow challenging this interpretation is in print, cf. Annette Schmidt-Klügmann, *Bernhard Wilhelm von Bülow (1885–1936): Eine politische Biographie* (Paderborn: Schöningh, 2020).

10 It is remarkable that Schubert actually inquired with Drummond how the latter would prefer the German delegation to the Assembly to look like. Cf. PA/AA, R 96803: Schubert's note, 15 February 1926, 5; Krüger, *Außenpolitik*, 354, 388.

11 Wintzer, *Deutschland und der Völkerbund*, 92–3.

12 Bernstorff was vice-president (1925–9), then president of the IFLNS (1929–36). Cf. Wintzer, *Deutschland und der Völkerbund*, 185–8; Jost Dülffer: Vom Internationalismus zum Expansionismus: Die Deutsche Liga für Völkerbund, in idem: Frieden stiften: Deeskalations- und Friedenspolitik im 20. Jahrhundert, Köln: Böhlau, 2008 [1989], 174–88.

13 Peter Weber, 'Ernst Jäckh and the National Internationalism of Interwar Germany', *Central European History* 52 (2019): 402–23.

14 PA/AA, R 96803: Bülow's note, 12 February 1926, Schubert's notes, 15/16 February 1926, Poensgen's note, 17 February 1926.

15 PA/AA, R 96860: table 'Verteilung der Beamten des General-Sekretariats auf die Mitglieds-Staaten,' (appr.) 21 November 1925.

16 Of the 484 civil servants included in the AA's table, 138 were English, 17 of which of high rank, 11 from the Dominions (7), 96 French (12), and 21 Italian (10). Cf. PA/AA, R 96803: AA's note (August 1926), 2.

17 PA/AA, R 96860: tables 'Maximum […]' respectively 'Minimum der Stellen[,] die Deutschland im Sekretariat anstreben soll', 21 November 1925. Wintzer, *Deutschland und der Völkerbund*, 455–60, 504–9, 548–54.

18 PA/AA, R 96854: Bülow's note, 18 February 1926; League of Nations [LoN] Distribution Branch: A [Assembly]. 1. 1926 X. [Extraordinary], Memorandum by the secretary-general 'Modifications in the Existing Organisation of the Secretariat', 9 February 1926.
19 PA/AA, R 96803: Aschmann to AA, 6 January 1926, 4–7; Max Beer, 'Drei Pöstchen für Deutschland', *Kölnische Zeitung*, no. 82, 31 January 1926 (cit.); see as well Beer's broader analysis of the League's allegedly anti-German personnel policies: 'Eine Personenänderung im Völkerbund. Wieder ein Beiseiteschieben Deutschlands', *Kölnische Zeitung*, no. 76, 29 January 1926.
20 PA/AA, R 96854: Bülow's note, 17 August 1925.
21 Peter Grupp, *Harry Graf Kessler – eine Biographie* (Frankfurt a. M.: Insel, 1999), 206–11. Kessler's draft dates to October 1920, reprinted as 'Richtlinien für einen wahren Völkerbund', *Die Friedens-Warte* 38 (1938): 45–9.
22 PA/AA, R 97535: Quidde: Bülow's note, 4 June 1926 (cit.).
23 Ludwig Quidde, *Völkerbund und Demokratie* (Berlin: Verlag Neuer Staat, 1922). Cf. Karl Holl, 'Ludwig Quidde und die deutsche Friedensbewegung in der Weimarer Republik', in *Der verlorene Frieden: Politik und Kriegskultur nach 1918*, ed. Jost Dülfer (Essen: Klartext, 2002), 273–85; Karl Holl, *Ludwig Quidde (1858–1941). Eine Biografie* (Düsseldorf: Droste, 2007).
24 PA/AA, R 97534: Ref. Völkerbund: Bewerbungslisten, complemented by individual applications, as documented in PA/AA, R 97535: Ref. Völkerbund: Verwaltungs- und technische Fragen: Bewerbungen speziell; PA/AA, R 96854: Ref. Völkerbund: Verwaltungs- und technische Fragen: Bewerbungen allgemein.
25 PA/AA, R 97535: Sächsisches Stenographisches Landesamt to AA, 17 December 1925 (cit.); Reichsverband der deutschen Industrie an AA, 2 February 1926; ibid., Bund der technischen Angestellten und Beamten to AA, 16 February 1926.
26 PA/AA, R 97535: Aschmann to AA, 28 October 1926.
27 This can be deduced from the League archives' database LONSEA. On that basis, Torsten Kahlert has drawn up a list of German civil servants and employees at the League and kindly provided me with it.
28 PA/AA, R 96860: table initialled by Bülow, presumably 17 February 1927. Isabella Löhr has recently used Schücking's League affiliation as a probing device for German participation in the organization: 'Deutschland im Völkerbund', in *Weimar und die Welt: Globale Verflechtungen der ersten deutschen Republik* (Schriftenreihe der Stiftung Reichspräsident-Friedrich-Ebert-Gedenkstätte, Band 17), ed. Christoph Cornelißen and Dirk van Laak (Göttingen: Vandenhoeck & Ruprecht Verlage).
29 On Renthe-Fink's biography see Corinna Franz, 'Renthe-Fink, Cécil von', *NDB*, vol. 21 (2003), 438–9; *Biographisches Handbuch des deutschen Auswärtigen Dienstes 1871–1945*, ed. Auswärtiges Amt, Historischer Dienst. Band 3: Gerhard Keiper, Martin Kröger: L–R. Paderborn: Schöningh, 2008. *Biographisches Handbuch des deutschen Auswärtigen Dienstes 1871–1945*, ed. Auswärtiges Amt, Historischer Dienst, vol. 3: Gerhard Keiper, Martin Kröger: L–R. Paderborn: Schöningh, 2007, 623–4.

30 PA/AA, R 96860: Renthe-Fink to Bülow, 19 January 1927; ibid., R 97531: Renthe-Fink: Renthe-Fink to AA, 25 November 1926, 12 June 1927 (with enclosed document on salaries within the secretariat, C. 48. 1927, 14 February 1927); ibid., Schubert to Renthe-Fink, 8 November 1927, Dufour to Bülow, 17/19 November 1927, Drummond to Renthe-Fink, 9 December 1926.
31 PA/AA, R 97531: Renthe-Fink: correspondence July to September 1931.
32 PA/AA, R 96806: Renthe-Fink to AA, 28 October 1932 (twice); ibid., R 97531: Renthe-Fink: Renthe-Fink to AA, 28 October 1933.
33 Iris Borowy, 'In the Shadow of Grotjahn: German Social Hygienists in the International Health Scene', in *Of Medicine and Men. Biographies and Ideas in European Social Medicine between the World Wars*, ed. Iris Borowy and Anne Hardy (Frankfurt: Lang, 2008), 141–70, here 158.
34 PA/AA, R 96804: Krauel's note (on German civil servants with the League and its organizations), 18 October 1933; Kamphoevener's notes, 25 October, 2/14/23 November 1933; Trendelenburg to Kamphoevener, 2 November 1933.
35 The phrase is derived from Peter Gay, *Weimar Culture: The Outsider as Insider* (New York: W. W. Norton, 1968).
36 PA/AA, R 96806: Schubert to Drummond (vice versa), 9/15 October 1926 resp. 13 October 1926; Aschmann to AA, 26/27 October 1926; Drummond to Dufour, 27 October 1926.
37 See the documentation of the press reporting: PA/AA, R 96806: *Kölnische Zeitung*, no. 810/811, 30 October 1926, *Journal de Genève*, no. 298, 31 October 1926; Sthamer (London) to AA, 1 November 1926, A. v. Bernstorff (London) to AA, 4 November 1926; Dufour to AA, 11 November 1926.
38 Lee, 'The German Attempt', 474–5 (cit.).
39 Maria Davion and Lucia Warnstedt were employed from 1927 to 1934 and 1926 to 1932 respectively. Cf. PA/AA, R 96806: Dufour to Bülow, 5 May, 21 June 1927, Bülow's note, 9 June 1927, Dufour to AA, 11 November 1926; ibid., Drummond to Dufour, 14 December 1926, 11/14 August 1927.
40 PA/AA, R 96806: Dufour's note, 31 May 1931.
41 Carl von Schubert, Dokumente, Schubert's note, 17 December 1928 (no. 199), stating that Dufour had written within his second year of employment at the secretariat more than 350 of his 'strangely confused' letters to Berlin (cit.).
42 PA/AA, R 97526: Beer: Dufour to Weizsäcker, 24 March 1930, 2–3.
43 Krüger, 'Carl von Schubert', 30–1, on the cooling of the personal relationship between Schubert and Dufour.
44 PA/AA, R 96806: Dufour's note, 3 December 1930, Weizsäcker to Bülow, 26 February 1931.
45 *Biographisches Handbuch des deutschen Auswärtigen Dienstes 1871–1945*, vol. 1 (2000), 470; Herbert Pönicke, 'Dufour-Feronce, Albert', *NDB*, vol. 4 (1959), 177–8.

46 Germania: Zeitung für das deutsche Volk, 'Eckbälle', 14 February 1926, speaks of a 'well-connected, influential man, a staunchly nationalist Jew'.
47 PA/AA, R 97531: Beer: Aschmann to Bülow, 18 April 1927, Bülow's notes, 16 April 1927, 10/14 May 1927, 22 June 1927 (cit.); PA/AA, R 97526: Beer: Dufour to Köpke, 1 November 1927.
48 PA/AA, R 97531: Beer: Dufour to Bülow, 4 August 1927.
49 Cf. the protracted discussion in PA/AA, R 97531: Beer: Bülow's notes, 10/14 May and 22 June 1927; see as well WTB, Eine Richtigstellung, no. 1094, 28 June 1927.
50 PA/AA, R 97531: Beer: Drummond to Beer, 3 June 1927, Comert to Beer, 11 June 1927, Dufour to AA, 28 June 1927.
51 PA/AA, R 97526: Beer: Dufour to Köpke, 1 November 1929, Beer to Weizsäcker, 8 November 1929.
52 PA/AA, R 97526: Beer: Weizsäcker's note, 12 November 1929.
53 PA/AA, R 97526: Beer: Dufour to Weizsäcker, 15 December 1929, Beer to Weizsäcker, 27 December 1929.
54 PA/AA, R 97526: Beer: Dufour to Weizsäcker, 29 January 1930, Beer's (2nd) resignation letter to Drummond, 24 January 1930, Beer to AA, 26 January 1930.
55 PA/AA, R 97526: Beer: Dufour to Weizsäcker, 30 January 1930.
56 PA/AA, R 97527: Beer: Contract (copy) between the AA and Beer, 2 June 1927; Weizsäcker's note, 15 February 1930.
57 PA/AA, R 97527: Beer: Weizsäcker's note, 14 February, 10 July 1930, 17 March 1931, Bülow to Köster (Bern), 9 January 1931.
58 Max Beer, *Die Reise nach Genf* (Berlin: Fischer, 1932).
59 'Nachruf auf Max Beer', *Vereinte Nationen* 13. 6 (1965): 212.
60 Madeleine Herren and Isabella Löhr, 'Being International in Times of War: Arthur Sweetser and the Shifting of the League of Nations to the United Nations', *European Review of History: Revue européenne d'histoire* 25 (2018): 535–52.
61 Wolfram Kaiser and Johan Schot, *Writing the Rules for Europe: Experts, Cartels, and International Organizations* (Basingstoke: Palgrave, 2014).
62 Borowy, 'Social Hygienists', 141–70.
63 PA/AA, R 96816: e.g. Zeiss to AA, 9/24 July 1925. On Zeiss's career cf. Wolfgang U. Eckart: Von Kommissaren und Kamelen. Heinrich Zeiss – Arzt und Kundschafter in der Sowjetunion 1921-31, Paderborn: Schöningh, 2016, 13–70.
64 Borowy, 'Social Hygienists', 150; idem., 'Wissenschaft, Gesundheit, Politik: Das Verhältnis der Weimarer Republik zur Hygieneorganisation des Völkerbundes', *Sozial.Geschichte: Zeitschrift für historische Analyse des 19. und 20. Jahrhunderts* 20 (2005): 30–56, here 40–4; David Macfadyen et al., *Eric Drummond and his Legacies – The League of Nations and the Beginnings of Global Governance* (London: Palgrave, 2019), 164.
65 Borowy, 'Wissenschaft', 44.
66 Borowy, 'Social Hygienists', 158–9.

67 Ibid., 161–3.
68 Lee, 'The German Attempt', 473–90.
69 Wintzer, *Deutschland und der Völkerbund*, 546.
70 Drummond criticized this point explicitly in 1931. Cf. Lee, 'The German Attempt', 475.
71 Madeleine Herren, 'Geneva, 1919–1945. The Spatialities of Public Internationalism and Global Networks', in *Mobilities of Knowledge*, ed. Heike Jöns et al. (Heidelberg: Springer, 2017), 211–26.
72 Stresemann, Vermächtnis, III, 579.

Chapter 11

1 See chapter by Bob Reinalda in this volume: 'Biographical analysis – insights and perspectives from the *IO BIO* dictionary project'.
2 *UN Charter*, Preamble.
3 Report of the Preparatory Commission of the United Nations, UN Doc. PC/20, 23 December 1945, p. 87.
4 Ellen Jenny Ravndal, '"A Force for Peace": Expanding the Role of the UN Secretary-General under Trygve Lie, 1946–1953', *Global Governance* 23, no. 3 (2017): 447–8.
5 This term has also been used by e.g. Peter Wallensteen to discuss Dag Hammarskjöld's diplomatic legacy, because, as he observed, some of the disputes were 'a crisis but not an active armed conflict'. Peter Wallensteen, 'Dag Hammarskjöld's Diplomacy: Lessons Learned', in *Peace Diplomacy, Global Justice and International Agency: Rethinking Human Security and Ethics in the Spirit of Dag Hammarskjöld*, ed. Carsten Stahn and Henning Melber (Cambridge: Cambridge University Press, 2014), 368.
6 Robert D. Putnam, 'Diplomacy and Domestic Politics: The Logic of Two-level Games', *International Organization* 42, no. 3 (1988).
7 Wallensteen, 'Hammarskjöld's Diplomacy', 366.
8 Ibid., 366–7.
9 M. Christiane Bourloyannis, 'Fact-finding by the Secretary-General of the United Nations', *New York University Journal of International Law and Politics* 22, no. 4 (1990).
10 Jacob Bercovitch, 'Mediation and Conflict Resolution', in *The SAGE Handbook of Conflict Resolution*, ed. Jacob Bercovitch, Victor Kremenyuk, and I. William Zartman (London: SAGE Publications, 2009), 347.
11 Arthur W. Rovine, *The First Fifty Years: The Secretary-General in World Politics 1920–1970* (Leyden: A. W. Sijthoff, 1970); Francis Paul Walters, *A History of the League of Nations*, vol. 1 (Oxford: Oxford University Press, 1952); James Barros,

Office without Power: Secretary-General Sir Eric Drummond, 1919–1933 (Oxford: Clarendon Press, 1979).

12 Bercovitch, 'Mediation and Conflict Resolution', 347.
13 Ibid.
14 Manuel Fröhlich, 'The "Suez Story": Dag Hammarskjöld, the United Nations and the Creation of UN Peacekeeping', in *Peace Diplomacy, Global Justice and International Agency: Rethinking Human Security and Ethics in the Spirit of Dag Hammarskjöld*, ed. Carsten Stahn and Henning Melber (Cambridge: Cambridge University Press, 2014).
15 Teresa Whitfield, 'Good Offices and "Groups of Friends"', in *Secretary or General? The UN Secretary-General in World Politics*, ed. Simon Chesterman (Cambridge: Cambridge University Press, 2007).
16 Kent J. Kille, 'Moral Authority and the UN Secretary-General's Ethical Framework', in *The UN Secretary-General and Moral Authority: Ethics and Religion in International Leadership*, ed. Kent J. Kille (Washington, DC: Georgetown University Press, 2007).
17 Ellen Jenny Ravndal, 'A Guardian of the UN Charter: The UN Secretary-General at 75', *Ethics & International Affairs* (forthcoming 2020).
18 Quang Trinh, 'The Bully Pulpit', in *Secretary or General? The UN Secretary-General in World Politics*, ed. Simon Chesterman (Cambridge: Cambridge University Press, 2007), 102–20.
19 Trygve Lie, *In the Cause of Peace: Seven Years with the United Nations* (New York: Macmillan, 1954), 28.
20 For more on the background and evolution of the conflict, see e.g. Neil Caplan, *Futile Diplomacy, Volume 2: Arab-Zionist Negotiations and the End of the Mandate* (London: Frank Cass, 1986); Ilan Pappé, *The Making of the Arab-Israeli Conflict, 1947–1951*, Paperback ed. (London and New York: I.B. Tauris, 1994; repr., 2008); Benny Morris, *1948: The First Arab-Israeli War* (New Haven and London: Yale University Press, 2008). For more on the process at the UN, see Ellen Jenny Ravndal, '"The First Major Test": The UN Secretary-General and the Palestine Problem, 1947–9', *The International History Review* 38, no. 1 (2016); Elad Ben-Dror, 'Ralph Bunche and the Establishment of Israel', *Israel Affairs* 14, no. 3 (2008); Jørgen Jensehaugen, Marte Heian-Engdal, and Hilde Henriksen Waage, 'Securing the State: From Zionist Ideology to Israeli Statehood', *Diplomacy & Statecraft* 23, no. 2 (2012); Marte Heian-Engdal, Jørgen Jensehaugen, and Hilde Henriksen Waage, '"Finishing the Enterprise": Israel's Admission to the United Nations', *The International History Review* 35, no. 3 (2013).
21 Ravndal, 'The First Major Test', 200.
22 Ibid., 205–7.
23 For more on the background and evolution of the Berlin blockade, see Avi Shlaim, *The United States and the Berlin Blockade, 1948–1949: A Study in Crisis Decision-*

making (Berkeley: University of California Press, 1983); Daniel F. Harrington, *Berlin on the Brink: The Blockade, the Airlift, and the Early Cold War* (Lexington, KY: University Press of Kentucky, 2012).

24 Minutes of meeting, 29 June 1948, S-0194-003-06, United Nations Archive and Records Management Section, New York.
25 Lie to Sissel Bratz, 27 October 1948. Letter in the Bratz family's possession. Copy provided by Guri Hjeltnes. Author's translation from Norwegian.
26 Ellen Jenny Ravndal, 'La mission la plus impossible au monde: Le Secrétaire général Trygve Lie face à la Guerre froide, 1946–1953', [The Most Impossible Job in the World: UN Secretary-General Trygve Lie and the Cold War, 1946–1953.] *Revue d'histoire diplomatique* 130, no. 2 (2016): 150–2.
27 Quoted in Ellen Jenny Ravndal, 'Trygve Lie (1946–1953)', in *The UN Secretary-General and the Security Council: A Dynamic Relationship*, ed. Manuel Fröhlich and Abiodun Williams (Oxford: Oxford University Press, 2018), 35.
28 Harrington, *Berlin on the Brink*, 185.
29 Philip C. Jessup, 'The Berlin Blockade and the Use of the United Nations', Article, *Foreign Affairs* 50, no. 1 (1971); Philip C. Jessup, 'Park Avenue Diplomacy – Ending the Berlin Blockade', *Political Science Quarterly* 87, no. 3 (1972).
30 David L. Bosco, 'Assessing the UN Security Council: A Concert Perspective', *Global Governance* 20, no. 4 (2014): 554.
31 Oral history interview with John D. Hickerson, 1972–3, Harry S. Truman Library: http://www.trumanlibrary.org/oralhist/hickrson.htm (accessed 8 August 2019).
32 Andrew W. Cordier and Wilder Foote (eds.), *Public Papers of the Secretaries-General of the United Nations: Vol. 1: Trygve Lie, 1946–1953* (New York: Columbia University Press, 1969), 20.
33 Simon Chesterman, 'Article 99', in *The Charter of the United Nations: A Commentary, Volume 2*, ed. Bruno Simma et al. (Oxford: Oxford University Press, 2012), 2016.
34 Ravndal, 'La mission la plus impossible', 156–7.
35 Lie, *In the Cause of Peace*, 329.
36 Memorandum of conversation (Ross, Hickerson), 28 June 1950, *Foreign Relations of the United States* 1950, vol. VII, pp. 221–2.
37 Ravndal, 'La mission la plus impossible', 158.
38 Ravndal, 'A Force for Peace', 456.
39 'Statement by Secretary-General Dag Hammarskjöld at a General Meeting of the Staff', UN Press Release SD/299, 1 May 1953.
40 Manuel Fröhlich, 'Dag Hammarskjöld, 1953–1961', in *The UN Secretary-General and the Security Council: A Dynamic Relationship*, ed. Manuel Fröhlich and Abiodun Williams (Oxford: Oxford University Press, 2018), 42. See also Brian E. Urquhart, *Hammarskjöld*, Paperback ed. (New York: W. W. Norton, 1994), 9–16; Brian E. Urquhart, 'The Secretary-General – Why Dag Hammarskjöld?', in *The*

Adventure of Peace: Dag Hammarskjöld and the Future of the UN, ed. Sten Ask and Anna Mark-Jungkvist (Basingstoke: Palgrave Macmillan, 2005), 14–22.
41 Kofi A. Annan, 'Dag Hammarskjöld and the 21st Century', *The Fourth Dag Hammarskjöld Lecture*: www.dhf.uu.se/pdffiler/Kofi%20Annan.pdf (6 September 2001).
42 Roger Lipsey, *Hammarskjöld: A Life* (Ann Arbor: University of Michigan Press, 2016), 319; Urquhart, 'Why Dag Hammarskjöld', 20; Wallensteen, 'Hammarskjöld's diplomacy', 372.
43 For more on the issue of American airmen in China and Hammarskjöld's mission to release them, see Urquhart, *Hammarskjöld*, 96–131; Manuel Fröhlich, *Political Ethics and the United Nations: Dag Hammarskjöld as Secretary-General* (London and New York: Routledge, 2008), 132–45; Lipsey, *Hammarskjöld*, 210–36.
44 Andrew W. Cordier and Wilder Foote (eds.), *Public Papers of the Secretaries-General of the United Nations: Vol. 2: Dag Hammarskjöld, 1953–1956* (New York: Columbia University Press, 1972), 416–17.
45 Fröhlich, *Political Ethics*; Lipsey, *Hammarskjöld*.
46 Barros, *Office without Power*.
47 A. James, 'The Role of the Secretary-General of the United Nations in International Relations', *International Relations*, October 1959, p. 627, quoted in Fröhlich, *Political Ethics*, 132.
48 Lipsey, *Hammarskjöld*, 232–3; Fröhlich, *Political Ethics*, 144.
49 Lipsey, *Hammarskjöld*, 230–4.
50 For more on the background and developments of the Suez crisis, see Keith Kyle, *Suez: Britain's End of Empire in the Middle East*, New ed. (London: I.B. Tauris, 2011); Wm. Roger Louis and Roger Owen (eds.), *Suez 1956: The Crisis and Its Consequences* (Oxford: Clarendon Press, 1989); Simon C. Smith (ed.), *Reassessing Suez 1956: New Perspectives on the Crisis and Its Aftermath* (Aldershot: Ashgate, 2008). For details on Hammarskjöld's activities, see Urquhart, *Hammarskjöld*, 159–94; Fröhlich, 'Suez story'; Lipsey, *Hammarskjöld*, 285–318.
51 Lipsey, *Hammarskjöld*, 293; Urquhart, *Hammarskjöld*, 165–9.
52 Fröhlich, 'Suez Story', 313–16.
53 Quoted in ibid., 315.
54 Ibid., 322–3.
55 Brian E. Urquhart, *Ralph Bunche: An American Life* (New York and London: W. W. Norton, 1993), 264–90; Fröhlich, 'Suez Story', 329–30.
56 For more on the background and development of the Congo crisis and the UN's involvement, see Alanna O'Malley, *The Diplomacy of Decolonisation: America, Britain and the United Nations during the Congo Crisis 1960–1964* (Manchester: Manchester University Press, 2018); Henning Melber, *Dag Hammarskjöld, the United Nations and the Decolonisation of Africa* (London: Hurst & Company, 2019).

57 Andrew W. Cordier and Wilder Foote (eds.), *Public Papers of the Secretaries-General of the United Nations: Vol. 5: Dag Hammarskjöld, 1960–1961* (New York: Columbia University Press, 1975), 20–3; Chesterman, 'Article 99', 2014–15.
58 Melber, *Dag Hammarskjöld*, 76.
59 Ibid.
60 Fröhlich, *Political Ethics*, 164–6.
61 Quoted in Cordier and Foote, *Public Papers, vol. 5*, 197–8.
62 Quoted in ibid., 200–01.
63 Alynna J. Lyon, 'The UN Charter, the New Testament, and Psalms: The Moral Authority of Dag Hammarskjöld', in *The UN Secretary-General and Moral Authority: Ethics and Religion in International Leadership*, ed. Kent J. Kille (Washington, DC: Georgetown University Press, 2007), 131–2; Fröhlich, *Political Ethics*, 166–74.
64 Wallensteen, 'Hammarskjöld's diplomacy', 381–5.
65 Manuel Fröhlich, 'The Special Representatives of the United Nations Secretary-General', in *Routledge Handbook of International Organization*, ed. Bob Reinalda (London: Routledge, 2013), 231–43.
66 Ravndal, 'A Force for Peace'.

Chapter 12

1 Linda Risso, '"I Am the Servant of the Council": Lord Ismay and the Making of the NATO International Staff', *Contemporary European History* 28, no. 3 (2019): 342–57.
2 SACEUR is at the same time Supreme Allied Commander of all NATO forces as well as United States Commander-in-Chief Europe (USCINCEUR). For key references, see Robert S. Jordan, *Norstad: Cold War NATO Supreme Commander: Airman, Strategist, Diplomat* (London: St. Martin's Press, 2000); and Robert S. Jordan (ed.), *Generals in International Politics* (Lexington, KY: University Press of Kentucky, 1987). See also Gregory Pedlow, 'Three Hats for Berlin: General Lauris Norstad and the Second Berlin Crisis, 1958–62', in *The Berlin Wall Crisis: Perspectives on Cold War Alliances*, ed. John P. S. Gearson and Kori Schake (London: Palgrave Macmillan, 2002), 175–98. Lawrence S. Kaplan 'General Lyman L. Lemnitzer and NATO, 1948–1969: A Deferential Leader', *Cold War History* 19, no. 3 (2019): 323–41.
3 Linda Risso, 'Writing the History of NATO: A New Agenda', in *NATO at 70: A New Historiographical Approach*, ed. Linda Risso (London: Routledge, 2019), 1–6.
4 Robert S. Jordan with Michael W. Bloome, *Political Leadership in NATO: A Study in Multinational Diplomacy* (Boulder, CO: Westview Press, 1979).

5   Ryan C. Hendrickson, *Diplomacy and War at NATO. The Secretary General and Military Action after the Cold War* (Columbia and London: University of Missouri Press, 2006).
6   Antoine Vauchez, 'The Force of a Weak Field: Law and Lawyers in the Government of the European Union (For a Renewed Research Agenda)', *International Political Sociology*, no. 2 (2008): 128–44. See also the chapters in this volume: 'Secretaries General and Crisis Management – Trygve Lie and Dag Hammarskjöld at the United Nations' by Ellen Ravndal; and 'The Making of the International Civil Servant c. 1920–60 – Establishing the Profession' by Haakon A. Ikonomou and Karen Gram-Skjoldager.
7   Michael G. Schechter, 'Leadership in International Organisations: Systemic, Organisational and Personality Factors', *Review of International Studies* 13, no. 3 (1987): 197–220.
8   Karen Gram-Skjoldager and Haakon A. Ikonomou, 'Making Sense of the League of Nations Secretariat: Historiographical and Conceptual Reflections on Early International Public Administration', *European History Quarterly* 49, no. 3 (2019): 420–44. Karen Gram-Skjoldager and Haakon Ikonomou, 'The Construction of the League of Nations Secretariat. Formative Practices of Autonomy and Legitimacy in International Organizations', *International History Review* (2017): 1–23.
9   'North Atlantic Council, Rome, 14–28 November 1951, Final communiqué', 28 November 1951. 'Record of a Meeting' 5 February 1952, NATO, DR(52)5 (Final). Lord Ismay, *The First Five Years, 1949-1954*: www.nato.int/archives/1st5years/chapters/6.htm (All links cited in this chapter have been last accessed on 20 October 2019); Final Communiqué of the Ninth Session of the North Atlantic Council ('The Lisbon Decisions'), 25 February 1952. And Telegram 740.5/2-2552. The United States Delegation to the Department of State. Lisbon, 25 February 1952, midnight. *Foreign Relations of the United States, 1952–1954* (henceforward *FRUS*), vol. V, part 1. See also Ismay, *Five Years*, chapter 6: 'The Civil Structure'.
10 Risso, 'I Am the Servant of the Council', 342–57.
11 Ronald Wingate, *Lord Ismay: A Biography* (London: Hutchinson, 1970), 192; 'Lord Ismay on His Plans Reorganization of NATO Staff', *The Times*, 19 April 1952.
12 Gram-Skjoldager and Ikonomou, 'The Construction'. Susan Pedersen, *The Guardians: The League of Nations and the Crisis of Empire* (Oxford: Oxford University Press, 2015). James Barros, *Office without Power: Secretary-General Sir Eric Drummond 1919–1933* (Oxford: Oxford University Press, 1979).
13 Risso 'I Am the Servant of the Council'. See also N. Piers Ludlow, *Roy Jenkins and the European Commission Presidency, 1976–1980: At the Heart of Europe* (London: Palgrave Macmillan, 2016).
14 Lord Ismay's speech to Abernethian Society, St Bartholomew's Hospital, 22 May 1958, LHCMA, Ismay 1/7/33a.
15 *NATO Letter*, vol. 5, special supplement to n. 6.

16 'Lord Ismay on His Plans Reorganization of NATO Staff', *The Times*, 19 April 1952. Ambassador Sergio Fenoaltea (Italy) headed the Political Affairs Division, M. Rene Sergent (France) the Economics and Finance Division, and Mr. Lowell P. Weicker (USA) the Production and Logistics Division.
17 The first deputy secretary-general was the Dutch Jonkheer Henri van Vredenburch.
18 'Vote of Thanks to Chairman and Board of Directors of Shell at the Annual General Meeting', 20 May 1958, LHCMA, Ismay 1/7/32/a.
19 *NATO Staff Manual*, 2 February 1953, item 3,000. The *NATO Staff Association Bulletin* started to be circulated from 1955.
20 Speech to Abernethian Society, St Bartholomew's Hospital, 22 May 1958, LHCMA, Ismay 1/7/33a.
21 There is a rich debate on the nature and limits of political cooperation within NATO. Among the most detailed studies that look at the long-term development of this question are Timothy Andrews Sayle, *Enduring Alliance: A History of NATO and the Postwar Global Order* (Ithaca, NY: Cornell University Press, 2019). Linda Risso, *Propaganda and Intelligence in the Cold War: The NATO Information Service* (London: Routledge, 2014).
22 Draft of Memorandum by the Assistant Secretary of State for European Affairs (Merchant) to the Secretary of State, Washington, 7 July 1953, FRUS, *Western European Security, 1952–1954*, V, part 1.
23 Winfried Heinemann, '"Learning by Doing": Disintegrating Factors and the Development of Political Cooperation in Early NATO', in *NATO and the Warsaw Pact: Intrabloc Conflicts*, ed. May Anny Heiss and S. Victor Papacosma (Kent, OH: The Kent State University Press, 2008), 43–57; Dionysos Chourchoulis, *The Southern Flank of NATO, 1951–1959* (New York, London: Lexington Books, 2014).
24 Wingate, Lord Ismay, 209.
25 'The Evolution of NATO Political Consultation, 1949–1962', 3 May 1963, NATO, NHO/63/1. 'Report of the Committee of the Three on Non-military Cooperation in NATO', 13 December 1953: https://www.nato.int/cps/en/natolive/topics_65237.htm (accessed 18 December 2019). See also 'The Evolution of NATO Political Consultation, 1949–1962', 3 May 1963, NATO, NHO/63/1. There is a rich historiographical debate on the impact of the Suez Crisis on the political cohesion of the West and on NATO in particular. Among the most important contributions are Heinemann, '"Learning by doing"'; W. Scott Lucas, *Divided We Stand. Britain, the US and the Suez Crisis* (London: Hodder & Stoughton, 1991).
26 As quoted in Jordan, *NATO International Staff*, 101.
27 Paul-Henri Spaak, *The Continuing Battle: Memoirs of a European, 1936–1966* (London: Weidenfeld, 1971). See also the chapter 'Learning across Institutions' by Katja Seidel, in this volume.
28 Paul-Henri Spaak, 'The Atlantic Community and NATO', *Orbis* I, no. 4 (1958): 397–427.

29 Ibid., 397–427.
30 Paul-Henri Spaak, Speech to NATO Parliamentarians' Conference, November 1959.
31 There is a rich body of literature on de Gaulle's approach to European security and to NATO, among which the most interesting contributions are Garret J. Martin, *General de Gaulle's Cold War: Challenging American Hegemony, 1963–68* (New York: Berghahn Books, 2013) and James Ellison and Oliver J. Daddow, 'Dealing with de Gaulle: Anglo-American Relations, NATO and the Second Application', in *Harold Wilson and European Integration: Britain's Second Application to Join the EEC*, ed. Oliver J. Daddow (London: Cass, 2000), 172–87.
32 Risso, *Propaganda and Intelligence*.
33 Francis A. Beer, *Integration and Disintegration in NATO. Processes of Alliance Cohesion and Prospects for Atlantic Community* (Columbus, OH: Ohio State University Press, 1969), 30. Jordan, *Political Leadership*, 48–9 and 82–3.
34 Paul-Henri Spaak, *The Continuing Battle: Memoirs of a European, 1936–1966* (London: Weidenfeld, 1971), 343–7.
35 Wörner also held a doctorate from the Ludwig-Maximilian University of Munich in international law specializing in military issues. He was a jet pilot and reserve officer of the Luftwaffe.
36 Ronald D. Asmus, *Opening NATO's Door: How the Alliance Remade Itself for a New Era* (A Council of Foreign Relations Book, Columbia University Press, 2002).
37 See for example Manfred Wörner, 'A Time of Accelerating Change' and 'North Atlantic Council Communiqué' both in *NATO Review* 37, no. 6 (December 1989).
38 For video footage of Wörner's visit to Russia: 'NATO Secretary General in Russia': https://www.youtube.com/watch?v=keUGR5P2Pnk (accessed 18 December 2019).
39 See 'Chronology' in the *NATO Handbook* (Brussels: NATO Office of Information and Press, 2001), 432–48 and articles published in the *NATO Review* at the time.
40 See Manfred Wörner, 'NATO Transformed: The Significance of the Rome Summit', *NATO Review* 39, no. 6 (December 1991).
41 The document stressed, 'At this time of unprecedented promise in international affairs, we will respond to the hopes that it offers. The Alliance will continue to serve as the cornerstone of our security, peace and freedom. Secure on this foundation, we will reach out to those who are willing to join us in shaping a more stable and peaceful international environment in the service of our societies.' 'Declaration of the Heads of State and Government participating in the Meeting of the North Atlantic Council. Brussels, 29–30 May 1989': http://www.nato.int/docu/comm/49-95/c890530a.htm (accessed 18 December 2019).
42 'Our determination to seize the historic opportunities resulting from the profound changes in Europe to help build a new peaceful order in Europe, based on freedom, justice and democracy. In this spirit, we extend to the Soviet Union and to all other European countries the hand of friendship and cooperation.' Message from

Turnberry. Ministerial Meeting of the North Atlantic Council. Turnberry, United Kingdom, 7–8 June 1990: www.nato.int/docu/comm/49-95/c900608b.htm. And we recognize that, in the new Europe, the security of every state is inseparably linked to the security of its neighbours. NATO must become an institution where Europeans, Canadians and Americans work together not only for the common defence, but to build new partnerships with all the nations of Europe. The Atlantic Community must reach out to the countries of the East which were our adversaries in the Cold War and extend to them the hand of friendship. LONDON DECLARATION, 5–6 July 1990, Declaration on a Transformed North Atlantic Alliance: https://www.nato.int/cps/en/natohq/official_texts_23693.htm (accessed 18 December 2019).

43 Manfred Wörner, 'The Atlantic Alliance in the New Era', *NATO Review* 39, no. 1 (February 1991); see also Wörner, 'NATO Transformed'.

44 Manfred Wörner, 'NATO Transformed: The Significance of the Rome Summit', *NATO Review* 39, no. 6 (December 1991). See also Michael Legge, 'The Making of NATO's Strategy' published in the same issue of the *NATO Review*. It may be worth reminding the reader that at the time the EU did include neither any proper common defence nor common foreign policy worth of their name.

45 'Study on NATO Enlargement', 3 September 1995: https://www.nato.int/cps/en/natohq/official_texts_24733.htm (accessed 18 December 2019).

46 Interviews with Michael Ruehle and Jamie Shea, Episode 7, *Tearing Down Walls* and Episode 8, *NATO Becomes Operations*: https://shape.nato.int/history/information/podcasts/episodes (accessed 18 December 2019).

47 Richard Holbrooke, *To End a War* (New York: Random House, 1998), 27.

48 Interviews with Michael Ruehle and Jamie Shea, Episode 7, *Tearing Down Walls* and Episode 8, *NATO Becomes Operations*: https://shape.nato.int/history/information/podcasts/episodes (accessed 18 December 2019).

Chapter 13

1 The literature that explores the profession of the international civil servant and its historical origins is often produced by practitioners with close ties to the UN. For an early example of this, see Dag Hammarskjöld's seminal: 'The International Civil Servant in Law and in Fact. Lecture Delivered by Dag Hammarskjöld, Oxford 30 May 1960', reprinted in *100 Years of International Civil Service*, no. 4, Dag Hammarskjöld Foundation, Stockholm 2019: https://www.daghammarskjold.se/wp-content/uploads/2019/10/ics_100_no_4_oxfordspeech.pdf (accessed 12 December 2019). There are a few exceptions though they tend to centre around the role of the UN in this process; see in particular: Norman A. Graham and

Robert S. Jordan: *The International Civil Service: Changing Role and Concepts*, Pergamon 1980; Robert S. Jordan, 'The Fluctuating Fortunes of the United Nations International Civil Service: Hostage to Politics or Undeservedly Criticized?', *Public Administration Review* 4, no. 4 (1991): 553–7.

2   Susan Pedersen, 'Back to the League of Nations', *American Historical Review* 112, no. 4 (2007): 1091–117.

3   Two interpretations that span the nineteenth and twentieth centuries are Mark Mazower, *Governing the World: The History of an Idea, 1815 to Present* (London: Penguin Books, 2013); Akira Iriye, *Global Community. The Role of International Organizations in the Making of the Contemporary World* (Berkeley: University of California Press, 2004).

4   For a comprehensive list, see the introduction to this volume.

5   See for instance Egon F. Ranshofen-Wertheimer, *The International Secretariat. A Great Experiment in International Administration* (Washington: Carnegie Endowment for International Peace, 1945), F. P. Walters, *Administrative Problems of International Organization* (Oxford: Oxford University Press, 1941); *The International Secretariat of the Future: Lessons from Experience by a Group of Former Officials of the League of Nations* (London: The Royal Institute of International Affairs, 1944).

6   See for instance James Barros, *Office without Power. Secretary-General Sir Eric Drummond, 1919–1933* (Oxford: Clarendon Press, 1979); Arthur W. Rovine, *The First Fifty Years: The Secretary-General in World Politics 1920–1970* (Leyden: Sijthoff, 1970).

7   Ranshofen-Wertheimer, *The International Secretariat*, 8.

8   Donald C. Stone, Administrative Aspects of World Organization: A Paper Presented at the Fourth Conference on Science, Philosophy and Religion Held at New York City, 12 September 1943 (mimeographed).

9   Ranshofen-Wertheimer, *The International Secretariat*, 8.

10 Ibid., 9.

11 Austen Chamberlain, 'Civil Service Traditions and the League of Nations, by the Rt. Hon. Sir Austen Chamberlain, K.G., M.P. [Being the inaugural address for the Session 1929–30]', *Public Administration* 8:1(1930): 5.

12 This connection is also made by Ranshofen-Wertheimer, *The International Secretariat*, 79. See also *Allied Shipping Control. An Experiment in International Administration* (Oxford: Clarendon Press, 1921) by the director of the League's Economic and Financial Section, J. A. Salter.

13 For an introduction to the bureaucracies of these bodies, see Bob Reinalda's chapter in this volume.

14 Karen Gram-Skjoldager, 'Drummond, Sir James Eric' in *IO BIO, Biographical Dictionary of Secretaries-General of International Organizations*, edited by Bob Reinalda, Kent J. Kille and Jaci Eisenberg: http://www.ru.nl/fm/iobio (accessed 18 December 2019).

15 Civil Service Traditions, 4–5.
16 League of Nations Archives, Geneva [Henceforth LONA], [Registry Files] R1455, Secretariat of the League of Nations. Draft of Provisional Organisation – Villa Majestic, Paris, 31 March 1919, M. Hankey; Salter 1921 pp. 278–80; Article in *The World Today*, March 1924, as quoted in C. Howard Ellis, *The Origin, Structure and Working of the League of Nations* (London: Allen & Unwin, 1928), 171–2. From Robert S. Jordan, *The NATO International Staff/Secretariat 1952–1957* (London: Oxford University Press, 1967), 5–6.
17 Karen Gram-Skjoldager and Haakon A. Ikonomou, 'The Construction of the League of Nations Secretariat. Formative Practices of Autonomy and Legitimacy in International Organizations', *International History Review* 41, no. 2 (2019): 257–79.
18 Article in *The World Today*, March 1924, as quoted in Ellis, *The Origin, Structure and Working of the League of Nations*, 171–2. From Jordan, *The NATO International Staff/Secretariat 1952–1957*, 5–6.
19 Ibid.
20 Zara Steiner, 'The Last Years of the Old Foreign Office, 1898–1905', *The Historical Journal* 6, no. 1 (1963): 59–90, 63.
21 Steiner, 'The Last Years of the Old Foreign Office', 67.
22 Ibid., 71.
23 Ibid., 89.
24 Haakon A. Ikonomou, 'An International Language: The Translation and Interpretation Service', in *The League of Nations – Perspectives from the Present*, ed. Haakon A. Ikonomou and Karen Gram-Skjoldager (Aarhus: Aarhus University Press, 2019), 30–9. See also Myriam Piguet, 'Gender Distribution in the League of Nations: The Start of a Revolution?' in *The League of Nations – Perspectives from the Present*, ed. Haakon A. Ikonomou and Karen Gram-Skjoldager (Aarhus: Aarhus University Press, 2019), 62–71.
25 Steiner, 'The Last Years of the Old Foreign Office', 88.
26 Letter from Herbert Ames to Louis Forrer, Director, L'Union internationale pour le transport des marchandises par chemin de fer, 24 November 1919, LONA-R1475. See also Correspondence with the Bureau International d'Hygiene, Correspondence with the Bureau international de l'Union Telegraphique, Berne, Correspondence with the Union internationale pour la Protection de la Propriete industrielle, Berne, all LONA-R1475.
27 Karen Gram-Skjoldager, Haakon A. Ikonomou and Torsten Kahlert, 'Scandinavians in the League of Nations 1919–1946', *Scandinavian Journal of History* 44, no. 4 (2019): 454–83.
28 On the creation of the Appointments Committee, see Gram-Skjoldager and Ikonomou, 'The Construction of the League of Nations Secretariat. Formative Practices of Autonomy and Legitimacy in International Organizations', 257–79, 264–5.
29 LONA-R1460: *Staff Regulations*, 1922, Article 1.

30 LONA-R1460: *Staff Regulations*, 1922, Articles 1–4.
31 Ranshofen-Wertheimer, *The International Secretariat*, 265ff.
32 Martin Hill, 'Immunities and Privileges of Officials of the League of Nations', in *Studies in the Administration of International Law and Organization* (Washington: Carnegie Endowment for International Peace, 1945), 9–12.
33 Hill, *Immunities and Privileges*, 13–39.
34 Douglas Gageby, *The Last Secretary General. Sean Lester and the League of Nations* (Dublin: Townhouse, 1999), 209–14.
35 On the German members of the secretariat, see Michael Jonas's chapter in this volume. On Italy's relationship with and presence in the secretariat, see Elisabetta Tollardo, *Fascist Italy and the League of Nations, 1922–1935* (London/New York: Palgrave Macmillan, 2016).
36 Ranshofen-Wertheimer, *The International Secretariat*, 27–31.
37 Quoted from ibid., 245.
38 Ibid., 246.
39 James Barros, *Betrayal from within. Joseph Avenol, Secretary-General of the League of Nations, 1933–1940* (New Haven: Yale University Press, 1969), 219 (quote), 238.
40 Gageby, *The Last Secretary General*, 188–249.
41 Glenda Sluga, *Internationalism in the Age of Nationalism* (Philadelphia: University of Pennsylvania Press, 2013), 89.
42 The pension plan of the League Secretariat was equally adopted, as were the High Administrative Tribunal to settle disputes between members of staff and the organization. Bob Reinalda, *Routledge History of International Organizations. From 1815 to the Present Day* (London, New York: Routledge, 2009), 319–20.
43 Karen Gram-Skjoldager 'From the League of Nations to the United Nations. Milestones for the International Civil Service', *100 Years of International Civil Service*, No. 3, Dag Hammarskjöld Foundation, 2019: https://www.daghammarskjold.se/wp-content/uploads/2019/09/ics_100_no_3_karin-gs.pdf (accessed 18 December 2019).
44 Benjamin Auberer, 'Digesting the League of Nations: Planning the International Secretariat of the Future, 1941–1944', *New Global Studies* 10, no. 3 (2016): 393–426; Royal Institute of International Affairs, *Secretariat of the Future*.
45 Aghnides was a real *éminence grise* of the UN's internal administration. Not only did he head the ICSAB, he was also chairman of the very influential Advisory Committee on Administrative and Budgetary Matters, balancing the fiscal priorities of the secretary-general, the assembly, the agencies and the Security Council members. Upon his retirement from the UN in the early 1960s, he was one of two officials that had served under *all* League and UN secretaries-general. Haakon A. Ikonomou, *The International Bureaucrat in the Twentieth Century – A Transnational Biography of Thanassis Aghnides* (London: Palgrave Macmillan, forthcoming 2021).

46　International Civil Service Advisory Board (hereafter ICSAB), 'Report on Standards of Conduct in the International Civil Service', *United Nations* (1954): 2; Auberer, *Digesting the League*, 424.
47　ICSAB, 'Report on Recruitment Methods and Standards for the United Nations and the Specialized Agencies', *United Nations* 18 (1950): 28–30.
48　ICSAB, 'Report on Recruitment Methods', 9–11.
49　ICSAB, 'Report on Recruitment Methods', 7, 11, 13.
50　ICSAB, 'Report on Recruitment Methods', 9–10.
51　Columbia Rare Books and Manuscripts, Cordier Papers, Box 82 'International Civil Servant Association'. 10 November 1952, Second Meeting 1952–3 Session, UN Headquarters. Standards of Conduct of the International Civil Servant by H. E. Thanassis Aghnides.
52　Haakon A. Ikonomou 'Thanassis Aghnides og skabelsen af den internationale embedsmand', *Baggrund*, 2 September 2019: https://baggrund.com/2019/09/02/thanassis-aghnides-og-skabelsen-af-den-internationale-embedsmand/ (accessed 18 December 2019).
53　Reinalda, *Routledge History of International Organizations*, 323–4.
54　UNESCO, *A Chronology of UNESCO, 1945–1985* (Paris: UNESCO, 1985), 60.
55　Yves Beigbeder, 'The United Nations Secretariat: Reform in Progress', in *The United Nations at Millennium. The Principal Organs*, ed. P. Taylor and A. J. R. Groom (London and New York: Continuum, 2000), 200.
56　Auberer, 'Digesting the League'.
57　Reinalda, *Routledge History of International Organizations*, 323–4.
58　Beigbeder, 'The United Nations Secretariat', 196–223, 201; Gram-Skjoldager, 'From the League of Nations to the United Nations'.

References

'Eckbälle' in *Germania: Zeitung für das deutsche Volk*, 14 February 1926.
'The Evolution of NATO Political Consultation, 1949–1962', 3 May 1963, NATO, NHO/63/1.
'Lord Ismay on His Plans Reorganization of NATO Staff', *The Times*, 19 April 1952.
'Nachruf auf Max Beer', *Vereinte Nationen* 13, no. 6 (1965): 212.
'North Atlantic Council, Rome, 14–28 November 1951, Final communiqué', 28 November 1951. 'Record of a Meeting' 5 February 1952, NATO, DR(52)5 (Final).
'Report of the Committee of the Three on Non-military Cooperation in NATO' (13 December 1953). Available at: https://www.nato.int/cps/en/natolive/topics_65237.htm (accessed 18 December 2019).
'Richtlinien für einen wahren Völkerbund', *Die Friedens-Warte*, 38 (1938): 45–9.
'Vote of thanks to Chairman and Board of Directors of Shell at the Annual General Meeting', 20 May 1958, LHCMA, Ismay 1/7/32/a.
Aghnides, N. P. *Mohammedan Theories of Finance. Studies in History, Economics, and Public Law. Columbia University*. New York: Long, Green and co., 1916.
Aghnides, T. 'Greek Art Itself Again', *The New World* (n.d.).
Aghnides, T. 'Vladimir Rosing and Greek Music', *The Musical Times*, 1 June 1918.
Akami, T. 'Beyond the Formula of the Age of Reason. Experts, Social Sciences, and the Phonic Public in International Politics'. In *The League of Nations – Perspectives from the Present*, edited by Haakon A. Ikonomou and Karen Gram-Skjoldager, 161–71. Aarhus: Aarhus University Press, 2019.
Akami, T. 'Experts and the Japanese Association of the League of Nations in the International Context, 1919–1925'. In *The League of Nations, Histories, Legacies and Impact*, edited by Joy Damousi and Patricia O'Brien, 158–78. Melbourne: Melbourne University Press, 2018.
Akami, T. 'The Limits of Peace Propaganda: The Information Section of the League of Nations and Its Tokyo Office'. In *International Organizations and the Media in the Nineteenth and Twentieth Centuries – Exorbitant Expectations*, edited by Jonas Brendebach, Martin Herzer and Heidi Tworek, 17–38. London: Routledge, 2018.
Akio, T. 'China's "Public Diplomacy" toward the United States before Pearl Harbor', *Journal of American–East Asian Relations* 17, no. 1 (2010): 35–55.
Amrith, S. S. *Decolonizing International Health India and Southeast Asia, 1930–65*. London: Palgrave, 2006.

Amrith, S. S., and P. Clavin. 'Feeding the World: Connecting Europe and Asia, 1930–1945. *Past and Present*, Supplement 8 (2013): 29–50.

Anderson, C. A. *A Critique of the UNESCO Statistical Program*. Ford Foundation, Series I: Subject Files. FA# 608, Box 7. Rockefeller Archive Center, 1959.

Ann Miller, C. *Lobbying the League* (unpublished PhD thesis, University of Oxford, 1992).

Annan, K. A. 'Dag Hammarskjöld and the 21st Century'. *The Fourth Dag Hammarskjöld Lecture* (6 September 2001). Available at: www.dhf.uu.se/pdffiler/Kofi%20Annan.pdf.

Archibald, G. *Les États-Unis et l'UNESCO 1944–1963*. Paris: Publications de la Sorbonne, 1993.

Asher, C. S. 'The Development of UNESCO's Program'. *International Organization* 4, no. 1 (1950): 12–26.

Asmus, R. D. *Opening NATO's Door: How the Alliance Remade Itself for a New Era*. New York: Columbia University Press, 2002.

Aster, S. P. *Policy and Personality: The Life and Times of Lord Salter, 1881–1975*. Lexington, KY: Aster, 2015.

Auberer, B. 'Digesting the League of Nations: Planning the International Secretariat of the Future, 1941–1944'. *New Global Studies* 10, no. 3 (2016): 393–426.

Auberer, B. '"From the Australian Bush to the International Jungle". Internationale Karrieren und der Völkerbund', PhD diss., Universität Heidelberg, Heidelberg, 2018.

Avant, D. D., M. Finnemore and S. K. Sell (eds.). *Who Governs the Globe?* Cambridge, UK; New York: Cambridge University Press, 2010.

Bailey, S. D. *The Secretariat of the United Nations*. New York: Carnegie Endowment for International Peace, 1962.

Barros, J. *Betrayal from Within. Joseph Avenol, Secretary-General of the League of Nations, 1933–1940*. New Haven: Yale University Press, 1969.

Barros, J. *Office without Power: Secretary-General Sir Eric Drummond, 1919–1933*. Oxford: Clarendon Press, 1979.

Becker, G. S. *Human Capital: A Theoretical and Empirical Analysis, with Special Reference to Education*. New York: National Bureau of Economic Research, 1964.

Beer, F. A. *Integration and Disintegration in NATO. Processes of Alliance Cohesion and Prospects for Atlantic Community*. Columbus, OH: Ohio State University Press, 1969.

Beer, M. *Die Reise nach Genf*. Berlin: Fischer, 1932.

Beer, M. 'Drei Pöstchen für Deutschland'. *Kölnische Zeitung*, no. 82, 31 January 1926.

Beer, M. 'Eine Personenänderung im Völkerbund. Wieder ein Beiseiteschieben Deutschlands'. *Kölnische Zeitung*, no. 76, 29 January 1926.

Beigbeder, Y. 'The United Nations Secretariat: Reform in Progress'. In *The United Nations at Millennium. The Principal Organs*, edited by P. Taylor and A. J. R. Groom. London and New York: Continuum, 2000.

Ben-Dror, E. 'Ralph Bunche and the Establishment of Israel'. *Israel Affairs* 14, no. 3 (2008): 519–37.

Benveniste, G. 'Creation of the International Institute for Educational Planning'. *Educational Planning* 16, no. 3 (2007): 1–9.

Bercovitch, J. 'Mediation and Conflict Resolution'. In *The Sage Handbook of Conflict Resolution*, edited by Jacob Bercovitch, Victor Kremenyuk and I. William Zartman, 340–57. London: SAGE Publications, 2009.

Bernhard, H. (ed.). *Gustav Stresemann: Vermächtnis. Der Nachlaß in drei Bänden*, vol. 2. Berlin: Ullstein, 1932.

Biermann, R., and J. Koops (eds.). 'The Palgrave Handbook of Inter-organizational Relations'. In *World Politics*. London: Palgrave, 2017.

Birebent, C. *Militants de la paix et de la SDN*. Paris: L'Harmattan, 2007.

Birn, D. S. *The League of Nations Union, 1918–1945*. Oxford: Clarendon Press, 1981.

Boel, B. *The European Productivity Agency and Transatlantic Relations, 1953–1961*. Copenhagen: Museum Tusculanum Press, 2003.

Boel, J. 'UNESCO's Fundamental Education Program, 1946–1958: Visions, Actions and Impacts'. In *A History of UNESCO: Global Actions and Impact*, edited by P. Duedahl, 153–68. London: Palgrave Macmillan, 2016.

Borowry, I. 'Wissenschaft, Gesundheit, Politik: Das Verhältnis der Weimarer Republik zur Hygieneorganisation des Völkerbundes', Sozial.Geschichte: *Zeitschrift für historische Analyse des 19. und 20. Jahrhunderts* 20 (2005): 30–56.

Borowy, I. *Coming to Terms with World Health: The League of Nations Health Organisation 1921–1946*. Frankfurt: Peter Lang, 2009.

Borowy, I. 'Maneuvering for Space. International Health Work of the League of Nations during World War II'. In *Shifting Boundaries of Public Health: Europe in the Twentieth Century*, edited by Susan Gross Solomon, Lion Murard, and Patrick Zylberman, 87–113. Rochester, NY: University of Rochester Press, 2008.

Borowy, I. 'In the Shadow of Grotjahn: German Social Hygienists in the International Health Scene'. In *Of Medicine and Men. Biographies and Ideas in European Social Medicine between the World Wars*, edited by Iris Borowy and Anne Hardy, 141–70. Frankfurt am Main: Lang, 2008.

Bosco, D. L. 'Assessing the UN Security Council: A Concert Perspective'. *Global Governance* 20, no. 4 (2014): 545–61.

Bourloyannis, M. C. 'Fact-finding by the Secretary-General of the United Nations'. *New York University Journal of International Law and Politics* 22, no. 4 (1990): 641–69.

Bourmaud, P., Chantal Verdeil and Norig Neveu (eds.). *Experts et expertises dans les mandats de la Société des Nations: figures, champs et outils*. Paris: Presses de l'INALCO, 2020.

Brendebach, J., M. Herzer and H. Tworek (eds.). *International Organizations and the Media in the Nineteenth and Twentieth Centuries. Exorbitant Expectations*. New York: Routledge, 2018.

Breuilly, J. *Nationalism and the State*. Manchester: Manchester University Press, 1993.

Bülow, B. W. v. *Der Versailler Völkerbund: Eine vorläufige Bilanz*. Berlin: Kohlhammer, 1923.

Bureau international des administrations télégraphiques. *Rapport de Gestion*, 1899.

Bürgi, R. 'Engineering the Free World: The Emergence of the OECD as an Actor in Education Policy, 1957-1972'. In *The OECD and the International Political Economy since 1948*, edited by M. Leimgruber and M. Schmelzer, 285-309. Cham: Springer International Publishing, 2017a.

Bürgi, R. *Die OECD und die Bildungsplanung der freien Welt. Denkstile und Netzwerke einer internationalen Bildungsexpertise*. Promotion 7. Opladen, Berlin & Toronto: Verlag Barbara Budrich, 2017b.

Bürgi, R. 'Learning Productivity: The EPA – An Educational Enterprise'. In *The OECD and the Rise of the Economic Paradigm in Education*, edited by C. Ydesen, 17-37. New York: Palgrave Macmillan, 2019.

Bürgi, R. 'Systemic Management of Schools: The OECD's Professionalisation and Sissemination of Output Governance in the 1960s'. *Paedagogica Historica* 52, no. 4 (2016): 408-22.

Byman, D. L. and K. M. Pollack. 'Let Us Now Praise Great Men: Bringing the Statesman Back'. *International Security* 25, no. 4 (2001): 107-46.

Caplan, N. *Futile Diplomacy, Volume 2: Arab-Zionist Negotiations and the End of the Mandate*. London: Frank Cass, 1986.

The Carnegie Endowment for International Peace. *Conference on Experience in International Administration, Washington, January 30, 1943*. Washington: The Carnegie Endowment for International Peace, 1943.

The Carnegie Endowment for International Peace. *Exploratory Conference on the Experience of the League of Nations Secretariat, New York City, August 30*. Washington: The Carnegie Endowment for International Peace, 1942.

Carnoy, M. *Transforming Comparative Education: Fifty Years of Theory Building at Stanford*. Stanford, CA: Stanford University Press, 2019.

Chamberlain, A. 'Civil Service Traditions and the League of Nations, by the Rt. Hon. Sir Austen Chamberlain, K.G., M.P. [Being the inaugural address for the Session 1929-30]'. *Public Administration* 8, no. 1 (January 1930): 3-9.

Chesterman, S. "Article 99." In *The Charter of the United Nations: A Commentary, Volume 2*, edited by B. Simma, D.-E. Khan, G. Nolte, A. Paulus and N. Wessendorf, 2009-21. Oxford: Oxford University Press, 2012.

Chourchoulis, D. *The Southern Flank of NATO, 1951-1959*. New York, London: Lexington Books, 2014.

Claude Jr., I. L. *Swords into Plowshares: The Problems and Progress of International Organization*. London: University of London Press, 1966.

Clavin, P. 'Defining Transnationalism'. *Contemporary European History* 14, no. 4 (2005): 421-39.

Clavin, P. *Securing the World Economy: The Reinvention of the League of Nations, 1920-1946*. Oxford: Oxford University Press, 2013.

Clavin, P., and G. Sluga. 'Rethinking the History of Internationalism'. In *Internationalisms. A Twentieth Century History*, edited by ibid., 3-16. Cambridge: Cambridge University Press, 2017.

Clavin, P., and J. Wessels. 'Transnationalism and the League of Nations: Understanding the Work of Its Economic and Financial Organisation'. *Contemporary European History* 14, no. 4 (2005): 465–92.

Conrad, S. *What Is Global History?* Princeton: Princeton University Press, 2016.

Cordier, A. W., and W. Foote (eds.). *Public Papers of the Secretaries-General of the United Nations: Vol. 1: Trygve Lie, 1946–1953*. New York: Columbia University Press, 1969.

Cordier, A. W., and W. Foote (eds.). *Public Papers of the Secretaries-General of the United Nations: Vol. 2: Dag Hammarskjöld, 1953–1956*. New York: Columbia University Press, 1972.

Cordier, A. W., and W. Foote (eds.). *Public Papers of the Secretaries-General of the United Nations: Vol. 5: Dag Hammarskjöld, 1960–1961*. New York: Columbia University Press, 1975.

Cory, R. H. 'Forging a Public Information Policy for the United Nations'. *International Organization* 7, no. 2 (1953): 229–42.

Cox, R. W. 'The Executive Head: An Essay on Leadership in International Organization'. *International Organization* 23, no. 2 (1969): 205–30.

Crump, L, and S. Godard. 'Reassessing Communist International Organisations: A Comparative Analysis of COMECON and the Warsaw Pact in Relation to Their Cold War Competitors'. *Contemporary European History* 27, no. 1 (2018): 85–109.

Dadej, I. *Beruf und Berufung transnational. Deusche und polnische Akademikerinnen in der Zwischenkriegszeit*. Osnabrück: fibre Verlag, 2019.

Davies, T. 'A "Great Experiment" of the League of Nations Era: International Nongovernmental Organizations, Global Governance, and Democracy beyond the State'. *Global Governance* 18 (2012): 405–23.

Davies, T. *NGOs: A New History of Transnational Civil Society*. Oxford: Oxford University Press, 2014.

Davies, Thomas R. 'The Experience of the International Federation of League of Nations Societies'. *Internationalism in a Divided World* 37, no. 2 (2012): 227–52.

Davies, T. R. 'Internationalism in a Divided World: The Experience of the International Federation of the League of Nations Societies, 1919–1939'. *Peace&Change* 37, no. 2 (2012): 227–52.

Davies, T. R. *The Possibilities of Transnational Activism. The Campaign for Disarmament between the Two World Wars*. Leiden: Brill, 2008.

De Tapia, A. A. *Orthodox Christians and Muslims of Cappadocia: Intercommunal Relations in an Ottoman Rural Context (1839–1923)*. Istanbul: Boğaziçi University, 2016.

Diepen, R. *Voor Volkenbond en vrede: Nederland en het streven naar een nieuwe wereldorde, 1919–1946*. Amsterdam: Bert Bakker, 1999.

Divani, L. H. *"ύπουλος θωπεία" Ελλάδα και ξένοι, 1821–1940*. Athens: Εκδόσεις Καστανιώτη, 2014.

Dorn, C., and K. Ghodsee. 'Cold War Politicization of Literacy: Communism, UNESCO and the World Bank'. *Diplomatic History* 36, no. 2 (2012): 373–98.

Draft of Memorandum by the Assistant Secretary of State for European Affairs (Merchant) to the Secretary of State, Washington, 7 July 1953, FRUS, *Western European Security, 1952–1954*, V, part 1.

Drange, M. 'Supervisor, Facilitator and Arbitrator. A Study of the Minority Department in the League of Nations Involvement in the Forced Population Exchange between Greece and Turkey in 1923', MA diss., University of Oslo, Oslo, 2017.

Dubin, M. D. 'Transgovernmental Processes in the League of Nations'. *International Organization* 37, no. 3 (1983): 473–5.

Duedahl, P. 'Selling Mankind: UNESCO and the Invention of Global History'. *Journal of World History* 22, no. 1 (2011): 101–33.

Dülfer, J. 'Vom Internationalismus zum Expansionismus. Die Deutsche Liga für Völkerbund'. In *Internationale Beziehungen im 19. und 20. Jahrhundert: Festschrift für Winfried Baumgart zum 65. Geburtstag*, edited by Wolfgang Elz and Sönke Neitzel, 251–66. Paderborn: Schöningh, 2003.

Dülffer, J. 'Vom Internationalismus zum Expansionismus: Die Deutsche Liga für Völkerbund'. In *Frieden stiften: Deeskalations- und Friedenspolitik im 20. Jahrhundert*, edited by Jost Dülffer, 174–88. Köln: Böhlau, 2008.

Düssel, I., and C. Ydesen. 'Jaime Torres Bodet and the Struggle over History Writing of the Americas: The Mexican Experience'. In *UNESCO without Borders: Educational Campaigns for International Understanding. Routledge Research in Education Series*, edited by A. Kulnazarova and C. Ydesen, 197–221. Oxford, UK: Routledge, 2016a.

Düssel, I., and C. Ydesen. 'UNESCO and the Improvement of History Textbooks in Mexico, 1945–1960'. In *The History of UNESCO: Global Actions and Impacts*, edited by P. Duedahl, 231–56. New York: Palgrave Macmillan, 2016b.

Dykmann, K. 'How International Was the Secretariat of the League of Nations?' *The International History Review* 37, no. 4 (2015): 721–44.

Dyroff, S. 'Avant-garde or Supplement? Advisory Bodies of Transnational Associations as alternatives to the League's Minority Protection System, 1919–1939'. *Diplomacy and Statecraft* 24, no. 2 (2013): 192–208.

Eckart, W. U. *Von Kommissaren und Kamelen. Heinrich Zeiss – Arzt und Kundschafter in der Sowjetunion 1921–1931*. Paderborn: Schöningh, 2016.

Eide, K. '30 Years of Educational Collaboration in the OECD. International Congress "Planning and Management of Educational Development"', Mexico, 26–30 March 1990', 1990. Available at http://unesdoc.unesco.org/images/0008/000857/085725eo.pdf (accessed 8 August 2020).

Elfert, M. 'The OECD, American Power, and the Rise of the "Economics of Education"'. In *The OECD's Historical Rise in Education: The Formation of a Global Governing Complex*, edited by C. Ydesen, 39–61. New York: Palgrave Macmillan, 2019.

Elfert, M. 'Six Decades of Educational Multilateralism in a Globalising World: The History of the UNESCO Institute in Hamburg'. *International Review of Education* 59, no. 2 (2013): 263–87.

Elfert, M. *UNESCO's Utopia of Lifelong Learning: An Intellectual History.* Routledge Research in Education Series. New York: Routledge, 2018.

Ellison, J., and O. J. Daddow, 'Dealing with de Gaulle: Anglo-American Relations, NATO and the Second Application'. In *Harold Wilson and European Integration: Britain's Second Application to Join the EEC*, edited by Oliver J. Daddow, 172–87. London: Cass 2000.

Ellwood, D. W. 'The Marshall Plan and the Politics of Growth'. In *OECD Historical Series: Explorations in OEEC History*, edited by R. T. Griffiths, 99–107. Paris: OECD, 1997.

Erdmenger, K. *Diener zweier Herren? Briten im Sekretariat des Völkerbundes 1919–1933.* Baden Baden: Nomos Verlagsgesellschaft, 1998.

Eriksen, S. 'Biografier som lakmuspapir. Overvejelser omkring den socialhistoriske biografi'. *Historisk Tidsskrift* 16 (1996).

Fahrenthold, S. *Between the Ottomans and the Entente. The First World War in the Syrian and Lebanese Diaspora, 1908–1925.* Oxford: Oxford University Press, 2019.

Faure, R. 'Connections in the History of Textbook Revision, 1947–1952'. *Education Inquiry* 2, no. 1 (2011): 21–35.

Ferguson, N., C. S. Maier, E. Manela and D. J. Sargent (eds.). *The Shock of the Global. The 1970s in Perspective.* Cambridge, MA: Harvard University Press, 2011.

Final Communiqué of the Ninth Session of the North Atlantic Council ("The Lisbon Decisions"), 25 February 1952. And Telegram 740.5/2–2552.

Finney, P. 'Introduction: What is International History?' In *Palgrave Advances in International History*, edited by P. Finney. Houndmills: Palgrave Macmillan, 2005.

Fischer, T. *Die Souveränität der Schwachen: Lateinamerika und der Völkerbund, 1920–1936.* Wiesbaden: Franz Steiner Verlag, 2012.

Fortna, B. *Imperial Classroom: Islam, the State, and Education in the Late Ottoman Empire.* Oxford: Oxford University Press, 2002.

Fosse, M., and J. Fox, *Sean Lester. The Guardian of a Small Flickering Light.* London: Hamilton Books, 2016.

Franz, C. 'Renthe-Fink, Cécil von'. In *Biographisches Handbuch des deutschen Auswärtigen Dienstes 1871–1945*, edited by Auswärtiges Amt, Historischer Dienst, Gerhard Keiper, Martin Kröger: vol. 3, L–R, 623–4. Paderborn: Schöningh, 2007.

Franz, C. 'Renthe-Fink, Cécil von'. *NDB*, vol. 21.

Fritz. V. *Juges et avocats généraux de la Cour de Justice de l'Union européenne (1952–1972). Une approche biographique de l'histoire d'une révolution juridique.* Frankfurt a. M.: Vittorio Klostermann, 2018.

Fröhlich, M. 'Dag Hammarskjöld, 1953–1961'. In *The UN Secretary-General and the Security Council: A Dynamic Relationship*, edited by Manuel Fröhlich and Abiodun Williams, 42–70. Oxford: Oxford University Press, 2018.

Fröhlich, M. *Political Ethics and the United Nations: Dag Hammarskjöld as Secretary-General*. London and New York: Routledge, 2008.
Frohlich, M. 'The Special Representatives of the United Nations Secretary-General'. In *Routledge Handbook of International Organization*, edited by Bob Reinalda, 231–43. London: Routledge, 2013.
Fröhlich, M. 'The "Suez Story": Dag Hammarskjöld, the United Nations and the Creation of UN Peacekeeping'. In *Peace Diplomacy, Global Justice and International Agency: Rethinking Human Security and Ethics in the Spirit of Dag Hammarskjöld*, edited by Carsten Stahn and Henning Melber, 305–40. Cambridge: Cambridge University Press, 2014.
Fukuyama, F. 'What Is Governance? Commentary'. *Governance* 26, no. 3 (2013): 347–68.
Gageby, D. *The Last Secretary General. Sean Lester and the League of Nations*. Dublin: Townhouse, 1999.
Garavini, G. *After Empires. European Integration, Decolonization, and the Challenge from the Global South 1957–1986*. Oxford: Oxford University Press, 2012.
Gass, R. 'The OECD as a "Culture", as seen by an "Old Timer"'. *@tmosphere* (October 2002).
Gass, R. 'Speaking Truth to Power. Reflections on the Future of the OECD'. *OECD Observer* (January 2013). Available at: http://oecdobserver.org/news/fullstory.php/aid/3951/Speaking_truth_to_power.html (accessed 8 August 2020).
Gay, P. *Weimar Culture: The Outsider as Insider*. New York: W. W. Norton, 1968.
Gilman, N. *Mandarins of the Future. Modernization Theory in Cold War America*. Baltimore and London: The Johns Hopkins University Press, 2003.
Gil-Riaño, S. 'Perturbed by "race": Antiracism, Science, and Education in UNESCO during the Cold War'. In *UNESCO without Borders: Educational Campaigns for International Understanding*, edited by A. Kulnazarova and C. Ydesen, 203–19. London: Routledge Press, 2016.
Goebel, M. *Anti-imperial Metropolis: Interwar Paris and the Seeds of Third World Nationalism*. Cambridge: Cambridge University Press, 2015.
Goodale, M. 'UNESCO and the United Nations Rights of Man Declaration: History, Historiography, Ideology'. *Humanity: An International Journal of Human Rights, Humanitarianism, and Development* 8, no. 1 (2017): 29–47.
Gorman, D. 'Ecumenical Internationalism: Willoughby Dickinson, the League of Nations and the World Alliance for Promoting International Friendship through the Churches'. *Journal of Contemporary History* 45, no. 1 (2010): 51–73.
Gorman, D. *The Emergence of International Society in the 1920s*. Cambridge: Cambridge University Press, 2012.
Gorur, R. 'Seeing Like PISA: A Cautionary Tale about the Performativity of International Assessments'. *European Educational Research Journal* 15, no. 5 (2016): 598–616.
Graham, N. A., and R. S. Jordan. *The International Civil Service: Changing Role and Concepts*. Pergamon, 1980.

Graml, H. *Bernhard von Bülow und die deutsche Außenpolitik. Hybris und Augenmaß im Auswärtigen Amt.* München: Oldenbourg, 2012.

Gram-Skjoldager, K. 'Drummond, Sir James Eric'. In *IO BIO, Biographical Dictionary of Secretaries-General of International Organizations*, edited by Bob Reinalda, Kent J. Kille and Jaci Eisenberg, http://www.ru.nl/fm/iobio (accessed 18 December 2019).

Gram-Skjoldager, K. 'From the League of Nations to the United Nations. Milestones for the International Civil Service'. *100 Years of International Civil Service*, No. 3, Dag Hammarskjöld Foundation, 2019. Link. Available at: https://www.daghammarskjold.se/wp-content/uploads/2019/09/ics_100_no_3_karin-gs.pdf (accessed 18 December 2019).

Gram-Skjoldager, K., and H. A. Ikonomou. 'The Construction of the League of Nations Secretariat. Formative Practices of Autonomy and Legitimacy in International Organisations'. *International History Review* 41, no. 2 (2019): 257–79.

Gram-Skjoldager, K., and H. A. Ikonomou. 'Making Sense of the League of Nations – Historiographical and Conceptual Reflections on Early International Public Administration'. *European History Quarterly* 49, no. 3 (2019): 420–44.

Gram-Skjoldager, K., H. A. Ikonomou and T. Kahlert. 'Scandinavians and the League of Nations Secretariat, 1919–1946'. *Scandinavian Journal of History* 44, no. 4 (2019): 454–83.

Grigorescu, A. 'Transparency of Intergovernmental Organizations: The Roles of Member States, International Bureaucracies and Nongovernmental Organizations'. *International Studies Quarterly* 51, no. 3 (2007): 625–48.

Grupp, P. *Harry Graf Kessler – eine Biographie*. Frankfurt am Main: Insel, 1999.

Guieu, J. 'La SDN et ses Organisations de Soutien dans les Années 1920. Entre Promotion de l'Esprit de Genève et Volonté d'Influence'. *Relations Internationales* 151, no. 3 (2012): 11–23.

Guieu, J. *Le Rameau et le Glaive: les Militants Français pour la Société des Nations*. Paris: Presses de Sciences Po, 2008.

Haas, E. B. *Beyond the Nation-state: Functionalism and International Organization*. Stanford, CA: Stanford University Press, 1964.

Haas, E. B. *When Knowledge Is Power: Three Models of Change in International Organizations*. Berkeley, CA: University of California Press, 1990.

Hall, N., and N. Woods. 'Theorizing the Role of Executive Heads in International Organizations'. *European Journal of International Relations* 24, no. 4 (2017): 865–86.

Hammarskjöld, D. 'The International Civil Servant in Law and in Fact. Lecture Delivered by Dag Hammarskjöld, Oxford 30 May 1960', reprinted in: *100 Years of International Civil Service*, no. 4, Dag Hammarskjöld Foundation, Stockholm 2019. Available at: https://www.daghammarskjold.se/wp-content/uploads/2019/10/ics_100_no_4_oxfordspeech.pdf (accessed 12 December 2019).

Handlin, O. *Truth in History*. Harvard: Harvard University Press, 1979.

Harrington, D. F. *Berlin on the Brink: The Blockade, the Airlift, and the Early Cold War*. Lexington, KY: University Press of Kentucky, 2012.

Hart, R. J. 'Battling Minds: Conservatives, Progressives, and UNESCO in Postwar United States'. In *UNESCO without Borders: Educational Campaigns for International Understanding. Routledge Research in Education Series*, edited by A. Kulnazarova and C. Ydesen, 35–52. Oxford, UK: Routledge, 2016.

Heian-Engdal, M., J. Jensehaugen, and H. Henriksen Waage. '"Finishing the Enterprise": Israel's Admission to the United Nations'. *The International History Review* 35, no. 3 (2013): 465–85.

Heinemann, W. '"Learning by doing": Disintegrating Factors and the Development of Political Cooperation in Early NATO'. In *NATO and the Warsaw Pact: Intrabloc Conflicts*, edited by May Anny Heiss and S. Victor Papacosma, 43–57. Kent OH: The Kent State University Press, 2008.

Hendrickson, R. C., *Diplomacy and War at NATO. The Secretary General and Military Action after the Cold War*. Columbia and London: University of Missouri Press, 2006.

Henry, M., B. Lingard, F. Rizvi and S. Taylor. *The OECD, Globalisation and Education Policy*. Oxford, UK: Pergamon, 2001.

Herren, M. 'Geneva, 1919–1945. The Spatialities of Public Internationalism and Global Networks'. In *Mobilities of Knowledge*, edited by Heike Jöns, Peter Meusburger and Michael Heffernan, 211–26. Heidelberg: Springer.

Herren, M. 'Gender and International Relations through the Lens of the League of Nations (1919–1945)'. In *Women, Diplomacy and International Politics since 1500*, edited by Glenda Sluga and Carolyn James, Women's and Gender History, 182–201. London: Routledge, 2016.

Herren, M., and I. Löhr. 'Being International in Times of War: Arthur Sweetser and the Shifting of the League of Nations to the United Nations'. *European Review of History* 25, no. 3–4 (2018): 535–52.

Herren, M., and I. Löhr. 'Gipfeltreffen im Schatten der Weltpolitik: Arthur Sweetser und die Mediendiplomatie des Völkerbunds'. *Zeitschrift für Geschichtswissenschaft* 62, no. 5 (2014): 411–24.

Herren, M., and I. Lohr (eds.). 'Lives beyond Borders. Toward a Social History of Cosmopolitans and Globalization, 1880–1960'. *Comparative* 23, no. 6 (2013).

Heß, Jürgen C. 'Europagedanke und nationaler Revisionismus: Überlegungen zu ihrer Verknüpfung in der Weimarer Republik am Beispiel Wilhelm Heiles'. *Historische Zeitschrift* 225, No JG (1977): 572–622.

Hill, M. 'Immunities and Privileges of Officials of the League of Nations'. In *Studies in the Administration of International Law and Organization* (Washington: Carnegie Endowment for International Peace, 1945).

Hogan, M. J. *The Marshall Plan: America, Britain, and the Reconstruction of Western Europe, 1947–1952*. Cambridge: Cambridge University Press, 1987.

Holbrooke, R. *To End a War*. New York: Random House, 1998.

Holl, K. 'Ludwig Quidde und die deutsche Friedensbewegung in der Weimarer Republik'. In *Der verlorene Frieden: Politik und Kriegskultur nach 1918*, edited by Jost Dülfer, 273–85. Essen: Klartext.
Holl, K. *Ludwig Quidde (1858–1941). Eine Biografie*. Düsseldorf: Droste, 2007.
Horowitz M. C. 'Leaders, Leadership, and International Security'. In *The Oxford Handbook of International Security*, edited by A. Gheciu and W. C. Wohlforth, 246–58. Oxford: Oxford University Press, 2018.
Howard, E. C. *The Origin, Structure and Working of the League of Nations*. London: Allen & Unwin, 1928.
Hucker, D. *Public Opinion and Twentieth Century Diplomacy – A Global Perspective*. London: Bloomsbury, 2020.
Iatrides, J. O. 'Missionary Educators and the Asia Minor Disaster: Anatolia College's Move to Greece'. *Journal of Modern Greek Studies* 4, no. 2 (1986): 143–57.
ICSAB. 'Report on Recruitment Methods and Standards for the United Nations and the Specialized Agencies'. *United Nations* (1950).
Ikonomou, H. A. '"He Used to Give Me Turkish Lessons in Constantinople": How to Get a Job in the League Secretariat'. In *The League of Nations: Perspectives from the Present*, edited by Haakon A. Ikonomou and Karen Gram-Skjoldager, 115–22. Aarhus: Aarhus University Press, 2019.
Ikonomou, H. A. 'Thanassis Aghnides og skabelsen af den international Embedsmand'. *Baggrund* (2 September 2019). Available at: https://baggrund.com/2019/09/02/thanassis-aghnides-og-skabelsen-af-den-internationaleembedsmand/ (accessed 18 December 2019).
Ikonomou, H. A. *The International Bureaucrat in the Twentieth Century – A Transnational Biography of Thanassis Aghnides*. London: Palgrave Macmillan, forthcoming.
Ikonomou, H. A. 'An International Language: The Translation and Interpretation Service'. In *The League of Nations – Perspectives from the Present*, edited by Haakon A. Ikonomou and Karen Gram-Skjoldager, 30–9. Aarhus: Aarhus University Press, 2019.
Information Section. *The League of Nations and the Press*. Geneva, 1928.
International Civil Service Advisory Board [hereafter ICSAB]. 'Report on Standards of Conduct in the International Civil Service'. *United Nations* (1954).
The International Secretariat of the Future: Lessons from Experience by a Group of Former Officials of the League of Nations. London: The Royal Institute of International Affairs, 1944.
Iriye, A. *Global and Transnational History. Past, Present, Future*. London: Palgrave Macmillan, 2012.
Iriye, A. *Global Community. The Role of International Organizations in the Making of the Contemporary World*. Berkeley: University of California Press, 2004.
Jackson, S. 'From Beirut to Berlin (via Geneva): The New International History, Middle East Studies and the League of Nations'. *Contemporary European History* 27, no. 4 (2018): 708–26.

Jakobi, A. P. *International Organizations and Lifelong Learning: From Global Agendas to Policy Diffusion*. London: Palgrave Macmillan, 2009.

Jensehaugen, J., M. Heian-Engdal, and H. H. Waage. 'Securing the State: From Zionist Ideology to Israeli Statehood'. *Diplomacy & Statecraft* 23, no. 2 (2012): 280–302.

Jensen, S. *The Making of International Human Rights: The 1960s, Decolonization, and the Reconstruction of Global Values*. Cambridge: Cambridge University Press, 2016.

Jerónimo, M. B., and J. P. Monteiro (eds.). *Internationalism, Imperialism and the Formation of the Contemporary World*. London: Palgrave Macmillan, 2017.

Jessup, P. C. 'The Berlin Blockade and the Use of the United Nations'. *Foreign Affairs* 50, no. 1 (1971): 163–73.

Jessup, P. C. 'Park Avenue Diplomacy – Ending the Berlin Blockade'. *Political Science Quarterly* 87, no. 3 (1972): 377–400. https://doi.org/10.2307/2149207. http://www.jstor.org/stable/2149207 (accessed 8 August 2020).

Johnson, G. *Lord Robert Cecil. Politician and Internationalist*. Farnham: Ashgate, 2013.

Jordan, R. S. 'The Fluctuating Fortunes of the United Nations International Civil Service: Hostage to Politics or Undeservedly Criticized?'. *Public Administration Review* 4, no. 4 (1991): 553–7.

Jordan, R. S. (ed.). *Generals in International Politics*. Lexington, KY: University Press of Kentucky, 1987.

Jordan, R. S. *Norstad: Cold War NATO Supreme Commander: Airman, Strategist, Diplomat*. New York: St. Martin's Press, 2000.

Jordan, R. S. *The NATO International Staff/Secretariat 1952–1957*. London: Oxford University Press, 1967.

Jordan, R. S. with Michael W. Bloome. *Political Leadership in NATO: A Study in Multinational Diplomacy*. Boulder, CO: Westview Press, 1979.

Judt, T. *Postwar. A History of Europe since 1945*. New York: Penguin Books, 2005.

Kahlert, T. '"The League Is Dead, Long Live the United Nations". The Liquidation of the League and the Transfer of Assets to the UN'. In *The League of Nations. Perspectives from the Present*, edited by Haakon A. Ikonomou and Karen Gram-Skjoldager, 254–64. Aarhus: Aarhus University Press, 2019.

Kahlert, T. 'Pioneers in International Administration: A Prosopography of the Directors of the League of Nations Secretariat'. *New Global Studies* 13, no. 2 (2019): 190–227.

Kaiser, W., and J. Schot. *Writing the Rules for Europe: Experts, Cartels, and International Organizations (Making Europe)*. Basingstoke: Palgrave Macmillan, 2014.

Kaplan, Lawrence S. 'General Lyman L. Lemnitzer and NATO, 1948–1969: A Deferential Leader'. *Cold War History* 19, no. 3 (2019): 323–41.

Keeves, J. 'IEA – From the beginning in 1958 to 1990'. In *IEA 1958–2008: 50 Years of Experiences and Memories*, edited by C. Papanastasiou, T. Plomp and E. C. Papanastasiou, 3–40. Amsterdam: The International Association for the Evaluation of Educational Achievement, 2011.

Kershaw, J. A., and N. M. Roland. *Systems Analysis and Education.* Santa Monica, CA: RAND Corporation, 1959.

Kille, K. J. 'Moral Authority and the UN Secretary-General's Ethical Framework'. In *The UN Secretary-General and Moral Authority: Ethics and Religion in International Leadership*, edited by K. Kille, 7–37. Washington, DC: Georgetown University Press, 2007.

King, A. *Let the Cat Turn Around. One Man's Traverse of the Twentieth Century.* London: CPTM, 2006.

Klabbers, J. *Advanced Introduction to the Law of International Organizations.* Cheltenham: Edward Elgar, 2015.

Knudsen, A., and K. Gram-Skjoldager (eds.). *Living Political Biography – Narrating 20th Century European Lives.* Aarhus: Aarhus University Press, 2012.

Kocka, J. 'Comparison and Beyond'. *History and Theory* 42, no. 1 (2003): 39–44.

Kocka, J., and H.-G. Haupt (eds.). *Comparative and Transnational History: Central European Approaches and New Perspectives.* New York: Berghahn Books, 2009.

Koselleck, R. 'Einleitung'. In *Geschichtliche Grundbegriffe: Historisches Lexikon zur politisch-sozialen Sprache in Deutschland*, vol. 1 (*A-D*), edited by O. Brunner, W. Conze and R. Koselleck. Stuttgart: Ernst Klett Verlag, 1972.

Koskenniemi, M. 'History of International Law, World War I to World War II'. In *Max Plank Encyclopedia of Public International Law*, edited by Rüdiger Wolfrum (online edition). Oxford: Oxford University Press, 2011.

Kott, S., and M. Lengwiler. 'Experts internationaux et politiques sociales'. *Revue d'histoire de la protection sociale* 10, no. 1 (2017): 9–21.

Kreuder-Sonnen, K. *Wie man Mikroben auf Reisen schickt: zirkulierendes bakteriologisches Wissen und die polnische Medizin 1885–1939.* Historische Wissensforschung 9. Tübingen: Mohr Siebeck, 2018.

Kreutzer, F., and S. Roth. 'Einleitung zu Transnationale Karrieren: Biographien, Lebensführung und Mobilität'. In *Transnationale Karrieren*, edited by Florian Kreutzer, 7–33. Wiesbaden: Springer, 2006.

Kröger, M. 'Carl von Schubert. Eine biographische Skizze'. In *Carl von Schubert (1882–1947). Sein Beitrag zur internationalen Politik in der Ära der Weimarer Republik (Ausgewählte Dokumente)*, edited by Peter Krüger, 9–31. Berlin: Duncker & Humblot.

Krüger, P. 'Die "Westpolitik" in der Weimarer Republik'. In *Deutschland und der Westen: Vorträge und Diskussionsbeiträge des Symposions zu Ehren von Gordon A. Craig*, edited by Henning Köhler, 105–30. Berlin: Colloquium Verlag.

Krüger, P. *Die Außenpolitik der Republik von Weimar.* Darmstadt: WBG, 1993.

Kulnazarova, A., and C. Ydesen. 'The Nature and Methodology of UNESCO's Educational Campaigns'. In *UNESCO without Borders: Educational Campaigns for International Understanding. Routledge Research in Education Series*, edited by A. Kulnazarova and C. Ydesen, 1–14. Oxford, UK: Routledge, 2016.

Kyle, K. *Suez: Britain's End of Empire in the Middle East.* New ed. London: I.B. Tauris, 2011.

Lagendijk, V. *Electrifying Europe: The Power of Europe in the Construction of Electricity Networks*. Amsterdam: Aksant, 2008.

Landahl, J. 'Small-scale Community, Large-scale Assessment: IEA as a Transnational Network'. Conference paper presented at the European Conference for Educational Research (ECER) in Copenhagen, Denmark, 22–25 August 2017.

Landsheere, G. 'IEA and UNESCO: A History of Working Co-operation'. 1997. Retrieved from http://www.unesco.org/education/pdf/LANDSHEE.PD (accessed 8 August 2020).

Laqua, D. (ed.). *Internationalism Reconfigured: Transnational Ideas and Movements between the World Wars*. London: Bloomsbury/I.B. Tauris, 2011.

Laqua, D. *The Age of Internationalism and Belgium, 1880–1930: Peace, Progress and Prestige*. Manchester: Manchester University Press, 2013.

Laqua, D., W. v. Acker and C. Verbruggen. *International Organizations and Global Civil Society: Histories of the Union of International Associations*. New York: Bloomsbury, 2019.

Laves, W. H. C. and C. A. Thomson. *UNESCO: Purpose, Progress, Prospects*. Bloomington: Indiana University Press, 1957.

Lee, M. M. 'Failure in Geneva: The German Foreign Ministry and the League of Nations, 1926–1933' MA diss., University of Wisconsin, Madison, 1974.

Lee, M. M. 'The German Attempt to Reform the League. The Failure of German League of Nations Policy 1930–1932'. *Francia* 5 (1977): 473–90.

Lee, M. M., and W. Michalka. *German Foreign Policy 1917–1933: Continuity or Break?* Leamington Spa: Berg, 1987.

Leffler, M. L., and O. A. Westad. *The Cambridge History of the Cold War*, vol. 1–2. Cambridge: Cambridge University Press, 2010.

Legge, M. 'The Making of NATO's Strategy' published in the same issue of the *NATO Review*.

Leimgruber M., and M. Schmelzer. 'Introduction: Writing Histories of the OECD', In *The OECD and the International Political Economy since 1948*, edited by M. Leimgruber and M. Schmelzer,1–22. London: Palgrave Macmillan, 2017.

Leimgruber, M., and M. Schmelzer. 'From the Marshall Plan to Global Governance: Historical Transformations of the OEEC/OECD, 1948 to Present'. In *The OECD and the International Political Economy since 1948*, edited by M. Leimgruber and M. Schmelzer, 23–61. Cham: Springer International Publishing, 2017.

Lengrand, P. *Le métier de vivre*. In Collection Histoires de vie, Série Histoire de vie d'acteurs. Paris: Peuple et Culture – Éducation permanente, 1994.

Lie, T. *In the Cause of Peace: Seven Years with the United Nations*. New York: Macmillan, 1954.

Lipsey, R. *Hammarskjöld: A Life*. Ann Arbor: University of Michigan Press, 2016.

Löhr, I. 'Deutschland im Völkerbund'. In *Globale Verflechtungen der ersten deutschen Republik* (Schriftenreihe der Stiftung Reichspräsident-Friedrich-Ebert-Gedenkstätte, Band 17), edited by Christoph Cornelißen and Dirk van Laak Göttingen: Vandenhoeck & Ruprecht Verlage.

Lord I. *The First Five Years, 1949-1954*. Available at: www.nato.int/archives/1st5years/chapters/6.htm.

Lord Ismay's speech to Abernethian Society, St Bartholomew's Hospital. 22 May 1958, LHCMA, Ismay 1/7/33a.

Louis, W. R., and R. Owen (eds.). *Suez 1956: The Crisis and Its Consequences*. Oxford: Clarendon Press, 1989.

Lucas, W. S. *Divided We Stand. Britain, the US and the Suez Crisis*. London: Hodder & Stoughton, 1991.

Ludlow, N. P. *Roy Jenkins and the European Commission Presidency, 1976-1980: At the Heart of Europe*. London: Palgrave Macmillan, 2016.

Lyon, A. J. 'The UN Charter, the New Testament, and Psalms: The Moral Authority of Dag Hammarskjöld'. In *The UN Secretary-General and Moral Authority: Ethics and Religion in International Leadership*, edited by K. J. Kille, 111-41. Washington, DC: Georgetown University Press, 2007.

Lyons, F. S. L. *Internationalism in Europe 1815-1914*. Leiden: A.W. Sijthoff, 1963.

Lyons, R. 'The OECD Mediterranean Regional Project'. *The American Economist* 8, no. 2 (1964/65): 11-22.

Macfadyen, D., Michael Davies, Marilyn Carr and John Burley. *Eric Drummond and His Legacies – The League of Nations and the Beginnings of Global Governance*. London: Palgrave, 2019.

Madariaga, S. *Morning without Noon*. Farnborough: Saxon House, 1973.

Mahon, R. 'In Conversation with Ron Gass: The OECD and the Crisis of Progress'. *Global Social Policy* 15, no. 2 (2015): 113-24.

Mangone, G. J. *A Short History of International Organization*. New York: McGraw-Hill, 1954.

Martin, G. J. *General de Gaulle's Cold War: Challenging American Hegemony, 1963-68*. New York: Berghahn Books, 2013.

Martin, S. F. *International Migration: Evolving Trends from the Early Twentieth Century to the Present*. Cambridge: Cambridge University Press, 2014.

Mathiason, J. *Invisible Governance: International Secretariats in Global Politics*. Bloomfield: Kumarian, 2007.

Mayer, A. J. *Political Origins of the New Diplomacy 1917-1918*. New Haven: Yale University Press, 1959.

Mazower, M. *Governing the World: The History of an Idea, 1815 to Present*. London: Penguin Books, 2013.

Mazower, M. 'Minorities and the League of Nations in Interwar Europe'. *Daedalus* 126, no. 2 (1997): 47-63.

Mazower, M. *No Enchanted Palace: The End of Empire and the Ideological Origins of the United Nations*. Princeton, NJ: Princeton University Press, 2009.

McAllister, W. B. *Drug Diplomacy in the Twentieth Century an International History*. London: Routledge, 2000.

McCarthy, H. *The British People and the League of Nations: Democracy, Citizenship and Internationalism, c. 1918–45*. Manchester: Manchester University Press, 2011.

McGrew, W. *Educating across Cultures. Anatolia College in Turkey and Greece*. Lanham: Rowman & Littlefield, 2015.

McQuade, J. *Terrorism, Law and Sovereignty in India and the League of Nations 1897–1945*. Unpublished PhD diss. Cambridge, 2017.

Melber, H. *Dag Hammarskjöld, the United Nations and the Decolonisation of Africa*. London: Hurst & Company, 2019.

Milward, A. S. *The Reconstruction of Western Europe 1945–51*. London: Methuen, 1984.

Morel, C. 'Le rêve d'un "gouvernment mondial" des années 1920 aux années 1950. L'exemple de l'Unesco'. *Histoire@Politique* 10 (2010): 1–18. Retrieved from www.cairn.info/revue-histoire-politique-2010-1-page-9.htm

Morris, B. *1948: The First Arab-Israeli War*. New Haven and London: Yale University Press, 2008.

Mourlon-Druol, E. 'Less Than a Permanent Secretariat, More Than an Ad Hoc Preparatory Group: A Prosopography of the Personal Representatives of the G7 Summits (1975–1991)'. In *International Summitry and Global Governance: The Rise of the G7 and the European Council, 1974–1991*, edited by E. Mourlon-Druol and F. Romero, 64–91. Basingstoke: Routledge, 2014.

Moynier, G. *Les bureaux internationaux des unions universelles*. Geneva and Paris: Cherbuliez and Fischbacher, 1892.

Müller, J. 'European Intellectual History as Contemporary History'. *Journal of Contemporary History* 45 (2011): 574–90.

Mundy, K. 'Educational Multilateralism in a Changing World Order: UNESCO and the Limits of the Possible'. *International Journal of Educational Development* 19 (1999): 27–52.

Murphy, C. N. *International Organization and Industrial Change: Global Governance since 1850*. Cambridge: Polity Press, 1994.

Murray, P. '"Can I Write to You about Ireland?": John Vaizey, the Ford Foundation and Irish Educational Policy Change, 1959–1962 [document study]'. *Irish Educational Studies* 31, no. 1 (2012): 67–75.

Nasaw, D. 'Introduction – AHR Roundtable: Historians and Biography'. *The American Historical Review* 114, no. 3 (2009): 573–8.

NATO Handbook (Brussels: NATO Office of Information and Press, 2001), 432–48.

NATO Letter, vol. 5, special supplement to n. 6.

NATO Staff Manual, 2 February 1953, item 3,000.

Nitzsche, T. *Salvador de Madariaga: Liberaler – Spanier – Weltbürger. Der Weg eines politischen Intellektuellen durch das Europa des 20. Jahrhunderts*. Baden-Baden: Nomos, 2009.

Noel-Baker, P. *The First World Disarmament Conference, 1932–1934, and Why It Failed*. Oxford: Pergamon Press, 1979.

Northedge, F. S. *The League of Nations: Its Life and Times, 1920–1946*. Leicester: Holmes & Meier, 1988.

O'Malley, A. *The Diplomacy of Decolonisation: America, Britain and the United Nations during the Congo Crisis 1960–1964*. Manchester: Manchester University Press, 2018.

Office Files of the Commissioner of Education. 'Memo to Mr. Francis Keppel regarding relation of OECD activities to Office of Education, RG 12, Entry No. A1122. Box 531'. Washington, DC: U.S. National Archives, 1963.

Organisation for Economic Co-operation and Development (OECD). *Policy Conference on Economic Growth and Investment in Education. Washington 16th–20th October 1961*. Paris: OECD Publishing, 1961.

Organisation for European Economic Co-operation (OEEC). *Investment in Education and Economic Growth*. Paris: OEEC, 1960a.

Osterhammel, J. *The Transformation of the World. A Global History of the Nineteenth Century*. Princeton Oxford: Princeton University Press, 2014.

Özsu, U. *Formalizing Displacement: International Law and Population Transfers*. Oxford: Oxford University Press, 2015.

Panter, S., J. Paulmann and M. Szöllösi-Janze. 'Mobility and Biography. Methodological Challenges and Perspectives'. In *Mobility and Biography (Jahrbuch für Europäische Geschichte/European History Yearbook)*, edited by Sarah Panter, 16 (2015): 1–14.

Papadopoulos, G. S. *Education 1960–1990. The OECD Perspective. OECD Historical Series*. Paris: Organisation for Economic Co-operation and Development, 1994.

Pappé, I. *The Making of the Arab-Israeli Conflict, 1947–1951*. Paperback ed. London and New York: I.B. Tauris, 1994.

Patel, K. K., and W. Kaiser (eds.). 'Continuity and Change in European Cooperation during the Twentieth Century'. *Contemporary European History* 27, no. 2 (2018): 165–82.

Pedersen, S. 'Back to the League of Nations'. *The American History Review* 112, no. 4 (2007): 1091–117.

Pedersen, S. *The Guardians: The League of Nations and the Crisis of Empire*. Oxford: Oxford University Press, 2015.

Pedersen, S. 'Metaphors of the Schoolroom: Women Working the Mandates System of the League of Nations'. *History Workshop Journal* 66, no. 1 (2008): 188–207.

Pedlow, G. 'Three Hats for Berlin: General Lauris Norstad and the Second Berlin Crisis, 1958–62'. In *The Berlin Wall Crisis: Perspectives on Cold War Alliances*, edited by John P. S. Gearson and Kori Schake, 175–98. London: Palgrave Macmillan, 2002.

Perth, E. of et al. *The International Secretariat of the Future – Lessons from Experience by a Group of Former Officials of the League of Nations*. London: RIIA, Oxford University, 1944. Appendix pp. 61–4.

Pettersson, D. 'The Development of the IEA: The Rise of Large-scale Testing'. In *Transnational Policy Flows in European Education. The Making and Governing of*

Knowledge in the Education Policy Field. Oxford Studies in Comparative Education, edited by A. Nordin and D. Sundberg, 105–22. Oxford, UK: Symposium Books, 2014.

Piguet, M. 'Gender Distribution in the League of Nations: The Start of a Revolution?'. In *The League of Nations – Perspectives from the Present*, edited by Haakon A. Ikonomou and Karen Gram-Skjoldager, 62–71. Aarhus: Aarhus University Press, 2019.

Ploß, C. *Die 'New Commonwealth Society'. Ein Ideen-Laboratorium für den supranationalen europäischen Integrationsprozess*. Stuttgart: Franz Steiner Verlag, 2017.

Pönicke, H. 'Dufour-Feronce, Albert'. In *Neue Deutsche Biographie* 4, 177–8. Duncker und Humblot, 1953.

Potter, P. B. 'League Publicity: Cause or Effect of League Failure?'. *The Public Opinion Quarterly* 2, no. 10 (1983): 399–412.

Prott, V. *The Politics of Self-determination. Remaking Territories and National Identities in Europe, 1917–1923*. Oxford: Oxford University Press, 2016.

Provence, M. *The Last Ottoman Generation and the Making of the Modern Middle East*. Cambridge: Cambridge University Press, 2017.

Putnam, R. D. 'Diplomacy and Domestic Politics: The Logic of Two-level Games'. *International Organization* 42, no. 3 (1988): 427–60.

Quidde, L. *Völkerbund und Demokratie*. Berlin: Verlag Neuer Staat, 1922.

Rachbauer, T. *Egon Ranshofen-Wertheimer: Chronologie eines bewegten Lebens*. München: GRIN Verlag, 2008.

Ranshofen-Wertheimer, E. *The International Secretariat: A Great Experiment in International Administration*. Studies in the Administration of International Law and Organization 3. Washington: Carnegie Endowment for International Peace, 1945.

Rasmussen, M. 'Legal History of the EU: Building a European Constitution?'. In *Oxford Encyclopedia of European Union Politics*, edited by D. Beach and F. Laursen, 1–19. Oxford: Oxford University Press, 2019. https://oxfordre.com/politics/view/10.1093/acrefore/9780190228637.001.0001/acrefore-9780190228637-e-1064.

Ravndal, E. J. '"A Force for Peace": Expanding the Role of the UN Secretary-General under Trygve Lie, 1946–1953'. *Global Governance* 23, no. 3 (2017): 443–59.

Ravndal, E. J. '"The First Major Test": The UN Secretary-General and the Palestine Problem, 1947–9'. *The International History Review* 38, no. 1 (2016): 196–213.

Ravndal, E. J. 'A Guardian of the UN Charter: The UN Secretary-General at 75'. In *Ethics & International Affairs* (forthcoming 2020).

Ravndal, E. J. 'La Mission La Plus Impossible Au Monde: Le Secrétaire Général Trygve Lie Face À La Guerre Froide, 1946–1953'. *Revue d'histoire diplomatique* 130, no. 2 (2016): 145–61.

Ravndal, E. J. 'Trygve Lie (1946–1953)'. In *The UN Secretary-General and the Security Council: A Dynamic Relationship*, edited by Manuel Fröhlich and Abiodun Williams, 22–41. Oxford: Oxford University Press, 2018.

Reinalda, B. 'The Evolution of International Organization as Institutional Forms and Historical Processes to 1945'. In *The International Studies Encyclopedia*, vol. III, edited by R. A. Denmark, 1903–21. Chichester: Wiley-Blackwell.

Reinalda, B., 'The History of International Organization(s)'. In *Oxford Research Encyclopedia, International Studies* (online edition). Oxford: Oxford University Press, 2019.

Reinalda, B. *Routledge History of International Organizations: From 1815 to the Present Day*. London and New York: Routledge, 2009.

Reinalda, B., and K. J. Kille. 'The Evolvement of International Secretariats, Executive Heads and Leadership in Inter-organizational Relations'. In P*algrave Handbook of Inter-organizational Relations in World Politics*, edited by R. Biermann and J. Koops, 217-42. London: Palgrave Macmillan.

Reinalda, B., K. J. Kille and J. L. Eisenberg (eds.). *IO BIO, Biographical Dictionary of Secretaries-General of International Organizations*.

Reinisch, J. 'Agents of Internationalism'. *Contemporary European History* 25, no. 2 (2016) (special issue).

Ren, K. 'The International Peace Campaign, China, and Transnational Activism at the Outset of World War II'. In *The Routledge History of World Peace since 1750*, edited by Christian Philip Peterson, William M. Knoblauch, and Michael Loadenthal, 359-70. Abingdon: Routledge, 2019.

Richard, A. 'Competition and Complementarity: Civil Society Networks and the Question of Decentralising the League of Nations'. *Journal of Global History* 7, no. 2 (2012): 233–56.

Richard, A. 'Huizinga, Intellectual Cooperation and the Spirit of Europe, 1933–1945'. In *Europe in Crisis. Intellectuals and the European idea, 1917–1957*, edited by Mark Hewitson and Matthew D'Auria, 243–57. Oxford: Berghahn, 2012.

Richard, A. 'Between the League of Nations and Europe. Multiple Internationalisms and Interwar Dutch Civil Society'. In *Shaping the International Relations of the Netherlands 1815-2000. A Small Country on the Global Scene*, edited by Ruud van Dijk et al., 97–116. Abingdon: Routlegde, 2018.

Risso, L. '"I Am the Servant of the Council": Lord Ismay and the Making of the NATO International Staff'. *Contemporary European History* 28, no. 3 (2019): 342–57.

Risso, L. *Propaganda and Intelligence in the Cold War: The NATO Information Service*. New York: Routledge, 2014.

Risso, L. 'Writing the History of NATO: A New Agenda'. In *NATO at 70: A New Historiographical Approach*, edited by Linda Risso, 1–6 London: Routledge, 2019.

Rockefeller Foundation, 'Memo "JM". UNESCO General Conference. Paris – second week. 17 November to 22 November 1952. Rockefeller Foundation Records. Field offices, RG6, SG1. Series 2: Post-war, sub-series 01: Post-war correspondence. FA# 395, Box 69, Folder 667 (General – UNESCO), 1952–1958'. Rockefeller Archive Center, 1952.

Rodogno, D. 'The American Red Cross and the International Committee of the Red Cross: Humanitarian Politics and Policies in Asia Minor and Greece (1922–1923)'. *First World War Studies* 5, no. 1 (2014): 83–99.

Rodogno, D., S. Gauthier and F. Piana. 'What Does Transnational History Tell Us about a World with International Organizations? The Historians' Point of View'. In *Routledge Handbook of International Organization*, edited by B. Reinalda, 94–105. London and New York: Routledge, 2013.

Rovine, A. W. *The First Fifty Years: The Secretary-General in World Politics 1920–1970*. Leyden: A. W. Sijthoff, 1970.

Royal Institute of International Affairs (RIIA). *The International Secretariat of the Future – Lessons from Experience by a Group of Former Officials of the League of Nations*. Oxford: Oxford University Press, 1944.

Rubenson, K. 'OECD Education Policies and World Hegemony'. In *The OECD and transnational governance*, edited by R. Mahon and S. McBride, 241–59. Vancouver: UBC Press, 2008.

Runciman, D. 'What Time Frame Makes Sense for Thinking about Crises?' In *Critical Theories of Crisis in Europe from Weimar to the Euro*, edited by Poul F. Kjær and Niklas Olsen, 3–17. London: Rowman & Littlefield, 2016.

Ruyssen, T. 'La propagande pour la Société des Nations'. In *Les Origines et l'œuvre de la Société des Nations 2nd vol.*, edited by P. Munch, 237–8. Copenhague: Rask-Ørstedfonden/Nordisk Forlag, 1924.

Salter, J. A. *Allied Shipping Control: An Experiment in International Administration*. Oxford: Clarendon Press, 1921.

Sayle, T. A. *Enduring Alliance: A History of NATO and the Postwar Global Order*. Ithaca, New York: Cornell University Press, 2019.

Sayward, A. L. *The United Nations in International History. New Approaches to International History*. London; New York: Bloomsbury Academic, 2017.

Scharpf, F. W. *Governing in Europe: Effective and Democratic?* Oxford, UK: Oxford University Press, 1999.

Schechter, M. G. 'Confronting the Challenges of Political Leadership in International Organizations'. In *Comparative Political Leadership*, edited by L. Helms, 249–71. Houndmills: Palgrave Macmillan, 2012.

Schechter, M. G. 'Leadership in International Organisations: Systemic, Organisational and Personality Factors'. *Review of International Studies* 13, no. 3 (1987): 197–220.

Schmelzer, M. 'A Club of the Rich to Help the Poor? The OECD, "Development", and the Hegemony of Donor Countries'. In *International Organizations and Development, 1945–1990. Palgrave Macmillan Transnational History Series*, edited by M. Frey, S. Kunkel and C. R. Unger, 171–95. London: Palgrave Macmillan, 2014.

Schmelzer, M. *The Hegemony of Growth. The OECD and the Making of the Economic Growth Paradigm*. Cambridge: Cambridge University Press, 2016.

Scheuermann, M. *Minderheitenschutz contra Konfliktverhutung? Die Minderheitenpolitik des Volkerbundes in den zwanziger Jahren*. Marburg: Herder Institut, 2000.

Schmidt-Klügmann, A. *Bernhard Wilhelm von Bülow (1885–1936): Eine politische Biographie*. Paderborn: Schöningh, 2020.

Schot, J., and V. Lagendijk. 'Technocratic Internationalism in the Interwar Years: Building Europe on Motorways and Electricity Networks'. *Journal of Modern European History* 6, no. 2 (2008): 196–217.

Schultz, T. W. *The Economic Value of Education*. New York: Columbia University Press, 1963.

Scott-Smith, G. 'Competing Internationalisms: The United States, Britain and the Formation of the United Nations Information Organization during World War II'. *International Journal for History, Culture and Modernity* 1, no. 6 (2018).

Secretariat of the League of Nations. *Ten Years of World Co-operation*. London: Hazel, Watson and Viney, 1930.

Seidel, K. *The Process of Politics in Europe: The Rise of European Elites and Supranational Institutions*. London: I.B. Tauris, 2010.

Seidenfaden, E. *Message from Geneva. The Public Legitimization Strategies of the League of Nations and Their Legacy, 1919–1946*. Unpublished PhD thesis, University of Aarhus, 2019.

Selcer, P. 'Patterns of Science: Developing Knowledge for a World Community at UNESCO'. University of Pennsylvania Dissertation, paper 323, 2011. Available at: http://repository.upenn.edu/edissertations/323 (accessed 8 August 2020).

Sellar, S., and B. Lingard. 'The OECD and the Expansion of PISA: New Global Modes of Governance in Education'. *British Educational Research Journal* 40, no. 6 (2014): 917–36.

Sewell, J. P. *UNESCO and World Politics*. Princeton, NJ: Princeton University Press, 1975.

Shlaim, A. *The United States and the Berlin Blockade, 1948–1949: A Study in Crisis Decision-making*. Berkeley: University of California Press, 1983.

Siotis, J. *Essai sur le secrétariat international*. Geneva: Librairie Droz, 1963

Skinner, Q. *Visions of Politics Vol 1: Regarding Method*. Cambridge: Cambridge University Press, 2002.

Slobodian, Q. *Globalists: The End of Empire and the Birth of Neoliberalism*. Harvard: Harvard University Press, 2018.

Sluga, G. *Internationalism in the Age of Nationalism*. Philadelphia: University of Pennsylvania Press, 2013.

Sluga, G. 'UNESCO and the (one) World of Julian Huxley'. *Journal of World History* 21, no. 3 (2010): 393–418.

Sluga, G., and P. Clavin (eds.). *Internationalisms: A Twentieth-century History*. Cambridge: Cambridge University Press, 2016.

Smejkal, T. *Protection in Practice. The Minorities Section of the League of Nations Secretariat, 1919–1934*. Unpublished Senior Thesis, Columbia University, 2010.
Smith, L. V. *Sovereignty at the Paris Peace Conference of 1919*. Oxford: Oxford University Press, 2018.
Smith, M. L. 'Venizelos' Diplomacy, 1910–1923: From Balkan Alliance to Greek Turkish Settlement'. In *Eleftherios Venizelos. The Trials of Statesmanship*, edited by Paschalis M. Kitromilides, 134–92. Edinburgh: Edinburgh University Press, 2008.
Smith, S. C. (ed.). *Reassessing Suez 1956: New Perspectives on the Crisis and Its Aftermath*. Aldershot: Ashgate, 2008.
Smuts, J. *The League of Nations. A Practical Suggestion*. 1918.
Spaak, P. 'The Atlantic Community and NATO'. *Orbis* I, no. 4 (Winter, 1958): 397–427.
Spaak, P. *The Continuing Battle: Memoirs of a European, 1936–1966* (London: Weidenfeld, 1971).
Spaak, P. Speech to NATO Parliamentarians' Conference, November 1959.
Spaulding, R. M. 'The Central Commission for the Navigation of the Rhine and European Media, 1815–1848'. In *International Organizations and the Media in the Nineteenth and Twentieth Centuries: Exorbitant Expectations*, edited by J. Brendebach, M. Herzer and H. Tworek, 17–37. London: Routledge.
Spaulding, R. M. 'Revolutionary France and the Transformation of the Rhine'. *Central European History* 44 (2011): 203–26.
Spenz, J. *Die diplomatische Vorgeschichte des Beitritts Deutschlands zum Völkerbund 1924–1926. Ein Beitrag zur Außenpolitik der Weimarer Republik*. Göttingen: Musterschmidt, 1966.
Spierenburg D., and R. Poidevin. *The History of the High Authority of the European Coal and Steel Community*. London: Weidenfeld & Nicolson, 1994.
Steiner, Z. 'The Last Years of the Old Foreign Office, 1898–1905'. *The Historical Journal* 6, no. 1 (1963): 59–90.
Steiner, Z. *The Lights That failed. European International History 1919–1933*. Oxford: Oxford University Press, 2005.
Stone, D. C. *Administrative Aspects of World Organization; A Paper Presented at the Fourth Conference on Science, Philosophy and Religion Held at New York City, September 12, 1943 (mimeographed)*.
Sweetser Clifford, S. *One Shining Hour*. Private publication, 1990.
ter Meulen, J. *Der Gedanke der Internationalen Organisation in seiner Entwicklung 1300–1800*. The Hague: Martinus Nijhoff, 1917.
Thelen, K. 'How Institutions Evolve: Insights from Comparative Historical Analysis'. In *Comparative Historical Analysis in the Social Sciences*, edited by J. Mahoney and D. Rueschemeyer, 208–40. Cambridge: Cambridge University Press.
Tollardo, E. *Fascist Italy and the League of Nations, 1922–1935*. London: Palgrave Macmillan, 2016.

Trinh, Q. 'The Bully Pulpit'. In *Secretary or General? The UN Secretary-General in World Politics*, edited by Simon Chesterman, 102–20. Cambridge: Cambridge University Press, 2007.

Trondal J. et al. *Unpacking International Organisations. The Dynamics of Compound Bureaucracies*. Manchester: Manchester University Press, 2010.

Tworek, H. 'Peace through Truth? The Press and Moral Disarmament through the League of Nations'. *Medien & Zeit* 4, no. 25 (2010): 16–28.

U.S. Department of Health, Education and Welfare. 'Letter to the Secretary of State from Nelson A. Rockefeller, 12 April 1954. RG 12 Records of the Office of Education. Office of the Commissioner 1939–1980. Education Missions Advisory Board, 1952–54. Box 37'. Washington, DC: US National Archives, 1954.

U.S. National Commission. 'Newsletter, 13 July 1956, Vol. III No. 11'. Washington, DC: US National Archives, 1956.

U.S. Office of Education. 'Proposed Programme and Budget – 1961–1962, Part II, dated 15 September 1960, RG 12 Records of the Office of Education, Office of the Commissioner 1939–1980, Education Missions Advisory Board, 1952–54, Box 37'. Washington, DC: US National Archives, 1960.

UNESCO. *50 Years for Education*. UNESCO: Paris, 1997.

UNESCO. 'Fundamental Education. Description and Programme'. *Monographs on Fundamental Education, I*. Paris: UNESCO, 1949b.

UNESCO. 'Organizing Programmes of Education for International Understanding, 27 September 1965, WS/0865.153 (EDS)'. Paris: UNESCO Archives, 1965.

UNESCO. 'Relations avec l'O.E.C.E. À M. Malcolm S. Adiseshiah, Director General. De Paul Bertrand, Chef de la Division des relations avec les Organisations internationales. ODG/RIO/Memo.24.903'. Paris: UNESCO Archives, 1961, 29 September.

United Nations Educational, Scientific and Cultural Organization (UNESCO). 'Records of the General Conference of the United Nations Educational, Scientific and Cultural Organization. Fourth session, Paris 1949'. Resolutions. November 1949a. Available at: http://ulis2.unesco.org/images/0011/001145/114590EO.pdf (accessed 8 August 2020).

United Nations Educational, Scientific and Cultural Organization (UNESCO). *A Chronology of UNESCO, 1945–1985*. Paris: UNESCO, 1985.

The United States Delegation to the Department of State. Lisbon, 25 February 1952, midnight. *Foreign Relations of the United States, 1952–1954* (henceforward *FRUS*), vol. V, part 1.

Urquhart, B. E. *Hammarskjöld*. Paperback ed. New York: W. W. Norton, 1994.

Urquhart, B. E. *Ralph Bunche: An American Life*. New York and London: W. W. Norton, 1993.

Urquhart, B. E. 'The Secretary-General – Why Dag Hammarskjold?'. In *The Adventure of Peace: Dag Hammarskjold and the Future of the UN*, edited by S. Ask and A. Mark-Jungkvist, 14–22. Basingstoke: Palgrave Macmillan, 2005.

Vauchez, A. 'The Force of a Weak Field: Law and Lawyers in the Government of the European Union (for a Renewed Research Agenda)'. *International Political Sociology*, no. 2 (2008): 128–44.

Wallensteen, P. 'Dag Hammarskjöld's Diplomacy: Lessons Learned'. In *Peace Diplomacy, Global Justice and International Agency: Rethinking Human Security and Ethics in the Spirit of Dag Hammarskjöld*, edited by C. Stahn and H. Melber, 364–86. Cambridge: Cambridge University Press, 2014.

Walters, F. P. *Administrative Problems of International Organization*. Oxford: Oxford University Press, 1941.

Walters, F. P. *A History of the League of Nations*, vol. 1. Oxford: Oxford University Press, 1952.

Waltz, K. N. *Theory of International Politics*. New York: McGraw-Hill, 1979.

Watenpaugh, K. D. *Bread from Stones: The Middle East and the Making of Modern Humanitarianism*. Berkeley, CA: University of California Press, 2015.

Watras, J. 'Was Fundamental Education Another Form of Colonialism?'. *International Review of Education* 53, no. 1 (2007): 55–72.

Weber, P. 'Ernst Jäckh and the National Internationalism of Interwar Germany'. *Central European History* 52 (2019): 402–23.

Weindling, P. (ed.). *International Health Organisations and Movements, 1918–1939*. Cambridge: Cambridge University Press, 1995.

Weindling, P. 'Philanthropy and World Health: The Rockefeller Foundation and the League of Nations Health Organisation'. *Minerva* 35 (1997): 269–81.

Weiss, T. G., T. Carayannis, L. Emmerij and R. Jolly. *UN Voices: The Struggle for Development and Social Justice*. Bloomington, IL: Indiana University Press, 2005.

Wertheim, S. 'Reading the International Mind: International Public Opinion in Early Twentieth-century Anglo-American Thought'. In *The Decisionist Imagination: Sovereignty, Social Science, and Democracy in the Twentieth Century*, edited by Nicolas Guilhot and Daniel Bessner, 23–63. New York: Berghahn, 2019.

Whitfield, T. '"Good Offices and 'Groups of Friends"'. In *Secretary or General? The UN Secretary-General in World Politics*, edited by S. Chesterman, 86–101. Cambridge: Cambridge University Press, 2007.

Williams, D. *The Specialized Agencies and the United Nations: The System in Crisis*. London: Hurst & Company, 1990.

Wingate, R. *Lord Ismay: A biography*. London: Hutchinson, 1970.

Winnick, R. H. *Letters of Archibald MacLeish: 1907 to 1982*. Boston: Houghton Mifflin Company, 1983.

Wintzer, J. *Deutschland und der Völkerbund 1918–1926*. Paderborn: Schöningh, 2006.

Wittner, L. S. *The Struggle against the Bomb*. Palo Alto: Stanford University Press, 1993.

Woehrling, J.-M. 'L'administration de la Commission centrale pour la navigation du Rhin'. *Revue Française d'administration publique* 126 (2008): 345–58.

Woodward, R. 'The Organisation for Economic Cooperation and Development (OECD)'. In *Global Institutions Series*. New York: Routledge, 2009.

Woolf, L. S. *International Government*. New York: Brentano's, 1916.

Woollacott, A., D. Deacon and P. Russell (eds.). *Transnational Lives. Biographies of Global Modernity, 1700–Present*. New York: Palgrave, 2010.

Wörner, M. 'The Atlantic Alliance in the new era'. *NATO Review* 39, no. 1 (February. 1991).

Wörner, M. 'NATO Transformed: The Significance of the Rome Summit', *NATO Review* 39, no. 6 (December. 1991).

Wörner, M. 'A Time of Accelerating Change' and 'North Atlantic Council Communiqué' both in *NATO Review* 37, no. 6 (December 1989).

Ydesen, C. 'Debating International Understanding in the Western World: The American Approach to UNESCO's Educational Campaigns, 1946–54'. In *UNESCO without Borders: Educational Campaigns for International Understanding. Routledge Research in Education Series*, edited by A. Kulnazarova and C. Ydesen, 239–55. Oxford, UK: Routledge, 2016.

Ydesen, C., and S. Grek. 'Securing Organisational Survival – A Historical Inquiry into the Configurations and Positions of the OECD's Work in Education during the 1960s'. *Paedagogica Historica* 56, no. 3 (2020): 412–27. https://doi.org/10.1080/00309 230.2019.1604774 (accessed 8 August 2020).

Yildirim, O. *Diplomacy and Displacement Reconsidering the Turco-Greek Exchange of Populations, 1922–1934*. London: Routledge, 2006.

Index

Adamawicz, Stanislawa 61–2
Aghnides, Thanassis
    and Drummond, Eric 38–9, 42, 44–5
    Greek Foreign Service 34, 38, 40, 45–7
    information and propaganda 152
    International Civil Service Advisory Board, the 226–7
    Megali Idea (the Great Idea/Greater Greece) 38, 41
    Minorities Section 39–40
    and Nicolson, Harold 37–8, 48
    Paris Peace Conference 38–9, 41, 47
    Political Section 42, 44–5
    and Politis, Nikolaos 40, 45
    and Venizelos, Eleftherios 38–40, 42–5
Arocha, Manual Juan 65
Aschmann, Gottfried 165, 173
Austria 57, 95
Avenol, Joseph 60, 66–7, 115–16, 133, 139, 154, 225

Beer, Max 171, 173–6, 178
Bellegarde, Dantes 157
Biraud, Yves 67
Britain. *See United Kingdom*
British League of Nations Union 146, 148, 149–50, 156–7
British Milk Marketing Board 114
Bülow, Bernhard Wilhelm von 165–9, 173
Bureau of the International Telegraph Union 24

Cardon, Philip 121–3
Cecil, Robert 148, 150, 156
Central Commission for the Navigation of the Rhine 22
Chatterjee, Amulya Chandra 64
Chisholm, Brock 30–1
Colban, Erik 47, 159
Cole, Sterling 31
Comert, Pierre 132–3, 139–40, 141, 174–5
Committee of Thirteen 224–5

Coombs, Philip 82
cooperative publicity 130, 135, 152
Crowdy, Rachel 27, 49
Curchod, Louis 24

Deutsche Gesellschaft für Völkerrecht und Völkerbundfragen 158
Deutsche Liga für Völkerbund 158, 166
Dickinson, Willoughby 160
diplomatic immunity 215, 223–4
Dodd, Norris 121–3
Drummond, Eric
    and Germany 165–7, 172–3, 175
    and Greece 42
    organization of the League of Nations Secretariat 26, 33, 50, 91, 95, 217–20
    recruitment of staff 38–9, 54, 61
    Second World War 140
    and the Greco-Turkish population exchange 44–7
Dufour-Féronce, Albert 170–4, 178

Economic Growth and Investment in Education (conference) 82
European Coal and Steel Community 91, 96–101, 108
European Commission for the Danube 23
European Economic Community 101–6, 108
European integration 91–2, 97, 99–102, 106–8
European Productivity Agency 75–6

FAO. *See Food and Agricultural Organization*
Felkin, Arthur Elliot 65
Food and Agricultural Organization 67, 109, 116–19, 122
Foreign Ministry, German 59, 64–69, 73–77
Foreign Service, British 203, 219–21

France
    second world war 98, 102, 139
    UN 194–5
    UNESCO 80
Freedom From Hunger, campaign 122–5
Frontierspersons (heads of international organizations) 21, 23–32
Fundamental education (UNESCO) 84–7

Gass, Ron 76–7, 82, 88
Gaus, Friedrich 164–6
Gerig, Orie Benjamin 64
Germany 51–2, 59–61, 97–9, 158, 163–77, 224
Gerritsen, Anne 36
Goedhart, Gerrit Jan van Heuven 31
Governance, input/output 87–9
Great Britain. *See United Kingdom*
Great Depression 51, 112, 120, 225
Greco-Turkish population exchange 34–6, 41–5, 47–8
Greece 38, 41

Haiti 157
Hallstein, Walter 101–6
Hammarskjöld, Åke and Hjalmar 57
Hammarskjöld, Dag 183–5, 187, 192–7
Handlin, Oscar 35
Hankey, Maurice 26, 32, 39, 219
Hill, William Martin 66
Hoffman, Paul 31
Hot Springs Conference 109, 118–19
Huxley, Julian 77

IIA. *See International Institute of Agriculture*
Inagaki, Morikatsu 53
International Association for the Evaluation of Educational Achievement 86
International Civil Service Advisory Board 34, 226
International Institute of Agriculture 111
International Peace Campaign 156
International public opinion
    and International Federation of League of Nations Societies (IFLNS) 145–6, 151, 154, 157
    and League of Nations Information Section 129, 131–2, 135–8, 142, 145
    and nutrition 114

IO BIO Project 15–18
Ismay, Hastings Lionel (Lord) 201–7, 212
Italy 51–2, 60, 160, 224, 230

Japan 51–2, 149–50
Jaurant-Singer, Marcel 97–9

Keenleyside, Hugh 31
Keishiro, Matsui 149–50
Kessler, Harry 168–9
Key-Rasmussen, Essy 67
Khrushchev, Nikita 195
Kohnstamm, Max 92–3, 99–101, 104, 107
Krabbe, Ludwig 65, 151, 156

Lange, Christian 152
Lausanne conference 34, 41–3
League of Nations Health Organization 111, 117
League of Nations Information Section
    and International Federation for League of Nation Societies (IFLNS) 135–6, 152–6
    legitimization 129–31, 134, 136, 141–3
    moral disarmament 135–6
    propaganda 130, 133–4, 137–8
    publications 137–8
    and the council and assembly 132–3
    and the press 134–5
    and United Kingdom 132
    and women's associations 135
League of Nations Secretariat
    and Austria 57
    career trajectories 51, 63–6
    central registry 221
    Economic Relations Section 52
    epidemiological intelligence service 61–2
    Eurocentrism 53, 61
    expertise on the Ottoman Empire 34–5, 40–2, 45, 48
    gender balance 61–3
    and Germany 51–2, 59–61, 164–77, 224
    and International Federation of League of Nations Societies 145, 148, 151
    and Italy 51–2, 60, 224
    and Japan 51–2

Legal Section 57
League of Nations Princeton team 57, 66-7
Minorities Section 39-40, 159-61
national composition 50-1, 53-61, 167, 222
oath of loyalty 225
pensions 224
publications and printing service 52, 60
and Scandinavia 55, 61
and South America 54-5, 61
staff appointments 33, 57, 60, 63, 221, 223
staff regulations 33, 223
and Switzerland 51, 224
and United Kingdom 58-9, 139-40, 172
and the US 150
League of Nations Union, India 154
Lester, Seán 57, 66, 139, 225
Liberal diet. *See optimum diet*
Lie, Trygve 29, 66, 183-93, 196-7
Loveday, Alexander 67

Madariaga, Salvador de 64
Mantoux, Paul Joseph 42, 45
Monnet, Jean 26, 68, 93-7, 99-101
Myrdal, Gunnar 31

Nansen, Fridtjof 27, 43
NATO. *See North Atlantic Treaty Organization*
New Diplomacy 145-7, 157, 160-1
Noël, Emile 92-3, 102-8
Nogueria, Julian 65
North Atlantic Treaty Organization (NATO)
    and Balkan 208, 211
    De Gaulle, Charles 207
    and Drummond, Eric 202-3
    and Norstad, Lauris 207
    North Atlantic Council 199-200, 202-8, 211, 213
    permanent representatives 202-3, 205, 207
    Post-Cold War 199-200, 208-13
    Rome Summit 210
    secretary-general 199-210, 212-13
    staff appointments 203-4
    staff nationality 204
    Supreme Allied Commander Europe 199-200, 207
    and the European Union 200, 209-12
    and the Suez Crisis 201, 204-6
    and the US 211, 213
    The Three Wise Men Report 201 205-6, 208
    and United Nations 212
    and Warsaw Pact 208-9

Octroi Convention 22
OECD. *See Organization for European Economic Co-operation*
OEEC. *See Organization for European Economic Co-operation*
Old Diplomacy 145
Olsen, Otto 171, 176-8
Optimum diet 113, 115, 117
Organization for European Economic Co-operation 5-6, 73-7, 81-9, 227
Orr, John Boyd 111-12, 114-115, 117-21
Ottoman Empire
    Anatolia 34, 37, 40-1
    collapse of 34-5, 38, 48
    Ottoman (Orthodox) Greeks 37-8, 41, 44-5
    post-Ottoman 40-1, 45, 48
    and the *Tanzimat* 37
    Treaty of Sèvres 41

Paris Peace Conference 61, 65
Pate, Maurice 31
Pearson, Lester 194
Pedersen, Susan 145-7, 161, 215, 217
Pelt, Adrianus 133, 139-42, 154-5
Permanent Central Opium Board 65
Pla, Joseph 154
Potter, Pitman 133-4

Quidde, Ludwig 168-9

RAND Corporation 75, 83
Radziwill, Gabriele 63, 135, 152, 154
Rajchman, Ludwik 27, 49, 61-2
Ranshofen-Wertheimer, Egon 64, 217-18
Renthe-Fink, Cécil von 170-3, 178
Rosenborg, Ansgar 57, 66
Ruyssen, Theodore 147, 158, 161

Salter, James A. 26, 65, 219
Scandinavia 39, 55, 61, 183
Schnabel, Fritz 53, 60–1
Schubert, Carl, von 164–6, 172–3
Schuman Plan 96, 99–100
Seipel, Ignaz 57
Sen, Binay Ranjan 122–4
Smuts, Jan 145, 162
South America 54–5, 61
Spaak, Paul-Henri 98, 201, 205–8, 212–13
Standard of conduct for international civil servants 29–30, 94, 108, 226–8
Starvation, prevention of 113
Stencek, Valentin 65–6
Stoppani, Pietro Angelo 52
Stresemann, Gustav 137, 159, 163–6, 169, 172–3, 178–9
Suez Crisis
  North Atlantic Treaty Organization 201, 204–6
  United Nations 184, 187, 192–4
Sweetser, Arthur 49, 132–3, 137, 139–42, 152, 174–6
Switzerland 24, 30, 51, 224
Sydenstricker, Edgar 62

Thomas, Albert 27, 153
Togoland 157
transnational epistemic communities 92, 109, 111–14
transnational history 2–4
Treaty of Lausanne 35–6, 41–2, 47
Treaty of Locarno 163–5, 174
Treaty of Versailles 138, 164–5

UN. *See United Nations*
UNDPI. *See United Nations Department of Public Information*
UNESCO. *See United Nations Educational, Scientific and Cultural Organization*
UNICEF. *See United Nations Children's Fund*
United Kingdom
  nutrition and public health 113–14, 117
  promotion of scientific and industrial research 76
  second world war 98
  and the League of Nations Information Section 132
  and the League of Nations Secretariat 58–9, 139–40, 172, 235
  United Nations 188, 193–5
United Nations
  and American Airmen in China 184, 192–3
  Charter 226
  Congo Crisis 184, 192, 195
  crisis management 183–8, 190–2, 195–6
  First Arab-Israeli War 184, 188–9, 194
  general assembly 186–95
  Korean War 184, 190–1
  and McCarthyism 228
  NGOs 146
  secretary general 183–97
  security council 185–92, 194–5, 197
  Suez Crisis 184, 187, 192–4
  and the Berlin-Blockade 184, 188–90
  and the dissolution of the League of Nations 66, 68
  and the US 188–93, 226, 228
United Nations Children's Fund 29, 31, 122–3
United Nations Department of Public Information 140–3
United Nations Educational, Scientific and Cultural Organization 73–89
United States
  European integration 98–9
  food and agriculture 124
  and international education policies 73–83, 88–9
  League of Nations 150
  NATO 211, 213
  UN 188–93, 226, 228
Universal Postal Union 30
Unwin, Stanley 60
UPU. *See Universal Postal Union*

Venkatsewaran, Manjapra Venkatkrishna 154–5
Vereengiging voor Volkenbond en Vrede 146

Walters, Frank 154
White, Eric Wyndham 31

WHO. *See World Health Organization*
World Disarmament Conference
 (1932–34) 34, 152, 159
World Food Board 120
World Food Survey 115, 120, 123

World Health Organization
 67
Wörner, Manfred 201, 208–13

Zilliacus, Konni 60

www.ingramcontent.com/pod-product-compliance
Lightning Source LLC
Chambersburg PA
CBHW072121290426
44111CB00012B/1739